Wounded Nation

Compliments about the book

"*Wounded Nation* by Bereket Habte Selassie is a gripping and troubling account of post-liberation politics in Eritrea. The book is both a personal memoir and an analysis of how a country's fate and future can be put into serious jeopardy by actions of a single individual or a group. Volume 1 of Bereket's memoirs traced his life up to the time of Eritrea's liberation in 1991 and the euphoria of independence after thirty years of independence war. Bereket who himself had been part of the liberation movement became Chair of the Constitutional Commission charged with the responsibility of writing a constitution for the newly liberated nation. Less than a decade after liberation, and only a few years after the adoption of the constitution, the promise of liberation and democracy had been thoroughly betrayed by the non-implementation of the Constitution, and the centralization of power in the hands of President Isaias Afwerki and a few of his collaborators in the Eritrean Peoples Liberation Front (EPLF). Bereket's honest account of how he, along with most Eritreans, trusted the liberation leaders and were not vigilant enough when the dictatorial and authoritarian tendencies of the EPLF leadership were apparent earlier on, is a good lesson for all of us to be always careful not to automatically or prematurely sing the virtues of liberation movements. But the memoirs are not just an account of betrayal and disappointment. They provide a basis for hope in the continuing struggle for democratic governance in Eritrea. Bereket firmly believes that one of the lessons to be gained out of the present crisis in Eritrea is the resilience of the Eritrean people as they struggle through economic decline, social deprivation and political betrayal. Their resilience is demonstrated by the spirit of nationalism which runs through all Eritreans both at home and in the diaspora. Bereket's memoirs are evidence of that spirit, giving hope to Eritreans wherever they may be."

--Julius E. Nyang'oro, Professor and Chair, African and Afro-American Studies, University of North Carolina at Chapel Hill

"The second volume of Bereket Selassie's unforgettable memoirs, *Wounded Nation*, is an outstanding analysis of the descent of Eritrea into personal rule and dictatorship. This beautiful land along the Red Sea is aptly described as a wounded nation, for its once promising quest for freedom, lasting peace and material prosperity has been betrayed by the denial of democratic rights and liberties, the destruction of constitutional government, and the lack of an aggressive pursuit of regional integration and development in the Horn of Africa through pan-African solidarity. Those who have read the first volume of these memoirs will continue to enjoy this rich narrative and the superb manner in which the author conveys it in writing. New readers have much to learn about Eritrea and postcolonial Africa."

--George Nzongola-Ntalaja, Professor of African Studies, University of North Carolina at Chapel Hill

"How did one of the most hopeful and admired revolutions of our time—one that included women's equality, children's education and democratic expression through the arts—win a thirty-year struggle against all odds, yet devolve into an anti-democratic one-party regime? This mystery is the subject of Bereket Habte Selassie's book, Wounded Nation, about post-liberation Eritrea. As the principal author of the country's constitution, Bereket has special knowledge of the hidden factors that led to war with Ethiopia, Eritrea's former occupier, betrayal of the original promise of democracy and progress, and transforming a once popular revolutionary leader into a despot. For all of us who supported Eritrea's fight for self determination—and who support such goals in other countries—this honest appraisal of how things went wrong should be required reading for the saving of hard work, hopes and lives."

--Gloria Steinen, Writer and Feminist Activist

WOUNDED NATION

How a Once Promising Eritrea was Betrayed and its Future Compromised

VOLUME II OF *THE CROWN AND THE PEN*

Bereket Habte Selassie

The Red Sea Press, Inc.
Publishers & Distributors of Third World Books

P. O. Box 1892
Trenton, NJ 08607

P. O. Box 48
Asmara, ERITREA

The Red Sea Press, Inc.
Publishers & Distributors of Third World Books

P. O. Box 1892   P. O. Box 48
Trenton, NJ 08607   Asmara, ERITREA

Book and cover design: Saverance Publishing Services

Library of Congress Cataloging-in-Publication Data

Bereket H. Selassie
  Wounded nation : how a once promising Eritrea was betrayed and its future compromised / Bereket Habte Selassie.
    p. cm.
  Includes bibliographical references and index.
  ISBN 1-56902-339-5 (hard cover) -- ISBN 1-56902-340-9 (pbk.) 1. Bereket H. Selassie. 2. Lawyers--Ethiopia--Biography. 3. Judges--Ethiopia--Biography. 4. Eritrea--Politics and government--20th century. I. Title.
  KRP110.B47A3 2011
  963.507'2092--dc22
  [B]
                    2010037439

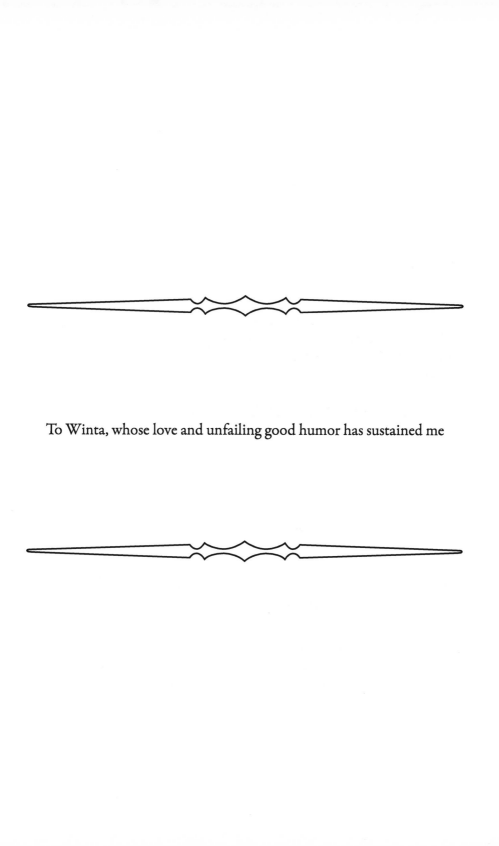

To Winta, whose love and unfailing good humor has sustained me

Table of Contents

Maps

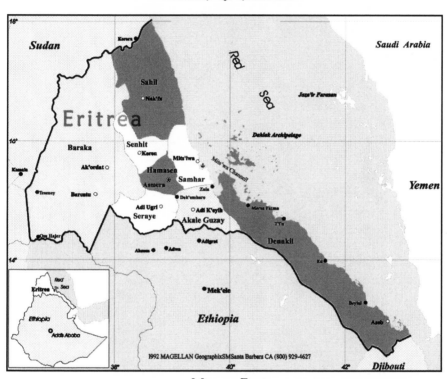

MAP OF ERITREA WITH NAMES OF REGIONS

A MILLENNIUM OF INTER-FAITH COEXISTENCE;
(TOP) ST MARY'S ORTHODOX CHURCH AND (BOTTOM) AL KHULAFA
AL RASHIUDIN MOSQUE, BOTH IN ASMARA

Preface

———————◇✕◇———————

This book is both a memoir and an attempt to answer a simple question: How did we Eritreans get into the present mess? It is the story of the current Eritrean reality and, in particular, the predicament in which we find ourselves in this post-Badme War era. To answer the question we need to look to the past; and as part of that attempt, we need to identify and question people who have been actors in the Eritrean drama from the early days of the armed struggle. As it happens, such questioning had begun in 2000 and 2001, i.e., when those wonderful young journalists pursued and questioned some of the former EPLF leaders (members of the G-15). In a series of dazzling interviews, the journalists took the leaders to task, quizzing them on how they allowed one man—their boss—to arrogate all power to himself, making decisions on war and peace with dire consequences to the nation. Some of the members of the G-15 made a clean breast of it, as if they had been waiting for an opportunity to confess; they put the shaken Isaias Afwerki on notice that he would no longer command their unquestioning obedience.

The ice was broken: The hitherto silent EPLF leaders started speaking volubly. Three of the G-15—Mesfin Hagos, Haile Menkerios, and Adhanom Gebremariam—who were fortunate enough to be abroad when their comrades were arrested and taken to an uncertain fate—were ready and eager to denounce Isaias as an autocrat and his rule as an unmitigated disaster. The interviews by the young journalists and the issues they raised were made possible by the fact that the G-15—all of them erstwhile comrades of President Isaias—had decided to challenge him, demanding democratic accountability and transparency. Isaias had been shaken by the outcome of the Badme War and the consequent popular dissatisfaction; and the expectation was that he would compromise and follow the line of least resistance—reconciliation. It was not to be; true to character, he defied the challenge and threw the gauntlet at the feet of his fifteen critics (see chapter 10 for details).

The suspense that ensued was palpable when Isaias became defiant warning his critics that they "were making a mistake"--with a hint of threat of dire consequences. Despite the threat, the critics persisted, appealing to the membership of the EPLF and the whole nation. In retrospect, it is clear that they gambled and lost; and most of them are paying for it—some have already paid with their lives.

Three from among the G-15—Mesfin, Haile, and Adhanom—later decided to continue the struggle by forming a political party. I joined them in that decision. My association with them in the founding of what eventually became the Democratic Party and the activities that this entailed has enriched my research for writing this book, enabling me to obtain valuable information and gain insight into many aspects of the liberation struggle. The research included taped interviews with some of them and with many others. I also had lengthy informal conversations with a number of Eritreans and some non-Eritreans interested in Eritrean affairs, taking notes as I went along. Such interviews and conversations took place in America and in Europe. Many of those I interviewed are serious academics and intellectuals in their own right. Others are former liberation fighters (from both the ELF and the EPLF) whose views and interpretations of events and comments on issues have been invaluable. I am most grateful to all of them; they are so many that mentioning some and leaving out others would not be fair.

I also wish to express a belated debt of gratitude that I owe to some people who did favors for me at difficult moments in my life. In *The Crown and the Pen* (2007), the first volume of my memoirs, I mentioned some of these, but inadvertently omitted a couple of others. One is Desta Wolde Kidan, who took me all the way from Addis Ababa to Mekele at a time of imminent danger to my life. Desta is alive and well; we met a few times in the early 1990s when I was able to visit Addis Ababa. Another person who did me a favor at a difficult moment of my life, during my banishment in Harar in the late 1960s, was Ato Kidane Adgoi. He extended his sojourn in Harar by a few days and gave me valuable counsel, advising me on how best to survive banishment and cheerfully relating stories of the early Eritrean immigrants to Ethiopia and the challenges they faced. I will never forget Aya Kidane.

Many readers of *The Crown and the Pen* encouraged me to write a second volume, some indeed constantly asking how far I had progressed in writing it. I thank them all for their encouragement and their kind words about *The Crown and the Pen*; and I sincerely hope that they and all readers of this volume will find it instructive as well as enjoyable. Many from among these read part of the draft of this book, making useful suggestions for improvement. I am grateful to them all; but I remain responsible for any defects of the book. I am thankful to Patricia Allen, my copy editor, who has done a superb job of editing this text. I am also grateful for a research grant from the African Center of My University (UNC- Chapel Hill). Last, but not least, my wife Winta, a born organizer, arranged my data, putting it in properly classified and accessible form. I am richly indebted to her in more ways than one. This book is dedicated to her.

One final note on names. Both in the body of the text as well as in the bibliography, I use first names for Eritreans and Ethiopians, whereas for the rest, I follow the usual practice of writing surnames first, followed by first names and initials, where applicable.

Bereket Habte Selassie
Chapel Hill, North Carolina
July 2010

Chapter 1

INTRODUCTION:
FROM THE PAST
BACK TO THE FUTURE

In the first volume of my memoirs, *The Crown and the Pen* (2007), I related the story of my life and times, including my childhood, schooling, government work, and finally my involvement in the Eritrean liberation struggle. The book ends in 1991, the year of Eritrea's military victory over Ethiopian armed forces. The present volume, for the most part, takes up the story from that point on; but it also looks back to the past, from time to time, in order to find clues to help explain the present.

This second volume is titled *Wounded Nation*, with the sub-title, *How a Once Promising Eritrea was Betrayed and its Future Compromised.* The earlier title of the book was "Trust but Verify." Trust is a critical element in the life of individuals and groups in society. It is a fundamental ingredient in human relations. In the medical profession, for example, trust underlies the Hippocratic Oath, which all medical doctors swear, promising to do no harm, to put the patient's interest above everything else. Speaking about doctors and the oath, Faith T. Fitzgerald, MD, a renowned American educator says, "It really means conducting themselves in such a way as to keep the patient's trust, because maintaining that trust cuts right to the heart of things—and it takes care of a lot of other issues along the way" (Doctor's Digest November/December 2008, 16). While consumers of medical services (at least in advanced societies) have become proactive about researching their own health conditions and even questioning the diagnosis of their physicians, most patients and society in general still place tremendous trust in doctors.

Similarly, people place trust in their priests or sheikhs and in others who provide services to them. By the same token, people place trust in the government they elect, expecting it to perform its duties according to the promises it makes and pursuant to the law. But human nature being what it is, promises are sometimes broken; and laws are broken with serious repercussions. The harm that results from a doctor's breach of ethics affects one person and his/her family. In contrast, a government's breach of promises or breaking the law may have far-reaching consequences affecting many more people. So, while it is necessary to place trust in the government that one elects, there are constitutional safeguards to minimize the harm, if not to avoid it completely. Such safeguards also include requirements of accountability and transparency. All this assumes, of course, a vigilant public.

As earlier mentioned, before settling on *Wounded Nation* as the final title, I had considered the phrase, "Trust, but Verify". The phrase is now part of the lexicon of international relations and has also entered that of national discourse. Governments must be trusted, with one important proviso; there must be principles and mechanisms for checking and correcting malfeasance. While trust is good, absolute trust does not make for healthy politics.

The choice of the title and subtitle is indicative of the bitter disappointments of a long-suffering people—a people whose government of former freedom fighters broke its promises. If life were fair, the dictum that a people gets the government it deserves should not apply to the Eritrean people, who, by any measurement, deserve better. Rather, the treatment of the Eritrean people at the hands of their government defies reason; in fact it confirms the wry judgment of social critic Eric Hoffer when he said that every great cause begins as a movement, becomes a business, and eventually degenerates into a racket. This is a distressing insight, one that contradicts the idea of human progress epitomized in the Age of Reason; in the belief that, given time, people would come to reason, and that finally history was on their side.

According to this insight, there is no certainty of a pleasant outcome to any human endeavor; no happy ending is guaranteed. Which raises the haunting question: Do the sufferings of the present and the past deny a future era of universal happiness? Put another way: Is evil a constant, ineradicable reality? Are a people—like the Eritrean people, who spent decades in the wilderness fighting for a better future—denied the hope of being rewarded with the (better) future for which they fought?

On the face of it, Eritrea's current predicament does not support a positive answer. Is it possible for things to change for the better and thus fulfill the promise of a better future, or is this a naïve and fallacious hope, which is a denial of the notion of the "audacity of hope" popularized in President Barak Obama's election manifesto? (See his book under that title). Time will tell. Meanwhile, we need to confront the reality of the present and try to make sense of it, comparing the promise with the performance.

This is indeed what this volume attempts to do.

In Eritrea today we have skeptics—bless their heart—who see the Eritrean armed struggle *(ghedli)* as a curse and the cause of our present predicament. Some, who have been called *ghedli* romantics, argue that the virtues of the experience outweigh its vices, and that it was the abandonment of these virtues that has landed Eritrea in its present crisis. Skeptics, on the other hand, see only vice in the experience of the *ghedli* and contend that the present crisis is a function of the continuation of the *ghedli* experience. That both of these points of view contain elements of truth is beyond argument, a pertinent question being: Which of them is nearer to the truth? I shall address the issues raised by these points briefly in this introductory chapter, and in greater detail, in the chapters that follow.

First of all, I begin with the injunction that "the truth shall set you free." Some may think this to be a naïve belief; my own firm view is that those of us who have been privileged to have an education bear a responsibility to speak truth to power—all the time. This means there must be no censorship of free speech; instead, there must be a free flow and clash of ideas. To those ends, a free and autonomous press is a necessary precondition: free people deserve no less as a guarantee against abuse by anyone, including would-be dictators. One of the aims of these memoirs—a modest one—is to encourage and, where it exists, sustain a culture of continual questioning and a quest for the truth in all aspects of life. We must all search for truth in every way we can in the here-and-now; we cannot wait for its revelation in the Second Coming. Truth must be told even when it hurts, as it often does. But as the inimitable Wole Soyinka has opined, to set you free, truth must be set free (Soyinka, *The Burden of Memory, The Muse of Forgiveness.* 1999, 31-34).

We Trusted Too Much

As Eritreans, what was absent from our world at the time when we were engaged in a liberation struggle was this culture of questioning. It was absent principally because we trusted too much. We erred on the side of trust by dint of the requirements of the *ghedli*, including, notably, the military necessity that imposed restrictions. Our leaders abused this trust, and we were played upon by them, like a harp. During those years, we were consumed by a burning desire for freedom and absorbed in efforts to realize the fruits of the struggle. We were encased in tunnel vision and unable to see anything outside of it. This continued during the first years after liberation because the same ethos of sacrifice and commitment to "the cause" reigned supreme, even when the cause seemed evanescent and its supposed guardians capricious.

Personally, it took me a long time to realize that the cause had become the monopoly business of a few determined power-hungry men that eventually degenerated into a racket. It took time because it is hard for a true believer in the cause of justice, equal rights, and self-determination to believe readily that those who fought for such a cause could abandon it with ease and degrade it into a racket. But that is what has happened, confirming the fear of the Eritrean teacher, and mother of martyred sons, who, when asked how she felt about the death of her children in the war of liberation, said that sad as she was, she accepted their fate with grace because they died in the cause of freedom; but that if and when the cause for which they gave their lives were to end up being the plaything of a few, then indeed, she would shed bitter tears.

The first volume of these memoirs ended with that mother's memorable words. This second volume is dedicated to exploring and fleshing out the causes and consequences of the country's present predicament. Much of the narrative in this volume is from the perspective of an observer/participant or of what I prefer to call an insider/outsider. An insider/outsider is a person who belongs to the category of members of the Eritrean Peoples' Liberation Front (EPLF) who made their contributions to the country's liberation on the basis of a shared national sentiment and a commonly-understood liberation (revolutionary) ethic. The central part of that ethic was grounded in each member's belief that the aim was the liberation of the land from alien occupation. At its more developed phase the shared sentiment also involved a progressive ideology of liberating the people from all forms of oppression or exploitation and the inauguration of an era of justice and equality. Whether this ideology was genuine or an immaculate deception is a question that needs exploration and one that I have attempted to examine. Marxism, with its emphasis on class analysis, was a dominant part of this ideology for much of the history of the movement.

In this narrative I have tried to bring out what I call the story behind the story—or more accurately, stories—that is to say, events and actors that should, in my view, be described and analyzed in the spirit of fidelity to historical truth (to the extent that this is possible), as well as to gain better understanding of the current Eritrean reality. The assumption is that my narrative will be different from the official historical account, which is the "victor's" narrative. The background story is, of course, Eritrea's national liberation with all its ups and downs, which has been the subject of scanty historical and social science-based narrative. In this volume, reference to the background will remain just that—a background history. However, in the attempt to understand—to make sense of the armed struggle and its aftermath—one cannot avoid frequent reference to relevant parts of that history.

The participants of the independence struggle, whom I call insiders/outsiders, representing the majority of the members of the Eritrean Peoples' Liberation Front took the EPLF at its word. They assumed, wrongly as it turned out, that in the liberation struggle (supposedly guided by revolutionary ethic) there would be no deception. They were shocked to find out, after liberation, that there was a secret party within the EPLF, known as the Eritrean People's Revolutionary Party, a secret party that controlled all matters concerning the EPLF—its politics and policy orientation, its management and decisions on political and organizational affairs; in short, everything. Above all, it was covert; only its members knew of its existence, and they were sworn to secrecy.

This is a prime example of what I have called immaculate deception. The ex post-facto explanation that it was created with the aim of national unity and the development of a democratic culture is a subject that must be examined closely and dispassionately. My discussion with some former members of this secret party revealed that opinion was divided as to is true purpose: Some believed in its value as a unifying and progressive organization that was abused and eventually degenerated into a power preserving device for its principal leaders. Others believed that it was a means of control from the very beginning. On this topic, Dan Connell's interview with Haile Woldensae (popularly known as Dru'E) is instructive, with its claim that the kernel of the idea of the secret party originated inside the ELF, at a crucial time when Haile, Isaias and other nationalists decided it was necessary in order to cope with the chaotic and self-defeating practices of the early ELF leaders. The idea was given shape and developed as a result of the sojourn of Isaias and Romodan Mohamed Nur in China in the late 1960s, where they had traveled for military/ideological training.

The revelation of the secret party raised many questions. To begin with, it led to disaffection among the majority of EPLF members—both guerillas and civilian members—who were bitter that they were treated as second-class citizens. Did it have a corrupting influence on the EPLF leadership? Did it create a culture of elitism and impunity; and if so, could it have contributed to the postliberation democracy deficit—the absence of accountability on the part of the leadership? Alternatively, might it have contributed to the success of the struggle, as the principal leaders contend? If so, in what way? These are serious questions that require answers, and I will return to the subject in the appropriate chapters.

The Ghedli *in Historical Perspective*

There is an urgent need for a sober reassessment of Eritrea's history of armed struggle, the *ghedli*. The word *ghedli* is used here as a referent to the armed struggle begun and waged with the aim of liberating Eritrea from Ethiopian occupation. Eritreans also use the word *sawra*, which on the face of it is interchangeable with *ghedli*. The distinction between the two as I understand it is that whereas *ghedli* is an armed movement aimed at liberating the land from foreign occupation, *sawra* includes that meaning as well as internal changes in the society. In other words, *sawra* includes liberation of a different kind; it involves revolutionary social change. In fact the word *sawra* is derived from the Arabic *thawra,* which means revolution.

It may well be that in the thinking of some Eritreans *ghedli* includes or implies *sawra*. One of the posters that I saw when I arrived in the United States in 1977, after a couple of years of involvement with the EPLF, carried the slogan written in large letters: "A Revolution to free the Land and the Man," referring to the Eritrean struggle. I am quite sure that the writers of that slogan meant man to include woman because by that time the notion of women's rights and equality with men was an established principle among Eritreans—well, at least in theory.

Why this discursive comment about words? I was first made acutely aware of the distinction during my early conversations with some young EPLF cadres in early 1975. It was in the Karnishim area of the highlands that I first made contact with the *tegadelti* (freedom fighters), during the time when I was involved in the public efforts to stop the "civil war" between the Eritrean Liberation Front (ELF) and the Eritrean Peoples' Liberation Front (EPLF). I had heard the word *ghedli* used by the ELF *tegadelti* in late 1974 in the Akeleguzai area (see map), which was where I first came in contact with Eritrean fighters after I escaped from the clutches of the Ethiopian military junta (the Dergue), as I describe in volume 1 of these memoirs. So when I asked the EPLF cadres why they insisted on using *sawra* instead of *ghedli*, one of them, named Araia Semere (one of the so-called Yamin group, later executed by Isaias), told me that *sawra* carries with it a different and revolutionary content. He went on to elaborate on it as he had been taught as part of the EPLF's political education, which was avowedly Marxist-Leninist.

In the extended discussion we held for a number of days, as we went from village to village in Karnishim, I mentioned to him that the ELF cadres use the term *ghedli* not *sawra*, he remarked with a smile that *ghedli* was what they use; but the EPLF has gone beyond that, he said, and went on to explain to me the distinction between the two words. Araia was a very intelligent young man, at the time in his early twenties, who had been captured by the ELF after a battle during the latest fighting. He was released and allowed to go back to rejoin his EPLF unit after Herui Tedla, the then ELF leader, intervened on his behalf and decided to let him go.

I remember Herui telling me that he had tried to convince Araia to join the ELF, and that he had refused on the strength of his conviction that there was a significant difference between the ELF and the EPLF. Herui said he admired his guts and his having the courage of his convictions even though he thought he was misguided. In releasing Araia from capture and letting him go back to his own EPLF unit Herui demonstrated decency and good sense. He repeated this gesture of goodwill, in the wake of the end of the first "civil war," by allowing EPLF members who were liberated from the Sembel prison by ELF fighters. I must say, in parenthesis, that the liberation of the prisoners from Sembel was a heroic deed representing one of the ELF's finest hours.

On the basis of the new awareness I gained from Araia Semere regarding the distinction between *ghedli* and *sawra*, I talked to some other EPLF cadres to test their own sense of the significance of the distinction. One of these cadres went so far as to say this was indeed what distinguished them from the ELF (or Jebha as the ELF was generally called) because, according to him, the EPLF believed in revolutionary change, whereas the ELF believed only in liberating the land without any change in society. Much later, when I raised this point to some of the more highly educated EPLF cadres, they put it in terms of Marxist ideology of class struggle as the engine of historical process, adding that the ELF did not subscribe to that ideology.

This partisan view was confirmed for me when I returned to the United States and came in contact with the group calling itself Eritreans for Liberation in North America (EFLNA), whose members were almost without exception supporters of the EPLF. They accepted the ELF as a genuine nationalist group in the struggle but as having a revolution deficit. There was an arrogant edge to this belief that characterized members of the EPLF and of EFLNA. As we shall see in a later chapter, the EFLNA and its European sister organization, the EFLE, became eventually carbon copies of the EPLF and provided them with material and human resources that made a significant contribution to its success and to Eritrea's liberation. At the same time they facilitated the hardening of the leadership's heart and in rejecting any compromise or in allowing opposition parties in postindependence Eritrea, as we shall see in more detail.

The difference between the words *ghedli* and *sawra* came to represent, to some people at least, the difference between ELF and EPLF. Whether those who entertained such belief were right or wrong is beside the point; the point is that they had become historical actors on the basis of such different consciousness and contributed to Eritrea's present predicament. Furthermore, foreign Leftist Parties, and organizations and individuals acting on that basis, contributed to the EPLF's success as well as to the negative developments of its policies and politics. They were thus enablers of EPLF's success as well as its debacle.

A General Reassessment

As previously noted, a promising public discourse has started among Eritreans on cyber space. It is promising, if sometimes acrimonious, involving as it does a healthy exchange of views on Eritrea's recent past, especially on the role of the *ghedli*. At the academic level also there have been some important publications reflecting on the Eritrean armed struggle. Gaim Kibreab's book, *Critical Reflections on the Eritrean War of Independence*, is an excellent representative of such academic endeavors. I am sure others will follow; I certainly hope that some of the veterans of both fronts will write memoirs about their experience in the *ghedli*.

I, for one, welcome this development of critical evaluation and hope that some parts of my memoirs will make a modest contribution to the ongoing discourse. I strongly believe that reexamining our past and bringing out what happened into the open—warts and all—are the only ways of healing our wounded nation. Though we know that in all such attempts the best balm is the healing hand of time, it does not mean that we should sit tight and wait for time to do everything for us. On the contrary, we need to be proactive and to take the necessary initiatives to help time help us.

Our recent past, particularly the years of the *ghedli*, have been full of dramatic events; some pleasant, others unpleasant. From the start, when the first shots were fired on Mount Adal in the Barka region of western Eritrea, by Hamed Idris Awate and his band of followers, and throughout the long armed struggle, the Eritrean public invested the *tegadelti* with an aura of romance. That was in the nature of things; young men (and later women) who went out to the bush to fight for the nation's freedom, leaving home and hearth, must necessarily be looked upon with admiration. The young men who remained behind—and who did not play a part in the urban resistance—invariably felt a sense of guilt, that sense of guilt also contributed to the elevation of the *tegadelti* to mythic heights of heroism to be admired and emulated by future generation of young men and even boys.

The first wave of exodus to the field of guerilla action (generally known as the *meda*) was voluntary. It was not until much later that the voluntary nature of the *tegadelti* changed when the leaders of the armed struggle felt the need for conscription by force. The years of peaceful resistance—what in Eritrean historiography has been called the Eritrean Liberation Movement (ELM)—created an acute public awareness (especially in the urban areas among students, teachers, and working people), about the bad hand Eritrea had been dealt by the international community assembled at the United Nations. A few of its historic leaders like Ibrahim Sultan Ali, Idris Mohamed Adam, and Woldeab Woldemariam had gone out to live as refugees in Egypt and had inspired peaceful resistance by different means including radio broadcasts from Cairo.

Thus, before the Eritrean armed struggle started, there had been peaceful urban resistance. Many of the young men who remained behind were veterans of the peaceful resistance during the UN-imposed years of federation (1952-1962) and, as such, felt kinship with and financially supported those who went to the bush to secure, through armed struggle, the freedom that their elders failed to bring about through peaceful means. Eritreans had felt a keen sense of betrayal when Emperor Haile Selassie forcibly annexed their country, erasing its identity as an internationally recognized legal entity.

The sense of betrayal and consequent anger that Eritreans felt was leveled as much at the Ethiopian government as at the United Nations. All their pleas for UN intervention had fallen on deaf ears, despite the fact that the UN resolution federating Eritrea with Ethiopia affirmed Eritrea's legal identity and autonomy, and that the UN-appointed commission on Eritrea had written in its report that the said UN Resolution would remain an international instrument. The commission also said that if the resolution were violated, the UN General Assembly "could be seized of jurisdiction," which Eritreans and their friends understood to mean that the UN would intervene if the federation were to be abolished as it was in 1962. Eritreans and their friends made peaceful appeals for such intervention—all to no avail. Cold war diplomacy and Ethiopia's close alliance with the United States at the time foreclosed the matter, leaving Eritreans no other choice but armed struggle.

It is important to reiterate that the moral outrage Eritreans felt had a basis of legitimacy rooted in international law. In later years when others, particularly Africans who feared Eritrea's potential as a source of inspiration to would-be secessionists within their own nations, described the Eritrean struggle as a secessionist movement not worthy of support, Eritreans answered by citing its legally grounded legitimacy. In other words, Eritrea's case is not one of secession, but of *illegally denied decolonization*. Eritrea's case is akin to that of Namibia, not that of Katanga or Biafra. But it took military victory to drive the point home; it took the victories at Afabet in 1988 and Massawa in 1990 before world opinion began to shift in favor of Eritrea, gradually seeing it in its proper historical and legal context. And then, of course, the total military victory of 1991 and the referendum of 1993 resulted in forcing world opinion into accepting Eritrea's case as legitimate and grant it its rightful place in the family of nations.

So, as we make a critical reappraisal of our nation's recent history, it is important not to lose perspective or to forget why Eritreans waged armed struggle. Let us also remember that to the deeplyfelt sense of betrayal was added the policies and politics of the Ethiopian government, and the practices of its officials, that further alienated the Eritrean population. Some of these policies and practices included arrests and detentions, dismissal, transfer of Eritrean officials and their replacement by Ethiopians, and control and censure of a hitherto freely working Eritrean press.

Above all, a critical and a most economically damaging policy of the Ethiopian government was aimed at weakening Eritrea's industrial base. This naturally led to more unemployment and social disaffection. Among those who joined the armed struggle were thus hundreds of unemployed youth, eventually to be joined by university and higher secondary school students, and even university graduates in the 1970s and 1980s.

Commenting on the critical role students played in the Eritrean liberation movement in the decade between 1958 and 1968, and providing a regional linkage to their role, Woldesus Amar has written as follows:

> The fact that the Eritrean Liberation Front (ELF) was established with an overwhelming participation of students in Cairo further attests to their overall contribution in the rebirth of the nationalist movement. Asmara students followed in the footsteps of those in Cairo and from the start played an important role in instilling nationalist feeling among the population. Between 1961 and 1965, in particular, they organized demonstrations almost yearly in the Eritrean capital and helped create awareness about the struggle for independence in part of the country where Eritreanism was initially weak. The same generation of Asmara students continued to contribute immensely in the growth and eventual victory of the liberation movement. Some of those students are easily identifiable and still active either with the government in Asmara or with the main opposition group so far kept in exile.

It is one of the sad legacies of the division and factional strife that characterizes Eritrea's history of armed struggle that the writer of the piece quoted above was a close friend and comrade of Isaias Afwerki, the current President of Eritrea (2010), during their student days at the Prince Mekonen Secondary School, and that he (Woldesus) is one of the leaders of the exiled opposition. Isaias became one of the founding members and leader of the EPLF, which splintered from the ELF; whereas Woldesus remained a member of the ELF, albeit outside the military field of action. Some have begun to write about the cause of the split that led to the creation of the EPLF and about the bitter "civil war" they fought. As yet nothing much has been written about the darker side within both fronts, including summary executions and disappearances.

The Truth Shall Set You Free

It is trite to say that Eritrea today is in crisis. In the chapters that follow this introduction, I will address different questions concerning the crisis, analyzing critical issues, and principal events and actors. Such analysis involves, at times, going back to the past to help explain the present. As a former member of the EPLF, in this the second part of my memoirs, I will focus on the policies and politics of the EPLF (and its successor, the People's Front for Democracy and Justice, or PFDJ) and its supreme leadership. I lay out the facts known to me in my different capacities as a former member of the EPLF as well as those obtained through research. I believe in the truism that the truth shall set you free. By the same token, I expect those Eritreans who have been privileged to have participated as members of the ELF in different capacities over the years to do the same. Indeed some have begun to do so in fits and starts. And the writing can take the form of historical or political analysis, or works of fiction, such as novels and plays. In the latter instance, Daniel Semere Tesfai's epic novel in Tigrigna, *Halaw'ta Weqawit Ghereb* (2009), and Saleh (Gadi) Johar's *Of Kings and Bandits* (2010) are good examples.

In these memoirs, seeking to bring to light some of the important events and the performance of important actors in the Eritrean story, I have endeavored to tell the truth as I found it from documents, from my own direct knowledge, and from interviews and other sources. Needless to say, bringing out the truth is critical in any effort to unravel the mystery of any story. This is of course easier said than done. First of all, there are different notions of truth. In any inquiry about disputed events in Eritrea's recent history, for example, the one involving the war between the ELF and EPLF that started in 1973, each side to the dispute can present different accounts of what happened. Each side may accuse the other of having provoked the war, as was also the case with the 1998-2000 war between Eritrea and Ethiopia, also known as the Badme War. Such a dispute is best left to neutral parties or to dispassionate analysis by historians. However, this does not mean that one cannot make attempts at revealing truths as one finds them or at offering interpretations. In doing so, one will inevitably be the subject of criticisms or controversy. But I do not fear criticism, nor am I a stranger to controversy.

In the spirit of fidelity to historical truth, I will begin by making a couple of confessions. The first concerns incidents that happened after I joined the Eritrean struggle in 1975; the second is related to events occurring during the early part of the postindependence years. My confession is not the kind that a devout Catholic is required to make to a priest: I neither seek nor expect absolution for any "mortal sin." My sin is one of omission that is part of a complex national story involving failure on the part of Eritrean society as a whole. In confessing my sin, therefore, I am claiming that, as a society, we bear a measure of responsibility for what went wrong. Just as people who played a part in the liberation struggle can lay claim to some of the positive achievements of that struggle, they must also bear their share of responsibility for some of the negative results issuing out of, or connected to, that struggle. Unfortunately, we find it hard to own up to our mistakes. This is what I have called our national failure; it seems to be embedded in our culture.

As I said before, I joined the Eritrean struggle in early 1975, first as part of the popular movement to help mediate in the ongoing "civil war" between the ELF and the EPLF; then as a relief organizer, and, finally, as a full-fledged member of the EPLF. One of the criticisms leveled at me, particularly by some former members of the ELF, is that I should not have decided to join the EPLF; in terms of personal favors, of the two, I should have joined the ELF because they got me out of a perilous situation in Ethiopia in late 1974, when my life was in grave danger. At the very least, these people contend, I should have stayed neutral and acted as mediator until the end.

I have tried to answer this criticism in volume 1; but it is worth reiterating for the record. Rightly or wrongly, I considered that staying neutral in that kind of situation was not only immoral but psychologically impossible for me. Both the ELF and EPLF had their positive and negative sides; but the EPLF seemed to me the better organized and better-led group to liberate Eritrea. So, after the failed attempt at reconciliation and creating a united organization, I had to decide to be with one or the other.

My decision to join the EPLF is, however, the least of my sins. I witnessed some wrongs being committed within the EPLF, and I failed to expose them. On two occasions, I witnessed a form of physical abuse being committed by EPLF cadres, and, though I protested at the time, admonishing the culprits on the rights and wrongs of handling detainees, I did not report this to anyone. Such failure was part of the self-imposed censorship that was justified as part of keeping the organizational dirty linen hidden. Although there were reasons advanced for such concealment, such as reasons of "national security" (!), I have always felt a sense of guilt about it.

This is part of a universal question as to whether such an act is justifiable on the ground of survival, as some government officials contend; it has been very much a matter of current discourse, especially in the wake of September 11 and allegations about the use of extraconstitutional (or unconstitutional) methods of extracting evidence by American investigators at Guantanamo Bay, allegedly used in order to save more lives. It involves knotty moral and legal questions— questions with which lawyers, juries, and judges grapple.

My other sin of omission committed in the postindependence period concerns the Mai Habar incident, the shooting of the disabled veterans by a government military unit, presumably by order of the president. I learned later that the officer in charge who gave the order to shoot is one known as Wedi Memhir. When I heard of the incident, late in 1995, I was leading the constitution making work, which was into its second year. I had gone back to the United States to fulfill my teaching obligations at my university, and when I returned to Asmara I heard about the official explanation to the effect that it was an unfortunate incident, which occurred on the spur of the moment, and that it was under investigion. Nonetheless, it is hard to believe that a veteran liberation fighter would order the shooting of a group of disabled veterans for any reason whatsoever. But that is what happened.

I remember a conversation I had about the incident with Bob Houdek, who was the American ambassador in Eritrea at the time. Houdek approached me at a reception where we were both guests, seeking more enlightenment on the subject. He informed me that Isaias had told him that it was an unfortunate incident that spiraled out of control, and that he regretted it. Houdek informed me that he then told Isaias to make a public statement about it, explaining it in the manner that he had explained it to him. Outraged by what happened I had momentarily considered resigning my commission; but when I heard that it was an unplanned and unfortunate incident, I decided against resignation. Besides, I thought that resignation would have been a cop-out, abandoning an important national project about which there were great expectations.

A major aim of this book is to help provide some answers to the nagging questions concerning the actions and decisions taken by the Eritrean leadership, notably its top leader, on a whole set of issues. As I noted above, the ongoing new critical reassessment of our recent history and current reality is encouraging. Its emergence has taken two forms: academic publications and cyberspace critiques. The first is exemplified by Gaim Kibreab's book, mentioned above. The second is exemplified by Yosief Ghebrehiwet's scathing critique of the *ghedli* appearing in a series of articles at Asmarino.com under the heading of *Romanticizing the Ghedli.*" Yosief's articles have been received with mixed reviews by readers, including critical responses by the Awate.com's Saleh Younis, Woldeab. Idris, and others.

Yosief's pieces are excellent; but, very useful as they are in helping us get our bearings on aspects of our present predicament, they can be—and have been—criticized as being untimely and too esoteric, and lacking a proper historical perspective. As such, they are not regarded as particularly helpful for our current need to unite in a common struggle against a dictatorial regime that has usurped our democratic rights and betrayed the cause for which our martyrs died. The criticism leveled at Yosief proceeds on the assumption that in our reassessment of the *ghedli* we need to distinguish between the *ghedli* and its cause, on the one hand and the leaders of the *ghedli* on the other. The argument goes along the line that the leaders may have made many mistakes and committed offenses for which they should be held answerable somehow or other, but the *ghedli* as a means of obtaining national liberation should not be blamed. In the politics of national liberation many errors were committed, including some serious crimes; but as we are engaged in the process of reexamining our past, we need to avoid the blame game and also free ourselves from the culture of victimhood.

On the role of the *ghedli* and its consequences, I refer the reader to my keynote address delivered at the founding conference of the Eritrean civic organization, CDRiE, on 11 January, 2009, under the title, "Unity for the Greater Good—Reflections of an Elder on His Nation's Predicament." (CEDRiE website, and Assenna.com, which also translated the piece into Tigrigna).

On the subject of the *ghedli*, one pertinent comment made by Saleh Younis is worth mentioning. In a posting at Awate.com, dated 3 June 2008, Saleh argues that the *ghedli* had vices as well as virtues, and that the "*ghedli*-skeptics" (as he calls people like Yosief Ghebrehiwet) committed an error of judgment by forgetting the virtues and focusing on the vices only.

He writes:

> The problem with Eritrea is not that it retained all the vices of the *ghedli*; the problem is that it forgot the virtues of the *ghedli* era. If we can own it as ours—not ELF's or EPLF's but ours—and if we can practice a fraction of its virtues—beginning with genuine love and care (not sympathy or pity, but love and care) for people, then we will begin the journey to making ourselves whole again....Here is another clue: "You might be a *ghedli* romantic if you really think the virtue acquired during the *ghedli* era sufficient to defeat authoritarianism....Now I sure would like to see how *ghedli*-skeptics will come up with their recipe for the movement without incorporating all the virtues of our *ghedli*."

The following questions need to be posed to both protagonists as a way of clarifying the terms of the debate—the terms of engagement—with a view to conducting a rational and fruitful future debate:

- For *ghedli* "skeptics": Are you saying that there were absolutely no virtues attached to the *ghedli*? If not, don't you think it would be fair and just to point out some of the virtues as well as in describing the vices?
- For the *ghedli* "romantics": Are you saying there were no vices committed during the *ghedli*? If not, don't you think admitting them and pointing them out is a necessary element in the healing process that Eritrea needs?

In my opinion, the emerging, critical reassessment of Eritrean history and current reality needs to be expanded and deepened. Any such reassessment needs to be done in a proper theoretical framework and historical context; and in my view, the above-cited book of Dr. Gaim Kibreab helps in providing such framework and context. I, therefore, end this Introduction by using it to frame some of the critical issues on which Eritreans can assess the record of the *ghedli* as well as the performance of the ruling PFDJ government. I will return to some of the issues in more detail in the chapters that follow.

From Self-censorship to Proclaiming the Truth

The principal point in Gaim Kibreab's book—indeed, the main thesis—is that a major casualty of the Eritrean armed struggle is what he calls social capital, borrowing the language of sociology. He argues that the destruction of Eritrea's social capital by the armed guerilla organizations (both the ELF and EPLF) and its replacement by totalitarian mentality that gives no quarter to different views and organizations is a major cause of Eritrea's predicament. In a meticulous examination, using the language of sociology, Gaim describes the loss of a valuable heritage of social capital that mediated all aspects of social life in pre-*ghedli* Eritrea. It is indeed depressing to be confronted with the truth that the organizations that waged the war to liberate their people from alien rule ended up destroying a vital value of their society. It is a devastating indictment and one that must be examined critically.

The ties that bind the component parts of our communities are values of caring and sharing and mutual concern, which place a high premium on consent, mutual respect, and consideration and frown upon violence and coercion. The Tigrigna word *nowri* sums up all things that society frowns upon such as the disrespect of people, especially of elders.

The values underpinning communal solidarity and cohesion (social capital) were under systematic attack by the *ghedli* leaders. A revitalized Eritrean society will need to make a sober assessment of the damages and both government and community leaders will need to work hard at rehabilitating the diminished values. In such tasks of assessment and revitalization, questions will arise. One such question is whether the damage was total and the diminished values irretrievable. Another is what was the replacement, Marxism? If so, how could they think they would succeed where others have failed, or are they unaware of the demise of this ideology in its place of birth, the Metropoles? Personally, I divide Marxism into, on the one hand an ideology—a kind of religion that has been the cause of much grief; and, on the other hand, a methodology of analysis. In the latter sense, Marxism has been a valuable tool in understanding the capitalist mode of production.

I wish also to register a note from my study of European colonial history and its impact on African customary law. The European colonizers began with the erroneous assumption that all African customs were barbaric and therefore must be rooted out, only to discover that it was neither possible nor desirable to abolish African customary laws. It was not possible because these laws governed the lives of the African people from the cradle to the grave; it was not, therefore, practicable to abolish them. It was not desirable because in the end the Europeans found that they could use the laws for their own imperial purpose.

In the postcolonial era, African's dual legacy of tradition-based laws and foreign-based laws live side by side. The conflict of the two systems is a story for another time.

A Summary of the Chapters' Content

In what remains of this introduction, I will provide a bird's eye view of the chapters of the book. Many of the issues raised in this chapter are taken up again in more detail in the ensuing chapters.

In chapter 2, titled PostLiberation Musings, I look back to the immediate preindependence period, while basking in the warm glow of victory. The point of departure chosen for this flashback is an event that constitutes the legal consummation of the armed struggle—the referendum of 1993. The Eritrean people were asked to deicide the future of their nation in an internationally supervised plebiscite. Next to that event I also reminisce about my first experience in a night march with the guerillas; I was asked to join the night march on my way to the village of my birth, where I went to say goodbye to my mother for the last time. I also use the flashback to comment on the last years of the war, including one of my diplomatic faceoffs with the adversaries, this time at the Palais de Nation in Geneva. The chapter ends with a reflection on the horrors of war and the prospects of peace expressed in the poem "The Scent of Peace." I end the chapter with a brief account of the July 1991 conference in Addis Ababa that I attended as a member of the Eritrean observer delegation. From that conference emerged the framework of the future Ethiopian political system.

In chapter 3, The Gold and the Base Metal, with the subtitle Leadership and the Fate of a Nation, I discuss some of the critical features of the making of Eritrea's political leadership, with a special focus on Isaias Afwerki. The metaphor of the two metals is designed to express the differing mettle of pre-and postindependence impressions about the promise of Isaias's leadership and the disappointment that set in. The chapter also discusses, in brief fashion, Marxism, class struggle, revolutionary theory and practice, and the place of women, the youth, and the traditional leaders as well as the nature of the economy and the social landscape. The issues raised here are some of those that are taken up in later chapters in more detail.

The title of chapter 4, Immaculate Deception, contains within it, in my view, the key to understanding what went wrong in Eritrea and why. The subtitle, The Original Sin of Eritrean Politics, gives a hint of this. The chapter tackles the question of crimes committed during the armed struggle and the responsibility for the commission of such crimes. Through the discussion of crimes and consequences, the chapter introduces the enduring issues of power and responsibility.

Chapter 5 deals with the EPLF-TPLF relationship, calling it the tangled web, and characterizing the history of the relationship in terms of Concord and Discord. The subject is taken up again in chapters 7 and 8, which deal, respectively, with the politics of national borders and sovereignty (chapter 7) and the protracted negotiations between the Eritrean and Ethiopian governments following the 1998-2000 war (chapter 8). Chapter 9 also takes up the border issue in terms of the unsettled dispute and the proxy wars the two governments accuse each other of pursuing.

Chapter 6 discusses the making of the constitution ratified in 1997. Later, chapter 10 takes up what became known (wrongly) as the Berlin Manifesto and the G-13, the group that drafted it, as well as the G-15, the high-ranking members of the government and the party who challenged Isaias Afwerki to implement the ratified constitution and to govern responsibly. The chapter raises the haunting question as to whether we have a missed an opportunity here for peaceful democratic change.

Chapter 11 discusses the opposition movement in the Diaspora, delving intio the historical background and significance of the Eritrean Diaspora; what constitutes the present Diaspora; the Diaspora and the opposition; and the Diaspora and the legacy of division.

Chapter 12 deals with the issues of state and religion in Eritrea, in historical and socio-cultural perspectives.

Chapter 13 takes up the issue related to ethnicity and regional politics. This includes pondering the historical phenomenon of false steps that result in disasters, exemplified by the fateful decision taken by the PFDJ government to remove highland Eritreans en mass to settle in the lowland areas of Barka.

Chapter 14 is a concluding chapter summing up and commenting on some recurrent problems and suggestions for resolution, including a problem common to most African countries, i.e., the artificially fixed boundaries that are a legacy of colonial rule.

Chapter 2

POSTLIBERATION MUSINGS

―――――◆◇◆―――――

In the Warm Glow of Victory

On 22 April, 1993, three elderly men were having breakfast and quietly conversing at the Keren Hotel in Asmara, Eritrea. The Keren Hotel used to be called Albergo Roma during Italy's colonization of Eritrea and for many years thereafter; and the management of its restaurant boasted of serving the best spaghetti and lasagna in the world. This belief was generally shared by its many clients, both native and foreign.

Those days of the restaurant's fame are long gone and what remains of the old glory is the structure of the building itself, which was one of the first to be erected by the Italian colonial government at the end of the nineteenth century. It is an architectural treasure, one of Asmara's landmarks. And in as much as Eritrea's postcolonial national identity is defined by its colonial history, this Italianate city forms an important part of Eritrean national consciousness—at least with respect to the urban population—and is emblematic of the sense of unity among Eritreans. This sentiment is reflected in the statement of a freedom fighter from the lowlands who expressed a desire to shed his blood on the streets of Asmara, upon seeing the city's lights from a distance, as we shall see below.

That April day, Asmara was in a festive mood. The population was jubilant and scores of foreign journalists and observers were moving about the streets or lounging in hotels. One topic dominated all conversations: the referendum. For we were sitting at the Keren Hotel that morning, the day after the referendum, which was internationally monitored, and the day after the vast majority of Eritreans had voted in favor of independence.

One of the three men having breakfast was the South African-born British journalist Colin Legum, who had written extensively on African affairs since the 1950s and was one of the foreign observers of the referendum; and my brother Tewolde-Birhan (Tewolde) and I were the other two. We were talking about the momentous event of the previous day and its historic significance. Two years earlier, Eritreans had scored a military victory over Ethiopian forces, and were determined to show a skeptical world that their people were solidly behind the guerilla army that brought victory. To that end, the Eritrean leadership had insisted on an internationally observed referendum, and the outcome amply justified their confidence and lent legitimacy to the military victory. What international diplomacy had denied them, the Eritrean people had achieved by force of arms, and now they demanded and received diplomatic recognition. The circle was complete; long-denied justice was vindicated.

Colin Legum, whom I had known since the early 1960s, when I was working with the Ethiopian government, had begun slowly to shift his position on the issue of Eritrea's right to self-determination, eventually supporting it wholeheartedly, which did not endear him to many "centrist" Ethiopians. Yet he was always suspicious of the Marxist hard core in the leadership of the Eritrean liberation struggle. When I met him in London in the summer of 1975, after I came out of the "field," having joined the Eritrean liberation struggle, he received me cordially, but as we sat down for lunch in the Strand, near his office of the London Observer, he shot a provocative question at me.

"So," he said, as he perused the menu, looking at me askance, with his eyes peering above his glasses, "so now you are a Marxist revolutionary!"

It was a probing question couched in the form of a statement followed by a teasing but friendly chuckle. I remember answering him tersely, "I am a freedom fighter."

For many years thereafter, whenever we met, Colin and I debated the issue of Marxism and liberation struggle. He repeatedly warned against Marxist dogma in our struggle. It became clear that, at breakfast that morning at the Keren Hotel, he wanted to reassure himself about the same issue.

"What is next?" he wanted to know.

"After the referendum, it will be democracy," I answered him.

"Yes, and that is the hardest fight."

"How so?" my brother Tewolde asked.

"Winning the peace is a lot harder than winning the war," Colin said and continued, "This is the curse of modern African history. Mind you, I am cautiously optimistic about Eritrea, but I have lived and worked in Africa long enough, and studied revolutionary movements seriously to be too optimistic. I am still skeptical; you need to be watchful, we all need to be watchful, that's all. Power can do strange things to people."

There was a long silence, which he broke by changing the subject.

"Now let us talk about you. What will you do next?"

I told him that I would continue to teach and settle down to enjoy my golden years in a peaceful life with my family. "I think I have earned that much, don't you?" I added.

"Oh without a doubt," he said, "without a doubt."

Then he added, "But you have lived a fascinating life, full of adventures and challenges. It would be a terrible waste it seems to me, if you don't put it down in writing. I think it is time for you to write your memoirs?"

"That is exactly what I have been telling him," Tewolde said.

"Where to begin! There is so much to tell," I said.

Colin looked surprised and said, "Start from the beginning, naturally; I don't have to tell you, of all people. Start from your birthplace, your childhood in Eritrea, your education and your involvement in Ethiopian government and in the Eritrean struggle."

He went on to say that the tension implicit in my Ethiopian government experience and my Eritrean nationalist leanings, culminating in my transition to become a freedom fighter is the stuff of dramatic stories.

"A book about your life would be a good read," he concluded.

"Easier said than done," I said. "In any case, I am too young to write my memoirs."

The last remark was not facetious; the truth is that all my adult life I have been involved in one struggle after another with not much time left, and none of the solitude for writing about myself, even if I wanted to. Also, I always thought of continuing the struggle, and writing could only come after the struggle is over. That was how I thought; I now know the struggle is never over; or rather it is over only when you are six feet underground.

Meanwhile, since that conversation over breakfast at the Keren Hotel, both Colin and Tewolde have passed away, and I decided to write my story. As some of my readers may know, the first volume has been out for three years now. In it, I wrote about events and people that touched my life from my childhood on, up to Eritrea's liberation in May 1991. As I have already pointed out, it is essentially a narrative of my life and times, beginning with an account of my youth and education and continuing with my work in government and later (out of government) as an Eritrean freedom fighter.

The present volume aims at providing a historical context to the Eritrean story and some of the principal actors and events involved in that story, viewed through the eyes of an insider/outsider. The term insider/outsider needs to be further explained, including its origin in the armed struggle, as it is key to understanding our present predicament—our postliberation blues.

Before I begin the narrative, I want to step back a few years to the past—to the days when I joined the armed struggle and especially to a particular event charged with emotion for me. It was the last time I saw and said goodbye to my mother.

Darkness and Silence: A Sobering Experience

This is about memories of a night march, my introduction to the active life of the guerillas—my epiphany.

As I write, I am going through the event in my mind's eye, as if it is happening now. It is a moment that connects, for me, the present with the past. It also happens to depict a typical event in the life of the guerillas and will thus give a flavor of a day (night) in a guerilla's life. It was no picnic ...

The EPLF guerilla unit, comprising three companies, picks its way along the narrow winding path, silently and in single file. It is a dark, cloudy night; the road is rough, strewn with boulders, and no flashlights are allowed. This much is certain; we are marching from the village of Quazien, going in a southerly direction along the edge of the escarpment, east of Beleza. I know the area from my childhood years as a sheep and goat herder, and Beleza is my mother's village of origin.

It is my first march of any kind with a guerilla army; more would follow, albeit for me, not involving actual combat. We had trudged on for about half an hour when someone comes rushing from behind and says in a half whisper, "The password tonight is '*Nato*.'" I am intrigued and conclude that we must have approached another guerilla encampment. He presses on forward, half running and repeating his declaration, though I can only hear the words the second time he utters them. Puzzled by the phrase and why he is uttering it, I am also amazed at his ability to move so fast in such darkness, bypassing the boulders.

"What does this mean?" I ask the fighter in front of me.

"Keep quiet; talking is not allowed," he answers curtly.

I withdraw into my private thoughts and follow this same man, gingerly stepping on the ground he treads. I assume the man behind me is doing the same thing, stepping on the ground that I tread. I imagine each fighter to be engrossed in his own thoughts, wondering what lies ahead. Then again, being veteran fighters, most of these people must be used to this kind of procedure and are, therefore, better prepared to cope with any eventuality. I am in the dark, both literally and figuratively, and thus less prepared for anything.

I imagine that the reason for the precaution must be because we are approaching the encampment of the other guerilla force. What other force?

Well, for over two years now, Eritrea has been the scene of a murderous war fought on two fronts. There was the war between the Eritrean liberation forces and the Ethiopian army of occupation. Then there was the "civil war" between two rival factions of the liberation forces—the Eritrean Liberation Front (ELF) and the Eritrean Peoples Liberation Front (EPLF). The two fronts had fought a bitter war for over two years by the time I arrived on the scene in late December 1974.

As I march with this particular contingent of the EPLF, the two fronts are under an unsigned truce, brokered by the general public. Of course there is no guarantee of peace; ambush is always a possibility. Mutual suspicions run deep, each side accusing the other of being the culprit for every tragic incident, including the question of who started the war and why. Mutual recriminations are hurled left and right, and the population is divided and confused. The ELF calls the EPLF a *tsere ghedli* or *thawra mudadda* (Tigrigna and Arabic, respectively, meaning counterrevolutionary). And the EPLF calls the ELF *Ama* (short for *Qiyada'l Amma*)—a pejorative term.

After my miraculous escape from the clutches of the Dergue (the Ethiopian military junta) in November 1974, the first thing I wanted to do was to be part of the public efforts to stop the fratricidal war between the two fronts. As soon as I became involved in the mediation efforts, I was able to find out that the ordinary fighters in both fronts wanted the fighting to end, and both wanted reconciliation and unity, just as the public did. The problem was with the leadership of both Fronts, with their own individual ambitions and secret agendas, though the EPLF leaders protested their innocence of any wrong-doing in terms of starting the war or wanting to continue it. In any case, in February 1975, following successful mediation efforts, I decided to join the EPLF. It proved a momentous decision with serious consequences for my life and career.

About an hour after we begin the march, we are told to rest; and we do so, halfway up a hill. We can see the lights of Asmara, and a squad leader, to whom I had been introduced earlier, is sitting, looking at the city lights, which seemed enticing. Suddenly he says, "I wish we could enter Asmara and engage the enemy in our very capital. How I desire to shed my blood on the streets of Asmara!" I remember thinking, why would a young man want to shed his blood in the city? This is one of many strange things that I would experience during the liberation struggle.

Earlier that day, I was told to get ready. At about seven in the evening, Iyob Gebrelul, the Russian-trained geologist and "commissar" of the Karnishim area, comes to where I am staying, having dinner at my cousin Letense'e's house in Quazien, and tells me to get ready to move. Iyob was my first contact from the EPLF side when I started my mediation efforts. I knew him in Addis Ababa in the early 1970s, when he was working with my cousin, Temesgen Haile, in the Ministry of Mining. My cousin, Letense'e, invites Iyob to sit down and join us for a meal. He sits down but says he just had dinner. When she goes into the *wushaTe* (the women's inner sanctum where they keep the good stuff and to which no man worth his salt can enter), Iyob tells me that I will be going with a guerilla unit that night. He says that I will be going with commander Ibrahim's unit.

I receive the news with excitement mixed with curiosity. Ibrahim Afa is one of the most popular guerilla leaders, beloved by his troops, whom he successfully led in countless battles.

"Ibrahim will take care of everything; we have agreed," Iyob says with a smile.

Letense'e emerges from the *wushaTe*, with two glasses of *siwwa* (local beer)—one for him and one for me. He takes one sip, and his face lights up. He compliments my cousin for her excellent *siwwa;* she responds with a beautiful smile of pride. Iyob sips a few times and then downs the remainder in one long gurgling sound, after which he wipes his mouth with the back of his hand, springs to his feet and tells me it is time to go. Just like that! He used to be a relaxed fun-loving type; now it seems that he is about all work and no play. It must be the life of a guerilla.

"Can I finish my *siwwa*? I can't drink it as fast as you," I plead, and he agrees to give me a few more minutes.

"We must not miss the train," he says cryptically.

I finish my *siwwa* and follow him out. We climb up the eastern hill of Quazien to a wooded area of cedar trees, further away from sight of the village, and join up with about a hundred guerillas. Seeing these Afro-haired, lean, and hungry-looking young fighters, and listening to their casual chit chat and friendly banter, one might think they are on a wedding picnic. But as a famous guerilla leader once said, revolution is not a tea party. Before we start our march, Iyob introduces me to the fighter in charge of logistics of the contingent to which I am attached.

After a couple of hours, we stop on the edge of an escarpment. The clouds had cleared and a half moon is rising from the eastern horizon. I can now tell exactly where we are—we are a few meters above what used to be a spring called *Mai Amus*, some three kilometers east of Adi Nifas, my birthplace. My childhood days flood my consciousness; I remember the time when a retarded girl called BriKti got lost. In the evening, upon hearing that she was missing, the entire lineage group to which I belonged was out looking for her with torch lights. Some one had seen her going in the direction of *Mai Amus*, so the villagers headed that way.

Lo and behold, BriKti was sitting by the spring singing her favorite song repeatedly. There were a pack of hyenas nearby; the hyenas ran away as they saw the search party approaching, and when she was asked how she managed to keep them away, BriKti said three men dressed in white had come and chased them away. It was generally believed throughout the village community that the three men in white were the Holy Trinity, the patrons of the village church.

A Mother's Last Goodbye

I am in reverie remembering these things and am only awakened when Ibrahim Afa appears with two companions. After the customary greetings, he said:

"So, here you are at last, in your own land." He then asks me to follow him and two others. I had met Ibrahim a few times before; after my escape from Ethiopia. In fact, he was among the first military leaders, along with Iyob and Weldenkiel Haile, with whom I spent more time a few weeks earlier, learning about the Eritrean liberation struggle and the cause of the "civil war."

The four of us walk in the direction of Adi Nifas, chatting about mundane things like how many goats and sheep I herded in my childhood, how do I find my homeland after a long absence, and so on. After the earlier experience when I received a curt response to my simple question as we began the march from Quazien, I wouldn't dare ask where we are heading. But I can tell from the general direction that we are heading towards Adi Nifas, the village of my birth and where I had spent my childhood until age twelve.

We are almost near the base of the village and Ibrahim whispers to me that we will stop and scout the area. No sooner has he finished whispering than one of his companions tells us to lie down. Ibrahim whispers something to one of them and the latter readies his AK-47 and runs forward in a crouched position. Minutes pass without a word spoken. Then the scout returns and says, "False alarm; it is villagers tending their flocks."

"*Yalla, niKid*," orders Ibrahim and pulls me forward by the arm, indicating that we are to resume our walk towards the village.

Eventually Ibrahim answers my silent question; he must be reading my mind. I had guessed but would not speak out.

"So," Ibrahim says, "you want to see mother." I say yes and thank him and his comrades for being thoughtful and for taking the risk. It was Iyob who had arranged everything without telling me. That is the way things are done.

"No risk at all. There is going to be no problem" Ibrahim says. "And there is no need for thanks; it is our duty and our pleasure. This is the least we can do for you."

The Guerilla fighters don't talk about their parents or other members of their families. They say that their comrades are their family. Also, they do not indulge in words like "thank you" or "excuse me," which most of them dismiss as "bourgeois" formality. I can tell them, but I don't, that this veneer of civilization acts as a lubricant to social cohesion. The new (alien) ideology has displaced customary values and habits. Such niceties are not the monopoly of the bourgeoisie; the simple farmers of traditional societies indulge in them. I could tell them, but I don't. I will return to this subject later.

"I have not seen my mother for many years, and I may not see her again," I say to break the silence.

"I am sure she will be happy to see you," replies Ibrahim.

"I am afraid she may die of shock to see me with you guys."

"I sincerely hope not; we don't want to be the cause of her demise."

"But is it really safe? Yesterday, I was told that there is an Ethiopian army unit stationed in the village. They have put a price on my head, you know"

"Really? I didn't know that. Anyhow, we have sent scouts to find out where they are camped. Don't worry; we will get you in and out without any problem.

One of the two companions, the one who has his AK-47 at the ready a while ago, says, "We have intelligence that they are camped far to the west of the village. And no one knows we are visiting Adey Letehaimanot."

"How did you know my mother's name ?" I ask, surprised.

"I know her as much as I know my mother. I don't blame you for not recognizing me in the dark; besides, I was a boy of ten when you last saw me, when you came with your bride."

"Who are you?"

"I am your cousin, MeHari."

"MeHari?"

"Yes, MeHari Habtegiorgis. They call me MeHari Sheqa, in the front."

"Our guerilla army is full of your kinsmen, Dr. Bereket," Ibrahim says, and my heart is filled with pride. But I make a perfunctory statement of protest, out of customary modesty. "You are all my kinsmen."

"Yes but how does the saying go? Blood is thicker than water."

I am pleasantly surprised to hear that.

The fourth companion, whom I heard them call Fiziz, goes ahead while we wait under the cover of a ridge at the edge of the village, some twenty minutes.

Fiziz comes back and says, "The coast is clear." He is accompanied by another man who turns out to be Ghidey, the husband of my niece Mehret. We walk silently towards the house where I was born. Fiziz and Ghidey are obviously childhood friends, for they are engaged in a warm exchange of greetings. Fiziz teases Ghidey for not joining the guerillas to which Ghidey apologetically responds that someone must look after the old people, an answer that does not convince the others, for they respond with a derisive laughter that embarrasses poor Ghidey. In the local lore, the freedom fighters known as *tegadelti,* occupy a place of honor; and those left behind are put to shame unless they volunteer to do underground work in the city, which can be even more dangerous.

We are led by Ghidey to the house through the back entrance and stand waiting for my mother to appear. Presently, my mother comes, wearing her *gabi* and with a puzzled expression, for she has not been told who the night guests are. Immediately upon seeing me, she lets out a scratchy ululation, our women's customary expression of joy. I must say, she used to ululate more sonorously in days gone by.

She then looks me over from head to toe and exclaims:

"My son, my son, what have they done to you? Look at you; you are wearing their rubber shoes without socks! Why did you decide to be with those who have abandoned life?"

"Adey Letehaimanot, please don't call us that; we are alive and kicking," Ibrahim says to her in a voice of gentle reproach.

"My son is worth more. He was made for something special. Do you know what he was, before those Amhara bulls received him with their horns?"

"Believe me, Adey, he is better off with us. They would have killed him by now had he not escaped and come to join us."

Though not convinced by Ibrahim's words, my mother lets it go at that and offers dinner to the group. But Ibrahim is already up and moving towards the door. She protests, asking him to sit down for a meal. He says he has urgent matters to attend to and leaves. Just as he is leaving he asks for her blessing, and she gives him and his companions her blessing very profusely. I see him and his group out. Ibrahim then tells me that I will spend the rest of the night at another place—just a precautionary measure. He adds that Fiziz has made all the arrangements for me to lodge in a secure place and to have me escorted back to Quazien early in the morning.

"So, goodbye for now, and see you next time," he says and disappears into the night.

That was the last time I spoke to the heroic Ibrahim, though I saw him briefly, from a distance, in 1981, during my brief visit to the front, four years before he was killed in mysterious circumstances. Shortly after I heard of his death at the Second EPLF Congress in March 1987, I wrote a poem dedicated to his memory. To my astonishment, I heard later that the poem was not favorably received by some in the EPLF leadership—there is no need to name names.

The Horrors of War

It would take another four years, after the EPLF's Second Congress before the war ended. A little under a year before it ended, I appeared before the United Nations Sub-Commission for Human Rights. The time was August 1990; the venue, Geneva.

It was a decisive moment in the Eritrean war of liberation, with the EPLF on the verge of victory, closing in on the entire Ethiopian regiment that had gathered and regrouped in and around Asmara. The regiment was encircled by the EPLF army. I had traveled from Washington D.C., via Bologna, where I delivered a speech at the annual Eritrean festival. From Bologna I went to Geneva to lodge a formal protest concerning the case of Eritrean victims of Ethiopian atrocities before the UN Sub-Commission on Human Rights. Geneva is the headquarters of the subcommission, and I had brought a video made by a Canadian filmmaker depicting the atrocities.

Earlier that year, the Ethiopian Air Force had dropped incendiary bombs on the port of Massawa, killing and maiming hundreds of civilians and destroying historic buildings. It was one of the last desperate acts of a dying regime, committed in the wake of its losses in several key battles, resulting in its loss of the port of Massawa. In the foyer of the Palais de Nations in Geneva, outside the hall where the subcommission was holding its meeting, the video depicting the atrocities was shown. Everyone who saw it, including members of the subcommission, was outraged. The video would prove useful in our fight for admission to lodge our complaint to the subcommission. We had made copies of the video and shown it to several government missions at the United Nations in New York.

Naturally, members of the Ethiopian diplomatic mission in Geneva protested loudly and made attempts to obstruct its viewing. The Ethiopian mission had relied on the Ethiopian expert member of the subcommission, Mr. Fisseha Yimer, to block our entry into the subcommission; and he had protested, raising technical reasons of accreditation to deny us admission. His contention was that I represented the EPLF, which he described as an unlawful rebel organization. But we had anticipated this and persuaded Centre Europe-Tier Monde, a Swiss nongovernmental organization, to sponsor us. So I appeared before the subcommission representing Centre Europe-Tier Monde. The previous evening, in a closed session, the subcommission overruled the objection and decided to admit me. The Ethiopian complaint continued, following my presentation; but the message had been delivered loud and clear. Even Fisseha's protests were perfunctory and did not carry much conviction, particularly since he had presumably seen the video and knew that it had been seen by most of the members of the subcommission.

The press release of the subcommission published the following day reported my appearance and speech with the following summary of my long speech:

> Bereket Habte SELASSIE (Centre Europe-Tier Monde) said that massive and grave violations of human right continued to be perpetrated by the Government of Ethiopia against the people of Eritrea. The Ethiopian air force had been engaged in massive bombing campaigns largely targeting civilians in residential and commercial centers. As a result hundreds of innocent children, women and men had been killed and thousands maimed and rendered homeless.

Those bombing raids had occurred on several occasions between 16 February and 10 June. The speaker said that the Sub-Commission should bear constantly in mind the historical and political conditions that caused and sustained the Eritrean people's 30 year struggle for freedom and justice. The Eritrean case was identical to that of Namibia and not of Biafra, as mentioned yesterday." [Press release HR/2628, 17 August, 1990].

The press release also published an interesting statement by Monsieur Louis Joinet, who was an expert jurist from France at the subcommission. I had mentioned his name in my written remarks, stating that he had been one of the jurists who had given an advisory opinion on Eritrea sitting as members of the People's Tribunal in Milan on 3 October, 1980. In their advisory opinion the panel of jurists had categorically supported the just demands of the Eritrean people for self-determination and independence. It seemed that now Joinet wanted to renege on his opinion; the press release reported him as saying that he regretted that his name had been mentioned as acting "as a witness at the International Peoples' Tribunal eleven years ago on the question of Eritrea." He said that his views had "evolved."

First of all, he was not a witness; he was a member of the tribunal. Then again, one wonders why and in what way his ideas had evolved? Did "evolve" mean he had revoked his support of the idea of self-determination, an idea he had supported in principle ten years earlier? We will never know. Nor will we know what he must have felt when the principle of self-determination that he had supported was vindicated ten months later when Eritrea won the war and two years later Eritrea was admitted as a member of the United Nations. It is possible that he was towing the official line of the then governing French Socialist party, which presumably assumed that the EPLF would never succeed. Most governments, including the U.S. government, made the same assumption, as I would be told repeatedly during my encounter in New York with members of the U.S. delegation to the UN.

At the time this was going on in Geneva, events back home were quickly producing their own momentum. History was being made, nations remade, and the people waiting with great expectations for better things to come. And those who saw the video graphically depicting atrocities being committed against innocent civilians could not have failed to be touched—even some who had the job of defending the indefensible—the carnage, children dead and wounded, half-buried bodies in the rubble of the crumbling buildings, women wailing amid the chaos and confusion. I would like to believe that Fisseha Yimer, who now (2010) represents the current Ethiopian government as ambassador in Geneva, was among such people.

Fast Forward: *Nineteen years later, in a recent meeting I had with an Ethiopian acquaintance, Samuel Assefa, Ethiopian ambassador to the United States, told me an interesting story. His recently- deceased mother, the illustrious Woizero Snidu Gebru, had shown him a poem she had written on the atrocities committed in Massawa. She must have seen the horrendous pictures that I showed in Geneva. The poem's refrain was: "Ilamawn satow!" (Miss the target!):*

> Ibak'hn Ilamawn satow!
> Yemmigodaw'ko Wondimh new
> *(Please miss the target*
> *The victims are your brothers...)*

In her poem, the good lady, whose humane sensibilities must have been outraged, was addressing the Ethiopian Air Force pilot whose order was to bomb Massawa.

I am dwelling on the atrocities covered by the video because I consider that such a horrendous sight should ideally induce compassion as well as outrage. It should become a factor for facilitating adversaries to think in terms of common interest. Victims of atrocities—indeed all victims—are not defined by national borders. This, after all, is the basis of humanitarian laws epitomized by the Geneva Conventions. Humanitarian issues should be above politics, and the essential point about the role of the UN Sub-Commission on Human Rights is based on this principle. That is why Geneva and the Geneva Conventions symbolize adherence to international norms that should govern the behavior of governments and their armed forces in time of conflict. The Geneva Conventions define the rules of conduct in times of armed conflict, prohibiting indiscriminate bombing of civilians and defining these as war crime or crime against humanity.

That is, of course, the ideal case scenario. In actual fact, the professional ethics of the country experts nominated by their governments does not mean they allow themselves to forget where they came from or to condone the acceptance of abstract ideals to prevail upon the interests of their respective governments. The national ideology that aligns people behind their government—my country, right or wrong—is a powerful force; hence Fisseha's attempts to defend the indefensible by resorting to technicalities.

The Larger Drama

A little historical perspective will be helpful here. By the time of my Geneva episode, the conflict in the Horn of Africa had been raging for almost thirty years—with tragic consequences to lives and devastation to property. At that time, the largest number of refugees in Africa was from that subregion. The internationalization of the conflict, with more and deeper foreign intervention had aggravated the situation as the world community, including the UN and the OAU (Organization of African Unity), watched with virtual disinterest. With military solutions imposed to solve political problems, the crisis intensified, increasing the level of violence tenfold since 1977, the time when the Soviet Union decided to intervene massively on the side of Ethiopia. That intervention, in turn, provoked American intervention on Somalia's side diplomatically as well as militarily, with the U.S. giving Somalia arms supplies to offset the Soviet intervention.

Two comments made reflecting on the fluid state of international relations at the time deserve mention here. One was a remark made by the then Somali president, Mohamed Siyyad Barre, who quoted the Somali proverb "Either be a mountain, or lean on a mountain" in order to justify his shift of alliance from the Soviet Union to the United States. The other comment was made in relation to the Soviets' intervention on Ethiopia's behalf and its impact on U.S.-Soviet relations. U. S. National Security Advisor Zbignew Brizinski said that SALT II (Strategic Arms Limitation Treaty) had been "buried in the sands of the Ogaden."

With prodigious aid of Soviet arms and Cuban troop involvement, the Ethiopians drove out the invading Somali army and threatened to cross the border and overthrow Siyyad Barre's government. This would have altered the balance of forces in the region and installed the Soviets in a strategic part of the world. America could not tolerate such a turn of events and warned the Soviets not to cross the border. .

Meanwhile the war raged on many fronts—in Eritrea, in Tigrai, and in parts of northern and southern Ethiopia, as the world watched seemingly unconcerned. In the face of the deafening silence of the international community on the impact of the continuing war to the people of the Horn of Africa, privately convened conferences were held, initiated by individuals and groups, principally university professors. The aim of such conferences was to help define and explain the main elements of the conflict in terms of the various issues of contention and the forces aligned behind the issues. The organizers and participants hoped that such conferences might elicit dialogue among concerned individuals and groups with a view to turning people's mind towards just and peaceful solutions. A conviction seemed to gain ground that military solutions were no answer to political problems, particularly when, as in the Horn of Africa, people were prepared to pay the ultimate sacrifice for their causes.

In the absence of official/government initiatives to help bring about a peaceful resolution of the conflict, some prominent individuals began taking initiatives to that end. The conflict seemed ripe for resolution, particularly as the liberation forces gained more ground, scoring spectacular victories over the

Dergue army and putting the Dergue government increasingly and desperately on the defensive. One such individual was former U.S. President Jimmy Carter, who organized mediation meetings between the Dergue government and the EPLF, once in Atlanta, Georgia and again in Nairobi, Kenya. Any effort for lasting solutions requires, as a precondition, an openness of mind, a readiness to talk and listen, and above all, an appreciation of what is at stake from all sides. As predicted, Carter's commendable initiative and efforts did not bear fruit. There was no readiness to compromise on either side.

As all these efforts were being undertaken, I frequently met Ethiopians at various forums and individually at private encounters. At such encounters, I experienced the absence of openness of mind and appreciation of the other side's contention. (Indeed, even in my own case, there was invariably some unmistakable resentment). One basic problem was ignorance of the roots of Eritrea's problems and the reason for our resort to arms, itself born out of a frustrated peaceful political movement—ignorance and an unwillingness to know and understand. An often-heard remark concerning my own involvement was: "How could a man who had been a high government official in Ethiopia become an Eritrean liberation fighter?" As readers of the first volume of these memoirs will have seen, my advent into the world of liberation struggle was not a first choice or a headlong leap into the guerilla option. There is a long and complex history behind it, but most Ethiopians have not been ready and willing to hear that story. Their mind is made up; they can't be bothered with the facts.

I met some of my old friends after the fall of the Dergue government, both in Addis Ababa and abroad. When they heard that I was convening a conference in 1993, titled "From Conflict to Concord: Regional Cooperation in the Horn of Africa," the fairminded and sensible among them showed a willingness to wait and see. Some even expressed generous sentiments of goodwill, wishing me success on the conference. Others were resentful, seeing such initiative as the moral bluff of a member of the liberation forces at the time of their victory. Prominent intellectuals that I invited to participate in the conference made excuses and declined to accept the invitation. But the wheels of history were turning, and there was no turning back. On 1 July, 1991, one month after entering Addis Ababa, Ethiopia's capital, Meles Zenawi and his EPRDF convened an international conference there. The eyes of the world focused on Addis Ababa for five eventful days. Before I take up the topic of that conference, let me conclude the narrative about the Geneva episode.

The Scent of Peace

After my presentation of the Eritrean victims of atrocities, which had a fairly good reception from the subommission, I found time to relax a little and unwind from a whirlwind of activities. We had all had enough of war—enough of senseless killing and devastation. Even Fisseha's feeble protest could not have come from conviction, if he had seen the video, as I was sure he did. And no one with any sense of decency could see the video and approve of what was clearly an egregious violation of human rights. An international law expert like Fisseha could not fail to see that the bombing of civilians constituted war crimes and crimes against humanity.

The war had touched all sides. So when it ended, the occasion signaled not only an end to hostilities but a new beginning in which human brotherhood would replace violent conflict. No wonder the muse visited me in Geneva, as it did from time to time, and a poem simply flowed from deep inside my soul. Some ten months later, I had that mysterious experience at the chapel of the Washington Cathedral, as I related in volume one of these memoirs, an experience that I could not explain rationally. And, as Albert Einstein once said, the most beautiful thing we can experience is the mysterious.

Immediately after I presented the case of Eritrean victims to the UN Sub-Commission, I went to a quiet corner in the delegates' lounge of the Palais de Nations and ordered a cappuccino with a croissant. And as I sat sipping the cappuccino, looking at Lake Geneva, I was seized by the muse; before I knew it, I started writing a poem, later edited and looking like the following, came out of me:

Scent of Peace

Sitting in the Hall of Nations
In leisurely Geneva,
I wait with hope and fear
As adversaries interface;
Dare I believe what I hear
That swords will turn to ploughshares
And brothers embrace,
And the foul stench of Death
Give way to the fragrance of peace,
In this tortured earth?
...All is possible in His Grace.

That I could think of "brothers embracing" is a function of not just my own sensibility, but above all of the exhaustion we were all feeling on both sides of the war. There was fatigue; there was general disgust, but few volunteered to say so; each side soldiered on fighting for its cause—the one for self-determination, the other for "territorial integrity," two seemingly opposed but equally valid principles of international relations.

Both causes demanded a heavy price, as countless lives were sacrificed in pursuit of those two causes. Well, *c'est la vie*, you might say; or rather *c'est la guerre*!

The war came to an end in Eritrea on 24 May, 1991, with the EPLF armed forces entering Asmara. In Ethiopia itself, the Ethiopian Peoples' Revolutionary Democratic Front (EPRDF) entered Addis Ababa four days later, on May 28. In the closing years of the war, when the forces of liberation—the EPLF and EPRDF—were scoring victories over the Dergue army, the leaders of these forces had begun to look to the future, a future of peaceful cooperation across national boundaries. Many members of the EPLF, myself included, had knowledge of some of the talks going on in that respect, if not the details of the discussions. There had been some unresolved differences and tension between the EPRDF and Oromo Liberation Front (OLF) over the question of power sharing in a postimperial Ethiopia. The EPLF leadership had helped mediate the differences.

During those heady days and in the first few years of Eritrea's postindependence period, much was said that gave grounds for hope of a peaceful democratic future. There was an unambiguous declaration of commitment to democracy and the rule of law and an implicit sense of hope for regional cooperation. Some even spoke of regional integration. I was in favor of the idea on the basis of sovereign equality gradually leading to regional integration. But first sovereign equality must be asserted and commonly accepted. I remember that when I was asked to draft the law establishing the Constitutional Commission of Eritrea, I was affected by this sentiment and decided to insert it in the preamble of the draft law in order to help create an environment of amity and comity among Eritreans and Ethiopians. It would help, I thought, to symbolize the movement away from conflict and toward concord. Evidently the Eritrean lawmakers did not approve of my decision, for the phrase was omitted from the final draft that was approved by the National Assembly. The long war had taken its toll in more ways than one.

As for the scent of peace that I envisaged in my poem, alas! Instead of it, I would experience, soon thereafter, "the stench of Death" in the wilderness of western Eritrea. A week after Asmara was liberated, some among those of us serving the cause of Eritrea's liberation abroad were summoned to come home; and, since there was no air service from anywhere to Asmara, my traveling companions and I flew from Washington, D.C. to Khartoum, Sudan, and rode all the way from Khartoum on the Tesseney-Barentu-Agordat-Keren road leading to Asmara. On our way, we saw a most frightful sight—thousands of Ethiopian soldiers lay dead, their rotting remains strewn all along the Keren-Barentu road. My mind flashed back to Geneva and the leisurely mood under which I wrote the poem. And here was I, traveling across this harsh terrain, past an endless, sorry spectacle of corpses wasting in a land they did not know. It is true that thousands of young Eritreans had died fighting for what they believed—for freedom and justice—but I thought that the death of these young Ethiopians was cruel and pointless. I was quite sure that many of these unfortunate Ethiopian youths, who were compelled to come to fight here, did not even know where or why they came to fight—why they paid with their lives.

I was confirmed in this conclusion after I gained an insight as a result of what my late sister Mebrat recounted to me in the story of a sixteen-year old Ethiopian soldier who was captured by shepherd boys, among them her fourteen-year-old son. The shepherds found the boy-soldier sleeping on the grass where their flock of sheep had been grazing. He was exhausted, hungry, and dehydrated and was probably suffering from sleep deprivation. He was armed but did not put up any resistance when the shepherds captured and corralled him with the use of mere sticks. Two of them took him to my sister's house, while one went to report his capture to the local EPLF authorities. My sister took pity on him, gave him water, tea, and bread before the EPLF people came for him. When I asked her why she treated him the way she did—after all, didn't his kind kill her husband and two of her sons?—she simply said, "He too has a mother somewhere, poor soul."

I looked at my sister in amazement, and thought, no wonder the villagers called her "*Maryam Shimanegus.*" (Mary of Shimanegus).

After the war, the victors promised peace, democracy, justice, and the rule of law. These are the values for which countless lives were lost and whole communities destroyed. The victors, who had come together for consultation, gave their solemn word to secure these values and live by them. As the war was winding down toward conclusion, the victors had come together, encouraged by American diplomacy, to discuss the postvictory political order. Indeed, the then assistant secretary of state for African affairs, Mr. Herman Cohen, convened a meeting in London to which were invited the leaders of the EPLF, EPRDF, the OLF, as well as the transitional prime minister of the Dergue's collapsing government. The dictator Mengistu Haile Mariam had run out of town and into exile in Zimbabwe one week before the guerilla army took Addis, presumably encouraged by the Americans. The Americans were anxious to avoid bloodshed and urged the EPRDF forces closing in on Addis Ababa to come in and take charge of the security. The EPRDF leaders were glad to oblige and ready and able to do so.

Thus did Addis Ababa fall into "rebel" hands, and thus did the seventeen-year reign of terror end, bringing with it great expectations of change for the better.

In his farewell pep talk to the "rebel leaders," at the end of the London meeting, Mr. Cohen harangued the leaders about the need of democracy. His admonition was laced with promises of American assistance to the new governments, predicated on the establishment of democracy. His parting shot was:

No democracy—No development aid! This was repeated time and again, like a mantra by American government aid donors.

From the vantage point of an academic-cum practitioner, I had occasion to write about aspects of the history and politics of countries of the Horn of Africa region. After I became involved as a full-fledged member of the EPLF, I had the advantage of acquiring some of the insights of a participant. And I was intrigued by the direction of events in research and writing topics about the fast-developing situation. That was how I decided to develop a research project and apply for a fellowship at the United States Institute of Peace (USIP). My research project was titled, "From Conflict to Concord: The Case for Regional Cooperation in the Horn of Africa." My project was accepted by the Board of Trustees of USIP, and I received the Jennings Randolph Distinguished Fellowship for 1992-1993.

As part of my project, I convened an international symposium on regional cooperation, funded by the U.S. Peace Institute and the United Nations Economic Commission for Africa, Addis Ababa, July 8-12, 1993. The symposium was convened at Africa Hall and formally opened by Ethiopia's minister of foreign affairs, Mr. Seyoum Mesfin. Among those invited to participate and present papers were ministers of Cooperation and/or finance of Eritrea, and Ethiopia, and representatives of Sudan, Djibouti, and Somalia. Judging by the official statements of the appropriate ministers as well as the climate of intellectual opinion as expressed by many of the participants, there seemed no doubt but that the region was ripe for cooperation, even eventual integration.

In fact, there were other important events preceding the conference that seemed to point towards a readiness by the new governments of Eritrea and Ethiopia for cooperation. The first of such meetings was a little gathering of the top leaders of the EPLF, EPRDF, and the OLF. Representing the EPLF were Isaias Afwerki and two members of the EPLF political bureau, namely, Ali Said Abdalla and Sebhat Efrem and two of us, myself and Amare Tekle, were included in an advisory capacity. Representing the EPRDF was Meles Zenawi, who came by car from Addis Ababa with some personal security details and a driver. Representing the OLF was Leenco Leta, deputy leader of the OLF, a man of wisdom and eloquence. I had met Leenco and Meles in Washington in the 1980s at different times. (See pictures)

The Addis Ababa Conference, 1-5 July 1991

The conference was called the Conference for the Peaceful and Democratic Transition in Ethiopia. The conveners were the EPRDF and OLF, but the EPRDF was the principal actor of this important conference.

Present at the conference were all the national opposition forces, with the exception of a couple of political organizations; the successor to the Ethiopian People's Revolutionary Party (EPRP) and another Marxist party known by its Amharic acronym, Meison. Both were invited to participate but made conditions that the EPRDF did not accept.

In his opening address to the conference, Meles Zenawi, head of EPRDF and president of the transitional government, explained the criteria for selecting the conference participants. Attempts were made, he said, so that the participants would "represent the various nations and nationalities and that the conference would be a forum in which the outlooks and tendencies of most sectors of the society would be reflected." He added that all opposing political attitudes and tendencies were represented "in the conviction that it would be vital and also valuable to involve those forces which had contributed to the downfall of the past regime despite the degree of their contribution...."

A charter came out of the conference that became the foundation of the future constitution of the federal democratic republic of Ethiopia, which included a federal structure granting regional power to the federating constituent units called *Kilils*. A spirit of reconciliation involving healthy realism and sensible compromise characterized the postimperial Ethiopian situation, a spirit that could have been, but was not, adopted in the Eritrean case, as we shall see.

A glance at the names of the cabinet members of the transitional government reflects this spirit of realism and compromise. In the cabinet list, one could see that, next to members of the EPRDF, OLF members figured prominently. Alas! The OLF and the EPRDF fell out on some issues barely a year following the formation of the transitional government, resulting in the pullout of the OLF from the government and resumption of its pursuit of the politics of liberation. Its aim was the creation of an independent state called Oromia. This was a serious setback for the postimperial democratic experiment in Ethiopia, a problem that has yet to find resolution.

The EPRDF's policy on Eritrea was based on the principle of the right of colonized peoples to self-determination. The EPRDF had issued its policy on Eritrea earlier and confirmed it during the conference, when the issue of the right of Eritreans to determine their political future through a referendum was raised. The conference passed a positive resolution on this issue with a couple of delegates abstaining. An EPLF delegation led by Isaias Afwerki participated in the conference in an observer capacity, and I attended as a member of that delegation.

As an important ally of the EPRDF, our delegation was given a place of honor in every respect, and Isaias gave a speech at the allotted time. His speech was in Tigrigna, and I was asked to interpret into Amharic, which led to an interesting incident. His rapid-fire speech was difficult to capture in all its essence; so on a couple of occasions I must have stumbled, and he stopped to complain that

I did not render his speech exactly, whereupon I said something to the effect that my training was not exactly in interpreting, which was greeted with raucous laughter. Meles came to the rescue, volunteering to do the interpretating, even while presiding over the conference! After a few moments, Meles turned to me and said, "you can now take over," to which I replied, "no no, you go ahead; you are doing a good job." Another raucous laughter and Meles called on Bereket Simon to do the interpreting, to my great relief. Nevertheless, I did not take kindly to Isaias's rude tone and remark, though I did not want to show it then.

In the evening of the same day, when we met for dinner in the palace where we were staying, Ali Said Abdalla, who had had one glass too many, made a snide remark about my fumbling in interpreting, to which I repeated my remark that I was not trained to interpret for anybody. Isaias was within hearing range and told Ali something in Arabic, which apparently Ali did not like, for he responded in kind, and the argument continued. They both rose to leave and left the dining hall arguing loudly in Arabic. So ended an interesting episode and my brief career as an "interpreter."

Years later, when relations began to harden between the two leaders, Addis Ababa TV program showed snippets of that incident repeatedly making Isaias look like an uncouth and rude boor who did not respect his elders. Many Ethiopian friends told me about the TV snippets; and I could imagine those who considered me as the *bête noire* who "betrayed" Ethiopia reveling at the spectacle of Isaias showing disrespect to me. Others were more discriminating and fair and were shocked to see an elder being rebuked by a younger man irrespective of his position.

At the end of the five-day conference, both Meles and Isaias held press conferences. At these press conferences, keen observers could see the difference of style in the two leaders. Whereas Meles spoke in a relaxed manner sprinkling humor in his remarks, Isaias was rigid and unsmiling. Overall, he was blunt and uncharacteristically obtuse. An American reporter, who had interviewed him before and knew he could be sharp, asked me later, "What was the matter with him? In fact why do I get the feeling that he wanted people to hate him? Why do I get the feeling that he wants me to hate him?" That was an astute observation. Nor did Isaias feel good about it. Later in the day, during our mealtime, I asked him how he thought the press meeting went; his immediate answer was, "it was bad."

Receptions were held at the National Palace (the former Emperor's Guenete Luul Palace) both on the opening night on July 1 and at the closing on 5 July 1991. I remembered the last time I attended a banquet given by Prime Minister Aklilu Haptewold, hosting on behalf of the Emperor; I believe it was on the occasion of the Emperor's eightieth birthday, if memory serves me well. What was formerly used as the palace of the privileged elites was now opened to the representatives of the "masses," signaling the dawning of a new era.

Will it be an era of peace, democracy and prosperity? Only time will tell.

Chapter 3

THE GOLD AND THE BASE METAL: LEADERSHIP AND THE FATE OF A NATION

A few years ago, when my sister Mebrat died and I was not able to be at her funeral, I expressed my lamentations on one of the Eritrean websites. On it I wrote the following words:

> Do I blame Isaias for my inability to be at my sister's funeral? I blame him for many other things, but not for this one. On the contrary, I find myself devoutly wishing for his redemption. Not the kind of redemption that the reverend Jesse Jackson usually invokes, although Isaias could probably benefit from such kind of redemption—who knows? The kind of redemption I wished for the supreme leader is a more mundane one, pertaining to the political kingdom—one that might help deliver the nation from its present predicament and possible catastrophe.

It was a statement made in an ironic spirit; but as ironies go, it did not carry a sting. In fact, in the paragraph following the statement, I made a wish: "Would that I could fly back to Asmara and, with a magic wand, transmute the base metal that Isaias has become into the gold that I thought he was."

These few words sum up my attitude and that of many others, regarding Isaias. Many still hope he will change back to his earlier self. (Full disclosure: I was one of these until 2000, as shown by the Berlin Letter that I helped draft in October 2000, in which I and twelve other Eritrean academics and professionals appealed to Isaias to act like a statesman). Others have given up any hope of redemption; to them he is a lost soul who has entered into a Faustian bargain with the devil. A few even believe that he never was a principled leader: that he was an egotistical maniac, out for power, not for the revolutionary ideal of liberation, which he used to his own selfish purposes. This belief has gained currency in recent times, particularly after the fallout resulting from the crisis of the Badme War.

Where does the truth lie? This is one of the crucial questions that must be explored. I will begin with the gold that I thought he was.

The Presumed Gold

Charisma of Dedication

When I first met Isaias in January 1975, at a place called Sabur Seghi in the then semiliberated area, he was a twent-nine-year-old striking figure—tall, sinewy, serious and unsmiling, wearing the green field jacket and rubber sandals, the "kongo." It was difficult not to be impressed by him. Diffident at first in conversation, his intelligence and command of facts and issues became apparent as we began to talk about the history of the struggle, and especially how and why the group he led out of the ELF came to form the EPLF. We talked the whole afternoon and evening the day I met him and continued the next day until noon. He had a quiet demeanor and spoke softly in what seemed to me a droning, monotonous tone; but his language was clear and concise, as he ranged over a number of issues in response to my questions.

Sabur Seghi formerly belonged to some local grandees who had concession rights on the fertile land where cash crops like fruits, vegetables, and coffee were cultivated. Naturally, there were no chairs or tables; so we sat on the ground outside a building that was built by concession owners. I remember that as we sat there, he brought out a piece of sack cloth and laid it on an elevated part of the ground, presumably to save my trousers from being soiled, as I was then a "city slicker." When I reported this detail to Herui Tedla Bairu, the leader of the rival front, during one of my meetings while I was engaged in "shuttle diplomacy," he dismissed the gesture as the act of a deceptive politician trying to impress me with feigned humility. I did not accept this dismissal; in fact I resented it at the time as being mean and unworthy of a freedom fighter. I would find more instances of such meanness later from all sides. For the record, despite the uneasiness of our relationship, Isaias exhibited similar courtesy toward me during our interaction over the years, keeping his real feelings about me to himself, until independece.

With respect to Isaias's behavior, two points need to be made. First, I heard later of conflicting stories as to the way he treated colleagues and subordinates, particularly when he was angry. Second, his patterns of behavior changed as he accumulated more power vis-à-vis his comrades-in-arms, a point that I take up in more detail in another chapter. All this raises the question: Did his behavior change, or had the anger and rage been there all the time, concealed beneath the surface? My interviews with some of his closest collaborators, help to shed some light on this question, as we shall see later.

A related question, one that is more relevant from the perspective of the aim of this book, of course, concerns what many consider a complete reversal of policy for which Isaias is answerable before history and perhaps before the law. I explore this in more detail later in this chapter. Meanwhile, let us look at different aspects of his role.

Leader of Party and Nation

A constant feature of the speeches Isaias made, especially those given in answer to the question of whether the EPLF will ever compete or share power with other parties, is his repeated proclamation of the unity of the party and the nation. I have heard him declare that the EPLF is Eritrea and Eritrea is the EPLF. This is no mere theoretical issue about nation and state or party and nation. It goes to the heart of the problem of power and accountability. I was present on one of his public meetings held at Asmara Municipality Hall in 1995, when he repeated this in answer to a question from a member of the public who wanted to know if and when the EPLF (by then renamed People's Front for Democracy and Justice, the PFDJ for short), would allow multiparty elections. In a tone of impatience and irritation, Isaias said that whether people liked it or not, the EPLF would remain as the ruling party for a long time. He capped his response by stating the now familiar mantra that the EPLF is Eritrea and Eritrea is EPLF.

After the meeting was over, an old friend of mine, who was a skeptic by nature and not an EPLF supporter, laughingly remarked, as we left the hall on our way to his house,

"Did you hear your leader?" I said, of course, I heard.

My friend said, "What Isaias did not say, but what I read from his statement is,

"The EPLF is Eritrea; I am the EPLF. Therefore I am Eritrea."

My friend (now deceased) was a history buff, and as we were walking towards his car, he added, with a hearty laugh, "What did the French king say? I am the state!... I don't know the French words for it, but I am sure you do." I did not join in my friend's joviality, but I had no answer to that perceptive comment. By that time, I had already started asking questions myself and entertaining grave concerns.

In the typical pattern of self-censorship from which all EPLF members suffered, I kept postponing the day of reckoning. The answer to my concern was that everything will be put in order after the constitution is promulgated, defining the limits to presidential power with checks and balances, and a Bill of Rights proclaiming peoples' rights. And all those who had similar concerns shared this hope of change with the coming of the constitution. There is a sense in which our hopes were wellfounded, as we shall see when considering the making of the constitution and the democratic promise undertaken by the

EPLF government. Little did we know then that the promise would not be kept. How could we? The promise was declared in the resolutions of two congresses, which were translated into laws.

As briefly noted above, it is an open question as to whether Isaias had always been a power-hungry autocrat who was waiting for an opportune moment to do away with the collective leadership that was the guiding norm throughout the liberation struggle, sideline his potential rivals, and bring everything under his control. Or did he change as he gained more personal and public attention, including the privilege of meeting world leaders as an equal; also enjoying the thrill of uncontested power and authority? I have personally witnessed incidents that may lend support to the theory that he changed with the accumulation of power. For example, as mentioned in the preceding chapter, I was a member of an Eritrean observer delegation, led by Isaias that attended the historic conference in Addis Ababa, which became the basis for Ethiopia's postimperial constitutional system. That conference also passed a near-unanimous resolution, agreeing that the Eritrean people have the right to legitimize their hard-won independence by referendum.

Towards the conclusion of the conference, I saw a delegation of Sudanese government ministers and diplomats visiting Isaias, on several occasions, on the palace grounds where we were lodged. They addressed him not as comrade Isaias, but as Mr. President (*Ya Said Al Rais*), with obsequious behavior to boot. This kind of attention, when repeated, could not have failed to bring about change in his behavior. The same was true with the visiting Ethiopian officials who came to do an interview with him. I could see the change in Isaias' body language in response to this changed protocol. I remember noting in my diary, "Ah, the corrupting capacity of protocol!" Nor was the attention limited to diplomats and other government officials. The press also had its corrupting impact, as a swarm of newspapermen closed in on both Meles Zenawi and Isaias, showering them with inordinate attention. In another chapter I will examine the issue of the relationship or more accurately, the rivalry between Isaias and Meles.

Guerilla Warfare and Marxism

Guerillas of most liberation movements in the 1960s and 1970s were influenced by the temper of the times, the dominant ideology being Marxism. Eritrea was no exception in this respect. The leaders of the EPLF and some of the ELF professed Marxism as their guiding ideology, replacing (or at best, working side by side with) a nationalist ideology. At one time, being Marxist became the badge of distinction among the elite in both the ELF and EPLF. When I decided to join the EPLF early in 1975, I remember some of the upper cadres telling me that they distinguished the EPLF as being Marxist, whereas the ELF was not! At that time, I saw no ELF publication that showed its political color, either Left or Right, although some of its leading cadres professed Marxism. Foreign journalists, like Dan Connell and the late Lars Bondestam, lent credence to this belief, distinguishing the EPLF as a Marxist organization and impliedly favoring it over the ELF. Several European Left groups, including notably the Italian *Il Gruppo Manifesto*, lionized EPLF members and seemed to pin their hopes on the EPLF as an authentic Marxist guerilla organization that would show the way to a Leftist world that had apparently lost its way, with the Soviets and the Chinese at logger heads and Western communist parties mostly toying the Moscow line.

Later, I learned that there was a secret Marxist group within the ELF called the Labor party. In the case of the ELF, the top leaders did not profess Marxism; far from professing it, they opposed the Marxist elements, sidelining them from any significant role. This is another murky side of Eritrean history that needs to be examined dispassionately. For this task nobody is better qualified than former ELF cadres now living in the Diaspora. For now, I leave it there.

As early as 1973, EPLF literature shows a dedication to a Marxist ideology and a determination to instruct the EPLF cadres, especially the young recruits, in Marxism. *Mahta* (Spark) was the ideological (theoretical) journal in which articles on the theory and practice of Marxism were discussed. Before Mahta, there was *Fitewrari* (Vanguard), which started as early as 1972. It carried news analyses and information on the development of the Eritrean struggle, often discussing timely issues. When I first reached Sahel, the base area of the EPLF, in March 1975, I found one of the highly educated new recruit from the United States, Haile Menkerios, translating Lenin's classic tract, "What Is to Be Done?" into Tigrigna. Another educated cadre and Arabic scholar, Mohamed Ali Oumaro, was also engaged in translating it into Arabic.

By the time of its First Congress in 1977, the EPLF had established a department of ideological guidance and a school for cadres to which selected young bright recruits were sent and instructed in the theory and practice of Marxism. Ten years later, by the time of the Second Congress, several hundred young cadres had graduated from the school, theoretically equipped and ready to do ideological battle with anyone challenging the official line. Even in 1975, when I started hearing the ideologically trained first batch of cadres, I realized that things were changing. Even the language had changed: New vocabulary had been invented many literal translations from Marxist literature. Some of the adopted language was imaginative, but it was foreign to the ordinary citizen. In daily conversation between the cadres and the peasants, it seemed at times as if the cadres were speaking a foreign language, leaving the peasants confused, often alienating them.

Class Struggle: Genuine Ideology or Instrument of Control?

As in all Marxist ideological discourse, class struggle was the dominant line controlling all discourse in the EPLF arena. Moreover, it was duly ordained that the alliance of the workers and peasants was to be the basic organization to help bring about a just society. The other classes—the petty bourgeoisie, the bourgeoisie, and the capitalists could be used for the end of the revolution, but had to be watched with care. The petty bourgeoisie, in particular, is an unstable class, forever changing with changing times and fortune and was, therefore, to be watched with special vigilance. The interesting thing was that the leadership of the EPLF and most of the important cadres came from that class; so who was watching whom! This incongruity did not seem to bother the ideologues, except perhaps some of the more inquiring and independent-minded cadres. But everyone exercised a peculiar species of self-censorship that marked the behavior of EPLF cadres.

When I spent time in the Sahel base area, these questions were the subject of conversation all the time, with the sons of peasants constantly teasing city types, most of them former high school and a few university students, about the untrustworthiness of the petty bourgeoisie. There have even been cases when some of the former city types, mostly better educated than the sons of peasants, could not tolerate the teasing, which most often amounted to harassment. Some of them committed suicide, while others defected. The tragic suicide of Dr. Bemnet, a brilliant medical doctor and a popular member of the EPLF, and another medical doctor, is a case in point. In the case of the two medical doctors, witnesses of former EPLF members that I interviewed boldly asserted that members of the top hierarchy of the EPLF leadership are answerable, if not for having a direct hand in their suicide, at least for not anticipating it and not discouraging indiscriminate harassment of educated types. Moreover, no satisfactory inquiry was made as to why these two doctors were driven to suicide.

Amilcar Cabral, the brilliant leader of the liberation struggle of Guinea-Bissau, proclaimed an unforgettable, if problematic, maxim about the petty bourgeoisie. He said that in order to be a true revolutionary, members of the petty bourgeoisie have to "commit class suicide." I always wondered if the EPLF cadres really believed in this maxim. Many repeated it like a catechism; some might have conceivably lived by it. There was a cruel joke that I heard in Sahel once regarding those who committed suicide, hinting that they did so because of their tragic misunderstanding of what Cabral meant about committing class suicide!

Now there is little doubt about the powerful mobilizing capacity of Marxism. It has been used to unite the greater mass of oppressed populations like the Eritrean people in a common goal of liberation. Its appeal consists in the promise that it offers to the larger mass of populations that their lives would be better off after they shake off the shackles of oppression of the dominant classes, be they feudal lords or exploiting merchant classes. Many in my generation, myself included, fell under the spell of Marxism because of this appeal. I still think that Marxist analysis of the capitalist mode of production is a valid tool. Marxism as a methodology is thus still relevant, in my view; but Marxism as an ideology—or rather as theology—has been discredited.

As it happens, Isaias studied military science in China for eighteen months in 1967-1968, which coincided with the Cultural Revolution that saw the purging of thousands of "capitalist-roaders," including Deng Tsiao Ping. Ironically, it was the purged Deng who later set China on the path of accelerated development following his reinstatement and triumph over those who had him purged. I don't know what lesson Isaias took from that experience, but there is no doubt that he imbibed Chinese methods on the use of the class struggle to his own power purposes, as we shall see. Whether this has benefited the masses is another question.

The Revolutionary as Father of Nation

Heads of state are invariably assigned paternal roles. This has been particularly true in African states that came out of colonial rule, where the men who held executive office were at the center of a network of state institutions dispensing patronage and distributing resources and favors. In newly created states like Eritrea, the national leader becomes the outward symbol of a new center of loyalty and national unity. The question of how ethnic or regional loyalties can be replaced by, or transformed into, a wider loyalty goes hand in hand with national leadership and the successful projection of new ideas and values connected with such leadership. Among the most potent ideas that colonized peoples in Africa and elsewhere used in their claim for independence were those of democracy and self-determination, as articulated by their leaders.

But then a new politics of revolution emerged, espoused in the former Portuguese colonies of Angola, Mozambique, and Guinea-Bissau as well as in Eritrea, that appeared to mark a break with the classical democratic mold. As pointed out earlier, its inspirational source was Marxism, with class struggle as its defining characteristic. In this new politics of revolution, displacing the alien ruler was only one goal, albeit a crucial one; a no less important goal was a socio-economic one aimed at establishing a new social and political order in which the government would be controlled by representatives of the working masses. The leader of the revolution sits at the summit of state power, virtually unchallenged, supported by the organized masses. In the context of a Marxist one-party state, the power of the leader is indisputable. In the theory and practice of Marxist parties, "democratic centralism" is used to buttress the uncontested power of the leader of the party. If one adds to this the context of a traditional, patriarchal society, the leader easily becomes the father of the nation in the mind of the masses.

Tradition and Revolutionary Change

Chiefs, Elders, and the Masses

A subject of controversy throughout the liberation struggle was the question of traditional modes of behavior and attitudes, including the place of women and youth in social relations. One famous EPLF slogan adopted by supporters in the Diaspora read: "A revolution to liberate the land and the man." Such liberation "of the man" included the liberation of women from age-old subjugation, as well as the liberation of groups within society that had been historically abused as vassals to local, self-appointed nobility.

In Eritrea the liberation of the Tigre from servitude to the ruling class known as "Shimagle" had been started by the British in the 1940s in which the Eritrean nationalist leader, Shiekh Ibrahim Sultan Ali, had played a prominent role. Ibrahim Sultan employed a famous slogan that served as a clarion call to the Tigre underdogs:

"Ni-Sheikh SheKshiko!
Ni-Shum Shemshimo!"

Roughly translated, these slogans mean, "Shake up the Seikh," "Challenge the Chief."

The attempts of changing old customs extended to challenging all elders, which sometimes took absurd forms. There was, for example, the notorious case that happened in the town of Dekemhare, during its brief occupation by the EPLF. A young cadre, blindly applying the notion of equality, ordered an old man who was sleeping on his bed to climb down from his bed (in his own house mind you) and sleep on the ground like the others. Other examples can be cited, but there is no need. The point is that inspired or fired by revolutionary ideology, some cadres have committed acts in relation to the elderly that sometimes amounted to deliberate humiliation.

Women and Revolution

The EPLF political indoctrination encouraged the young to defy elders, in the name of the revolution, and women were encouraged to defy male domination. Old social habits and attitudes were subjected to systematic challenges. When I was traveling in the Hamasien highlands, engaged in a mediation effort,

I began to hear stories of young women joining the struggle in droves to fight for national liberation side by side with their male compatriots.

I heard about the case of one particular girl who had become the subject of conversation with women mostly applauding her, while older men condemned her. I met this young woman in Sabur Seghi when I went to meet with Isaias in January 1975, as I related before. Her comrades there referred to her as Comandis, because of her sturdy build and size. When I heard that she was in Sabur Seghi, I expressed a desire to talk to her because I was intrigued by her story. This remarkable young woman, a newly-wed in the village of Weki, had seen the *tegadelti* (freedom fighters), including a few women, come and go in her village. A few days after her wedding, she disappeared, leaving her unfortunate husband dazed and shamed.

I met her on the day of my visit there. Isaias made the arrangement for me to talk to her; only she was accompanied by a "minder," a *tegadalai* nicknamed Somal, whom I was to see on another occasion. It was clear to me that Isaias wanted to know what I wanted to know and what she would say. The controlling side of his character, for which he became well known, was understandable in the circumstances. I asked Comandis why she disappeared, leaving her bridegroom. She gave me a catechism, chapter and verse, of what she was taught at the orientation course for new recruits—how the oppressive social system has to be challenged, smashed, etc. I have always been a supporter of women's rights to equality; so I had no problem with the EPLF line of political education. Indeed, there is a marked difference between what was promised during the struggle and their status after liberation. But no issue should be considered outside the overall context of a society. I heard Isaias argue in this vein one evening on the occasion of the launching of the constitution making process in 1994. It was at the Ambasoira Hotel, and he was arguing this point surrounded by a phalanx of ex women-*tegadelti* who were complaining that their expectations had not been fulfilled. Listening to the heated informal debate, I couldn't help feeling that the women were pleading with their leader in the manner of disappointed daughters complaining to their father who had not delivered on his promise of giving them a prized object. Isaias' manner was that of an irate father trying to control his temper, strict but indulgent.

The Youth and Revolution

Another issue concerning tradition and change concerns the place and role of youth. Like all revolutionary leaders committed to social change, the EPLF leadership, and especially Isaias, attached great importance to this issue. Apart from the obvious need to replenish the fighting force in a situation of war with its hazards of decimation, the youth serve as useful instruments, as passionate vanguards. Their purity and single-mindedness, unencumbered by family ties and other worldly concerns of older people, proved extremely important in advancing the aims of the struggle. They take things literally and become true believers, which makes them useful instruments for any cause. But this means that they can be the unwitting tools of a ruthless leader to advance his private agenda. To that end they can serve as his eyes and ears, spying on unsuspecting older people who share confidences with them. Isaias used some youthful cadres to spy and report on a group that was eventually charged and liquidated for "Rightist" (*Yamin*) tendencies, whatever that meant. The case of the Moscow-educated Mehari Girmatsion comes to mind. In the mid-1970s, Mehari shared with a young *tegadalai,* a close relative, some information about a reformist movement that he had secretly helped launch. The latter reported him to the *Halewa Sawara* (security), resulting in his liquidation as a "Rightist conspirator."

This incident, as well as that of the so-called *Menka'E* movement of the early 1970s, whose leaders were also liquidated, has yet to be explained in full. These incidents constitute only two of the hidden skeletons in Isaias's closet. In this respect his close collaborators have also a lot of explaining to do. As we shall see in chapter 10, many of them have expressed a willingness to answer before a proper tribunal, if and when they get a chance to do so under a regime following the rule of law. Whether Eritreans should insist on retribution or agree on a general amnesty for crimes committed during the armed struggle is a question that needs to be debated.

The youth in revolutionary situations have also been used to humiliate elders, though such acts are not limited to the youth. One of the most important values in traditional African societies, Eritrea being no exception, is the respect accorded to elders. Indeed, the constitution makers of Eritrea, in recognition of the importance of this value, included it as one of the clauses of the preamble to Eritrea's constitution as follows:

> Appreciating the fact that for the development and health of our society, it is necessary that we inherit and improve upon the traditional community-based assistance and fraternity,....etc.

Yet, there were unfortunate incidents during the struggle in which elders were humiliated by true believers who took some of their lessons literally as the following story illustrates. In 1978, I had a phone call from the late Dr. Goitom Petros, a respected Eritrean elder whom I addressed as *"Ayya."* *Ayya* Goitom, who happened to be visiting Washington, called me from the residence of a relative of his. He could not meet with me personally for fear of retribution because he lived in Addis Ababa during the reign of the Dergue; but he called to tell me a sad incident in his home town, Dekemhare, the incident cited above.

He said that one of his relatives who lived in his house in that town was ordered by a young EPLF cadre to get out of his bed and sleep on the floor. Clearly, he said, that a young true believer took it upon himself that equality demanded that the old man sleep on the floor like the rest. He characterized the act as that of a misguided fanatic who had wrong ideas about equality. He did not believe, he told me, that this would be countenanced by the senior leaders. That was why he called to tell me to warn the leaders because he assumed this would not be favored by them. He said he was full of admiration for the liberation fighters, but they needed to control their members or give them proper instructions on how to handle the elderly.

It is tempting to note here, parenthetically, George Orwell's famous summation of a false revolutionary notion of equality: All animals are equal, but some are more equal than others. Indeed I had seen one enlightened cadre of the EPLF reading Orwell's *Animal Farm* and I remember engaging him in a conversation on the subject of equality in theory and practice. He made a comment that even in liberal democracy some are more equal than others. He went on to amend his remark by saying, "I mean especially in liberal democracy." He is right. All men are created equal, but in reality, such foundational notion of equality is accompanied by a spacious liberty that entails unequal outcomes. Some become more equal than others, to use the hackneyed phrase. The emergence of inequality may thus be a consequence of the different application of different talents and energy by some, resulting in a differentiation in riches and an elevated standard of living.

But I digress. As I said before, some *tegadelti* mistreated people under their custody. Toward those under their custody, whom they presume to be guilty, even high-ranking EPLF cadres have been known to be merciless. The use of violence, or threat of its use, in the investigation of suspected spies or other wrongdoers was sanctioned by "revolutionary justice." Even as their supporter or their member, I had problems with their notion of "revolutionary justice."

Ironically, the EPLF treatment of prisoners of war was strictly in accordance with the standards required under the Geneva Conventions, and they have been rightly praised for this. In fact I heard some of the youth (the *fitawrari*) doing guard duty complain as to why the prisoners who "had come to kill us" should be treated well. The older cadres had a difficult time explaining the reasons for the better treatment of the prisoners of war.

The lesson for all concerned is that when mobilizing and indoctrinating the youth in revolutionary politics, setting them up against the old and the "other," it is necessary to instruct them in the intricacies of differentiation. Like Frankenstein's creature, a mobilized, politicized revolutionary youth can turn against its creator.

The Base Metal

Before I continue any further, I need to say a word on my chosen metaphor and its application to Isaias. Gold is a precious metal and thus more valuable than base metals like copper and zinc; yet base metal has its use too. Those with a literal bent of mind may want to translate the metaphor and ask if Isaias could have any use as base metal. Put another way, if he is found to be falling short of the quality of gold, might he have other uses as do copper and zinc? In anticipation of a final judgment on his record, my answer is yes indeed—he might play a role as a former president advising his successors. To those who are adamantly anti-Isaias, I would counsel patience and urge them to lighten up. (Laughter is welcome anytime). After all, rabid Isaias fans have already tried and convicted me of treason for suggesting that he could be a base metal. To them, he is more than gold: He is a demigod and unassailable by the rest of us mere mortals

As I write these lines some foreign mining companies have been issued license from the Eritrean government to start gold mining in western Eritrea (and perhaps elsewhere). The Chief Executive of one mining company went out of his way to lavish praise upon the Eritrean government for its program of infrastructure development. He also said that he expects gold mining will start earning his company, by fiscal year 2009, some $200 million annually. Then he added that after the first few years, the gold will presumably be exhausted and replaced with copper and zinc mining.

Gold, replaced by copper and zinc! The metaphorical plot thickens!

Did Isaias turn from gold to base metal, i.e., did power change him, or was he always a base metal externally covered by glittering gold , which is to say other than what people thought he was? These are not easy questions to answer. Some who knew him intimately during the struggle say that he had dictatorial tendencies, but that he was able to hide them behind a mask of revolutionary dedication. But none offer any credible proof, beyond isolated incidents of bizarre behavior that he exhibited when angry. Some who knew him during his childhood tell stories of temper tantrums and authoritarian tendencies, for example like his possessiveness of household items like his *dukka* (a small wooden stool), which he would never share with any one of his siblings. One of his own brothers is reported to have told stories about the duka and warned that he would not share the national duka, namely the presidency.

Such anecdotal psychosocial narratives may not offer substantive evidence to help in explaining the behavior patterns of the mature person. More important is what a person does in practice, in fulfillment of the solemn undertakings that he made, or what he fails to do in violation of principles or in breach of solemn promises. Among the narrative given to the author in interviews with former comrades, the constant factors are his controlling nature, his methods of divide and rule practiced with meticulous care, his secretiveness and ruthlessness, and a restless mind that plans tactics of control in later years refined by the use of the computer.

Leaving the personal psychosocial profile aside, I will focus on the performance of Isaias and his government in post liberation Eritrea, by reference to the record on political, economic, and social issues, comparing the performance with the of promises given.

Playing with the Democratic Card

The maxim "The Price of Liberty is Eternal Vigilance," attributed to American founding father and sage, Benjamin Franklin, is one that should be written on the doors of every citizen everywhere. Franklin was also attributed with another witticism worth recalling. As he was coming out of the Constitutional Convention in 1787, someone asked him what he and his fellow convention members had done; he said, "We have given you a republic, if you can keep it." Where some nations failed, the United States managed to keep its republic—and develop it.

The reason for my reference to Franklin's gems is that I think we Eritreans could do with a good dose of such wisdom. Indeed, we have discovered that we were lacking in vigilance, consumed as we were with patriotic zeal, to consider pondering the hazards of uncontrolled power in our national life. One of our assumptions was that our heroic *tegadelti* could do no wrong, like the kings in English constitutional fiction. I will be the first to cry *mea culpa* in trusting that Isaias and his PFDJ inner circle would abide by their promise to implement the constitution ratified in 1997. As I explain in detail later, my colleagues of the Constitutional Commission and I believed in the letter and spirit of the law and the EPLF's solemn undertaking, given in two congress resolutions, that Eritrea would institute a democratic system of government in which there would be pluralism, the rule of law, parliamentary checks on the executive, an independent judiciary, and a Bill of Rights.

Government accountability and competitive parties are guaranteed in the constitution. The reason given by Isaias and his PFDJ inner circle for breaking their promise and refusing to institute a multiparty system is that a multiparty system is a luxury Eritrea cannot afford because it would impede rapid economic growth. Our response was relating the cautionary tales of the corruption of African one-party systems in which governments promised an era of plenty on the condition that people exchange liberty for bread. The obvious answer to the proposed exchange is that bread and liberty are not—and should never be—mutually exclusive; that democracy and development go hand in hand. As we shall see in more detail, the controversy remains unresolved, with the PFDJ government and its leader, Isaias Afwerki, adamantly opposed to multiparty democracy, contrary to the requirements of the ratified constitution, and in opposition to much of the public sentiment, as well as to a significant faction of the governing party.

The controversy, aggravated by the 1998-2000 war with Ethiopia, precipitated a serious political crisis ending in the September 18, 2001, arrest of twelve high-ranking government and party leaders, including three former foreign affairs ministers. These and several others demanded the implementation of the constitution and a democratic opening. The president also ordered the closing of the free press, and the arrest of all their editors and reporters. As the world now knows, all those arrested are still under detention, held incommunicado, and have not been charged with crime. Many have been reported dead due to lack of medical care.

In violation of the constitution, the government of Eritrea is thus based on the monopoly of power by a single party. The executive dominates the two other branches of government, a nominal parliament and an intimidated judiciary; its chief justice was summarily dismissed by the president after he complained of executive interference in judicial matters. Needless to say, as head of state and commander-in-chief of the armed forces, the president controls all aspects of the military and the associated security services and thus presides over a militarized and traumatized society.

A Mixed-up Mixed Economy

Immediately after independence, the EPLF government announced that the "command economy" followed by the occupying Ethiopian regime would be replaced by a market-based economy. Has this policy thus proclaimed been followed in practice? The short answer is no. The command economy inherited from the military-Marxist government of Ethiopia has not been abandoned by the PFDJ government, which is itself led by recovering (or rather unreconstructed) Marxist ideologues. Contrary to the earlier government rhetoric, far from being encouraged, private enterprise has been restricted almost into nonexistence. In an extensive interview he gave as late as November 1997, a few months before the Badme War, President Isaias spoke of the government's commitment to privatization of government-owned industries. As we shall see below, however, the contrary is true.

The government's originally professed aim was to harness a disciplined and hardworking population toward a Singapore-style development project; this has clearly failed. To begin with despite the proclaimed aim, there was no credible government program that made human power development its central feature, unlike that of Singapore. To the contrary scarce financial resources were wasted on non-profitable policies and programs, including the never-ending "national service" that pinned hundreds of thousands of youths in the wilds of Sawa, thus depriving them of educational and social development. There was an environment of anti-intellectual bias that discouraged educational attainment and self-improvement. Moreover, the hopes pinned on marine resources, minerals, tourism, which were expected to draw foreign investments and provide employment, have been shattered on the rock of bad policies and politics. Above all, an obsessive national security prioritization has driven a whole generation of youths to abandon home and country in mass exodus to foreign countries that raises questions about the future of the state and its viability.

The promised income from gold mining is a far cry from the earlier promise of large-scale investments from foreign sources. Eritrea's economy—agriculture, livestock, light industry, and fishery—does not provide a sufficient base for a "takeoff." Judging by the interview Isaias gave to Al Jazeera TV on 22 May 2008, the PFDJ economic development policy seems to be torn between an inordinate desire to be free of the control of foreign interests, as expressed in the much-vaunted idea of self reliance, and the need to expand the revenue base. In the interview, Isaias boasted of the country's mineral resources, while having a preoccupation to be free of foreign involvement in developing the mining sector. This preoccupation stems from the realization that there cannot be an expanded mining sector and the consequent increase in the source of revenue, in contrast to the fact that the mining industry requires the infusion of high-tech and foreign finance. If you want your gold dug out of the bowels of the earth, you need the involvement of foreign finance and technology. If foreign finance and technology is involved, out goes your pet philosophy of self reliance. It is either stubbornly adhering to your pet philosophy, or having foreign involvement. You can't have your cake and eat it too.

The government's earlier rhetoric emphasizing the importance of privatizing government-held enterprises and giving free rein to private enterprise has been abandoned. What has happened instead is the rapid growth of enterprises owned and managed by the economic arm of the government party, the Red Sea Corporation and its many affiliates, covering all sectors of the economy. At first, an illusion was created in the mind of the public, fostered by the government, that the PFDJ's economic wing would offer reasonable, competitive prices of goods and services and thus alleviate the people's economic hardship. The Red Sea Corporation had also justified its expansion in terms of redressing the existing imbalance by reducing the gap in the standard of living between the urban and rural populations, and by asserting that the corporation would be involved in areas where the private sector did not take part.

To be sure, in their earlier operations, the Red Sea Corporation and its affiliates somewhat eased the economic problems of a long-suffering people by selling consumer goods below market prices. This reinforced the illusion entertained by the public of better days to come. However, the public would soon find out that it was all a clever hoax, and that the PFDJ enterprises were engaged in unfair competition both in the formal and informal sectors of the economy. Not only were these enterprises given all kinds of government support, but it was widely believed that they did not pay taxes. Such favored treatment of the PFDJ-owned enterprises put many private enterprises out of business. The inordinate growth and expansion of the PFDJ-owned enterprises were revealed following the 1998-2000 war with Ethiopia. Their involvement became clear for all to see in different economic activities, including construction, manufacturing, transportation, agriculture, health services, tourism, energy, and foreign exchange. The number and scope of their activities have grown exponentially. According to statements of PFDJ officials, the Red Sea Corporation and its affiliates owned and managed thirty-eight enterprises in 2002; there is no sign that they will curb their expansion..

Given its narrow revenue base, it is quite clear that the government of Eritrea depends on much foreign aid for its economic development, despite its much-vaunted policy of self reliance. Taxes and other sources of revenue are considered high, and government attempts of changing this through a more liberal investment policy have not had much success. The failure is principally due to the monopolization of the PFDJ-owned business enterprises and the consequent weakening of the private sector. What the many foreign enterprises that had shown interest in investing in Eritrea, particularly in the mining sector, will do is a question no one can answer. The anti-private enterprise ideology of the government creates uncertainty that does not encourage a positive outlook. It is reasonable to assume that all interested investors are waiting for the clarification of the legal/constitutional regime and stabilization of the political and security situation. So far only multilateral economic institutions like the World Bank have been consistent in their policy of encouraging investment, but even in their case, insistence on "good governance" and the rule of law as preconditions for financial assistance is proving an obstacle for obtaining such assistance in the requisite amount and time.

In sum, judging by the economic performance of the past few years, the outlook for the future appears bleak. Growth measured by GDP (gross domestic product) is expected to remain as low as 2 percent. (Ethiopia, by comparison, recorded a growth rate of 10 percent in the same period). Given the discouraging business environment as well as the recurring trend of drought, the main source of growth so far has been donor-funded projects. Remittances from abroad (from Eritreans in the Diaspora), which were the largest source of foreign exchange, are expected to decline because of the protest movements demanding democratic transition and the government's resistance to such demands. Such decline can cause strain on the economy and aggravate the social crisis.

The Social Landscape

A country's social condition is naturally impacted by worsening economic and political situations. This has been the case in Eritrea over the past few years, particularly in the wake of the 1998-2000 war with Ethiopia. Even before the onset of that devastating war, the policy and politics of domination and exclusion—political domination by the PFDJ, excluding other political parties as well as the monopolization of the economy practiced by the one-party government—had foreshadowed the current social crisis. Judged by the standard of the United Nation's Human Development Index (HDI), Eritrea is ranked very low. Eritrea's HDI in the year 2004 is 0.454, placing it as number 157 out of 177 countries—right in the bottom rung, trailing behind 156 other countries. (UNDP HDI Report, 2006).

Let us put this revealing statistic along side of the government's often-cited project of infrastructure development to the realization of which a whole generation of Eritrean youth have been committed (*condemned* is the truer term). The HDI is a useful measure of human wellbeing, going beyond the GDP—beyond the production of goods and the building of roads and bridges, important though these are. The HDI embraces different dimensions of human development, most importantly: the availability of affordable and adequate nutrition, provision of affordable education, access to good health services and to affordable housing in safe neighborhoods. Eritrea's extremely low HDI score in the 2004 survey demonstrates, beyond question, failure in the provision of these services to the vast majority of the population.

A proud and hardworking people have become dependent on the generosity of external donors for their survival in items as basic as food. Though drought has exacerbated their predicament, today as before, the cause of the distress of the majority of Eritreans cannot be blamed on nature alone; bad policies and politics are the real culprits. It is paradoxical that a government that proclaims its abhorrence of dependence on outsiders has steadily become dependent on outside aid, even as it denies international nongovernmental organizations' (NGOs) a role in the provision of basic needs.

A disturbing development is the government policy and practice of forcible appropriation of farmers' produce and paying the farmers an arbitrarily determined price. In this Pharonic practice, the government's security services take the grain from the field after its harvest, or out of the grain stores on individual farms and homes and take it to government stores, paying throw-away prices to the farmers. In response to this outrage, and determined to defeat the government's policy, farmers devised different tactics, including immediate grinding of the grain and turning it into dough. In this race between government outrage and peasant survival tactics, the government has brought the full force of the law and security apparatus to bear on the issue, imposing heavy penalties on those who try ty to beat the government at its own game. Popular complaints on this and related problems forced Isaias to issue a statement that is as bizarre in its content as it is heartless in intent. He instructed the public on nutrition questions telling them that of 250 calories intake is too much; they can survive on 180!

A tragic dimension of the social crisis in Eritrea concerns the plight of the elderly who have been left to fend for themselves at a time in their lives when their children were expected to look after them—and would have looked after them. Scores of thousands of Eritrean men and women (mostly men) have been pinned down in the trenches or have been working in the wilderness on national service, wasting their youth, foregoing educational opportunities or getting married and raising children, leaving their parents to penury and desperately lonely old age. Many thousands have escaped to neighboring countries; others, not so lucky in their attempts to escape, have been imprisoned under extremely harsh conditions. The government makes demands on parents of those who escape, either to bring them back or face imprisonment or heavy fines.

Hardly a decade after the promising start by a government on which the world pinned so much hope and to which it showed so much good will, the social landscape of Eritrea is distressing. The shops may be stocked with foreign imported goods, but the sight of long breadlines in the cities has become common, a visible symbol of things gone awry. People line up starting as early as 5 am and may wait for hours, only to be told there is no bread and to come back the following day. The overcrowded schools do not have sufficient books and other educational materials; and teachers are paid salaries that cannot carry them to the end of the month. The health services are so poor that those who can afford it travel abroad for medical treatment—this in a country that boasted of miraculous health services in the valleys of the liberated areas during the armed struggle.

I will end this section with the words of an astute observer who reported on the Eritrea's sad state of affairs in 2003.

> In the Eritrea of today, where the burden of one crisis after another crisis are mercilessly weighing down on the people, the rapid deterioration in the material and emotional wellbeing of the people cannot escape the eye. The sudden increase in the number of beggars, the women in the late hours of the night—their infant babies sleeping

on their backs—as they struggle to sell their meager merchandise on the streets of Asmara, the skinny boys you pass on the road, the villages that are devoid of any able-bodied men, the fields that remain unattended....while demobilization is indefinitely deferred, leaving a whole generation of young men and women desperately counting the days in the wilderness, and mothers and wives longingly wait for the return of their loved ones, people are aging at a fast rate as standards of living take a nosedive...." (A Tale of Life under a Tyranny, *Events Monitor*, September 6, 2003. Awate.com).

In view of this reality, one wonders, what is the role of the Eritrean government employees? I have met some of these employees on their trips abroad, and I have come to realize that they live an agonized existence. Some desperately try to get in touch with those of us in the Diaspora as if to lighten their grief-stricken bad conscience. Such meetings and information obtained through various means has convinced me that, despite the disheartening reality, most Eritreans in positions of responsibility, below the ministerial level, have been doing their best to meet the challenges of the worsening situation of their people. But their best efforts fall far short of what is required simply because they operate under a reality defined by the policies and politics over which they have little control. Any attempts at influencing or demanding for policy change is met with dire consequences, as demonstrated by the fate of the G-15 as we shall see. All they do is complain and wait for better times.

As for the select few—the ministers and generals as well as high-ranking party stalwarts—there is no evidence of any of these members of the new class making attempts in the direction of change. They all do the bidding of the supreme leader. As I wished in my metaphorical whimsy, at the beginning of this chapter, all one can do, short of getting involved in an opposition movement, is to wish for their redemption. *Ab lbom kmllessu Nxiliyellom* (we will pray for their rectification). Either that or let them drum up courage, and join the opposition camp.

Chapter 4

Immaculate Deception:
The Original Sin
of Eritrea Politics

First, I must apologize to all Catholics for using the word *immaculate* as part of the title for this chapter, even though it is only half of their hallowed doctrine of the immaculate conception. The operative word in the present instance is *deception*.

I decided to use this title because, for me, it describes, better than any other words, the cunning with which the system and dynamics of power was conceived, developed, and sustained for over two decades by the architect(s) of the EPLF. Deception has been the defining characteristic of the EPLF guerilla leaders' mode of operation from the start. It is even suggested by some that the principal architect(s) of the EPLF learned the art of deception from the leaders of the ELF, from whom they broke away in 1969-1970.

The most dramatic illustration of deception was the revelation in 1993 that there was a secret party guiding the EPLF to which only a select few would be admitted and were sworn to secrecy, as I indicate in the preface to this book. There, I use leadership in the plural sense because the principal actor, Isaias, though the main culprit, was assisted by a few trusted followers.

It will not be hard to prove that this immaculate deception has been at the root of practically all of Eritrea's problems. Eritreans and their friends know for certain that Eritrea is in serious trouble; only the few blind Isaias supporters will deny this fact. Take the question of governance, for instance. Let me state two obvious facts about Eritrea's governance today.

Fact number one: Isaias Afwerki is an unelected dictator who has ruled the country, with an iron fist, for almost two decades. In a rare interview with Reuters on 13 May 2008, he answered the question as to when he would allow elections to be held in Eritrea; his answer was: "I will stay as I long as it takes." A week later, on May 22, when he was interviewed in Al Jezeera and asked the same question, he said that there would be no elections for thirty or forty years, or even longer. He took the opportunity afforded by an Arab media to ridicule elections held in other countries and seemed to defy all generally accepted principles of governance. It was an incredible act of irrational and arrogant defiance of world opinion—a kind of verbal sticking of his middle finger up to everybody. It was so vulgar that even those of us who are opposed to his dictatorial rule are ashamed of him, ashamed because he is Eritrean.

Isaias Afwerki is addicted to power and will not relinquish it. As a dictator, he has absolute power, unrestrained by any constitutional limiting mechanisms of checks and balances. During the armed struggle, people accepted his dictatorship because of military necessity; and also because there was a modicum of "collective leadership" that acted at times as a check. There are things that you do in a military situation that you don't in normal times. We hoped and expected that there would be changes with the coming of independence, when the people would elect their leaders. Our hopes have been dashed. He broke a solemn promise. Not only did he break a solemn promise to be governed by democratic principles defined in the 1997 ratified constitution, he seems to revel in defying all common standards of morality and civilized conduct. Evidently, he holds the people who were his comrades-in-arms—nay, the entire nation—in contempt.

This leads to fact number two: Isaias unabashedly trashed a constitution that was ratified by a Constituent Assembly—a constitution prepared by the Constitutional Commission that his own National Assembly (i.e., himself) appointed. He used his time-tested game of deception, leading all concerned, including this writer, to believe that he would honor his word—the word of the law—and implement the constitution; only to use the pretext of a "border war" to trash it and continue his dictatorial rule.

Much has been said and written about this disturbing fact, with many people hoping that he would change his ways; that he would give effect to the people's will and implement the constitution—all in vain. One particularly bold, if belated, attempt by his closest comrades to effect some change in him ended in their imprisonment, as we all know, and as we discuss in detail in chapter 8. Isaias has made it clear that he will remain president as long as he can; until he is forced out. Like the proverbial leopard that does not change its spot, Isaias will not change his color—the chameleonlike deceptive color. In moments of flight of fancy, I imagine Dante's immortal words posted at the gates of our fair city, Asmara: "Abandon all hope ye who enter." But then I relent; for hope is the ultimate weapon of the oppressed—hope springs eternal, as the saying goes.

A question that everybody asks—one for which there has been no clear and unequivocal answer thus far is: How did Isaias succeed in convincing everybody to let him do as he pleased, whatever he wanted, for all those years? Clearly, he did not do it alone; he had helping hands. And it did not suddenly happen; it started in the Sahel wilderness, where he transformed himself into a prophet and gained the upper hand over the armed political organization—the EPLF.

The EPLF was essentially a military organization with a political objective, i.e., Eritrea's liberation. That political objective united everyone and afforded him the framework for his own power schemes; and the discipline that military training gave him enabled him to enforce his will.

Moreover, according to some of his close companions, Isaias demonstrated a command of ideas and issues that impressed most of those who came in contact with him. The reference to ideas includes a command of the dominant ideology among the freedom fighters at the time, i.e., Marxism. For example, Mesfin Hagos mentions in an interview that in a meeting between the top leaders of the ELF and EPLF held in Port Sudan once, Isaias dominated the discussion of all issues, covering matters about which the top ideologues of the ELF, like Azien Yassin were supposed to excel. The same is true, evidently, with regard to the top leaders of the EPLF like Mesfin himself whom Isais dominated throughout the organization's history. He always came to meetings thoroughly prepared and dominated the discussions. This included even matters over whch others claimed expertise and had been assigned to research and prepare. He excelled and intimidated everyone so that nobody could challenge him. It was a case of domination of minds. If for any reason, another seemed to challenge him, he would use tactics of ridicule to belittle the views of that person; if the person persists, Isaias demotes or freezes him, as he did in Dr. Tesfai Girmazion's case. His disrespect of people with higher degrees is well-known. As chancellor of the Asmara University, he never once attended a graduation ceremony; indeed, he destroyed the university breaking it up into several community college-type institutions. This earned him the charge of being anti-intellectual.

As to how he convinced his comrades-in-arms to go along with what he did there is, as yet, not a clear answer. Obviously, he used other tools in addition to deception or as an integral part of it. One was what may be called the charisma of mystery. For most of the years of the armed struggle that he led with aplomb and dedication, Isaias Afwerki affected a convincing indifference to publicity. It turns out that he is in fact an avid seeker of the very thing he seemed to shun. His feigned indifference was a shrewd tactic of myth-making, and an indirect way of discouraging others from seeking what he appeared to deny himself. In the political education that he and his upper cadres conceived and practiced, *anennet* (individualism, stressing the notion of *I* or *me*) was taught as a cardinal sin. All this was billed as an aspect of communistic, collective thought and action. Every EPLF member was enjoined to use the plural pronouns even when referring to the work of an individual effort. At a time and in the context when Leftist politics was the order of the day, this was considered the proper pattern of behavior. Occasional protests voiced in the name of individual dignity and self regard were shouted down to silence.

Among the many foreign guests who visited Sahel, the base area of the EPLF, only one writer—Australian novelist Thomas Kineally—knew by intuition that the self-effacement and meticulous avoidance of the media was a shrewd device of myth-making. He suspected that a personality cult was being assiduously cultivated, as his friend and countryman Dr. Fred Hollows confessed to me in Sydney during my visit to Australia in 1988. Another visitor, British writer and friend of Eritrea, Basil Davidson, described Isaias in his correspondence with me as a "hard man with a saving sense of humor."

I remember writing Basil back, admonishing him to see below the hard surface, where I said he would find a gentle soul. *Mea culpa*. It took me some time after that to find out that Basil was right. I don't know about the saving sense of humor, but I do know Isaias is a hard man. Yes, a very hard man with sheathed claws at the ready to pounce at anytime when necessary for his own purposes. The story of the arrest of Aster Yohanes illustrates this. Who but a heartless man, with a deceptive mind, would entice a mother of innocent children to return home from her studies abroad, as he did with Aster, only to order her arrest upon her arrival at the Asmara airport, even denying her the chance to see her children who were waiting for her there? Yes indeed, he is a hard man; deceptive and vindictive. The arrest of Aster was done in order to hurt her detained husband, Petros Solomon, a member of the G-15 who called on him to implement the constitution and keep his promise of democratic rule. Isaias considers Petros to be his main rival for leadership and hence a threat to his power. By detaining his wife and depriving his children of their mother he aims to destroy Petros psychologically, and thus disable him, preventing him from ever challenging him.

To the question, what is his purpose today as he presides over a tottering regime and a confused society with mourning mothers and angry, disaffected youth, the answer is that Isaias is a power-hungry man who cannot live without power. Power is his reason for existence—he has power, therefore he is. As a leader of the EPLF, his declared purpose, proclaimed to a gullible youth hungry for salvation, was revolutionary reconstruction of society and the establishment of a democratic order of free men and women. But then a funny thing happened on the way to those noble ends. Or had it been in the making from the getgo in Sahel? I don't know the answer to this question, nor do any of his comrades whom I have interviewed; but I am sure of one thing: The debate on it will remain unresolved till the day he dies.

When I think of the tragic conditions Eritrea is facing today, as outlined in the preceding chapter, two images press themselves on my mind, stirring in my troubled psyche feelings of remorse and intimations of calls for action—action to bring an end to this, our winter of discontent. There is, first, the image of the heroic guerilla fighters who defied the military might of a superior enemy (defied death itself)—a young *tegadalai* throwing himself at an advancing enemy tank, holding a hand grenade, and exploding with it in the nick of time to save his comrades. There is also the squad of *tegadelti* running for attack, ululating their battle cry in the manner of celebrants at a wedding; yet there is the image of another squad dancing in the evening at a *guayla* following a successful day of battle. Images of our heroic past that I cannot forget, and that no denigration of the *ghedli,* now fashionable among some, can erase!

In times of distress, like the one we Eritreans have been experiencing, and still experience, the mind has a way of succumbing to its power of evocation, recalling pleasant things that happened. More often than not, it is the pleasant things that the mind evokes; for, otherwise, if we remember only the unpleasant things, madness would set in. I remember the heroic deeds of our freedom fighters not only to celebrate their courage and sacrifice, but for my own sanity. The mind filters out the few times that I witnessed the carnage, the pain and suffering, and recalls instead the pleasant event. This is one reason why works of literature like *Halaw'ta Werqawit Ghereb* has a healing power, and why we need more of such works.

Another pleasant image that presses on my mind is the public euphoria in Asmara on liberation day, with holy madness taking over—wives forgetting their daily chores of preparing their families' meals, as they left home and hearth to take part in the massive celebration going on everywhere, with youths and elders alike dancing all night. It was the spectacle of a liberated nation delirious with joy. To witness the ecstasy of the birth of one's nation at the end of a long period of labor—a labor of liberation—was like being born again. The people lionized the liberation fighters, whom they viewed as though they were messengers sent from heaven to deliver them from bondage. And at the head of these heroes was the super hero, Isaias Afwerki, whom people saw as a demigod who could do no wrong. I was among those who believed Isaias to be an outstanding leader with sterling qualities—brilliant, dedicated, incorruptible, and committed to democracy and justice. As I discuss in more detail in chapter 6, my belief in him was strong enough to induce in me a sense of trust that he would honor his word and implement the constitution and abide by its strictures. As mentioned before, we now know that he did not plan to honor his word; it was a devilish ruse, heartless and reckless.

That euphoria continued for a few years even in the face of economic hardship and the emerging bizarre behavior of some of the *tegadelti* who loudly decreed the existence of a distinction between *tegadalai* and *ghebbar*—that is to say, between freedom fighter and other citizens. It was the beginning of an unhealthy development of a new class; but the people readily excused such bizarre behavior, and even some of the brutality and rudeness they experienced in government offices. It was the kind of indulgence that parents of spoiled children accord their offspring out of sheer love. Excuses and generous explanations were heard aplenty— it would all change, it was said, as the *tegadelti* resumed normal life and adjusted to the city life that they must have forgotten, poor souls, deprived as they had been all those years roaming in the desert.

Excuses, excuses... Extenuations... Explanations...

Actually, it was self-induced deception, aided and abetted by guilt for having stayed behind while the heroic *tegadelti* went forth to do battle against an occupying enemy. This is no longer the case. All of that has changed—no more excuses for the egregious "mistakes" that the government and its operatives are making. No more blank checks for Isaias and his minions to write upon their lives. Even the *adetat* (mothers), those gentle souls who used to swear by Isaiais's name and bestowed upon him daily blessings and offered prayers for his long life and wellbeing, even they are no longer doing so. How can they when their own sons, or those of their friends and neighbors—thousands of them—have been voting with their feet, escaping his rule and seeking refuge in neighboring countries?

That is another image that oppresses me: the image of thousands crossing the wilds of western Eritrea over into the Sudan or Ethiopia; some of them, daring fate, crossing the Sahara Desert into Libya to an uncertain destiny; and from there crossing the Mediterranean Sea into Malta or to Italy. They might be considered lucky ones, though many have perished, devoured by the desert or drowned at sea. I have had emails and phone messages sent to me from Libya by some of the lucky ones who, fearing deportation by the Libyan government back to Eritrea, asked me to appeal on their behalf to anybody who can come to their rescue. An unlucky batch had been deported by Ghadafi's order back to the mercy of his brother dictator, Isaias, to be beaten and put in containers or sent to the Dahlak Iislands for indefinite detention.

Crimes and Consequences

To some observers, knowledgeable about the history of the EPLF, what is going on in Eritrea today is a continuation, in a different form, of what I have called the Sahel Syndrome—that complex phenomenon that includes the unexplained disposal or disappearance of freedom fighters in mysterious circumstances. In that history it is sometimes difficult to separate fact from fiction. For example, some claim that Isaias killed the EPLF's first martyr, Abraham Tewolde, who was the first leader of the group that splintered from the ELF (of which Isaias was a leading member), the group that would later morph into the EPLF by merging with other splinter groups.

Those who make the claim that Isaias killed Abraham argue that he did so because Abraham stood in the way of his burning ambition to become the leader. Isaias has a pathological zero tolerance for being number two; he simply has to be number one. If true—and let me reiterate it has never been proven—Abraham's murder would indeed be the original sin, so to speak, the origin of what went wrong and what ails Eritrea today. The "official" version of Abrham's demise is that he died of a sudden heart attack. No one knows where the truth lies; Isaias certainly would deny the charge, though he has not, to my knowledge, been confronted with the question. He named his own son Abraham in memory of his deceased comrade; and the cynics say that this is a clever ploy, typical of Isaias' game of deception.

In 1989, during his North American tour, Isaias was asked in a Los Angeles public meeting about allegation of crimes he committed in Sahel. His response was that he will answer if and when he is charged with the crime. The reference by the questioner was regarding the so called Menka'E group. Isaias' treatment of both Abraham and the Menka'E evokes Cain's murder of his brother Abel—a stain that emanates from Adam and Eve's original sin.

The Menka'E group was tried and sentenced to death by a committee of the EPLF appointed by the leadership. Was the death sentence ratified by the Central Committee of the EPLF? Clearly, the leaders of Menka'E, the first to challenge Isaias's power in the name of democratic accountability, were tried and found guilty of crimes that were defined by Isaias and his followers. Unless evidence to the contrary is forthcoming, it seems that there was a unanimous decision to pass the guilty verdict. There are unconfirmed reports that Mesfin Hagos and Ibrahim Afa voiced a dissenting opinion on the sentence, pleading instead for indefinite imprisonment. According to the same unconfirmed reports, Ibrahim Afa was later persuaded by Romadan Mohamed Nur to change his mind and accept the death sentence. It was not the only time that Isaias relied on Romadan to advance his own agenda; until he outlived his usefulness and was discarded like a used lemon.

In an interview with the author, Mesfin Hagos neither confirmed nor denied this report. Unfortunately, he keeps a Sphinx-like silence on these things for reasons that are not clear to me, but certainly not because he likes Isaias; I happen to know that he does not, contrary to some ugly allegations. Mesfin contends that he liked many of the Menka'E group, especially Musie, their presumed leader, whom he described as dedicated but impetuous. Mesfin said that he agreed with the demands of the group for accountability, but he disagreed with their timing and the manner of their demands at a time when the very survival of the EPLF was at issue.

Among the executed members of the Menka'E were Musse Tesfamichael and Yohannes Sebhatu. Musse was a popular and fearless fighter whom Isaias feared, even physically, as some claim, Isaias being unable to speak in front of him. He was considered the leader of the group, though Yohannes Sebhatu was intellectually head and shoulders above everybody, including Isaias. Yohannes was a brilliant Addis Ababa University graduate whose intellect apparently intimidated Isaias, as evidenced by several challenges he made during his brief sojourn in Sahel. Some say that Isaias' well-known anti-intellectualism is due, in part, to those defiant episodes.

Speaking of Ibrahim Afa, it is also rumored that his death was not caused by enemy action, as officially reported, but that Isaias had him murdered. Again, this is also rumor for which there is no credible evidence advanced. It is generally known, however, that Ibrahim and Isaias did not see eye to eye on some issues, including (but not limited to) military strategy and tactics. One witness related to me an incident at a meeting where Ibrahim was heard loudly denouncing Isaias as selfish and greedy. That charge was also loudly and clearly made by the so-called Menka'E group, whose crime was calling for democratic accountability because, they argued, Isaias had monopolized power. This was as early as 1973. Their supporters comprised many among the educated elements of the EPLF, including Petros Solomon and Sebhat Ephrem; but they were made to recant in exchange for pardons. It is ironic that as members of the Central Committee of the EPLF these elements sat in judgment of the accused, and approved the death sentence. This may also explain the fact that some of them (like Mesfin and Petros) expressed willingness to be judged by the appropriate tribunal for any wrongs they might have committed.

In raising these examples as part of the sordid record of the EPLF's past, I am trying to confront our collective guilt and examine the obstacles that stood in the way of the fulfillment of the dreams of Eritreans, including freedom fighters both martyred and living. Naturally, although we all share in the blame, a major aspect of this probing concerns prominent figures in Eritrea's recent history, notably the current president, who carries a heavy burden of historical responsibility for much of what went wrong. Such responsibility cannot be shielded by the significant role he played in the armed struggle for Eritrea's liberation.

The failure of the dream cannot be traced only to individual deeds. Another aspect that helps to explain the failure of the dream is context. This is not to excuse or in any way to justify the guilt of individuals who committed crimes. A time may come when they are brought to justice; or, if the country opts for dealing with this problem through the mode of a truth and reconciliation commission, it may dispose of the issues and bring closure to this sad episode.

One thing is certain: We need an open and extended national debate on the subject. In such a debate, the record of the ELF as well as that of the EPLF should be examined in the same way and with the same end in mind. The skeletons rattling in the hidden closets of both Isaias Afwerki and Abdella Idris, his ELF nemesis, need to be exposed. To that end, people with intimate knowledge of facts regarding this must come forward and testify. The question is: In what forum? There's the rub. We need to start thinking seriously of a national convention in which a decision must be made on how to bring closure to this tragic past. One way is to use the South African model of truth and reconciliation commission, with an open invitation to people to come forward and confess their crimes in exchange for pardon and amnesty. Such a proposal would include Isaias and Abdella Idris as well as others who may have been involved in crimes during our long history of armed struggle.

All this assumes that both those in government and in opposition would come to an agreement on this and other national issues, which may be far-fetched. It also assumes that the presumed guilty parties will be forthcoming and admit guilt in exchange for pardon and reconciliation for the sake of the nation. Then again, this too may be farfetched. What other alternative can there be to bring to an end this interminable, moral, and intellectual national crisis?

In the introduction of this volume, I mention the need for all of us to own up to mistakes or wrongs committed in the course of our involvement in the Eritrean liberation struggle. The important thing is to understand why we made mistakes or committed wrongs, wittingly or unwittingly. It is my view that much of what went wrong in our story can be explained in terms of our refusal to admit mistakes or own up to defects, hard as that might be. This is what I mean by context; each one of us being affected by the cultural heritage and historical circumstance in which we find ourselves and over which we may have little control.

The Imperative of Responsibility

There is a generally accepted principle that those who wield power must be held accountable for its use or abuse. Even in old monarchies, there was a class of elders or the priesthood that exerted a measure of influence and control over the scope of kingly powers by virtue of unwritten rules of conduct.

Addressing the question of responsibility, German philosopher, Karl Jaspers discusses three types of responsibility in a concise but brilliant book, titled *The Question of German Guilt* (1947), published in the aftermath of World War II. He wrote the book to explore the responsibility of the German people and their leaders for the crimes committed by Hitler's Nazi party. Germany, following World War II, faced not only huge material hardships as a result of the war's devastation, but also a serious moral crisis because of the horrendous Nazi crimes. Jaspers delineates these types of responsibility: legal, moral, and what he called metaphysical responsibility.

He writes first and foremost, about the legal responsibility faced by the Nazi leaders who were tried at Nuremberg, most of them convicted and sentenced to death for genocide, war crimes, and crimes against humanity. The international tribunal at Nuremberg used the laws of war as defined under international treaties and also under accepted norms of international law. The Nuremberg principles, as they are now called, have initiated a new international law of criminal responsibility, now epitomized in the treaty that established the International Criminal Court.

The irony of ironies is that the United States of America, the very country that led the Nuremberg trial, and the leader of the postwar international community, has so far refused to sign on to this treaty for domestic political reasons.

Second, following legal responsibility, is moral responsibility. Jaspers poses the question, as others have done then and since that time, whether the German people jointly and severally bore a moral responsibility for the crimes. This is a difficult question to answer with certainty; and opinion is divided on the answer to the question. An obvious issue in this respect is what kind of sanctions would be attached to such lack of moral responsibility. Would sanctions effect or produce any form of an embarrassment, a sense of shame vis-à-vis friends and relatives, and to what end? Yet friends and relatives, in the case of the Nazi experience of Germany, went along with the program without raising any objections, with the exception of some heroic souls who protested and perished in the attempt.

Even absent such dire consequences, modern psychology teaches that it is wellnigh impossible to withstand the pressure of a powerful propaganda machine of the kind wielded by Dr. Goebel's Ministry of Propaganda in Hitler's Germany. The same is true of the Stalinist propaganda machine (agit-prop) of the Soviet Communist party. Nor is this kind of pressure limited to the Nazi or Stalinist experience; many a dictator in our times has adopted the model to his advantage, as people follow the official line and march lemming-like to the tune of official propaganda.

Third comes metaphysical responsibility. If the sanction for legal responsibility is different kinds of punishment, and the criticism or censure of friends and relatives the punishment for moral responsibility, what is the sanction for metaphysical responsibility? Here, Jaspers introduces his own existential philosophy and maintains that you are responsible either to your own inner conscience or to a higher being—God or another manifestation of a superior entity before whom man presumably hangs his head in shame. The obvious questions that follow are: What if a person does not believe in religion? What if a person does not have conscience?

In situations of war or any intense conflict extended over a long period, there follows, inevitably, a coarsening of human sensibility. This is borne out by experience and is backed by experiments in modern psychology. It may indeed be the key to understanding the absence of opposition to outrageous behavior by psychopathic personalities in war, as exemplified in Eritrea's experience under Isaias Afwerki, in which all his comrades-in-arms kept silent while he decimated democratic elements for the "crime" of demanding accountability and transparency. Exhibit A in this charge is the case of the so called Menka'E group. Exhibit B is the case of the so called Yamin, educated members of the EPLF who wanted democratic accountability from Isaias and were rounded up and murdered on Isaias' order. They were called Yamin (Arabic for *Rightist*) in contrast to the earlier victims (the "Menka'E") who were dubbed ultra-Leftists by Isaias' secret ideological war machine.

In all war situations, people face hard questions that test their morality or their conscience. The best-known incidence of the Vietnam War experience was the Mai Lai massacre, in which American soldiers were seen killing people indiscriminately, mainly women, children, and older people. A young helicopter pilot named Hugh Thompson saw the massacre being committed while he was on a flying mission. He landed his helicopter on a spot between the soldiers engaged in a killing spree and their victims and he faced his American comrades, daring them either to shoot him or to stop the killing. They stopped the killing, and the pilot flew several Vietnamese on his helicopter to safety and also saved many more, evincing an act of moral courage at the risk to his life.

Years later, he was honored by a school, where he gave a keynote address at the graduation ceremony. When he was asked what made him do what he did, his answer was that he came from a simple folk in the mountains of Georgia and attended church every Sunday, where, he said, he was taught the difference between right and wrong. How many Thompsons were there in Vietnam at the time of the Mai Lai massacre? Obviously not many; perhaps none, or else the massacre would not have occurred, at least not to the extent it did.

The story of Mai Lai can happen anywhere to any armed force in similar circumstances, and for that reason, among others, military schools study Mai Lai and the psychology operating in that kind of situation.

Nationalism, Power, and Responsibility

In analyzing problems and their causes one is often tempted to look for someone to blame for what has gone wrong. Faced with a catastrophic situation, people tend to look for a culprit; and, in extreme circumstances, extreme positions are adopted. As an example of such extremes, I cite the case of Gunter Rutenborn, a German Lutheran minister, who wrote and produced a play titled *The Sign of Jonah*. The reference to Jonah is from the Gospel of Luke, chapter 11, verses 29-32.

The play takes place in a Germany still reeling from the devastation of the Second World War. A group of German refugees are arguing about the cause of the disaster as a result of the war. Who is to be blamed? Some blame Hitler; others blame the manufacturers who financed Hitler; still others say that the German people, in their apathy, bear responsibility for the destruction of the country. Suddenly, a man breaks through the crowd and says, "Do you want to know who is really to blame for all the suffering we've been through? I'll tell you who is responsible. God is to blame. God created this world. He placed all of this power in such unworthy hands. He allowed all of this to happen."

And so God is brought down on stage and put on trial for the crime of creation. He is found guilty as charged and sentenced to suffer the worst possible punishment. He is sentenced to live on this earth as a human being. He is to die the most painful and humiliating death imaginable.

Need I remind those who know that at the heart of the Christian faith is the belief that God became man and died on the cross, suffering arguably the most horrible form of death ever designed by man's punitive imagination. Why the crucifixion of Christ? To rescue mankind from the sentence of death incurred by Adam's sin. But this is not the point of Rutenborn's play. The point is that in the face of the horrors of the Second World War, the human mind dispensed with rational thinking and morality in order to cope with matters beyond its control. In making God the culprit, the play transcends logic and rational thinking. Although there is a certain logic in holding the Creator accountable for the sins of His creatures, normally, human beings tend to attach blame to fellow humans, often to those weaker than themselves.

Expanding this examination of power and responsibility beyond one country, I must ask: Can we Africans justifiably put the Europeans colonizers and their American cousins in the same position that our Lutheran minister put God? After all, they acted like God; they colonized Africa and they are responsible for the Atlantic Slave Trade and the horrors of slavery? Indeed, the reparation movement for obtaining redress for the crimes involved in colonialism and slavery is based on such belief. Leaving aside the question whether reparations will ever be paid, and to whom, the fact of making the claim imposes a moral burden and acts as a reminder of horrendous crimes committed. In my view rather than ask recompense for crimes of the past, we should instead, focus on crimes being committed in our own time.

Transparency International, an international coalition committed to fighting corruption, has urged the recently established International Criminal Court (ICC) to link business corruption and war crimes in its trial of defendants charged with war crimes in the Democratic Republic of the Congo (DRC). It also urged the creation of mechanisms for sanctioning the illegal exploitation of natural resources and other forms of corruption and plunder (www. Transparency.org, 7 February 2007). Human Rights Watch, for its part, has sent an appeal urging that the ICC, in the DRC case, should widely disseminate information on the trial. The appeal was launched in the belief that such information has an empowering effect on the general population. The aim is to encourage the creation of institutions and mechanisms for holding those in power accountable.

The aim of the foregoing remarks is to place emphasis on the question of responsibility and accountability in our social and political life. What is its relevance to the subject under discussion, namely crime and punishment? One of the consequences of the sovereignty principle, which underlies the nation state, is that it shelters wrong doers; it protects errant heads of state or those who act for them. Will a move away from this condition, and opting for regional arrangements designed to avoid wasteful or destructive competition, lead to better government accountability? There is no way of telling, unless it is tried. Perhaps it may if appropriately tied to the evolving international law of criminal responsibility for war crimes and crimes against humanity.

Africa has had its share of monsters that abused national sovereignty and gave nationalism a bad name, though, granted, there are two kinds of nationalism. There is fanatical and destructive nationalism; then there is responsible and balanced nationalism. Monsters like Idi Amin Dada (Uganda), self-proclaimed Emperor Bokasa (Central African Republic), Red Emperor Mengistu Hailemariam (Ethiopia), to mention a few. These and others who came after them, unelected rulers who have abused their people's trust and ruled by royal decree, deserve a place in Madame Tussaud's Chamber of Horrors. We have mediocrities that will be mere footnotes in modern African history; and we have, on the other hand, giants like Mandela (South Africa), Nkrumah (Ghana), Neyerere (Tanzania), and Senghor (Senegal) whose place is in the Hall of Celebrities.

Consigning abusive leaders who committed crimes against their people to the Chamber of Horrors is an important emblematic act; but is it enough? What should be done to leaders who are the cause of much tragedy and human suffering? And what is the role of ideas and institutions, both modern and traditional that enable such leaders to commit unconscionable acts of inhumanity?

To start with the question of personal responsibility, which has been touched upon above, historically, there have been different responses to the challenge of power and its abuse. I have been particularly interested in the spiritual and artistic responses to the problem of settling scores with earthly monsters because it represents a more profound answer to the question of responsibility than legal (or constitutional) provisions. This subject has been a fertile ground for religion, myth, and literature.

Two examples to illusrate the point

The examples I will cite are: one from Ethiopia, the other from Italy. The first comes from Ethiopian religious tradition. There is a passage in the Ethiopic religious literature, *Te'amire Mariam* (The Book of the Miracles of Mary) in which the Virgin Mary, mother of Jesus, is taking Jesus round in a tour of hell. Jesus sees some people bound to a column of fire, and He asks His mother who those people are. She tells Him they were princes who abused people when they were rulers on earth. The column of fire never goes out, and the bound creatures are subject to eternal suffering—a very effective deterrent, one would think; or is it? To what extent did Ethiopian rulers desist from doing harm to their subjects as a result of this imaginative theological admonition? No one knows; all we know is that there have been some just monarchs and many unjust ones. The story demonstrates the role of religion in instituting a system of moral or metaphysical responsibility to guide princely behavior.

In European literature, an example of metaphysical responsibility is found in Dante's *Divine Comedy*. In a peculiar manner of settling scores metaphysically, Dante consigns to purgatory those who wronged him, like the count Ugolino. Again, what restraining effect such religious imagination might have had on the behavior of Florentine princes is open to question. But it couldn't have failed to arouse public glee and thus conceivably impart on at least the educated elites of Florence a sense of empowerment.

In our own time, if the example of censorious literature like some of Wole Soyinka's work is anything to go by, it does not seem to have had any impact on the presidential behavior of Nigeria's Obasanjo, and certainly not on that of Abacha. But then, Obasanjo, like George Bush, has no need of any counsel of the wise; he needed no guidance from mere mortals like Soyinka or, in Bush's case, his own somewhat wiser father. Both Obasanjo and George Bush had a Higher Father to guide them. Hence Nigeria's plight, and America's predicament in Iraq!

In Eritrea's case, our unelected, self appointed national redeemer bases his power not on a higher being; it is derived from "revolutionary" legitimacy and is backed by the force of arms. His power came literally out of the barrel of the gun. That revolutionary legitimacy is the mother of terror and has consumed much in its wake. It has been said that a revolution devours its children. The origin of this notion is the phase of Reign of Terror during the French Revolution, and many a blood-thirsty dictator has quoted this notion to justify egregious violations of human rights, including massacres and disappearances. The quote was a favorite of Ethiopian dictator, Mengistu Haile Mariam (1977-1991), who used "Red Terror" to decimate thousands of Ethiopia youth, mostly members of the Ethiopian Peoples' Revolutionary Party (EPRP). His propaganda agents used to say that the arm of the revolution is long, and "the revolution will knock at every door." I have often wondered if dictators emulate one another, because the propaganda agents of Isaias Afwerki used to say, and still say, the same thing. It all boils down to this: All dictators are chips from the same block—the sociopathic block.

One thing that dictatorial regimes dislike is law—the very idea of law, which necessarily implies restraint, goes against the grain. The only law they welcome is one that amplifies their power. When Isaias and his Central Committee of the EPLF debated the introduction of a legal system in the Sahel wilderness, and after independence, the lawyers in the EPLF were hard pressed to justify the idea of legal restraint. Heading the department of law, at the time, was Taeme Beyene, who became the chief justice of the Supreme Court after independence and came to grief because he protested against executive interference with the judicial branch. He was summarily dismissed by the president.

All systems have laws to guide their actions. In the Sahel environment of "jungle law" in which the gun rules, there was an element of legality supposedly governing the actions of the members. In the formal sense, the structure of that legal system was as follows. The congress of the EPLF was, according to its founding charter, the highest organ of the organization between congresses. The congress meets every three years according to the charter; and, during those three years, the Central Committee (CC) is the next highest body, which is mandated by the charter to meet every three months. The CC acted as the legislative body. Then there was the Political Bureau (Politburo, for short), which was the body with the next highest authority, but which in effect exercised the supreme power of the organization, with the secretary general as chair of both the CC and the Politburo.

During the ten years between the first congress of 1977 and the second congress of 1987, Isaias was the deputy secretary general of the EPLF, with Romadan Mohamed Noor acting as the secretary general. Two points must be noted. First, the legality was breached in that the meeting of the congress was not held on time. The reason given was that there was a war situation involving a succession of Ethiopian campaigns. That reason might be acceptable if the due date for holding the congress was a matter of going beyond the required time by one or two years. But ten years, instead of the mandated three years, is too long an interval and leads to reasonable suspicion that the motive for the failure lies elsewhere, just as the failure to implement the ratified constitution was not caused by the 1998-2000 war. This pattern of defiance of rules requires explanation and suggests reasons that go beyond logistical or practical problems. It goes to the heart of the matter of the deception and obfuscation that is characteristic of Isaias' mode of operation altogether. This mode of operation is conveniently facilitated by the cultural indisposition to challenge authority.

The Secret Party

The second point concerns the secret party and its power over the EPLF. What outsiders did not know until 1993, when the existence of the secret party was revealed at the third congress, was that in fact Isaias, as the secretary general of the secret party, was the one who had the supreme power over the EPLF. Romadan was head of the EPLF in name only; in actual fact, Isaias did everything, including lead the EPLF behind the scenes.

Isaias makes and breaks the rule at will, and when the rules serve his purpose he is adamantly insistent on obedience to them; when they don't serve his purpose, rules and laws in general are dismissed as bourgeois preoccupation with technicality. The revolution is not about technicality; it is about the imposition of the will of the masses, and as the one who embodies the will of the masses he can make and break the rules in the name of the masses. *Awet N'Hafash*—Victory to the masses!

I had occasion to observe the working of the organization in one congress and in a couple of in-between- congress conferences. I was also in Sahel several times and observed the mode of operation and attitudes to law on the part of the EPLF leaders. I once took a text book on criminal law of the Somali Republic written by a friend of mine, Martin Ganzglass. The lawyers in the EPLF, Taeme Beyene and Eden Fassil, in particular, were deeply appreciative of the gesture, and we discussed briefly the idea of law making in revolutionary situations. Both lawyers and others present were concerned that the attitude of many among the EPLF leadership toward law and principles of legality (rule of law), was cavalier, to put it mildly. They were doing their best in the circumstances to instill the idea of the rule of law carefully and timorously, as I could observe. When I broached the subject to Isaias himself, the reaction was vintage Isaias— of course we are governed by the rule of law; we are all for law, he wanted to assure me. But in the situation of the war, he continued, law has to be subject to conditions. "*Highi Kem Shamu*" was the phrase he used. He might not have realized that I was making mental notes of everything he said and did, and that I noted down all significant statements and acts. I did that all the time.

My overall conclusion is that to Isaias law is an inconvenience at best, and at worst, an obstacle to be removed at an opportune moment. That was why I was pleasantly surprised when he undertook to translate the congress resolution of a multiparty democracy into law and passed the interim constitution in 1993, under which the framework for a future constitutional government was drawn and a constitutional commission created to prepare a constitution.

As it turned out, it was all a gigantic hoax on the nation, an immaculate deception of the worst kind, but one that will lead to his undoing sooner or later.

Chapter 5

CONCORD AND DISCORD: THE TANGLED WEB OF THE EPLF–TPLF RELATIONSHIP

Hopeful Beginnings

When I think of the relationship between the two new governments of Eritrea and Ethiopia I am reminded of a famous statement by the midnineteenth century British statesman, Lord Palmerstone. He said that in international relations, there are no permanent friends and permanent enemies; only permanent interests. This is as true today as it was during the Crimean War when the statement was uttered; in much of human relations, interest trumps all other considerations, be it at the individual or corporate or national level. To all observers, except to a few discerning eyes, Eritrea and Ethiopia began with enviable amity and comity in the first years following Eritrea's independence in May 1991.

The liberation organizations that formed the governments of the two countries jointly defeated the army of the military government of Ethiopia (the Dergue). After the Addis Ababa Conference of July 1991, the two new governments showed every sign of translating their proclaimed commitment to peaceful cooperation into practice. From the very beginning the leaders of the two victorious liberation fronts assured each other and the world that they would be a positive factor for peace and cooperation. The EPLF issued a press release three days after it entered Asmara, declaring that Eritrea was "ready to contribute toward the promotion of peace and stability in the region." The same press release assured the Ethiopian peoples "that the Eritrean people bear no animosity toward them. As neighbors, the ports of Massawa and Asseb are open to them for passages of goods needed in the heartland of Ethiopia." Indeed, the EPLF and EPRDF signed a protocol at the conclusion of the July conference, assuring Ethiopia a free passage of goods through Eritrea's ports, requiring only payment of service charges.

This hopeful beginning was rooted in conditions shared by the governments of the two countries. There is, first of all, a common historical experience and cultural heritage. In fact, the shared experience goes beyond the two countries and embraces the Horn of African region in terms of certain commonalities in cultural heritage and material conditions of life. Second, there is the recent shared experience of struggle against a common enemy, accompanied by a sense of the need for common aims and combined efforts in the face of the harsh reality of devastated economies and impoverished peoples.

It appeared to some citizens of the two countries that in view of the shared conditions it would behoove the new governments and their populations to think in terms of cooperative efforts in the postwar situation. It was in this spirit that, as previously mentioned, an international conference was held in July 8-12, 1993, in Addis Ababa, convened by the present writer and hosted by the United Nations Economic Commission for Africa (UNECA) and cosponsored and supported by the United States Institute of Peace.

The conference was opened by a keynote address by the minister of Foreign Affairs of Ethiopia, and ministers and other high-ranking members of the governments of Eritrea and Ethiopia were invited as participants of the symposium. Also invited to the conference were other high-ranking members of governments of the Horn of Africa region, including Djibouti, Kenya, Sudan, and Uganda as well as observers from many other governments. Representatives of the European Union, and the UN and envoys from different embassies also attended as observers.

The time was propitious; it was during the halcyon days in the wake of the victories scored against an oppressive government when hopes ran high and an infectious spirit of optimism was palpable, affecting even a skeptical international press. The conference came out with a communiqué that caught the spirit of optimism and spoke about a vision envisaged by the participants as the following paragraph demonstrates:

> Drawing insights from the many shared experiences between the people of the sub-region in terms of certain commonalities in cultural heritage and material conditions of life...we have spelt out the components of this vision, namely: the need for a durable and lasting peace based on tolerance of diversity and heterogeneity; the need for a human-centered approach to development policy planning and implementation; the closely related need for accelerated sustainable development based on human and natural resources of the region; *the need for cooperation between countries in the sub-region in critical areas of mutual benefit to advance their development prospects*; and the need to establish an effective linkage between emergency assistance, rehabilitation and long-term development in

intervention by the international community. (Page 2 of Final Communique, "From Conflict to Concord," UNECA, Addis Ababa July 12, 1993.). [Italics supplied].

The vision of the participants was shared by the concerned governments as demonstrated by the papers presented by the government Ministers who took part in the symposium, and especially by the opening address of Foreign Minister Seyoum Mesfin. A memorable point in the speech was his statement that cooperation and eventual integration is not one of the options; it was the only option. Nor was this spirit limited to rhetorical statements. In the years between 1993 and 1997, agreement was reached between the governments of Eritrea and Ethiopia covering issues of security, trade, communications, and education. These agreements were designed to facilitate freer movement of goods and services across the boundaries of the two countries. To all interested observers, it seemed as if a new era was dawning in the region, raising great expectations among people in the two countries.

A formalization of the relation between Eritrea and Ethiopia took place with the signing of the Asmara Pact in 1993. It has been reported that the two countries had signed twenty-five protocol agreements aimed at reinforcing and expanding the cooperative relations developing between them. The Asmara Pact of 1993 created the framework for the implementation of the various agreements and established three joint technical committees and a ministerial committee to monitor the implementation of the agreements. According to authors, Tekeste Negash and Kjetill Tronvoll, the Ethiopian Ministry of Foreign Affairs gave them access to the agreed minutes of the joint ministerial commission meetings between 1993 and 1997. (Tekeste et al. *Brothers at War* 2000. 31). The most important protocol of the Asmara Pact, the authors contend, were those on harmonization of economic policies and on trade, including, investment, monetary and fiscal policies.

The Asmara Pact reflected the ideal of interstate relations in the context of regional cooperation envisaged by a new leadership that stepped into the shoes of a repressive regime. This ideal of a cooperative framework of international relations had not taken into account, in the case under discussion, some of the tensions and contradictions simmering below the surface and subsumed under the borders that define the African nation-states. Apparently, the euphoria of the post-Dergue days had blinded many, including the present writer, to the belief that there was a Horn of Africa exceptionalism that would transcend the national or ethnic politics besetting the rest of Africa.

State Boundaries and Identity Politics

Identity politics is a continent-wide African phenomenon. It is a function of the colonially-fixed boundaries that defined the postcolonial states of Africa, boundaries that enclosed within them ethnic/linguistic groups of people. In the case of Eritrea and Ethiopia, the boundaries divide Tigrigna-speaking as well as Kunama-speaking people on the Eritrea-Ethiopia border, Afar-speaking people on the Eritrea-Djibouti border, and Tigre-speaking and other Beja people on the Eritrea-Sudan border.

One of the ironies of this phenomenon is that despite the artificial nature of the boundaries that define the postcolonial states, people belonging to the same ethnic group, living across the artificial boundaries, have accepted the new identity to the point, at times, of engaging in deadly fights against one another. In other words, the artificially forged identity has become the basis of a new national consciousness, transcending or trumping primordial ethnic identity.

In order to accommodate different ethnic groups in a new national state, governments have adopted systems of administration that suit their national objectives. Eritrea and Ethiopia have adopted different models for decentralizing state power on the basis of their differing historical and political conditions and needs. In Eritrea a policy of regional autonomy was the chosen model in which central government power would be equitably shared and reasonably balanced with local power, such that it would instill confidence in the idea of one nation, one united people. That at least was the idea of the constitution drafters. In Ethiopia, by contrast, a federal framework has been adopted designed to accommodate ethnic demands and concerns.

In the final analysis, whatever the model adopted, there are two powerful motives that animate people, particularly at the regional level. First, there is the desire for recognition as worthy members of their communities. Second, there is the desire to be part of a larger, more efficient and dynamic modern state. The first involves, in the words of a noted scholar, Clifford Geertz, "a search for an identity, and a demand that the identity be publicly acknowledged as having import." (Geertz: 1993, 258). Ethnic federalism is designed to fulfill this demand. The second is a demand for better life, which can be best realized in a larger unity, transcending regional boundaries of power or socioeconomic interaction, and beyond that (ideally) of playing a part in the larger arena of global politics.

These two motives are linked in the concept of citizenship, which in the modern state has become, to quote Geertz again, the most broadly negotiated currency of personal significance, connecting the person and his or her place of origin with the center of power. The two motives are nonetheless different and respond to different pressures. They are held in tension, which can be constructive as well as obstructive to national progress. A successful arrangement of the center-region relation must thus take account of this inherent tension. Needless to say, all allocation of powers and responsibilities must be designed to encourage constructive efforts at all levels leading to a common good. It is also worth noting that much of the political process in developing states turns on the constant effort by leaders to maintain a working relationship between regional peculiarities and common national goals.

In Eritrea, nationalism united the various ethnic groups in a common struggle, and nationalism now acts as a matrix of the larger political community bound up with the state. Nationalism also mediates the conflict between local sentiments and interests with those of the larger community forged in a common struggle against alien domination.

It would be rare today for ethnic or regional groups to entertain a burning desire for a separate existence from one another outside the larger community, for they recognize the advantage of remaining together as one state. In Ethiopia, the new leaders who have embarked on a federal structure based on ethnic/linguistic ties have taken a calculated risk. If they succeed, they will have contributed to Africa a new politics of constitutional government. In Nigeria's federal structure, the jury is still out as to whether or not the federal experiment has succeeded in forging a sense of national belonging, particularly in view of rampant corruption as well as the unanswered demand by the people of the Delta region for equitable distribution of wealth.

In the case of Ethiopia, there are some outstanding issues that need to be faced. Concerning the federal experiment, two points must be made. The first concerns the Oromo question—the fact that the Oromo Liberation Front (OLF) still claims the right to form a separate nation of Oromia, breaking away from Ethiopia, despite the fact that many Oromo argue that they would fare better in a democratic Ethiopia, being the single most numerous ethnic group. The second point relates to the fact that the new Ethiopian leaders have gone one step beyond previous experiments in federalism by inserting an article in the constitution (article 39) providing for the right of any aggrieved ethnic group to secede from the Ethiopian state in the case of fundamental disagreement between such group and the federal government. This is indeed one of the points that has provoked bitter criticism from a significant number of Ethiopians, especially from those belonging to the Amhara nationality.

Critics of a federation based on ethnicity argue that ethnicized politics can lead to ethnic cleansing. They claim that, as a result of the ethnic-based division of the country, there have been massacres of people whose ancestors had settled in Oromo areas. This claim may be well founded and if so poses a serious problem. At the same time, as I was able to observe during an extensive research tour of Oromo-speaking parts of Ethiopia in February-March 1998, there was a hitherto unknown sense of autonomy and control of one's destiny and resources. I posed the question to local leaders and, later, to OLF leaders: Why secede; why not amplify your rights and expand your autonomy within a democratically restructured Ethiopia? It was my contention, based on rational arguments on demographic facts, that in such a restructured Ethiopia the Oromo would be controlling the government; for they are the majority. The response to my contention was a polite smile and silence, smile and an intriguing silence that spoke volumes.

Ethnic Politics and Eritrea-Ethiopia Relations

I posed another question, this time to my Tigrayan friends who are members of the government of the Ethiopian Peoples' Revolutionary Democratic Front (EPRDF), the party of which the TPLF is the senior partner: Why did the EPRDF government insert the article on secession in the constitution? I also raised this question, among many other questions, in interviews with Prime Minister Meles Zenawi, House Speaker, Dawit Yohannes, and other high-ranking members of the government. The answer was framed in terms of the principle of the right of people to self-determination. Didn't we fight for the same fundamental right? So why not put it in the constitution if we are serious about this right? These "in-your-face" questions directed at me, an Eritrean who has written on the subject and also fought for that right for my own people, was quite a challenge in terms of principle. What can an Eritrean say to answer such a challenging question?

Well, this happens to be one of the questions on which the leadership of the two governments has registered serious disagreement. The disagreement goes beyond the issue of secession; the Eritrean government is highly critical of the new ethnic-based federal system of Ethiopia. In their book *Brothers' at War*, Tekeste Negash and Kjetil Tronvoll quote Yemane Gebrerab, the Eritrean government's chief ideologue as follows:

> For us the ethnification of politics, creating regions on an ethnic basis, is wrong, and it is going to create problems tomorrow. It is not just going to create problems for Ethiopia, it is also going to create problems for the TPLF, because now these (ethnic states) may be junior allies because you are stronger, you have more resources. But tomorrow, when these people become stronger they will think about themselves not as Ethiopians but as Oromos or whatever, and they will say why are we being dominated by TPLF and the Tigreans? So the approach is wrong and counterproductive. They (the TPLF) would not accept the argument. We also talked about the Ethiopian constitution and its idea of secession and its ethnic-based

> participation. We told them (the TPLF) you are doing a disservice
> to Ethiopia just because you want to have an independent Tigray
> as a fall-back position if your agenda in Ethiopia does not work.
> You shouldn't impose that agenda on Ethiopia and it's wrong. They
> wouldn't listen to that either. (Negash and Tronvoll. 2000: 15-16).

As far as Eritrea is concerned, Yemane's views on ethnic federalism are shared by Eritrea's constitution makers, as I explain in my book, *The Making of the Eritrean Constitution*, perhaps one of the few points on which we agree these days. The Constitutional Commission of Eritrea recommended that Eritrea have a unitary government consistent with our goal of building a unified and strong nation. In deciding which system to adopt—federal or unitary—the size of the country was one consideration, along with the historical and cultural conditions. In the case of Eritrea, in addition to the small size of the country, the history of unified struggle of the Eritrean people against a succession of alien occupiers was taken into account in opting for a unitary state.

The commission also recommended that the existence of local governments be essential in order to ensure the people's initiative and participation. The commission's major concern in that regard was that the issue be handled in a way to maintain the right balance between centralization and decentralization, taking into account the condition of the country and aiming at orderly development over time, taking practical needs into account. In accordance with the recommendations of the commission, the final draft of the constitution frames the issue in concise terms, leaving detailed elaboration to future legislation. Thus article 1(5) provides: "Eritrea is a unitary state divided into units of local government. The powers and duties of these units shall be determined by law." In this connection it is worth reiterating that the commission made a determination that a concise constitution is better for the conditions of the country, leaving details to future legislation and judicial interpretation.

As we saw above, Yeman Gebreab made a comment that the secession provision in Ethiopia's constitution is a "fall-back" position, which is interesting. It raises at least two questions. First, why would the TPLF (if not the allied parties of EPRDF) want a fall-back position? Second, in what way might it have an impact on Eritrea?

I will start with the second point. With regard to this point, Negash and Tronvoll have written that the Eritrean government "perceives a direct link between border skirmishes...and the ongoing process of ethnogenesis in Ethiopia." The same writers have also opined that the government of Eritrea is "trying by all means and policies to subdue and neutralize ethnicity in Eritrea," and that it "places great emphasis upon creating a national, homogeneous and all-embracing nation with an Eritrean identity." (*Brothers at War.* 16).

This is a damning judgment, and if it is right, then the government of Eritrea has indeed violated one of the founding principles and committed an offence against its own people: It has violated their fundamental right and betrayed a pledge implicitly made to them during the long struggle for independence, which necessarily included a human right. Such a human right places an obligation on the government to recognize and maintain the integrity of each citizen and to protect and sustain them. The well-worn slogan of long duration throughout the struggle, which also guided the constitution makers, is *unity-in-diversity*. This principle places a high premium on the integrity of all the component parts making up the Eritrean polity; the reported policy of "subduing" and "neutralizing" any ethnic group would thus militate against the cherished principle of the democratic and human right of the people.

Identity and Nationality

As to the respective policies and perspectives of the EPLF and TPLF with regard to the question of ethnicity and nationalism, other scholars of the Horn of Africa have offered different comments and interpretations. Richard Reid has, for example, studied documents issued by both the EPLF and the TPLF dealing with the issues of ethnicity and nationalism or nation building. On the basis of his analysis of these documents, Reid traces the existence of "tensions, contradictions and misunderstandings" between the EPLF and the TPLF from the time of the liberation struggle. He asserts that the documents he analyzed highlight a number of problems that "would come back to haunt the movements in government, and demonstrate the lengthy genealogy of certain issues which can be understood as having contributed to uneasy relations at the time—the height of the struggle—and more specifically to the outbreak of war between two sovereign states over a decade later." (Richard Reid, 2003: 73).

Concerning the definition of Tigrayan nationalism , the writer makes reference to an earlier TPLF manifesto that defined a Tigrayan as anyone who speaks Tigrigna, the language of central highland Eritrea as well as of Tigray itself. According to Reid this earlier definition of what constitutes a Tigrayan was considered by the EPLF as a dangerous new form of Tigrayan nationalism that would impinge on the integrity of Eritrean nationalism. It was later abandoned by the TPLF, when the idea of separating Tigray from the rest of Ethiopia was itself abandoned in favor of a multiethnic federalism, embraced by the TPLF and the larger party of which it became the core leader, the EPRDF.

Reid speculates interestingly that it might have been this earlier view of Tigrayan nationalism, narrowly defined but later abandoned, that impelled the the TPLF to launch its campaign in favor of Eritean national self-determination, focusing on the people of Tigray, presumably to persuade them that Eritreans are not Tigrayans, despite the fact that they share the Tigrigna language and culture with a significant number of Eritreans. Indeed, the author states that the TPLF asserted that "from the outset it had supported the Eritrena cause, which it believed to be a just anticolonial struggle.(ibid, p.383). The author adds, with a note of irony, "It is significant that the 'Tigrayan people' needed the most persuading, while the extent to which the TPLF actually persuaded itself of the justness of the Eritrean cause is a mater of some debate."(ibid).

As for the idea of a fall-back position for the TPLF, this matter is connected to the whole notion of an independent Tigray in case the TPLF-led government is overthrown. From the start when the EPLF and the TPLF became allies in the war of liberation, there was a time, as mentioned above, when the TPLF entertained the idea of an independent Tigray state one separated from Ethiopia. The EPLF did not accept this, and it was for a time one of their points of disagreement until the TPLF changed its mind and became a leading all-Ethiopian liberation movement.

To return to the notion of unity-in-diversity, which is a mediating principle guiding Eritrea's constitution makers, the question arises as to how a government like that of Eritrea should respond to any demand for secession by anyone of its component ethnic minorities. Indeed, this was at one time a bone of contention between the EPLF and the TPLF with respect to the Afar people. When the TPLF earlier believed the Afar of Tigray to be an integral part of a future Tigrayan nation-state as propounded in the 1975 manifesto, they opposed the Afar liberation movement then in operation. At the same time the TPLF supported the idea of Eritrean Afars seceding, a matter that became a sticky wicket between the two fronts. In recent years, the TPLF have used article 39 of the Ethiopian constitution to encourage Eritrean minority groups, including the Afar and Kunama, to seek self-determination up to and including secession. Obviously, this has been a point of disagreement between the two governments; and it is the one TPLF policy on which the vast majority of Eritreans are united in opposition to. It is also one on which the dominant opposition groups are in agreement with the government of Eritrea, which they nonetheless seek to overthrow.

Isaias Afwerki and Meles Zenawi—A Study in Contrast

From the first years of their victorious entry in their respective capitals, Isaias Afwerki and Meles Zenawi appeared to be good friends. Their personal relationship was very cordial—so cordial, in fact, that it led to idle speculation; some saying that they were cousins. Such speculation was fueled by the fact that Meles's mother is Eritrean, and Isaias is partly of Tigrean origin.

Needless to say, personal relation alone, outside the overall context, including the structure and ideology of the respective organizations, is not sufficient to explain what seemed to be developing friendly relations between the two countries. Nevertheless, personal relation between leaders is a crucial element in interstate politics. I will briefly note here my own personal observations of the two leaders.

I have met Meles Zenawi, the prime minister of Ethiopia, five or six times on various occasions between 1991 and 1998; and during that period, I have seen the two leaders together at close quarters on a few occasions. On one of those occasions, they were joking and "pulling each other's legs" like two old friends whether while playing snooker or while simply chatting over beer or coffee. It is impossible for me to avoid drawing comparisons and contrasts on their differing personalities and social skills. Apart from their contrasting physical features—with Isaias's 6-foot, 4-inch height and Meles's diminutive figure and balding head—they have quite dramatically different personalities. One Ethiopian intellectual close to Meles, who later became Ethiopia's ambassador to the United States, once described Isaias as having a "dangerous charisma." Why describe the charisma as dangerous? Could he have in mind Meles' "charisma" deficit? Anyway it was a deeply revealing statement, uttered in a moment of anger.

Since I have already described my first meeting with Isaias in January 1975, when he was a twenty-nine-year-old guerilla leader; there is no need to repeat it here. I will only add to what I have already said; that Isaias has a domineering personality with a tendency to reject out of hand, often with sarcasm, any views that do not seem to tally with his own. This character trait has defined his relationship with all people dealing with him, especially his close aides and Ministers. One former cabinet minister described his experience to me; when he had made a statement regarding a housing policy that contradicted Isaias'dictates and would not bend to repudiate his earlier statement in defiance of Isaias's demand, he was "frozen" for months, and eventually kicked upstairs. Isaias cannnot tolerate anyone boldly asserting a principled position that happens to contradict his own position.

By contrast, Meles Zenawi has an ingratiating personality that places a high premium on civility and persuasive argument instead of domination. Not that Isaias cannot sustain a winning argument when he is in a good mood; but that is a rare phenomenon. Nor is Meles all sweetness, devoid of a hard edge when it comes to principles or opinions that he holds dear. I met Meles for the first time in 1989, when he was thirty-four. Our meeting took place in Washington, D.C., following his emergence as the leader of the TPLF, and he was touring the United States. He came to visit me in Howard University, accompanied by Berhane Gebrekristos, the then TPLF representative in North America. I took them to a local coffee shop for a pleasant chat. I found Meles easy to talk to, very engaging in conversations, witty, and extremely articulate. Our conversation was very cordial and ranged over a number of issues. Throughout the extended conversation, there was no controversy except at one point; when he showed a different mettle after I asked him pointedly why the TPLF had given quarter to an ELF splinter group that was hostile to the EPLF. His response was as surprising as it was terse and uncompromising, albeit delivered with a smile and in an even tone. He said the TPLF had the right to give quarter to anybody it wanted, and that the group in question had a democratic right to voice opposition even against the EPLF. *Period.*

I remembered this statement when, in 1999, he uttered that curious remark about Ethiopia's right to expel anybody on the basis of the color of his eyes—if it so chose. This statement was given in response to a question about his government's expulsion of Eritreans and Ethiopians of Eritrean origin.

During our conversation, he maintained that the relationship between the two fronts should be based on mutual respect for the principled positions that they held on all issues even where they disagreed. This was a foundational principle, he seemed to say, and nothing would change it. Clearly, I was dealing with a man of destiny whose soft demeanor deceptively concealed an iron will. This trait has been subsequently demonstrated time and again.

An additional clue to the differences between the two may be found in their educational background or rather in their scholastic record. Meles was a second-year medical student when he joined the TPLF in 1975. He was a brilliant student at the General Wingate Secondary School in Addis Ababa, an elite British-run school; and he achieved the highest score in the national examination for entry to the university. After the victory over the Dergue army, Meles and many of his colleagues enrolled in the British Open University, obtaining a degree in business administration. His command of economic and financial issues can be seen in all the interviews he gives; and the Nobel Laureate for economics, Joseph Stiglitz, is on record for saying that Meles is equal to any of the best students he ever taught.

As for Isaias, according to accounts I heard from former students of the Prince Mekonen Secondary School of Asmara, he was an average student. He did not take part in sports. According to someone who was one of his teachers, when he was asked why he did not participate in the football game others were playing, Isaias was dismissive, displaying an attitude of contempt for those who were playing. His answer was: "*Mis Men?*" (with whom?) He left Prince Mekonen School in 1965 and entered Addis Ababa University, then known as Haile Selassie I University, enrolling in the engineering department. In October 1966, he left the university to join the ELF. There is an unconfirmed report that he failed his examination to pass to the second year, and that he decided to join the armed struggle partly (if not mainly) because of this failure. In fairness, it should be said first of all that the story has not been confirmed; moreover, even if it is true, the temper of the times was such that students bent on struggle did not give much weight to education. In 1967, Isaias was sent to China for military and political training, together with Romodan Mohamed Nur and three others.

In addition to the differences in political ideology and military doctrines between the EPLF and TPLF that have been noted by writers on the subject, a point of great interest to all concerned with the recent history of the two countries is the difference in leadership styles of the two men, including their attitudes toward the rule of law and modes of governance. Where Meles relies on his powers of persuasion, with full confidence on his oratorical and analytical skills, Isaias prefers imposing his will by sheer dominance over all around him. Where Meles is tolerant and allows some space for those who hold different views, even while maintaining a hawk-eyed vigilance, Isaias is intolerant and eliminates or freezes into insignificance anyone who disagrees with him. Where Meles pays more than lip service to the rule of law and brings errant opponents to justice through the normal legal process, Isaias shows no respect for the rule of law and has detained opponents without trial, often for several years. Where Meles believes in adhering to the law and the constitution, Isaias has shelved a ratified constitution and rules by decree, not unlike kings of old. Indeed, when a Swedish journalist asked him why he did not introduce democratic governance, he responded by asking the journalist why the Western commentators do not ask the same question of the king of Saudi Arabia, thereby betraying a monarchical predilection.

At the time of our 1989 Washington meeting with Meles there was no lingering problem or hostility between the EPLF and the TPLF; the two fronts had just mended fences a little while before our meeting after a few years of frozen relations (1985-1988). And a year after our meeting, they would launch a coordinated campaign on the Ethiopian army that would end in a joint final assault that doomed the Dergue's rule in May 1991. However, as events would reveal later, the sharp response that Meles gave me in our Washington meeting, regarding the ELF splinter group to which his party gave quarter, was indicative of some unresolved underlying tension not apparent to most observers. Indeed, most of us had been persuaded that after their successful triumph over the Dergue army, there were no lingering differences between the two fronts.

We were in for a rude awakening as the "Badme War" was to show. By "we" I mean citizens of both countries as well as members of the scholarly community of the Horn of Africa. In fairness to this optimistic view, as I noted above, the governments of the two countries had agreed to make cooperation the cornerstone of their relationship. They had established joint ministerial commissions to resolve any disputes between them. All eyes were focused on these two promising young leaders and their touted talk of cooperation, leaving behind them years of conflict that had devastated their countries. The Badme incident of May 1998 and the ensuing full-scale war put the lie to all this optimism. Evidently, the joint commission on security did not do its job in the Badme area and elsewhere, which escalated into an all out war in 1998. Or perhaps there was no real sincerity behind the pronouncements of cooperation, which is worse.

From Concord Back to Discord

The failure of the Joint Commission on Security indicates a failure of the original, much-heralded policy of cooperation. As to the reason why the policy of cooperation failed, the two sides have different interpretations, as they do also on the cause of the Badme War, as we shall see. It turns out that the two governments had, by the end of 1997, even before the Badme incident that triggered the war, gone their separate ways on practically all issues. The final straw that broke the (cooperation) camel's back was the issue of currency, which is a key factor in trade relations between the two countries.

Matters came to a head on this issue in the autumn of 1997, some six months before the outbreak of the war, when Eritrea issued its own national currency, naming it *Nakfa*. As I will explain in more detail below, the symbolism was not lost on Ethiopians who never reconciled themselves to the idea of an independent Eritrea, as the city of *Nakfa*, the capital of the Sahel region, the base area of the liberation struggle, was emblematic of the struggle.

Why was the currency issue so problematic that it caused the two governments to go their separate ways, abandoning the trajectory of cooperation and integration?

Several writers have offered explanations. One of these is the Eritrean academic, Professor Tekie Fessehatzion. In the introductory chapter of his 2002 book, *Shattered Illusion, Broken Promise: Essays on the Eritrea-Ethiopia Conflict (1998-2000)*, Tekie (to use the customary Eritrean mode of appellation) has called the currency issue "the seed of discord." Tekie describes the disagreements between the governments of Eritrea and Ethiopia as the system of payment in trade between the two countries.

This disagreement occurred in the wake of the introduction of the *Nakfa*. Tekie reports that in the final meeting between negotiating teams of the two governments (April 18—19, 2007), the two sides could not agree on how the payments should be settled and in what currency payments should be made. Ethiopia's position was that with the exception of limited cross-border trade, all other trade with Eritrea must be paid in hard currencies, not in Ethiopian *birr* or *nakfa*. Eritrea, on the other hand, wanted the use of a combination of *birr, nakfa,* and hard currency. Eritrea's view was that bilateral trade should be free and open with few restrictions, and that market forces should determine the value of the currencies in relation to each other. Ethiopia thought this too risky and was instead in favor of more restrictions. As a result of this policy, there would be restrictions on the export of certain commodities from Ethiopia to Eritrea, and the movement of currencies in and out of Ethiopia would be controlled. The reason given by the Ethiopians was that the two countries were pursuing two different policies on trade, investment, and development. (ibid, pp.1—2).

Toward the end of the negotiations that led to the decision to go their separate ways in the matter of currency, the governors of the national banks of the two countries were interviewed by the Amharic weekly, the *"Reporter."* One of the points of information that Mr. Dubale Jallie, governor of the State Bank of Ethiopia, revealed in the interview was that the Eritrean government had informed the Ethiopian authorities of its intention to have its own national currency ahead of the day of the change. (*Reporter*, Hidar 1990, Ethiopian calendar, i.e. October 1997 A.D., page 5.). That was why they synchronized the day of issue of their new currencies.

One week later, the same weekly magazine interviewed Tekie Beyene, the then governor of the Eritrean National Bank.

Without getting into too much detail on how the two sides explained the causes of the war, I will note here interviews that I had conducted with Isaias and Meles, a few months before the outbreak of the war, on the then looming crisis connected to currency and trade issues. My interview was concerned with a research project I had planned on democratic transition in the two countries as well as in Uganda; and the issue of democracy and development was among the items included in the research, which I later abandoned after the war broke out. The interview also included other officials of the two governments whose work at the time involved trade and currency issues.

Both Isaias and Meles appeared to view the looming crisis as exaggerated; that it would be resolved soon in the spirit of the cooperative spirit that they said was the defining characteristic of the relationship between the two countries. In my interview with him, Meles used the word *hiccup* to describe the problem, insisting that it would be resolved soon. I was also informed by an eye witness that a few weeks before the Badme incident, Isaias and Meles and their wives were seen in Massawa, enjoying a vacation that included a boat trip to the Dahlak islands. Was Isaias doing an Alula number on Meles, lulling him into believing all is fine and dandy while thinking of springing a trap, or did everything happen all of a sudden? We will probably never know, given Isaias' secretive personality.

On the causes of the mistrust that led to the debacle and a reversion from concord to discord, consider the following, based on random sampling of various opinions.

First, some observers believe that the cause of the debacle lies in the clashing ambitions or colliding egos of the two leaders. On the Ethiopian side, or on the part of those who support Ethiopia's case, the belief lies in the conviction that President Isaias had (and may still entertain) regional hegemonic ambitions to be the master of the Horn of Africa in general, using Eritrea as a base and Eritrea's resources as a means to achieve his ambitions.

The earliest murmurs of such suspicions appeared at the time of the Congo (Zaire) adventure in which Ethiopia and Eritrea, as well as Uganda, played key roles in helping to overthrow the Mobutu regime. Isaias, it is claimed, used the military prowess of the EPLF armed forces and his influence in Ethiopian affairs through his comradely relationship with Meles to push his hegemonic agenda in the Congo. Such claims also include allegations that his party (the PFDJ) derived much material benefit in the course of that adventure.

Differences began to emerge between the two leaders when Eritrea made headway in inserting itself in Congolese affairs even before the fall of Mobutu. Meles himself wrote a lengthy and controversial paper titled "Bonapartism" (in late 1997) for the TPLF Central Committee to discuss, aiming it at what was considered the hegemonic ambitions of Isaias. Eritreans on their part contend that there was (may still be) a Tigrayan hidden agenda of a Greater Tigray that would include much, (and perhaps even all) of Eritrea, thus obliterating Eritrea's national identity.

Another view is that both leaders have their own ambitions. One observer gave an astronomical analogy thus: When two objects are in overlapping orbits, the bigger one inevitably pulls the smaller into its path. Sooner or later they collide. In terms of the analogy, Isaias might have thought he could tame and dominate Meles; if he did, he failed because he underestimated the latter's guile and tenacity. Is history repeating itself, one would inevitably ask on the basis of the analogy; Ras Woldemichael of old underestimating Ras Alula's guile and falling into a trap?

The question inevitably arises: Can the cause of the war be reduced to a single factor such as the clash of ambitions? Surely it is more complex than that. Were newly liberated Eritrea and Ethiopia, Eritrea's former occupier, on a collision course from the start, or did the conflict emerge after Eritrea's liberation? If the latter, on what grounds? What about the economic factor—the economic factor and its complications by competing political motives? What was presumed "done deal" in terms of harmonious cooperation between the two regimes proved to be elusive.

By and large, Ethiopians did not accept the fact of Eritrea's separation; such separation was anathema, especially to the central Ethiopians or centrists (the Amhara). It should also be pointed out that the centrists monopolized most of the key government positions—including the sensitive posts in finance and banking, at the key subministerial, technocratic level. Eritrean negotiators on the currency-harmonization policy discussions complained (in informal talks with the author) that there was stiff resistance by these technocrats to requests by Eritreans to have a fair share in currency and other financial policy making while Eritrea still used Ethiopian currency.

From the protracted and frustrating negotiations that spanned many months, the Eritrean negotiators came to one bitter but obvious conclusion: Their Ethiopian counterparts were determined to subject Eritrean economic autonomy to Ethiopian requirements. This, they realized, was a rearguard action of a political nature, masked with economic rationality; it was aimed at undermining the political self-determination and independence that had been won with so much sacrifice, independence that was still not accepted in the minds of these Ethiopians.

The *Nakfa* and Ethiopian Reaction

This frustrating experience was critical in Eritrea's decision to sever its ties to the *Birr* and issue its own currency, the *Nakfa*, in November 1997. As already noted, that happened six months before the Badme War broke out. To those Ethiopians who were not reconciled to the "loss" of Eritrea, the creation of the currency "*Nakfa*," named after the town that was a symbol of Eritrean armed resistance and triumph, only served to aggravate resentments. It was like pouring salt on Ethiopians' wounded political pride. A frequently-heard remark of Ethiopians addressing Eritreans who lived in Ethiopia was, "You want independence, good riddance; see if you can feed yourselves." Many Ethiopians, including highly educated ones, thought of Eritrea as a resource-poor region that could not sustain itself without help from Ethiopia. This is not to suggest that serious policy makers at the top necessarily shared such views, but only to indicate the depth of resentment felt with regard to Ethiopia's "loss" of Eritrea. It also confirms the view that one cannot put the blame on a single cause, like personal ambitions or colliding egos, important though it may be as contributing factor.

Given the history of cooperation between the two governments, albeit brief, including Eritrea's use of the Ethiopian *birr*, the decision by Eritrea to issue its own national currency in 1997 may have come as a surprise to some Ethiopians outside government circles. That decision is, of course, a manifestation of Eritrea's sovereign right, and the two governments coordinated the timing of the issue of their new currencies, which shows that even as sentiments were hardening, there was a significant degree of cooperation between the two governments on the eve of the Badme conflict that led to an all out war.

Ethiopia issued a new currency on the same day as Eritrea's issue of the *nakfa*. In view of the earlier hopes, however, the event demonstrates the depth of the problem attendant upon regional cooperation and economic integration, which requires, first and foremost, the political will and determination to those ends. It also requires the establishment of the requisite institutions and mechanisms to reinforce and continue cooperation on the basis of mutual benefit. Clearly, the governments of Ethiopia and Eritrea had failed to create such institutions for reasons that are complex and that explain the failure of a promising start.

All this assumes that there was a genuine commitment to cooperation in the first place. Institutions of interstate cooperation must be based on mutual trust and a spirit of give and take. It is now clear that such a spirit of trust was lacking in this instance. Eritrea's decision to issue its own currency was made because of "irreconcilable differences" on trade and investment policies between the two governments. What followed was a classic case of protectionist trade policy on Ethiopia's side, which is a logical consequence of Eritrea's decision to go its own way, but a consequence Eritreans interpreted as a punitive measure taken against them by Ethiopia for daring to exercise a crucial function of their sovereignty. Ethiopia decided that all trade between the two countries, which had been paid for in Ethiopian currency would henceforth be paid for in hard currency.

The resentment felt among some Ethiopians is not limited to centrists; it applied to Tigrayans, at least to some of them. There is anecdotal evidence that the issuance of the *Nakfa* was resented not only as a manifestation of Eritrea's will to develop separately from Ethiopia, but also the very choice of *Nakfa* grates nationalist feelings. There were some unfortunate incidents illustrating such resentment, including the refusal by Ethiopian (Tigrayan) custodians of the Holy Church of Saint Mary of Axum to accept contributions from some Eritrean Christian pilgrims who offered to pay in *Nakfa* to the Church.

Commenting on the tensions reflecting the "problematic" nature of the historical relationship between Eritrea and Tigray, Richard Reid offers a concise summing-up. In his article, "Old Problems in New Conflicts," he wrote that the relationship involved:

> such issues as land, identity, and ultimately, destiny, as well as mutual misconceptions and misunderstandings as to the other's mental outlook. This has been, perhaps, most visibly manifest in the

common Tigrayan resentment of a perceived Eritrean superiority complex, the origins of which are unclear but most likely stem from Eritrea's Italian colonial experience. Above all, the new reality of an independent Eritrean state from 1991, its very existence a refutation of much received wisdom concerning the region's history, threw the relationship under examination into sharp relief. (ibid, 733-4).

Nothing more need be said here, except to hope that time will heal the mutually inflicted wounds, that all have learned a lesson from the costly and unnecessary war, and that cooler heads will prevail in setting the relationship of the two peoples on a proper foundation. To those ends, a rational reexamination of the "received wisdom" and a realistic assessment of present policies and politics needs to be made, aimed at a common good—the mutual benefits of the two peoples.

አባላት ፖለቲካዊ ቤት ጽሕፈት ህ.ግ.ሓ.ኤ. 1977-1987

ኮፉ ኢሎም ዘሰዉ ካብ ጸጋም ንየማን።
ብርሃነ ገብረኢዮር፡ ስዉስ ኢብራሂም ነፉ፡ ሮመዳን መሓመድ ኑር፡
ኢሳያስ አፈወርቂ፡ ግእሙድ ሻራር።
ጠጠው ኢሎም ዘሰዉ ካብ ጸጋም ንየማን።
ዑቅበ አብርሃ፡ ዓሊ ሰይድ ዓብዱላ፡ ሰብሓት አፍሬም፡ ሃይለ ወልደትንሳኤ፡ እጥሮስ
ሰለሞን፡ መሓመድ ስዒድ ባርሁ መሰናኔ ሓጎስ፡ አልአሚን መሓመድ ስዒድ።

EPLF POLITBURO

EPLF SOME MEMBERS OF THE CENTRAL COMMITTEE

IBRAHIM AFA

MEMBERS OF THE EXECUTIVE COMMITTEE
OF THE CONSTITUTIONAL COMMISSION

AUTHOR WITH PRESIDENT OF IRAQ'S CONSTITUTIONAL COMMISSION, DR. HUMAM HAMOUDI (BAGHDAD SUMMER OF 2005). DR. YASH GHAI IS ON DR. HAMOUDI'S RIGHT AND MS. JILL COTTRELL IS ON AUTHOR'S LEFT.

SENAFE, JUNE 1991. MELES ZENAWI AND OLF DEPUTY LEADER LEENCO LETA

SENAFE, JUNE 1991. GROUP: L/ TO R. SEBHAT EFREM, AUTHOR, MELES
ZENAWI, UNKNOWN INTERLOPER, LEENCO LETA, MELES' SECURITY
DETAIL, ALI SAID ABDELA

AUTHOR BEING INTRODUCED BY PRESIDENT OF SIMMONS UNIVERSITY
DURING AWARD CEREMONY OF DOCTOR OF LAWS OF SIMMONS

DINNER PARTY AT AUTHOR'S HOME FOLLOWING INTERNATIONAL CONFER-
ENCE ON AUTHOR'S ACHIEVEMENT, AT UNC CHAPEL HILL. AT TABLE'S
HEAD IS SITTING GLORIA STEINEM. TO HER LEFT IS YALE LAW PROFESSOR
OWNE FISS. WITH THEIR BACK TO THE CAMERA ARE: DR. MOHAMED
NURHUSSEIN, KASSAHUN CHECOLE, AND AUTHOR'S WIFE, WINTA.

AUTHOR CHATTING WITH DR. ARAYA DEBESSAY AND WIFE SEMRET,
DURING THE DINNER PARTY AFTER THE UNC CONFERENCE. I DON'T
REMEMBER WHAT JOKE I CRACKED THAT IS CRACKING UP HUSBAND AND
WIFE!

BOSTON MASS. AT THE PARTY WITH DAN CONNELL, AUTHOR'S DAUGHTER, SEBENE, AND DAN'S WIFE DEBBIE.

SOME OF MY STUDENTS AT UNC.

Taken in the spring of 1998 at the mini conference convened by my colleagues Julius Nyang'oro and Michael West who are sitting to my right in front. To my left are Gloria Steinem and James (Jim) C. N. Paul, a long time friend. Standing (L. R.) are: Said Samatar, Ruth Iyob, Rich Rosen, Hussein Adam, Mohamed Hassan, Kassahun Checole, and Senait Bahta

Oqbe Abraha at his office in the Ministry of Social Affairs (November 1997).

TAKEN IN KHARTOUM (JANUARY 1987). IN PICTURE ARE: (L. TO R.)
PAULOS TESFAGIORGIS, YESHI, PETROS SOLOMON AND THE AUTHOR.

MAHMUD SHERIFO AT HIS OFFICE IN THE MINISTRY OF REGIONAL
GOVERNMENT (NOVEMBER 1997).

MEMBERS OF THE CONSTITUTIONAL COMMISSION DURING BREAK OF
MEETING. SPRING 1995

AUTHOR IN HIS OFFICE AT THE HQ
OF THE CONSTITUTIONAL COMMISSION

AFABET, SPRING 2006, AUTHOR WITH THE
LEGENDARY POET MAMA ZEINEB

Chapter 6

THE CONSTITUTION
AND THE BROKEN PROMISE

Hopeful Beginnings

Eritrea's constitution was ratified by a constituent assembly on 23 May, 1997, on the eve of the seventh anniversary of Liberation Day. A year later, about the time when it was expected to be implemented, war broke out between Eritrea and Ethiopia, and the constitution has been shelved ever since—detained or locked up would be perhaps a more appropriate word: locked up like the Eritreans who demanded its implementation. The government used the war as the reason for the detention of the constitution; but that explanation did not satisfy the majority of thoughtful observers, including Eritreans. As we shall see in chapter 10, the behavior of the central organ of the ruling party (the PFDJ) and especially its chairman, Mr. Isaias Afwerki, when challenged by high-ranking members of the government and the party, gives an indication as to the real reason for such failure.

As one who headed the commission that was charged with the making of the Eritrean constitution, I have been at the receiving end of continual inquiries about its creation, about its misadventure at the hand of Isaias Afwerki, and about some of its main features. In what follows, I will give a brief account of its making, its major elements, and its impact on Eritrean politics over the last few years, ending with a prognosis as to its future place in Eritrean politics. But first, a little background on my assumption of the charge.

Background to My Appointment to Head the Commission

I will begin by giving a brief background on how I came to be head of the commission. It was generally expected, particularly among members of the EPLF, that I would be chosen to head the Constitutional Commission—and this for two main reasons. First, constitutional law and constitution making is an area of my expertise, and I have done some writing on it, including my doctoral dissertation, which was published in 1974 as a book with the title *"The Executive in African Governments."* (London. 1974) Second, it was perhaps natural for Eritreans especially those who were members of the EPLF, to entertain such thoughts, for I had not only been a member of the EPLF since 1975, but represented it at the United Nations between 1995 and 2001. Many of such members openly expressed their dismay to me when another Eritrean—a recent arrival to the EPLF fold—was chosen to head the referendum commission. My response was that the person who was chosen to head the referendum commission was equal to the task, and that in any case, it was time for me to attend to the needs of my family, who had suffered during much of my absence, especially as I discharged my duties as the EPLF representative at the United Nations.

Then in 1993 I received a telex message sent by Isaias, care of Hagos Gebrehiwet who was his envoy in Washington at the time. In the telex Isaias asked me to chair a commission to draft the constitution for Eritrea. Since undertaking such a task would mean going back to Eritrea for some time, I declined the offer because of the family reasons mentioned already. Hagos relayed my response to Asmara and came back to say that Isaias is insisting that I accept and would I contact him. I did not respond as requested.

When I told the story to one of Isaias' close friends, a businessman in Washington, he told me that Isaias had actually first asked Seyoum Haregot to head the commission, but that Seyoum declined and suggested to Isaias that, for many reasons including expertise, it would be better to ask me to do the job. According to my informant, Seyoum had added: "After all, isn't Bereket one of your members and valuable assets?"

My informant, who also happened to be close to the Haregot family, said that Seyoum had expressed surprise that Isaias called on him instead of me to head the commission; and my informant agreed with him on that point. What neither Seyoum nor my informant did not know was that Isaias has had reservations about me, which is to say that he questioned my loyalty to him and perhaps even suspected that I had ambitions that might clash with his own. After all, loyalty to the cause of Eritrean liberation is not necessarily the same as personal loyalty to its leader. I say necessarily because at times the two loyalties converge, but frequently do not. In fact Isaias and I have always had an uneasy relationship, mainly because I tend to express my views openly, which he did not always like; he could see this when I was going back and forth between the ELF and the EPLF in 1974-75 in attempts at stopping the on-going "civil war" between the two fronts and at helping to unite them. As I tried to demonstrate in the preceding chapter, deception and subterfuge are only two of the tools he employed from way back.

Isaias was torn between, on the one hand, his need of my services to the struggle that he was leading and, on the other hand, my being in the way of his own dictatorial tendencies. The last straw was when I published a booklet titled, *Reflections on the Future Political System of Eritrea* (June 1990) where I proposed, among other things, that the ELF be considered as a future opposition party in a democratic Eritrea with multi-parties in which the EPLF would be the dominant political party for the first few years. A witness who saw Isaias in Sahel, after he read the booklet told me that he was extremely upset.

At different times during the last few years before liberation, I had indications—some subtle, others not so subtle—that Isaias was not comfortable with my positions and atitudes, including my explicit advocacy of the rule of law and democratic governance with a multiparty system. I was, therefore, not surprised to learn that he chose Seyoum Haregot, a man who was not a member of the EPLF or any other Eritrean organization, and who had his own cross to bear after suffering a long period of imprisonment by the Dergue, and whose father had been one of the victims of the Dergue massacre in 1975. Seyoum, whom I met in Washington after his release from prison, was later employed by the United Nations and his principal goal was to lead a peaceful life with his family. At least that was my impression.

After he received a negative response from Seyoum, Isaias—who knew of my friendship with Seyoum—decided to call on me, presumably for fear that complaints similar to those expressed regarding the choice for the referendum commission might surface again. Meanwhile, I met Yemane Gebreab in Addis Ababa who was on a mission during the time when I was participating in the symposium that I convened at Africa Hall in July 1993. Many in the government knew that I was in Addis; indeed I had invited some of the ministers to take part in the symposium. Yemane, who was obviously aware of the symposium I had convened, told me that Isaias wanted me to head the constitution commission—would I travel to Asmara and meet with Isaias? I told him about my family situation and stressed the fact that my family needed me and it was time for me to attend to their needs. He said that he was sure Isaias knew this, and that appropriate arrangements would be made to take care of that problem. Why didn't I at least go to Asmara, meet with Isaias and discuss these problems with him? After much debate with Yemane, I agreed to go to Asmara and see Isaias.

The meeting with Isaias took place in his office. After the preliminary banalities, he asked me point blank if I would accept the charge. When I raised the question regarding my family, he went on to say that there should be no problem in finding financial assistance for them should I accept the charge. I then told him that I would need a release from my university and that I would need a letter signed by him asking for an extended leave from my university.

He asked me to draft the letter; I drafted a letter addressed to the president of Howard University, which he signed without change. Howard University's response was not to my satisfaction; in fact it was outrageous. So I decided to leave Howard; in fact I thought it was time to look for a more congenial place. I joined the University of North Carolina at Chapel Hill (UNC-CH). UNC not only obliged me, but gave me leave with pay and, six months later, established an endowed Chair for me with a salary one third more of what I was getting at Howard! Such is the paradox of life in American higher education.

Constitution Making of a Special Kind

I had become aware that constitution making and constitutionalism had achieved the status of paradigm in scholarly discourse or were at least regarded as the bases for a paradigm shift. In the realm of statecraft, constitutional engineering is increasingly relied upon as a promising enterprise in the search for bridges of understanding among factions in divided societies as well as between civil society and the state based upon a foundation of consensus. The assumption is that constitution making with extensive public participation can play a crucial role in the building of such consensus. It is also assumed that in postconflict situations constitution-making can provide a framework for resolution of ongoing conflicts.

In the Eritrean constitution making scheme, emphasis was given to the process, with public participation as the primary element. One of the reasons for this emphasis was the belief that a participatory process creates an enabling environment that helps the public to gain a sense of ownership of the country's constitution. Such a sense of ownership, it is further assumed, increases the likelihood that the public would seek to control the government. In Eritrea, the EPLF-based transitional government expressed commitment to democratic transition and constitutional government. The government formalized its commitment to democracy and popular participation in the making of the constitution with Proclamation No. 37/1993. The Constitutional Commission of Eritrea was established under Proclamation No. 55/1994 in fulfillment of this commitment.

After our meeting with Isaias, and while I awaited a response from the president of Howard University in the autumn of 1993, I was asked to draft the law that would establish the Eritrean Constitutional Commission, a draft law that became Proclamation No. 55/1994. The National Assembly accepted my draft making only a few changes. Under that law, the Constitutional Commission of Eritrea (CCE) comprised a fifty member Council and a ten-member Executive Committee drawn from the Council. The CCE was charged with the duty of organizing and managing a "wide-ranging and all-embracing national debate and education through public seminars and lecture series on constitutional principles and practice." Following public debate, the Commission was required to submit the draft to the National Assembly, having taken the views of the public into account. The approved draft would then be submitted to a Constituent Assembly for ratification.

The public consultation took over two years, and, following a debate on the draft by the public and the approval of the National Assembly, the draft was submitted to the Constituent Assembly three years almost to the day after the establishment of the Commission.

The Dialectic of Process and Substance

No analysis devoted to process can avoid reference to substance. There is a sense in which the process and the product are dialectically linked: The ends prescribe the means, and the means impinge on the ends. Public participation in the making of a constitution necessarily raises questions of substance. The contemporary debate on the meaning of democracy underscores this point. The debate has largely focused on two aspects of democracy: its substantive aspect (its source and purpose) and its procedural elements. The classical approach defines democracy in terms of its source and purpose, with the will of the people as democracy's source and the common good as its purpose.

Extending this analysis to the dynamics of democratic praxis, we can agree to consider elections and electoral politics (including electoral laws and institutions) as prerequisites of democratic (representative) government. But once elected, parliaments have responsibilities that do not end with the conclusion of an election. In short, election is a means to an end. The end—the functioning of representative institutions—constitutes the substantive aspect of democracy. The procedural imperative, though essential, must be analyzed in relation to the role of representative institutions in the totality of the constitutional order.

An eloquent articulation of this point, one of my favorite quotes, is from Chicago University professor, Jean Bethke Elshtain:

> Democracy is not and has never been primarily a means whereby popular will is tabulated and carried out but, rather, a political world within which citizens negotiate, compromise, engage and hold themselves and those they chose to represent them accountable for action taken. Have we lost this deliberative dimension to democracy? Democracy's enduring promise is that citizens can come to know a good in common that they cannot know alone.

The point of the above quoted comment about democracy in general applies with equal force to constitution making in the sense that the latter engages, or should engage, citizens to negotiate and compromise in framing the issues concerning their rights and duties and the powers and responsibilities of government to be defined in the constitution by which they will be governed.

The task of the Constitutional Commission of Eritrea of organizing wide-ranging public debate and soliciting expert opinion placed an unusually heavy emphasis on the direct and active involvement of people outside of government during the drafting phase. The law establishing the CCE enjoined, for example, the chairman of the CCE to encourage the participation and contribution of Eritrean and foreign experts and to organize ad hoc committees and advisory boards to help expedite the process of preparing the draft constitution and to advise the commission on the experience of other countries in constitution making. The board of foreign advisors was chaired by Professor Owen Fiss of Yale Law School, and comprised lawyers and poltical scientists plus one anthropologist. There was supposed to be an economist in the person of renowned Nigerian economist, and my friend, Dr. Ojetunji Aboyade, who died suddenly of a heart attack.

Needless to say, the role of the advisory board was purely advisory, and the members were keenly aware of the limits of their role, as were also those of the advisory board on Eritrean customary laws, a board comprising members representing the nine ethnic groups of Eritrea. Some of the latter mistakenly entertained the idea that the constitution would incorporate all their respective customary laws. Nor was such expectation limited to traditional ethnic-based customary laws; some elders from the Islamic segments of Eritrean communities also expected the Sharia (Islamic law based on the Qur'an) to be incorporated into the constitution. We had to disabuse people from such erroneous assumptions or expectations, which we did through various modes. These included education materials such as a concise booklet explaining the nature, purpose, and scope of the constitution and the mission of the commission.

For a more detailed consideration of Eritrea's experience in constitution making, including the uses of consultation as well as the issue of legitimacy in constitution making, and I refer the reader to my work "*Constitution Making in Eritrea: A Process Driven Approach*" (2010), a chapter in a volume published by the U.S. Institute of Peace on the experience of constitution making in nineteen countries including Eritrea. It is a matter of honor (and a humbling one) to mention that I was chosen by the U.S. Institute of Peace of to chair the panel of experts that oversaw the study of the constitution making experience of nineteen countries, including that of Eritrea (mentioned above).

Eritrea's Specific Approach

Organizing debates on the most fundamental political questions facing a nation is far more than a technical or logistical matter. It involves issues of substance concerning the most appropriate literature to be translated and distributed and the best way of communicating essential ideas about democracy and constitutional rule. The participation of Eritreans in making their constitution relied on the inherent wisdom of encouraging and organizing people to become involved in decisions affecting their lives.

This made sense theoretically and conforms to universal principles of democracy. It also accords with the historically evolved system of village democracy in much of Eritrea, where village communities governed themselves democratically through periodically elected village assemblies. This village democracy forms a central part of Eritrean traditional law and was preserved and utilized during much of the long period of armed struggle.

The CCE worked out a strategy and organized research and public consultation efforts on the conviction, as already mentioned, that the process is as important as the product. A great deal of attention was paid to preparing the public to make the fullest and best-informed contribution possible. Equal emphasis was placed on the need to record, collate, and eventually analyze the views that emerged during the public debate. This step has a twofold importance, for not only might such views be used in drafting the constitution; the very fact of keeping track of them gave people a sense of ownership of the constitution—a crucial element of the process-driven mode of constitution making.

The CCE began its work by posing a series of questions that it set itself the task of answering before launching the public debate and drafting the constitution. The essence of the major questions may be summed up as follows:

1. What lessons, if any, do historical experiences of other countries offer?
2. Do such experiences yield helpful models or guidelines?
3. Is it desirable, or practicable, to use models? Are they transferable, like some technology?
4. What, after all, are the values and goals that a nation needs most emphatically to promote, nurture, and protect? And how should these be incorporated into a constitution?
5. Should such values and goals be so incorporated, or should they be left to be determined in the crucible of political and social interaction in the daily discourse of culture?
6. What form of government would be best suited for Eritrea?
7. What degree of centralization should there be? Is federalism appropriate for a small country like Eritrea?
8. Should there be an official language or official languages? If so, which ones should be selected and why?

It was apparent from the outset that some subjects could be left out of the constitution while others could not, which made the question of what to include susceptible to debate. There were questions of detail, including some pertaining to technicalities such as the size of the constitution—should it be long or short? How detailed should the chapter on the Bill of Rights be? Should the constitution, for instance, incorporate international covenants on human rights by reference or by detailed inclusion? There were, in all, twenty-three questions that the commission listed for consideration at its earliest meeting. The proposals that were ultimately submitted to the public for debate were based, to a great extent, on these twenty-three questions but were also enriched by research and expert consultation.

There was consensus in the commission from the outset that there should be no reliance on ready-made models, whatever their source or merit. Rather, it was thought better to take stock of the reality and paramount needs of the country. The CCE's research and consultation activities were designed with that objective in mind. To the often-asked questions whether there are universally applicable criteria on what to include in a constitution, or should it be left for each country to determine on the basis of its specific historical condition, the answer is both. From the writing of the American Constitution in 1789 onwards, constitutions of the modern era have been based on preceding models or experiences. At the same time, the historical conditions of a given country—its culture, social structure, and government policies—inevitably play a modifying role. How much this modifying role affects the universal principles differs from case to case.

Scholars and statesmen have wrestled with this question, and some have attempted to provide general rules for good constitution writing. The British scholar Lord Brice, for example, affirms the rule of brevity in constitution writing. He adds simplicity of language and precision as essential requirements for writing a good constitution. He ranked the U.S. Constitution above all other hitherto written constitutions "for the intrinsic excellence of its scheme, its adaptation to the circumstances of the people, the simplicity, brevity and precision of its language, its judicious mixture of definiteness in principle with elasticity in detail."

Drafting a constitution can thus be likened to both a work of art and an engineering exercise, because it can test the writing skill of the best draftsman in terms of choice of language, precision, and clarity; that at the same time requires craftsmanship in building the edifice of state institutions. An edifice is built to last, and in the case of a constitutional edifice, it has to be built to weather the storms, as it were, of changing political fortunes.

French cleric and statesman-scholar Abbe Sieyes, who influenced the making of the constitution of postrevolutionary France counseled to "keep the constitution neutral" or at least open ended in political/ideological terms. This would be particularly true in the provision concerning the Bill of Rights; for otherwise, they may be too closely identified with *"transient fortunes of a particular party or pressure group, and rise and fall with them."* (Emphasis added). This wise counsel, born out of the white heat of the experience of revolutionary France helps to justify and explain the need for a core of professional legal personnel to lead the drafting of a constitution. "Neutrality" may be disputed as a controlling concept in this respect, but not objectivity. Even a partisan of a ruling party or group can objectively see the rationale behind Sieyes' counsel if he/she is forward looking and can see the perils of being wrapped in only present or parochial concerns.

In the constitution making experience of Eritrea, the commission met these questions head-on. It insisted that the contents of the constitution must reflect present realities as well as be mindful of future development of the society, to cite the words of the CCE's proposals. The concluding paragraph of Part I of the commission's proposals states:

> Our constitution has to be concise, clear and forward-looking; it has to be written in a general way rather than in detail, such that it will be amenable to future developments through a process of interpretation in response to future events. Its detailed implementation should be left to ordinary legislation.

The Executive Committee of the CCE, which had turned itself into a drafting committee, had these points in mind when it sat down to review the mass of documents—the product of over two years of research, seminars, conferences, and public debate— before writing the first draft. The draft that came out of the discussions of the Executive Committee and that was submitted for the approval of the entire commission reflected the outcome of the previous two years debate and the thinking of the members of the commission.

In order to accomplish its task, the CCE established four working committees at its first meeting on 17 April 1994:

- Committee on Government Institutions and Human Rights
- Committee on Social and Cultural Issues
- Committee on Economic Issues
- Committee on Administrative Questions

It was also on that day that the CCE appointed two advisory committees: one to consult on domestic customary laws, the other to consult on foreign experience of constitution making. Later, the CCE also established five regional offices throughout the country and a central office in Asmara. An office responsible for the nearly one million Eritreans in the Diaspora was also established, for it was decided that they would be part of the popular participation in the constitution-making process, which

1. is based on the realities of our society;
2. reflects the aspirations and interests of our people; and
3. guarantees human rights, justice, prosperity, and development.

Eritreans in the Diaspora are found in Ethiopia, Kenya, and Sudan, and nowadays in South Africa, Europe, and North America.

About the same time, the CCE sent a message to the Eritrean people, urging them to get actively involved in the process of constitution making. The Commission tried to impress upon the public that its primary responsibility is to ensure broad participation of people in the process.

The message ended with the following words:

> Writing a constitution is just the beginning of a long historical process toward establishing a constitutional system. We are starting this process in Eritrea now, and the way we start the process impacts the rest of our journey to establish and strengthen a constitutional system in the country. Thus, we strive to institute a process that builds confidence right from the beginning and ensure patience and far-sighted efforts throughout.

The Commission and the Government— Autonomy and Legitimacy

One thing I wanted everyone to understand right away when we started the commission work was that the CCE was going to be autonomous. In my speech at the inaugural reception on 16 April 1994, which was opened by President Isaias, I made this point clear. Having first expressed my thanks to the president and the National Assembly for electing us to the commission, I said that it was "a great honor and a privilege to be part of this historic process. It is also an awesome responsibility and a challenging task." I added: We pledge to those who entrusted us with this task and to the Eritrean people that we will do everything humanly possible to be worthy of the trust and to fulfill our mission.

I then issued the following caveat to all interested parties, including the President and his party and government:

> I would like to make it clear at the outset that as an independent entity of two year duration, the Commission will depend for its

operation on funds from the international donor community. This coming week we will hold a donor's meeting in which we will present and explain a budget estimate that will enable us to fulfill our mission satisfactorily.

That statement was the talk of town for the days that followed. Some who were close to Isaias questioned the wisdom of the statement in view of the fact that Isaias is adamantly opposed to any entity associated with his government declaring such autonomy. Well, I said, he just has to live with that; it is either that or I will tender my resignation. *No one wanted that to happen. That was my trump card.*

Concerning the notion of autonomy, there are a couple of episodes that are not generally known but that had rankled Isaias and his closest aides. One concerns my refusal to attend the second EPLF congress. The usual notice was issued to members of the EPLF who were designated as eligible to attend the congress. I had attended the second congress in March 1987, which took place in Sahel. This time, the congress was to take place in independent Eritrea, and the notice for me to attend as a delegate was issued care of the EPLF office in Washington after I had been asked to head the constitutional commission. I told the office that I would not attend. Some weeks later, Hagos Gebrehiwet, the head of the office, told me that my refusal to attend had caused a stir in higher circles. (The Tigrigna version of what he said was: *Iza neger'zia, bizuH azariba'lla.*)

He asked me to reconsider, and I reiterated that I would not attend and gave him the reason. As chairman of the Constitutional Commission I wanted not only to be autonomous, but also wanted to be seen to be autonomous in order to ensure the widest possible participation of Eritreans in the making of the constitution, embracing non-EPLF members. I was still a member of the EPLF, but as head of a national commission drafting a national constitution, I wanted to be more than an EPLF member. To some, this may appear to be sophistry or even disingenuous; and I would not blame people if they thought so. However, my reason is connected to my original but unsuccessful efforts to involve non-EPLF organized groups to take part as legitimate groups in Eritrean political life. In my own mind, appearing to be autonomous to the general public was in the service of a higher cause.

The other episode occurred after we began work on the Constitutional Commission. Sometime in 1995, the EPLF leadership ordered a membership registration campaign. The order was given to all heads of ministry departments and commissions to organize and supervise such a campaign, and as head of the CCE, I was asked to do so for the commission. Again I declined, giving the same reason as for when I was asked to attend the third congress. I suggested that one of the members of the CCE Executive Committee do the job. Accordingly, Musa Naib was assigned and that was the end of the matter. The incident gave rise to rumors that I had resigned my membership in the EPLF, and one busybody came to my office to ask me if the rumor was true; I told him it was not.

Some members of the Eritrean opposition have raised questions about the autonomy of the Constitutional Commission, suggesting that it was an appendage of the EPLF and that the constitution would have been made to order according to the EPLF's prescriptions. Such views were expressed in postings to Eritrean websites in response to a series of interviews I gave in early 2001 to Saleh A. Younis, one of the prolific writers of Awate.com. In my response, I pointed out the fact that any entity commissioned to draft a constitution has to be appointed by the legitimate authority of the state; that the CCE was appointed by the EPLF government, which was (at the time, anyway) the legitimate national government. The constitution was not written to the specifications of the EPLF, though it (renamed PFDJ in 1994) was duly consulted on a number of issues as a governing party and therefore a legitimate stakeholder.

A governing party has every right to be consulted; but that is different from such a party or its government dictating to the constitution drafting entity. *The autonomy of the CCE was never compromised at any time during the three-year period of constitutional consultation.* There were two or three occasions when the president as head of the PFDJ, who also happened to be the chairman of the National Assembly, the body that appointed the CCE and to which the draft constitution would be submitted for approval, raised questions about the CCE's work. The questions concerned the manner and direction of the commission's conduct of its business.

I remember that in one of the few written communications he addressed to me on our work at the commission, the president posed a question regarding the work of the CCE among the Eritrean Diaspora; he inquired into whether too much attention was being diverted abroad as compared to what was going on inside the country. Isaias knew that if he acted in a way that would compromise the integrity of the process of constitution making over which I presided, I would tender my resignation; and he had no desire for that to happen.

It bears repetition that I had made it clear to the EPLF/PFDJ people that once appointed, the commission was to act with complete autonomy both in terms of the conduct of the process and in the content of the draft constitution. They could, of course, change the draft when it is submitted to the National Assembly, which they controlled; but they could not dictate to me or to the commission how to conduct the business of the making of the constitution or how to draft it.

In January 1995, ten months into the start of the process of constitution-making, the CCE convened an international conference on constitution making to which all the members of the Foreign Board of Advisors and other scholars and practitioners were invited to participate. The conference was aimed at benefiting from the experience of other countries as well as sensitizing all concerned on Eritrea's historical and sociocultural reality. All the members of the CCE, except one who died in the meantime, participated, some actively as paper presenters and the majority as interested observers. It was a highly educational conference that enriched the process, helping us to sharpen and modulate our original proposals. It also galvanized Eritrean public opinion as the media, both print and electronic, reported the proceedings daily and interviewed many of the participants.

At the same time—actually for the same reason—it also heightened the sense of paranoia of President Isaias Afwerki, who could not resist coming to the conference venue to "feel" the events. He did not enter the conference hall, but summoned a senior party cadre who acted as his eyes and ears inside the CCE. Exactly what he told him is not known; but I could tell from the cadre's state of depression in the wake of the dreaded visit that he had been given a good dressing down by the boss. This happened fairly often throughout the duration of the process. Isaias was allergic to the whole idea of an international conference but had no choice but to live with it.

There had been a miniconference the previous July 1994 to which we invited four representatives of other countries to speak on the constitution making experiences of their respective countries. These were from Egypt, Ethiopia, Namibia, and Switzerland. The Namibian and Swiss representatives were the ambassadors of those two countries to Ethiopia and Eritrea. The Egyptian was a professor of law at Cairo University, and the Ethiopian was the former chairman of the Constitutional Commission of Ethiopia.

It was the first time in which Eritreans were treated to a free flow of ideas and open discussions of issues like the rule of law, government accountability and transparency, multiparty democracy, et cetera et cetera.

I chaired the first day's session in which the four foreign scholars and practitioners talked about their respective countries' experiences and gave answers to hard questions about law and politics. I remember the look of disbelief and apprehension on the face of the head of the government's security service. He looked incredulous as did many of the party cadres, high and low, who had not been used to this kind of free discussion of controversial issues and subjects, which were taboo in EPLF circles. One of these was a sister-in-law of mine who confessed to me the evening of the same day that she could not believe her ears and expressed fear and anxiety about what might happen to me. I reassured her that nothing would happen to me, adding a bonus that she better get used to this now that we are going to live under a constitutional democracy! How could I anticipate the breach of promise that would surprise us all and launch Eritrea on a perilous trajectory? How could I be aware of the immaculate deception that was the guiding principle of Isaias Afwerki's mode of rule!?

CCE, Democracy, and the Immaculate Deception

As noted before, the Russians have a saying, "Trust but Verify." It is a saying that Ronald Reagan learned from Mikhail Gorbachev when they were negotiating nuclear issues. It is a saying that we—the members of the CCE, the Eritrean nation, and everyone else who trusted Isaias—could have used, but didn't. *How do you verify whether a solemn promise, like the commitment to democratic transition made in two party congresses, was for real or if it was another hoax, another immaculate deception?* We chose to trust. Like the dying Othello whose last words were that he loved "not wisely but too well," we trusted too well—not out of love for Isaias, but because we believed that a government of freedom fighters must be trusted. Our unquestioning confidence in our national heroes induced in us a working principle that not to trust a government of freedom fighters would be tantamount to draining the soul out of the body politic of which we considered ourselves an integral part. For if we did not trust, our work would be hollow.

Our act of trust can also be expressed in terms of the proverbial Tigrigna saying: *"Mi'inti Megogo tHlef AnChuwa"* (Let the mouse go free for the sake of the clay oven). This saying reflects the wisdom of the ages that allow the guilty to go free for the sake of social harmony or solidarity. In trusting a man who was and is not worthy of our trust, what we were doing—those of us who by then had an inkling that he could be deceptive—is that since he had the nation by the throat, we had no choice but to go along, hoping one day to remedy the situation. It was pragmatism adopted for a higher cause.

The signs were there for us to be distrustful. The party gave mixed signals. Though they passed resolutions promising democracy in two congresses and recommitted themselves to the same end by translating the resolutions into law, they issued a pamphlet on June 10, 1995 titled "Clarification of Our Views on the Constitution." I had a suspicion this was written in response to the kind of pragmatic openness that reigned in Asmara during and immediately after the international conferences, especially the one held in January 1995. I had received a few barbed comments from some members of the Central Council of the party after the January conference. One of them blurted out the buzz words that appeared in the pamphlet of June 10; the words were "Guided Democracy." That is what Eritrea needed, he said, not "Western style democracy." It is a term that I would hear again and again by party cadres close to Isaias, though he never said it to me himself.

In my response to these interjections, invariably made in a sarcastic tone, I never tired of giving my interlocutors a piece of my mind and a historical perspective on the origin and use (and abuse) of the notion of a guided democracy. It was first used by President Sukarno of Indonesia, I told them; and it did not save him from being overthrown by the military in 1965. "Guided democracy" is another term for one-party rule, I explained and one-party rule has been tried in Africa and has failed. It was also rejected in two EPLF resolutions. I also reminded them of some of the pertinent points I made at the CCE's inaugural meeting and thereafter; that there was much that we can learn from our people, from the accumulated wisdom of the ages.

All too often, I said, we Africans have tended to devalue or ignore some of the time-tested and valuable mechanisms and values of governance. We have found, perhaps too late, that not everything Western or "modern" is congenial to our needs. At the same time, we cannot avoid the universally recognized principles and mechanisms of governance summed up in the idea of democracy, which is the paramount political value of our epoch, and to which even dictators pay lip service.

The PFDJ's June 10, 1995 pamphlet is immaculate deception at its most desperate because, as already pointed out, it openly and unabashedly goes against the solemn resolutions of two party congresses and the law (Proclamation 37/1993). Isaias and his top political aides endeavored to demean the importance of the constitution as a store of value and source of rights and responsibilities. The principal point they labored to push was that the constitution is just an instrument of political power. In fact in one of his latest statements when asked why he suspended the constitution, Isaias made an outrageous comment that embarrassed even his supporters. In an interview with a Los Angeles Times reporter, he said that a constitution is [just] a piece of paper. Why all this fuss about a constitution! It was one of those times when he showed his true colors, and it gives the lie to the awkward explanations given earlier; that the implementation of the constitution was delayed because of the war with Ethiopia.

The June 10, 1995 pamphlet was written by Isaias himself, judging by the blunt language and convoluted style of writing. In it he addressed two principal points: the question of government power and the question of democracy. With regard to the first point, he stated that government in a developing country must be all powerful: Restraints imposed by constitutions will act as debilitating government in its development agenda. In other words, the restraints encouraged by Western sources, and the principles and mechanisms of accountability that the 1997 constitution provided for are not acceptable. As it happens, the CCE never advocated a weak government; in view of that fact, but also of the CCE's insistence on providing for principles and mechanisms of accountability (as contained in the draft constitution), what Isaias and his top party cadres wanted was uncontrolled government. Which is to say, they wanted a dictatorial government; and they got that by suppressing the constitution.

On the related point about democracy, the pamphlet argued that multiparty democracy is messy and divisive, and that it has to be postponed indefinitely. What we need, Isaias concluded, is "guided democracy." No wonder he jettisoned the constitution. But then why go through the motion of conducting a protracted and costly constitution-making process in the first place? Obviously, he needed to be in the good books of the donor community. It will be remembered that the U.S. assistant ecretary of state for African affairs, Herman Cohen, had warned him and Meles in London, in May 1991: "No Democracy—no development assistance." Isaias must have been torn between two courses of action—either reject Cohen's demand or accept it and find ways of vitiating it. He chose going along with it, believing that he could control the process and the product of constitution making. But he couldn't; so he waited.

Partly as a result of the June 10 pamphlet and in part because of the continual provocations of some of the higher cadres denigrating "Western notions of democracy," obviously acting as surrogates of Isaias, I asked for a meeting between the CCE Executive Committee and the PFDJ highest echelons. The latter comprised the "gang of five," as some people referred to them, plus, of course, Isaias himself. A meeting was held at the party headquarters attended by Isaias and the gang of five—Alamin Mohamed Said (PFDJ Secretary General), Yemane Gebreab, Abdalla Jabir, Hagos Gebrehiwet, and Zemihret Yohannes. On the CCE's side, out of the ten members of the Executive Committee, six of us were present; two had died by then and two were absent because of travel.

The tension was palpable before Alamin broke the ice by asking us if we would like some tea or coffee. I noticed that when Isaias arrived a few minutes late, the earlier joviality with which we were greeted dissipated, replaced by an uneasy silence. The eerie silence was broken later as the server entered, carrying a tray of tea and coffee. I cracked some joke which helped reduce the intolerable tension.

I began the meeting by thanking the party chieftains for giving us their time. After a brief preliminary introduction, noting the progress of the constitution-making work, I said the reason for requesting the meeting was to ask of the PFDJ leadership one simple but important question. I prefaced my remarks by stating that there had been some mixed signals coming from the PFDJ hierarchy concerning the issue of democracy and multi-party system. I referred to the resolutions of the EPLF congresses about multiparty system, after which I asked a question point blank. I remember the exact words of my question posed to Isaias: "Are you in favor of a multiparty system—yes or no?"

There was a stunned silence. The "gang of five" all looked at Isaias with evident trepidation as though they expected him to explode. I trained my gaze on Isaias. He shifted a little in his chair; he breathed heavily but did not show any sign of irritation—the man is nothing if not a consummate actor, a characteristic essential for immaculate deception. He then said something to the effect that he thought the meeting was called for us to raise some logistical questions, perhaps asking for government help to expedite the process. As for the question I posed, he said with apparent sincerity, the matter had been decided by the party congress, and it would be carried out accordingly. And that was the end of the matter. We were elated and went back to our respective duties in high spirits. We trusted too well—*deqqi gerhi libba*!

Some Controversial Issues of the Constitution

Some issues gave rise to more controversy than others during the debates throughout the process. The language question was one. As mentioned before this was one of the twenty-three questions with which the commission started the process; asking whether there should be an official national language or official languages, and if so, which ones. The majority of the members of the CCE took the view, supported by the majority of the people during the debate, that as a matter of principle, it is better to declare the equality of all Eritrean languages, leaving Arabic and Tigrigna as the working languages of the government. A minority of the CCE members strongly argued in favor of adopting Arabic and Tigrigna as official languages. The majority voice prevailed.

There have been strong reactions against this majority view among some members of the opposition movement and even among some members of the EPLF, now members of the opposition, who feel that the language question may have to be revised, and that it might be one of the issues on which a constitutional amendment will be made in the future. More on this later.

Another controversial issue concerns land. The constitution's provisions on land have been subject to a good deal of debate both during the process of constitution making and since the constitution was ratified. According to article 23(2) of the constitution, "all land and all natural resources below and above the surface of the territory of Eritrea belong to the state. The interests citizens shall have in land shall be determined by law." This provision of the constitution affects the vast majority of the population whose livelihood depends on land. This reflects the socialist orientation of the majority of the members of the commission who were EPLF members, and state ownership of land was one of the cardinal principles of the EPLF. It is also one on which most of us have now been considerably chastened.

Historically, the ownership of land fell into two main categories: (1) community land inhabited and owned by village communities having kinship ties and claiming a common ancestor; (2) *gulti*—land that belonged to feudal authorities or their retainers, granted by a king or regional chieftains. Changing fortunes of local grandees and their overlords could, of course, cause a transformation of *guilti* into *risti,* land owned by other citizens with the result that there were, side by side, two types of land tenure systems: Diesa, communally owned village land, on the one hand, and *xilmi,* privately ownership land, on the other. After 1977, the Dergue government of Ethiopia declared all land to be state property and abolished private ownership of both urban and rural land.

The EPLF-based (later PFDJ) government of Eritrea issued a law declaring all land to be state owned, making provision for conditions under which citizens, both private and village communities, can acquire use (usufruct) rights. The law also provides for incentive systems to encourage investment in developing projects. Under the preexisting land- holding system, particularly in communal land, the periodic reallocation of land rights among villagers had the effect of inhibiting any investment in land, thus creating obstacles to development. The new law allows investors to be granted lease-hold concessions for development, provided such land lies outside that reserved for subsistence farming and housing of the village community.

The law referred to in article 23(2) of the constitution, determining the interests of citizens, was in fact already in existence at the time of the making of the constitution. One of the people interviewed by members of the Economic Committee of the CCE was the minister in charge of land. The CCE members also reviewed the report of the Economic Committee and debated the matter before adopting the provision cited above. The recent record of the government in handling land issues, especially urban land, has given all concerned ground for review of their previous opinions on state ownership of land. The fact is that the government has used its ownership of land for patronage and revenue collection for purposes other than for development. An example of this abuse of its ownership of land is the distribution of former communal lands to citizens who made contributions to its war efforts in the 1998-2000 war with Ethiopia. The government distributed urban land in and around the Asmara area, instead of paying the bond holders their money upon the maturation of the bonds. An important result of the new positions taken by Eritrean opposition parties regarding the land issue is to declare that the land proclamation must be abolished, and that the provision of the constitution related to land must be amended.

Other issues of controversy concern the election of the president; some advocate direct election, whereas others agree with the constitution, which provides for an indirect election by the National Assembly. Related to this issue is the type of government—a parliamentary or a presidential system? The constitution's provision is a compromise, a hybrid system under which the president is elected by the National Assembly and thus accords to the parliamentary system, but that once elected he/she acts as an executive president and does not sit in parliament unlike dispensations under a parliamentary system. It is of interest to note that under the 1952 constitution granted under the UN General Assembly Resolution to Eritrea, there was a more or less similar arrangement; under that constitution, the chief executive was elected by the Assembly. The Eritrean constitution makers of 1997 examined that system and the historical reasons that formed its rationale and drew a similar lesson.

The two issues first mentioned above—language and land—are the most important. For the rest, the reader may consult the text of the 1997 constitution and make up his or her mind on the merits or demerits in each case. It is interesting to note that on the system of government, Eritreans living in Europe under the parliamentary system tend to favor that system; whereas Eritreans living in the United States favor a presidential system with direct election of the president and a strict separation of powers.

Some Memorable Episodes

There were many incidents throughout the constitution-making process, especially during the civic education phase, which made the exercise interesting and even rewarding. One memorable incident concerned a question posed by a Muslim, a simple peasant-cum-camel herder in Nakfa, the capital of the Sahel region. He asked the question following a long lecture I had given on the central principles of the constitution like the rule of law, sovereignty and separation of powers. He said he was an avid listener of the Arabic program on the British Broadcasting Corporation (BBC), and he had learned a good deal from it, more than from what the Eritrean radio program offered. Then, referring to my remarks about the importance of the concept of separation of powers, he wondered why the press, and the radio in particular, was not made a separate branch of government. I was astounded by the intelligence and intellectual curiosity of that simple peasant; I was reminded of the concept of the press as the fourth estate in my reading of American history and politics.

Another incident occurred in the Christian highlands of the country. Again, it happened during the question and discussion session following my lecture. This time, an old man gave a lengthy expose, interspersed with rhyming couplets, on the idea of accountability. It is summed up in one word—*lugam* (harness). It is important to have *lugam*, he said, to control the government, but we should be careful not to hobble or otherwise constrict leaders, or else they would not be able to perform their function. His address was a counsel of the wise advocating balance and moderation in all spheres of life. He summed it all up by saying that the concepts we talked about, using new words, already existed in our traditional legal system. These kinds of caveats were expressed at different times and places in different languages exemplifying a rich heritage.

There were, of course, questions asked or assertions made expressing grave doubts about some of the proposed new constitutional principles and concepts. Of these, none was more controversial and challenging than the question of Sharia (Islamic law) and its place in the constitutional order. This was particularly challenging, as it concerns the issue of women's rights. An incident that brought this question to the fore, raised by Muslim elders with alacrity, occurred in Aqurdet (Agordat), in the western lowlands, during the early part of our civic education campaign. The meeting took place in the afternoon in a local cinema hall, which was filled to standing room only. Naturally the Muslim elders, including a couple of former leaders of the ELF took the front seats. The women, including former fighters took their seat at the back or in the middle.

As I stood to open the meeting, I asked how many of the women present were liberation fighters? A few of them raised their hand. Dramatically shaking my head in disapproval, I asked them to please come forward and take their rightful place in the front row, where there was enough room left. They hesitated, following traditional modesty; I insisted and asked the elders if they would mind if their daughters and sisters sat by their side. None objected, and upon my vigorous insistence, the women fighters started filing forward to take their seat not quite in front beside their elders but close, still showing some embarrassment.

The reason for this rather melodramatic move on my part was to instill confidence in the women, who still had a long way to go to break the gender barriers; and also to shake the confidence of those elders who were presumptuous to take their seat in the front row. It was an act of psychological warfare that I thought needed to be waged at a time when we were boldly asserting equal rights for both men and women. The women fighters had proven their mettle in the armed struggle side by side with their male comrades, and had earned their rightful place by virtue of that fact. Now we were affirming that right in principle; the constitutional proposals that were the basis of the civic education campaign stated the principle in no uncertain terms. At the end of my introductory lecture, I expected questions on that very issues from some of the elders, and the questions kept coming.

What is the place of Sharia law in the constitutional order, one elder wanted to know. I gave the standard answer that the constitution guaranteed freedom of worship of all religions, and that there was going to be separation of state and church/mosque. The tricky question of women's rights and the Sharia was raised as expected. In answer to this question on that occasion, as in other situations, we made it clear to all of the audiences that the constitution would provide for equality. During the latter part of the process, the issue of women's equality was discussed, citing the relevant articles of the constitution and explaining their scope and application. What about our rights over our children and property rights? Another wanted to know.

A little background is in order on these questions. According to information I garnered from those knowledgeable of the Sharia system, a divorced wife has no right of custody over her children and gets only a third of the value of the property. [*N.B. Following the posting on the Internet of a version of this chapter, I was criticized by one writer for committing error concerning this issue. Evidently, it is a burning question involving differing views; but we should not avoid debating the issues openly*]. There is a clash between the Sharia and the civil law systems and the constitution, which affirms equal rights for men and women. So a woman insisting on her equal rights as guaranteed under the constitution has the option of going to the civil courts to secure those rights. The down side to this option is that she may risk social ostracism from members of her Muslim community. It will all take time, government commitment to help secure these rights, and social action on the part of members of society committed to equal rights.

The Constitution and Eritrean Politics

As a document drafted with wide popular consultation, the Eritrean constitution is generally regarded as belonging to the people. Indeed, as mentioned before, a major reason for popular participation is to instill a sense of ownership of the constitution in the people. As we shall see in a later chapter, in a letter written to President Isaias, a group of Eritrean academics and professionals (popularly known as the G-13) implored him to implement it. A passage in the letter gives the following poignant summing-up:

> Eritrea has a constitution—the most sacred document of the nation. This constitution represents the consummation of the Eritrean struggle which was fought for self-determination, democracy, social justice and the rule of law. It was crafted with the participation of the people and ratified by their elected representatives. It is the people's document and no one has the right to suspend it or otherwise tamper with it. (Letter to President Isaias Afwerki, October 2000)

I thought I heard a collective "Amen" to these sentiments, presuming that these were almost universally shared among Eritreans. Not quite. Those who felt excluded from the constitution-making process did not claim ownerswhip of the constitution. But that is a point to be taken up on another occasion, though a summary view is given below, for the record, in response to one particular critique.

In an essay posted on one of the Eritrean websites, I stated: "The defining issue of current Eritrean politics concerns the constitution that remains unimplemented three-and-a-half years after its ratification. It has fired the political imagination of Eritreans and engaged them in a search for answers as to why it remains unimplemented...." The three-and-a-half years have now become thirteen years and the constitution is still a prisoner of the whims and caprice of a president who clearly means to continue to rule dictatorially. After all, he called the constitution just a piece of paper!

In view of this reality, one issue that unites most Eritrean opposition parties and all civic society organizations is the implementation of the constitution. Some of them have reservations about some of its features like language, but that is an issue that can be accommodated through the amendment procedure ordained in the constitution. If the majority of the Eritrean people or their legitimate representatives agree on such an amendment, it can happen. The same would be true with regard to other issues of controversy.

A mild, but persistent complaint about the process of constitution-making expressed by an important ELF-based party (ELF-RC) is articulated in terms of two related issues—inclusion and legitimacy. In an extensive exchange of views with me, on the Internet, a team of the ELF-RC, called Nharnet, argued that their group and those of other ELF-based groups were excluded from the process; therefore, the process lacked legitimacy. My response was to ask: Who was included and to the exclusion of whom? Now it is a matter of common knowledge that the vast majority of the Eritrean public participated in extensive debates and consultation in town and village meetings. The Nharnet team's answer to the question was that the public was captive to the PFDJ's will, and that that process excluded other political and social forces.

As to the notion of a captive population, no one disputes the historical fact that the entire Eritrean population was not only supportive of its liberation fighters but was euphoric. In this respect, we must distinguish between the years before 1998 and what followed thereafter. Up until the 1998-2000 war and its tragic consequences, the people, including those of us who are elderly and more discriminating, lived and worked with great enthusiasm and in great expectations of happy days ahead. That period (1998-2000) was confusing and complicated, charged with the collective sense of threat to the country's sovereignty and territorial integrity, despite the fact that many felt that the war should and could have been avoided.

In those euphoric days of the postliberation period, with the exception of some negligible pockets of resistance, the entire Eritrean population welcomed the EPLF liberators with immense jubilation and indeed considered them angels descended from heaven. This sentiment of blind admiration would of course become a source of our problems, just as our unilateral trust in Isaias' promise of democratic transition became a source of our current crisis. As noted already, the promise of democracy had been expressed in two EPLF congresses and translated into law, which was why so much hope was pinned on the constitution-making exercise and the resulting document. It was also the ground upon which the G-15 would base their demands for change, as we shall see.

It is curious that the Nharnet team chose to ignore these historical facts. The team used the writings of Professor Vivien Hart in their attempts to counter my arguments. Vivien Hart is an eminent scholar whose work I respect. We had met during her fellowship at the US Institute of Peace during the last phase of the work of the Working Group, which I had the honor of chairing, on the constitution making experience of several countries. The Nharnet team's contention, citing Professor Hart, that the process of constitution making is as important as the constitution itself, if not more important, is a view that I not only share but one on which the work of the Constitutional Commission of Eritrea was based.

In the atmosphere of factional politics—of suspicion and retroactive recrimination for past deeds—it might be pointless for me to issue a declaration assuring my compatriots, both ELF-RC and others, of our sincerity and dedication to democratic transition. I can reiterate that the constitution-making process of Eritrea as conceived and managed by the CCE, as well as the product of the process, with all its imperfections, was the result of a sincere and scrupulous search for the mechanism that would be best suited to our historical condition; but the double-edged sword of factional politics would defeat such a declaration, however sincere.

At the very least, I can pose a question to all interested parties: Are we to ignore three years of dedicated work involving knowledgeable Eritreans among both members of the constitutional commission and those of appropriate research committees that were organized to achieve optimum results in terms of imparting the necessary knowledge to enable the public to give their input to the process? Are we to ignore the participation of the vast majority of the Eritrean people simply because a minority of representatives of opposition groups chose not to participate, despite their right to do so?

I will leave the judgment to the fair and discerning reader.

The prognosis on the future place of the constitution is that it will remain intact in its major parts. As the above account shows, a branch of the opposition movement has registered reservations about the constitution as a document prepared under the aegis of the PFDJ and its President, Isaias Afwerki. This reservation is also coupled with a complaint that the opposition was not consulted as an organized group in the making of the constitution. There is a sense in which this complaint is justified because the PFDJ party and its president did not accept the idea of organized groups taking part in the process as organized groups. As was mentioned before, Isaias is viscerally opposed to political opposition parties. In the circumstances, the best that we at the CCE could do was to invite members of the opposition to participate in the debate individually and make their contribution as such, and many did make such a contribution.

The recent aggregation of the thirteen opposition groups under the Eritrean Democratic Alliance has brought the issue of the constitution, with a significant majority accepting it as a working document with reservations on some of its features. This is a promising trend because the constitution can provide a framework to unify the efforts of the opposition. Even in the opposition, however, the curse of militarism, a legacy of the armed struggle, bedevils Eritrean politics. In the case of Isaias Afwerki, in addition to his personal predilection toward autocracy, the militarism he imbibed during his virtually unchallenged reign over the EPLF, from its inception, was a contributing factor to his rejection of the constitution and constitutional rule. At least among members of the opposition, especially among the remnants of the former ELF, there was a modicum of democratic debate; however, the military ethos was palpable even there, especially under the reign of Abdalla Idris. An objective history of that era has yet to be written; some former cadres like Antonio Tesfai have made some sporadic attempts, which though useful, tend to be partisan.

The emergence of civic organizations has begun to impinge on the behavior of the opposition parties, particularly as regards the constitution, because the civic organizations almost unanimously demand the implementation of the constitution and have urged the political parties to accept the 1997 constitution as a working document. This is a very encouraging trend, and more organized civic organizations and their consolidation will help expedite a reassessment of the conduct of political parties in the future. Just as in late 2007, the various Eritrean civic organizations established an umbrella organization, the civic organizations in Europe also created a similar umbrella body, the Citizens for Democratic Reform in Eritrea (CDRiE), founded on January 11, 2009. A similar trend began in North America also, exemplified by the Eritrean Global Solidarity (EGS).

Despite the fact that it remains unimplemented, the constitution of Eritrea is alive in the mind of many Eritrean citizens, especially those who participated in its making. The question of its validity has been raised in legal circles, not only in theoretical terms, but for practical reasons of legal responsibility. As to whether the constitution is legally binding, opinion is divided between two schools of thought. One view is that upon its ratification it came into force and effect, and therefore it is a legally binding document. The other view, one supported by this writer, is that the provisions of the constitution concerning fundamental human rights and duties, for instance, as contained in its chapter 3 are binding on all concerned.

This raises some serious questions about government liability for acts (and omissions) that infringe on the rights of citizens. Cynics may ask who is to sanction an all-powerful and irresponsible government for violating constitutionally protected rights? Didn't the President remove the chief justice of the Supreme Court for mere criticism of executive interference in judicial matters? In the absence of democratic accountability, what guarantee do citizens have when making claims on their rights?

There is no easy answer to these questions; but when the current dictatorial regime is changed, acts committed or measures taken by it, in violation of the constitution on fundamental human rights, can be challenged in a court of law. To give one example, a government contract transferring a citizen's property in violation of his or her rights would affect the party to that contract, which should raise an alarm to anyone seeking government contracts. The government replacing the current one, would be hard put to justify such contracts and might need to review all the measures taken by the previous government in violation of the constitution.

In the new situation, there might be cases of demands for compensation or restitution of property, which would fall hard on a new government perhaps inheriting a near-bankrupt treasury. There will be not only social and economic but also legal challenges galore facing an incoming government, and it behooves all concerned citizens, especially those inside Eritrea (and within the government), to keep tabs on all such measures. There is is a moral obligation and, in the case of some in the government, there may also be legal obligation to keep such records. Just to be on the side of the angels on the day of reckoning!

Before I end this section of the closing remarks, let me say why I subscribe to the second school of thought; why I do not think that the constitution's binding validity does not extend beyond fundamental human rights and duties. In my work, *Constitution-Making in Eritrea* (2003), and in the article I mentioned, posted in an Eritrean website (Asmarino.com), I raise this issue in relation to the question of constitutional transition that the Constitutional Commission of Eritrea discussed in its final meeting. We were faced with the question of whether to include an article providing for an effective date by which the constitution would come in force or whether we should leave it open. We chose to leave it open on the understanding, given to us verbally, that the government would remove from the statute book all laws that did not conform to the constitution. We did this on the strength of that promise and our trust. As I have been saying repeatedly, that promise was not kept; our trust and that of the Eritrean people was, and remains, betrayed.

I have written before, and I say now, that we made a mistake and are answerable for that mistake. In our defense, in extenuation for the mistake based on trust, it can be said that, in view of the determination by Isaias and his party loyalists to install a one-party system and to jettison democracy and the rule of law, it would not have made any difference even if we had written into the constitution an article providing for an effective date.

Now for the connection of this issue with my view on the binding effect of the constitution: It is a matter of legality pure and simple. In Eritrea, the law establishing the Constituent Assembly charged that body with ensuring, either directly or through the creation of an entity, that all the necessary steps be taken to implement the requirements of the constitution, including the election of a government. Now the election of a government would require the enactment of an electoral law and the establishment of an Electoral Commission to organize and supervise such an election as required by the constitution. It would also include passing a law authorizing the existing government to continue in office, pending the election of a government on the basis of the new constitution.

Article 32(1) of the constitution provides that all legislative power be vested in the National Assembly. This provision came into effect on May 23, 1997 when the constitution was ratified. The problem arises because there is no elected National Assembly as stipulated under the constitution. For such an assembly to be in office, it has to be elected. For it to be elected, an election has to be held on the basis of an electoral law, and an electoral law has to be passed by an entity with legislative power. Under the constitution, the only entity with legislative power is the National Assembly, and, as yet, there is no National Assembly.

It is a vicious circle. It was in anticipation of this legal dilemma that Proclamation No. 92/1996 was enacted, providing that, in addition to the ratification of the constitution, the Constituent Assembly have power "to take, or cause to be taken, all the necessary legal steps for the coming into force and effect of the constitution." The legal imperative—"the legal steps that the Constituent Assembly must take"—requires, as noted already, the passage of a law providing that, until a new government is formed on the basis of the new constitution, the existing government continue in office, exercising governmental power. There can be no power vacuum, not only for theoretical reasons that may be esoteric but for practical reasons.

Another step that the Constituent Assembly was required to take in order to break the vicious circle is to enact laws that create institutions necessary for implementing the constitution. One such institution is the Electoral Commission. To that end, the Transitional National Assembly was formed out of the Constituent Assembly in the wake of the ratification of the constitution. The Transitional National Assembly authorized the appointment of a drafting committee to draft an electoral law. As we know, this never happened. In chapter 10, we discuss the attempts made to realize that objective and the subsequent fallout.

In consequence of this failure, the requirements of the constitution regarding the legitimate constitution-based institutions of the state, like the National Assembly, have not come into being. To the extent that this did not happen, that part of the constitution cannot, in strict legal terms, be said to have come into effect. For that failure the government (and in particular the Constituent Assembly, as the entity charged with the responsibility) must be held accountable. The members of the Constituent Assembly are jointly and severally liable in law and answerable to history

The Constitution and the Opposition Movement

As was mentioned above, there have been some opposition parties that expressed reservations about the constitution on the ground that it was made under the aegis of the Isaias government. This writer has occasionally engaged some leading members of such opposition parties in debate on this issue; in some of such debates they were asked: If the objection is based on the ground that the constitution belongs to Isaias, then why, in heaven's name, did he suppress it? Isn't that the crux of the matter—didn't Isaias refuse to implement the constitution because he does not believe in it; because he doesn't believe in constitutional democracy? This is a challenge that they cannot answer; indeed, the majority of their members believe that the constitution can and should be used as a potent weapon in the struggle to change the regime. One of the opposition parties, one the present writer helped launch (the Eritrean Democratic Party), made this point an important item at its second congress. The constitution as a weapon of struggle cannot fail to disturb Isaias and his ruling party because this resonates with the Eritrean people and their aspirations. Despite some criticism on aspects of the process leveled by some opposition groups, there is a general consensus that the constitution and demands for its implementation can be a potent force to mobilize the opposition.

Chapter 7

WHAT PRICE SOVEREIGNTY? NATIONAL LEADERSHIP AND BORDER POLITICS

———◇×◇———

T.S. Elliot, in a poem in The Waste Land, wrote "April is the cruelest month." He had his own reason (poetic license) for saying so. For Eritreans and Ethiopians, the fateful month is May—but in our case, it represents a mixture of joy and sorrow. May is a crucial month in the calendars of Eritrea and Ethiopia, bringing with it some momentous events. It was in May 1991 that the current governments of the two countries made history by jointly overthrowing the dictatorial military government of Mengistu Haile Mariam. They would make history again, but this time it would not be pleasant.

One sad day in May 1998, the people of Eritrea and Ethiopia woke up to face a disturbing new reality—their two countries were at war once again. Their two leaders, allies of yesterday, were now at each other's throats and dragging their peoples to a disastrous conflict, a conflict that many describe as absurd. Beginning with a fatal shooting incident that occurred on May 12, it blew up to a wide-ranging conflagration involving scores of thousands of troops on both sides. It has been described as a World War I type of deadly trench warfare, leading to a combined death of over one hundred thousand people.

To "objective" observers, it is just an unfortunate tragedy. Years later, historians would give their cold analysis, citing statistics of the casualties on both sides and the pile of armory and weaponry deployed by each. Military historians would discuss the strategies and tactics employed, the military forces deployed, which side did what, where, and how, etc., etc. Then there is the human dimension to the story, for those who returned fresh from the field of action as well as for the anxious mothers and fathers waiting to know if their son or daughter was dead or maimed—endless days and nights of waiting.

Meanwhile, journalists reporting from the battlefield would provide a grim picture of casualties and loss—of priceless human loss and enormous material cost. Among the carcasses of tanks and APCs and twisted artillery, there also lay a hidden casualty, invisible to the naked eye. It is invisible because it is not a physical object; it is metaphysical—truth. Truth is the first casualty in war, as the saying goes; and this particular war is no exception. But there is more: Lying prostrate beside the bodies of the fallen young men and women is a certain promise—a promise of a bright future for the peoples in all the countries of the Horn of Africa.

I have a copy of the *Hadas Eritra* (Eritrean Tigrigna Daily) of Thursday, 27 May 1993, carrying pictures of the leaders of Eritrea's three neighbors—Ethiopia, Sudan, and Djibouti. The occasion was the postreferendum celebration of Eritrea's *de jure* independence in which all three leaders gave congratulatory speeches. The speech delivered by Meles Zenawi, at the time president of the transitional government of Ethiopia, was particularly poignant. In warmly congratulating the Eritrean people for the achievement of their hard-won independence, Meles made reference to the emerging peaceful and fraternal cooperation demonstrated during the preceding two years between the peoples of Ethiopia and Eritrea as a harbinger of better days for a people and region that had longed for the peace and development that they had been denied for too long. It was a memorable speech, much of it delivered *ex tempore* and with deep feeling.

Following the Badme conflict and the devastating war, many Eritreans remembered that speech: Those given to stereotypes and negative sentiments spoke of "classic Tigrayan perfidy," while others with more charitable views lamented the tragedy of an unnecessary war without placing blame on anyone individual.

One thing is certain—the 1998-2000 war has shattered the dream of a generation, a dream of a peaceful and prosperous region based on democratic, postimperial dispensation. It was a legitimate dream engendered by the fall of the Dergue, because the allied forces of the present belligerents had waged war and defeated one of the best armies of Africa and had overthrown the oppressive regime of Mengisu Haile Mariam in May 1991. And, as previously mentioned, the leaders of the victorious forces had met, immediately thereafter, to lay down what was thought to be the foundation of a better future for their peoples. But things were not as they seemed to be. Friends became enemies as suddenly as the breaking of a summertime storm.

What went wrong? What is it that has stripped the veneer of civilization and good neighborliness from the leadership of the two governments and turned them into sworn enemies engaged in a fratricidal war? The resort to arms, in lieu of peaceful dialogue, reflects a military mentality with its consequent loss of a sense of balance that is worth probing a little further. An examination of the Badme War will, it is hoped, provide useful perspective to the ongoing tragedy.

The Real Question

I happened to be reading William Golding's novel, *The Lord of the Flies*, at the time when the war was raging, and I found similar questions in the book as the ones being raised here. In the novel, a character named Ralph poses questions regarding a group of children in a middle school who had savagely killed his friend. He finds no answer to the question why the children became merciless killers; and in the end all he does is weep. He wept "for the end of innocence and the darkness of man's heart." That was all he could do, and it is an insight that speaks to the story of the leaders of a once promising region being perennially subject to endless crises; and it speaks to the impotence of the rest of us in the face of that tragedy.

In the scholarly analysis of the origin and implications of the 1998 war fought between Eritrea and Ethiopia, can we avoid asking this haunting question: Why did we become merciless killers? And will the question not lead us inevitably to an inquiry into the state of the mind of the leaders concerned? Can questions of national interest, border dispute, economic competition, trade policies, currencies and the like provide the only answer? Can these issues adequately answer the real question: Why have such erstwhile allies resorted to such a devastating war only seven years after jointly winning a decades-old war?

At first glance, the cause of the war seemed to be over a disputed territory around a place called Badme. The border between the two countries was not completely demarcated at the time of Eritrea's formal independence in 1993; but nowhere in Africa had there been a war fought on such a scale over a border dispute. All thoughtful people in both countries, and knowledgeable people interested in African affairs, found it hard to believe that the war was caused by such a reason. It was one of those times when scholars and practitioners experience a keen sense of helplessness, not being able to find solutions to a problem. Not only because of the enormous human tragedy that war entailed, but also because their helplessness in the face of the crisis implied a crisis of relevance— their own relevance as citizens and professionals.

As someone who was involved in the Eritrean independence struggle, and who knew the leaders of both countries, I was willing to suspend disbelief for months in the face of the spiraling violence that began in Badme because I hoped against hope that reason would prevail. I held the view that in all attempts to end the war the question of who is to blame for causing the tragedy must be put aside to await the judgment of history. I continued to hold the view that any effort toward a solution must concentrate on ending the war first, while also addressing the humanitarian issues and preparing the mechanisms for peaceful resolution.

When the war broke out, I had just returned to the United States from a research trip to Eritrea, Ethiopia, and Uganda. A couple of months before, I had conducted a long interview with Prime Minister Meles Zenawi and several other high-ranking members of his government on matters of relations between the two countries, including the problems surrounding issues of trade and currency, as I mentioned before. In all these conversations, I did not see or feel any sign of emerging disaster. Indeed, all interested observers were shocked and astounded by the sudden eruption of war.

None of those with whom I exchanged views believed that we were in for the long haul—that the protagonists were engaged in a deadly row, and that the war would continue for a long time.

"Man Learns from History..."

Whatever its cause, war had become, once more, the arbiter of dispute, reminding us of the statement attributed to Hegel: "Man learns from history that he cannot learn from history."

Different parties began attempts at mediation, including the United States government, later joined by the United Nations and the Organization of African Unity (OAU). As all these parties made efforts to bring the leaders of Eritrea and Ethiopia to the conference table to resolve the crisis, I was approached by several individuals representing the U.S. government who were anxious to know what could be done to stop the war from escalating and the situation deteriorating.

As it happened, the members of the US government team engaged in the diplomatic efforts at the time were known to me in one way or another; some from my previous work as EPLF representative at the United Nations, and others from my travels to mobilize financial support for Eritrea's constitution-making process. These were: Anthony (Tony) Lake, Robert Houdek, Gayle Smith, and John Prendergast. Most of them contacted me in their sincere efforts to help find a solution to the crisis—alas, all in vain. There was a fifth person who was anguished at the sight of two leaders whom Clinton had described as members of Africa's new renaissance leaders. He was Dick McCall, deputy head of the U.S. Agency for International Development. I became friends with Dick McCall when he helped me secure a half million US dollars for the Eritrean constitution making project. McCall had also met with and was impressed by Isaias. I have never met a high-ranking American official more eager to help resolve a problem concerning others, a problem not of his own making, and so despondent when he realized he could do nothing to help.

It was clear to me that all these good people were anxious to do the right thing in terms of helping to bring an end to the unfortunate war. Tony Lake was brought in to lead the team later, replacing Susan Rice (at the time assistant secretary of state for African Affairs).

I must say, for the record, that it was with a profound sense of sadness and frustration that each one of them approached the matter. Some contacted me informally, as an interested friend, inquiring if there was anything that I could do to help them unlock the diplomatic door that kept being shut in their faces. Perhaps they thought that because of my seniority and past service to the Eritrean cause, I held a key to the solution. One of them even thought that I was very close to Isaias, and that I could persuade him "to give diplomacy a chance," as he put it. He did not know—how could he?—that I was equally frustrated and helpless to furnish the magic key. I could not cry open sesame to obviate their Herculean task! Isaias does not take kindly to people who have the temerity to give him advice.

In searching for the real cause of this absurd war, the insight offered by the story cited above from William Golding's novel seems to me to be most helpful in pointing to the real cause. Let us call it the Golding insight; and of the array of supposed causes of the war mentioned earlier, the one that approximates to the Golding insight concerns the so called "Greater Tigray" hypothesis believed by many Eritreans, on the one hand, and the allegations of "Bonapartist" ambitions leveled at Isaias by Meles, on the other. There have been allegations made by Tigrayan leaders of Eritrea's ambition to make Eritrea the Singapore of the region, thus reducing Tigray and the rest of Ethiopia into the dumping ground of Eritrean manufactured goods. Even these allegations make little sense unless they are analyzed in terms of the belief that Isaias suffers from delusions of grandeur, or from a messianic complex, wanting to become master of the Horn of Africa region and even "savior of Africa."

With regard to the Eritrean allegations of the TPLF's hidden agenda of a Greater Tigray to which Eritrea would be incorporated, the TPLF (EPRDF) leaders' response is a flat denial. In lengthy interviews conducted in Tigrigna, in 2008, and broadcast on the Tigrigna program *Dimtsi Woyane Tigray* (The Voice of Tigray's Revolution), both Meles Zenawi and Sebhat Nega (popularly known as Aboy Sebhat) not only denied this but claimed that the TPLF fought for Eritrea's independence equally ardently with the EPLF. They argue that the inclusion in the Ethiopian constitution of an article providing for the right of self-determination, up to and including secession, is an article of faith of the TPLF, theoretically applicable to all the component parts of the Ethiopian federation.

In the same broadcast, Meles repeatedly observed that the TPLF has not now, and never had, a design to take any part of Eritrea; and that the problem of implementing the Hague Tribunal's verdict concerned only issues of the need of mutual adjustment of areas inhabited by village communities along the border that the verdict left divided. His argument is that left unadjusted, these divided communities—some of them living on the Eritrean side, others living on the Ethiopia side—would face immense difficulties and thus be potential causes of future conflict. He used a catchy, homely Tigrigna phrase to describe the primordial bond uniting these people, calling them *Melamnti Hawwi* (people who share fire). Using a variation of the fire metaphor, Meles warned that, left unadjusted, such a border condition leaving people divided would be like leaving fire buried underneath, risking future conflagration. All attempts to persuade the Eritrean leadership to agree on border adjustment, he said, were rejected outright, despite the TPLF's undertaking to abide by the Hague verdict in all respects.

To turn back to Badme and the cause of the war, every thoughtful observer of the situation now thinks that the border dispute is not the real cause of the war. Badme is symptomatic of a deeper problem confronting Eritrea and Ethiopia. When the war broke out, it brought out the worst in people, as partisans on both sides raked muck and threw it at one another. Some even carved careers out of it in the manner of merchants who speculate and who make a fortune in war. Those who kept their distance from the partisan fray and occasionally made truthful comments that one or the other of the antagonists disliked were pilloried and smeared as traitors to the cause of one or the other side to the war. This confirms the saying that the first casualty in war is truth.

The Badme-Sawa Nexus

There is a significant connection between Badme and Sawa, the one as the locus or flashpoint of an absurd and costly war and the other as the center of military training. Their significance in Eritrean life and politics lies as symbols of something beyond their geographical location. If we take a sanguine view of Eritrean politics, the defense of the country's sovereignty and territorial integrity would be uppermost in our mind when we think of these two places. The Badme dispute over the national border inevitably raised questions of defending territorial integrity. In Sawa hundreds of thousands have been involved in obligatory military training and subsequent service for "national development." The same youths form a reserve army available for the defense of nation; indeed thousands of Sawa service veterans died in the Badme War.

The symbolism of the Badme-Sawa nexus can also be interpreted as symptomatic of defensive-aggressive behavior on the part of a leader obsessed with territorial aggrandizement and imperial ambition. That is the interpretation given by the Ethiopian leaders. This subject of alleged Eritrean (Isaias') expansionist ambition must be juxtaposed with the opposed charge advanced by some

Eritreans about "Greater Tigray" ambition. In this connection, a word of explication of the notion of sovereignty and territorial integrity is in order.

State sovereignty is a sacred cow in contemporary international relations along with the companion concept of territorial integrity. Both are defined by boundaries recognized in international law. In Africa's case, states have been created on the basis of boundaries that were fixed arbitrarily by Europeans during the colonial era, for the most part in the late nineteenth century. In the postcolonial era, African leaders accepted these boundaries to define their postcolonial nation-statehood. It is a paradox of African history that national sentiments have been formed and wars fought on the basis of such artificially constructed boundaries.

One is reminded of the strenuous efforts made by the Panafricanist and first president of Ghana, Dr. Kwame Nkrumah, who fought a lone battle to persuade his African brethren to accept the idea of a united African continent. His last effort to that end was made at the founding conference of the Organization of African Unity (OAU) in Addis Ababa in May 1963. He continued the battle at the second meeting of the OAU in Cairo in 1964, but failed; the assembly of African leaders passed a resolution in Cairo accepting the colonially fixed boundaries to define their postcolonial nation-statehood. The colonial boundaries have thus become sacrosanct, and the deadliest war in our times has been fought between Eritrea ands Ethiopia over a boundary.

In the case of this particular war, the border question about the Badme area divides people who speak the same language and share an ancient cultural heritage. The mother tongue of Isaias Afwerki and Meles Zenawi is Tigrigna, a language they use in their meetings and correspondence, even though Meles, as Ethiopia's leader, uses Amharic in his communications to Ethiopians. Perhaps the separate development of Eritrea as an Italian colony for the better part of a half a century forged a different national psychology and identity. Some Eritreans say, "We may share the same language with the Tigrayans, but we have different mentalities." It is also possible that such sentiments when voiced aggressively may impinge on Tigrayan sensibilities, which exacerbates the relationship by hardening the "differences."

When discussing sovereignty, it is worth remembering that in earlier times the idea of sovereignty was linked to kings and their dominions—"I am the master of all I survey; my right there is none to dispute... etc." Then with the advent of the democratic idea and the rise of parliamentary rule, sovereignty shifted from the crown to the people who supposedly exercise it through the agency of their elected representatives. In modern times, national sovereignty is thus linked to people's sovereignty, which, when coupled with territory defined by recognized boundaries, brought with it the concept of territorial integrity.

The notion of territorial boundary is part of the human condition, from the fence separating a house to the agreed lines dividing villages and districts within a country. Normally any dispute arising out of borders, whether it is one dividing a house from a neighbor or a village from another village, is resolved by judicial or administrative tribunals. Occasionally in a dispute over territory, hot heads may prevail over cooler heads, causing violent confrontation; but this is not the norm.

In days gone by, when kings or chieftains ruled over people, territorial greed or ambition might lead one king or chief to expand his domain by force, unless and until he is stopped by superior force, with the help of allies or others concerned with the implications of such expansionist ambitions. Are the current Eritrean and Ethiopian leaders susceptible to such temptations? All we can say at this point is that they accuse each other of such ambitions. One way of gaining an insight, though not in a conclusive way, is to examine how the Badme confrontation led to war.

As already mentioned, the flashpoint that caused the fighting in May and June 1998 was a shooting incident. In that incident, an Ethiopian military unit in the Badme area killed a member or members of an Eritrean military patrol that, according to Eritrean accounts, was on peaceful mission. According to these accounts, the ten-man unit approached Ethiopian authorities in the area, seeking to explore ways in which the two sides could solve some outstanding problems. The main problem in the Badme area, according to the Eritrean side, concerned repeated complaints by Eritrean citizens, mostly nomadic herders, of harsh treatment at the hands of Tigrayan authorities, including detention, beatings and demands for payment of exorbitant sums of money as penalties for trespassing. The victims of such mistreatment claimed that they were not trespassing, since they had considered the territory as part of Eritrea; and that their repeated petitions requesting the Eritrean government to intervene on their behalf had been answered with pleas for patience. Eritrean government authorities had told the complainants that the matter was being handled by Eritrean authorities with their Ethiopian counterparts at the highest level. Nonetheless, the complainants kept coming with more stories of maltreatment, and apparently Tigrayan authorities kept encroaching on Eritrean territory.

The interested reader can find a detailed account of the treatment of Eritreans at the hands of Tigrayan authorities in the Badme area in Tekie Fessehtzion's book *Shattered Illusion, Broken Dream*, especially chapter 3, titled Genesis of the Border War (2002). Tekie's account, presumably based on data obtained from official Eritrean sources, is a compilation of a chronological report of events and the steps that were taken to resolve the border dispute. Tekie issues a caveat that the report should be taken "as one person's reading of what took place." The chronology starts with the earliest recorded border incident in Badme, then goes on to other parts of the border including the Bada area of eastern Eritrea. Tekie reports that as early as 1992 officials of the Tigray Administrative Region (later called Kilil One) "unilaterally crossed into Eritrean territory at Badme. They put new border markers deep into Eritrean territory. Tigrayan police charged thirty-three Eritrean farmers with trespassing and 'illegally' cultivating the land the Administrative Region recently declared as part of Tigray. The police confiscated the farmers' crops."

He also reports that in 1993 the Tigray Administrative Region launched a "Border Rectification Project," and that Eritreans in areas that the Administrative Region had claimed as Tigray's were expelled; and those that stayed were continually harassed. Tigrayan settlers moved in, armed militias were set up, and new civilian administrative structures run by demobilized TPLF fighters were established. All livestock that crossed the "new" border were impounded.

This condition continued through 1997, raising the question: What was the government of Eritrea doing all this time while its citizens were being maltreated, their property confiscated and dispossessed of land they considered their own? Apparently, in the absence of any effective response from the central government, local "diplomatic" efforts were undertaken, but to no avail, until finally a local military unit took the initiative to make a show of force in what the Eritrean side says was a peaceful patrol mission. And that, as we know, was what led to the shooting incident of 6 May 1998 in which Eritrean soldiers and officers were killed and wounded. That incident became the flashpoint of the disastrous war.

In his 2008 interview with Dimtsi Woyane Tigray, cited above, Meles claims that the Eritrean patrol was sent to arrest the Tigrayan militia, and that was how the shooting incident started. According to the Eritrean version, the patrol was a peaceful one, aimed at diffusing the quickly escalating violence in which Tigrayan militias and local authorities continually harassed and detained and penalized Eritrean farmers.

In the circumstances of claims and counterclaims over disputed land, one reasonable presumption is that the aforementioned ten-man unit of Eritrean defense forces had decided to try local-level diplomacy. This presumption is supported by the fact that at the time of the incident a bilateral commission was holding talks in Addis Ababa. The Eritrean delegation was led by Sebhat Efrem, minister of defense. Speculations as to whether he knew about and authorized the local diplomatic initiative taken by the ten-man unit have been neither confirmed nor denied. Eyewitness accounts of people who saw him in Addis Ababa at the time when he was informed of the incident apparently reported that he was shocked to learn about it. If such reports are true, then the unit either acted on its own initiative or had received authorization from a higher authority.

On May 12, 1998, six days after the shooting incident, the Eritrean military commander of the region moved troops to occupy Badme and its environs, displacing Tigrayan civilians and militias. In the interview Meles claimed that the Tigrayan militia was crushed, and that several of its members were executed by the attacking army. Several brigades, including tanks, were involved in the attack. Things went from bad to worse, events producing their own momentum. Prime Minister Meles Zenawi called President Isaias, who was traveling to Saudi Arabia and could not be reached. Meles convened the Ethiopian Parliament on May 13 to report on the situation and to seek approval for putting his country on a war footing. Immediately thereafter, Meles announced that Eritrea had committed an act of aggression on Ethiopian territory and demanded that Eritrea withdraw its troops or face the consequences of total war. According to Meles, the military balance favored Eritrea, which had a force of 150,000 against Ethiopia's 54, 000.

Serious Questions

Three related questions arise with regard to the above-cited set of events.

First, was it necessary for the Eritrean side to make such a massive military move on May 12, following the killing of the member(s) of the ten-man unit?

Second, was it necessary for the Ethiopian side to declare all-out war? Then too, was it not possible for each side to have exercised restraint and tried peaceful means?

Third, why did mediation fail to stop the war earlier?

Each side claimed to be the victim of aggression. The Ethiopian version of the Badme incident and its response is based on an assertion that Badme is part of Ethiopia, and that the Eritrean invasion was therefore an act of aggression. The Eritrean response to this charge is that Badme is part of Eritrea, and that the treaty maps between Ethiopia and Italy prove it. In other words, the issue turns on treaty maps and borders, an issue that could have been, and can still be, resolved through joint boundary commissions, or, failing that, through mediation or arbitration with the help of a neutral body of cartographic experts.

Speaking of treaty maps, apart from the Badme area, there is another area under dispute between the two governments—the Bada area, further east. Ethiopia signed several treaties with European colonial powers, including Italy, at the end of the nineteenth century and the beginning of the twentieth century. Of these treaties, three main ones were signed between Italy and Ethiopia, marking off the boundary of Ethiopia and Eritrea. The treaty of July 10, 1900, established a boundary along the Mereb River and two tributaries. *On the west, a straight line was drawn between Tomat-Todluc-Mereb-Belessa-Muna,* traced on the map annexed to the treaty. Two years later, the 1902 treaty moved that straight line into the east which, according to Eritrean claims puts Badme inside Eritrea. Then in the 1908 treaty again between Italy and Ethiopia, established a line along eastern border running in a south-easterly direction parallel to, and 60 kilometers west of, the Red Sea.

The boundary dispute was resolved by the arbitral tribunal at The Hague, as we shall see in more detail below. As far as Badme is concerned, Eritrea's claim that the reference to the coordinates would place Badme inside Eritrea was vindicated by the arbitral tribunal whose award placed Badme inside Eritrea.

One thing seems to be certain: An arbitrarily drawn, artificial boundary cannot, in and of itself, lead to such a horrendous mutual massacre as the Badme War. If both sides were convinced of the justice of their cause based on treaty maps, why didn't they give diplomacy a chance, as the mediators had asked them? Which is to say, the border issue is not the real cause of the war; it just provided the pretext for acting out other motives. The question is what motives?

Many Tigrayans believed that after severing its currency from the Ethiopian *birr,* the Eritrean economy was on the verge of collapse; and that the war was launched by Isaias because of that. In a private conversation with the Ethiopian ambassador to the United States, Berhane Gebrekristos with the present writer, Berhane made this point on the eve of the outbreak of the war. Sebhat Nega, former chairman, and gray eminence of the TPLF, in the interview he gave to the Tigrigna radio/tv program mentioned above, claimed that the primary motive was economic. He cites the expert opinions of members of the TPLF who attended an international conference convened by the EPLF in Asmara in 1992, a year after independence. The conclusion of the TPLF members, based on papers presented at the conference, was that the Eritreans were bent on becoming the economic power house of the region, and that in their scheme they expected Tigray and the rest of Ethiopia to become the dumping ground of Eritrean goods, as already noted. Sebhat was expressing a view shared generally by other members of the TPLF who regard Eritreans in general, and EPLF members in particular, as inordinately ambitious, arrogant, and obsessed with Eritrean "exceptionalism."

Eritreans counter such accusations as the sentiments of a group (the TPLF) that is itself obsessed with its own sense of deprivation and inadequacy vis-à-vis Eritrea and Eritreans, thus making unfounded accusations about Eritrean designs to dominate Tigray and Ethiopia in general. Eritrean economists, who believe in the interdependence of the two countries, argue that the TPLF economic development policy of creating manufacturing industries in Tigray, duplicating those existing in Eritrea, is not based on sound economic rationality, but on a sense of deprivation and resentment that would prove to be wasteful in the end. Whether such arguments are wellfounded or not remains to be seen; but they reflect an unhealthy relationship that will not be helpful in advancing future cooperation and friendly relations. And they certainly do not help in resolving the ongoing crisis. The challenge for the two countries is for experts and seasoned professionals from both sides—economists, lawyers, political scientists and others—to create an environment that will facilitate rational arguments based on a mutuality of interests and, as much as possible, one free from partisan politics.

There is intriguing correspondence, which the leaders of the two countries exchanged before the outbreak of the war, centered on the dispute over the Bada area. The letters are brief and seemingly cordial but have the eerie appearance of a dialogue of the deaf. The exchange was initiated by the Eritrean president, Isaias, who begins his letter with "Comrade Meles," followed by "Greetings."

The letter is sufficiently brief to be reproduced here.

> The purpose of my writing you today is the grave situation in the Bada area. The border between us is not clearly demarcated. In view of the current and future [good] relations we did not pay much attention to it. Even in the future I don't see its importance or urgency. This being the case, there have been many incidents on many occasions and in different places. So far, effort has been made to solve the problem on site by local authorities. Recently, the resort to force by your military at Adi Murug is very sad. There was no justification for military action. Even if it is believed that the situation warranted serious attention, it would not have been difficult to solve the problem amicably. If there is any need for drawing demarcation lines it can be handled in a calm atmosphere. To prevent the step taken so far from leading to a deterioration of the situation, I am writing you to request [that] you take appropriate action.
>
> Regards—Your comrade, Isaias Afwerki [signature]. August 10, 1997.

In view of what happened after the outbreak of the war, including the general "free for all" and obscene media extravaganza, two things are striking in Isaias' letter. First, his tone is not only conciliatory, but comradely, reminiscent of the days when they were comrades-in-arms against a common enemy. Indeed, he signs his letter with "Your comrade." Secondly, he urges calm and a resort to peaceful settlement of the border issue.

In response, Meles wrote a long letter, which dealt not only with the Bada issue but with economic and financial matters. The first paragraph of the letter is again brief enough to be reproduced here. He begins with "Greetings" and interestingly enough does not reciprocate with the word, "comrade." It goes on as follows:

> I have seen the letter you wrote. I also have heard that the border situation is not good. I also know that when Yemane and his team were here they discussed the issue with Tewelde and his team. There was no expectation that the situation would develop (sic). Because we thought there was no disagreement about the territory held by our comrades, and the agreement reached was on disputed areas only. We moved into the area to drive out the *Ugugumu,* who were disrupting our distribution effort, from the area. At any rate, on all matters pertaining to border issues, there is an understanding reached between Tewelde and his team, and we are of the opinion that[understanding] should be the starting point for resolving them. Perhaps it may be necessary for both of us to get prepared and bring the border issue to a conclusion.
>
> With Good Wishes,
> Meles [signature]

In sum, despite the reassurances expressed in the letter written by Meles, the Eritrean government took the view that in July 1997 the Tigrayan forces used the pretext of pursuing the Afar Revolutionary Democratic Front (ARDF), commonly known as Ugugumu, to occupy a part of Eritrea and to dismantle the civilian administration in the Bada area. President Isaias' letter is a milder version of what was to come after the war broke out in May-June 1998—the unambiguous charge of Ethiopian invasion of Eritrean land. The accusation further stated that the Meles government unilaterally changed the treaty-based map by issuing a new map of the Tigray region, incorporating large parts of Eritrean land in the Badme area in violation of international law. The Eritrean side saw the Badme incident as a provocation to test Eritrea's will to resist what Eritreans saw as a pattern of encroachment that had started earlier.

As Prime Minister Meles' letter indicates, Ethiopia's response to this accusation was a denial of any act of aggression, and that the territory held by Ethiopian forces (those referred to as "our comrades" in Meles' letter) was not in dispute. Where there had been dispute, there was an understanding (according to Meles) to resolve them through the mechanism of joint discussion. Alas! Joint discussion had long ceased to produce any mutually agreeable results, as the failure of discussions on the currency issue demonstrated.

After the war broke out the polite diplomatic language was replaced by an escalation of an ugly media war. The media war, involving accusations and counteraccusations of aggression, complicated matters, making mediation and peaceful settlement doubly dificult. An examination of the contents of the media exchange gives an idea of some of the deep-seated prejudices and mutual suspicions that had been simmering below the surface of the much-vaunted EPLF-TPLF alliance. A constant feature of the media war was *ad hominem* attacks on the leaders and some of their principal aides. The Ethiopian media continually asserted the real source of the problem as being the inordinate ambition and authoritarian nature of President Isaias Afwerki.

Some press statements went so far as to assert that there would be no peace in the region unless and until Isaias is removed from the scene and, with him, his PFDJ party. Well, the Eritrean side reciprocated in kind. It was an altogether dismal spectacle. The media abuse on both sides was obscene. To all democrats it was like passing through the Stations of the Cross. This writer, who was a target of hostile attack by a TPLF-affiliated media outlet on at least one occasion, was present at a conference of Eritreans in North America in the Washington, D.C. area in August of 1997 when Alamin Mohamed Said, the secretary general of the PFDJ, made a statement to the same effect about the TPLF. He said, in unambiguous terms, that they must be removed from power. It is virtually impossible for Alamin to make such a drastic statement without receiving a green light from Isaias; at least he must have heard Isaias express such sentiment during one of the meetings of the PFDJ inner circle. Alamin's statement was made nine months before war broke out, but at a time when relations had been deteriorating on many fronts. And in private conversations among Eritreans, one constantly heard expressions of the underlying mistrust—of the TPLF's hidden agenda of Greater Tigray.

Impact and Ramifications of the War

Eritrea and Ethiopia along with Uganda were considered by U.S. policy makers as strategic allies in stemming the tide of Islamic fundamentalism in the region. This was particularly true during the time when Hassan el Turabi and his Islamist party dominated Sudan, and were seen as posing a threat to the stability of the region, even before the advent of Osama Bin Laden and his Al-Qaeda.

Thus from the standpoint of US strategic and geopolitical interests in the region, the war between Eritrea and Ethiopia marked a signal failure. All violence marks a failure of politics; but the war between these two erstwhile allies was particularly galling to the U.S. strategists who had dreamed of a Greater Horn of Africa Strategic Initiative, anchored by the continuance of the alliance between Eritrea and Ethiopia under the leadership of Eritrea's Isaias Afwerki and Ethiopia's Meles Zenawi with Uganda's Musseveni adding to these presumed "axis of good regimes." Indeed, Musseveni was one of the African leaders who traveled to Addis Ababa and Asmara to appeal to Meles and Isaias to resolve their differences and settle their dispute peacefully.

The failure of the attempts at peaceful settlement and the resulting two-year, devastating war practically vitiated the US-inspired regional strategic initiative. A major effect of the war has been the militarization of society in the two countries with the consequent drain on their scarce financial resources. Before the end of the war, between the two of them Eritrea and Ethiopia mobilized some half a million troops with the enormous cost that this implies. Both Ethiopia and Eritrea spent several hundred million dollars on arms, all paid for in cash, including significant amounts of heavy artillery, tanks, armored vehicles, and aircraft. All this has severely affected the economies of the two countries.

Apart from the cost involved, the militarization has lead to the spread of arms within the region with future implications of instability over and above the adverse impact it has had on the economies of the two countries. The social impact of the war includes not only the scores of thousands of dead and wounded but left families without any support system.

Another negative effect of the war was the diminished role of regional organizations especially the Inter-Governmental Authority on Development (IGAD), which links Djibouti, Eritrea, Ethiopia, Kenya, Somalia, Sudan, and Uganda. The promising role previously played by a regional organization like IGAD was severely affected in terms of regional peacemaking and peacekeeping. The continued crisis in Somalia demonstrates, with its anarchic statelessness and clan-based Hobbesian condition shows the effect of IGAD's diminished role.

The Eritrea-Ethiopia war, as well as the continuing crisis in Somalia, has resulted in immense humanitarian crises. Soldiers are not the only casualties in war. The corpus of international humanitarian law is concerned not only with the war wounded and prisoners of war. The International Committee of the Red Cross (ICRC), commonly known as the International Red Cross, which is mandated by its charter and under international law to deal with such issues, called on the warring parties to abide by the rules of international law with regard to the wounded, prisoners of war, and civilian populations on both sides. Within the first year of the Badme War thousands of soldiers were killed and wounded.

No one can tell whether in the heat of battle—in the fog of war—the rules of international humanitarian law are observed. What is known, though not widely reported, is the fact that the ICRC requested the parties to the conflict to allow the wounded and the sick to be evacuated from the battlefield and given appropriate medical care. It also demanded that combatants killed in the fighting be identified and afforded a decent burial and their place of burial duly marked.

Alas! Unlike cases where war crimes or crimes against humanity were committed, there is no sanction for failure to observe the ICRC rules on the evacuation of the sick and wounded and the decent burial of the dead. In this respect, the code of conduct to be followed by the military leaders of each side with regard to the evacuation of their sick and wounded and the burial of their dead will depend on their respective training, discipline, and sense of right and wrong. It will also, obviously, depend on the situation, on the conditions on the battlefield, including the logistical capacity of the concerned parties to perform what is required.

With respect to the treatment of civilian populations, the most controversial in the Eritrea-Ethiopia war was the expulsion of over 70,000 Eritreans and Ethiopians of Eritrean descent from Ethiopia. Several international organizations, including Amnesty International and the UN Human Rights Commission, condemned both the fact of the expulsion and the manner in which the Ethiopian government carried it out. Ethiopia's reason for that unfortunate act was consideration of national security. Both Prime Minister Meles Zenawi and other prominent leaders of the government have said that the Eritrean government was on record for saying that the battlefront extended beyond Badme and went as far as Addis Abba, meaning that they were going to use the large presence of Eritreans in Ethiopia to undermine the Ethiopian government. The Ethiopians also countered the charges by claiming that Eritrea had expelled Ethiopians from Eritrea.

Subsequently, following the Algiers Accord, the Ethiopian government has expressed regret for the manner in which some of the expulsion was carried out. It has also made an offer to any Eritrean who thinks of himself/herself as Ethiopian to come back to Ethiopia and has made an offer to any other Eritrean to come and live in Ethiopia as a lawful foreign resident and do business as such. How expelled Eritreans will respond to this gesture remains to be seen. But a great deal of bitterness persists among those who suffered under Ethiopia's harsh treatment while being expelled. As in all other matters, the healing hands of time will take care of this too.

Another impact of the war on civilian populations is the massive displacement from the war zone. This occurred on the Eritrean side much more than on the other side. An estimated 300,000 to a half million Eritreans were displaced. The situation of displaced Eritreans was complicated by the fact that the peace agreement included the area occupied by Ethiopian military forces after the war ended, including the Temporary Security Zone (TSZ), which extends 25 kilometers into Eritrean territory. This has continued long after The Hague Tribunal gave its decision awarding Badme to Eritrea. Despite declarations by both governments that they do not intend to go to war, some doubt remains as the impasse continues unresolved. Eritrea contends that the "virtual demarcation" legally entitles it to take possession of the areas awarded to it.

Now within the parts awarded to Eritrea there are pockets of areas that had been the subjects of counterclaims, which are still under Ethiopian occupation, with Ethiopia demanding that there should be dialogue for readjustments, and Eritrea insisting on unconditional withdrawal of Ethiopian occupation troops. A generally expressed fear is that if Eritrea decides to repossess these areas, Ethiopia may decide to take action in "defense" of these territories, which would mean another round of fighting. In the current "no war—no peace" situation, all it takes for renewal of hostilities is one hasty move by either side. As things stand, there is massive mobilization of forces on both sides, staring at each other across the "virtual," and as yet undemarcated, boundary—with tensions building up.

In chapter 8, I deal in more detail with the Algiers Agreement under which the Ethiopian and Eritrean governments agreed to submit their case for binding arbitration by an international tribunal at The Hague and the consequent verdict of the Ethiopia-Eritrea Boundary Commission (EEBC) and the post-verdict situation.

Sovereignty and Self-determination

Like most African countries, Eritrea is a creation of European colonial history. Implicit in the postcolonial African legal order are two seemingly opposed principles—territorial integrity of a state, on the one hand, and self-determination of peoples, on the other. States, not peoples, are represented at the international system epitomized by the United Nations as well as its regional organizations like the African Union (AU), formerly OAU, and the Organization of American States (OAS). Enclosed within the confines of artificially created boundaries, Africans of different ethnic groups were left to fend for themselves as best they could in all matters, including the matter of forging a nation out of diverse groups.

The experience of common oppression at the hands of alien rulers and the need to fight that oppression, in addition to the powerful economic system imposed by the colonizers brought the colonized African populations, forcing them to be mobilized in the face of a common adversary. Despite their ethnic differences, the primordial sentiment of outraged dignity suffered by Africans and their thirst for freedom acted as a matrix for the birth of a unifying African nationalism, the ideology that the new leaders used to forge an idea of common destiny, a sense of nationhood. This is the origin of the present African state system, defined by artificially created boundaries and allocating citizenship and identity to its members on that basis. This new identity has replaced old tribal identity for all practical purposes, though in times of crisis the old identity may appear to provide support system to kinsmen in distress. In our case, Eritreans in the highland share linguistic and cultural features with their kinsmen across the Ethiopian border; but each people on the two sides have different citizenship, which defines their political allegiance. I call this the border ideology.

What Price Sovereignty

There is an organic connection between the concept of sovereignty and the border ideology described above. The ideology is a powerful force animating people's actions, and underlying it is an inherent tension built along the boundaries with far-reaching implications in terms of interstate conflict. The tragic Eritrea-Ethiopia war of 1998-2000 serves as an extreme illustration of this phenomenon. I conclude this chapter by asking the question: Can there be common ground in terms of the needed search for a lasting solution to the problems associated with national borders and some of its grotesque applications and effects on ordinary people's lives?

As the border conflict morphed into an all-out conflagration, what can only be described as war psychosis set in, distorting everything. The two sides had reached a point of no return, and nothing short of third party intervention could reverse it. The half-hearted, if sincere, attempts at mediation that the U.S. government had made had to be replaced by a more vigorous and systematic act of mediation.

Chapter 8

FROM ALGIERS TO THE HAGUE: MEDIATION AND BINDING ARBITRATION

———————◇✕◇———————

Before considering international and regional mediation efforts, mention should be made of attempts by local groups to encourage peaceful settlement through dialogue between the two leaders. Such attempts reflected the deep disappointment of the public on both sides of the conflict. The sudden irruption of a deadly war shocked and surprised everybody, particularly in view of the history of cooperation between the two fighting fronts and the postconflict efforts made to deepen cooperation and give it institutional form on various fields of endeavor.

Top church leaders and other concerned elders of the region, both Eritreans and Ethiopians met to discuss ways of inducing a peaceful solution. Prominent civic leaders wrote to the leaders and eventually coalesced their efforts towards a systematic approach by forming a group representing both sides, comprising professional and academic leaders and retired civic persons of substance. One such group was organized by Professor Ephraim Isaac of Princeton University. Isaac's group traveled to Addis Ababa and Asmara and met the leaders of Ethiopia and Eritrea. But they drew a blank at both ends. War had become the final arbiter.

A Japanese organization known as Peace Boat also made serious efforts at peaceful resolution. It organized joint meetings between Eritrean and Ethiopian scholars, and offered financial resources with Japanese government backing to build development institutions around the disputed area as an incentive, in order to encourage the warring states to resolve the conflict through peaceful means. I was invited together with Dr. Assefaw Tekeste to meet two Ethiopians, Mr Kifle Wodajo and Dr. Andreas Eshete in Japan for a dialogue. This effort too drew a blank as the war escalated.

The Algiers Negotiations

First, a word about the chapter title. Though the protracted mediation ended in Algiers with a final accord under which the two parties agreed to submit their case for binding arbitration, the route to Algiers and thence to The Hague went through Ougadougou, the capital of Burkina Faso. Perhaps a more accurate, though clumsy, heading would be—From Ougadougou to Algiers and to The Hague.

Why Ougadougou and Algiers? This is so, because the respective presidents of the two countries happened to be the chairmen of the OAU at the time—Burkina Faso in 1998-1999, Algieria in 1999-2000.

The route was tortuous and the negotiations tedious and costly, with diplomats shuttling from Washington to Addis Ababa, from Addis to Asmara, and back to Addis again; and then from these two capitals of the belligerents to Ougadougou and later to Algiers. Back and forth, again and again. It was costly not only in monetary terms but also—and above all—in the loss of human lives. Every twist and turn resulting from the refusal of one or the other leader to sign on to solutions proposed by the mediators, over a period of two years, was the cause of such egregious loss. It is when considering the loss that the question of who started the war becomes relevant. It becomes relevant because it raises issues of responsibility, both in the legal and moral sense. And the battle of words between the belligerents is waged partly to avoid facing such responsibility.

The loss was keenly felt by all persons of conscience, especially people from the Horn of Africa region. So, while statesmen of different nations engaged in the mediation efforts, puzzled over the intricacies of diplomacy to find a solution to the war between these two poor countries, shuttling from capital to capital and holding urgent meetings, there were other kinds of meetings taking place involving both politicians and ordinary citizens. I was privy to some of these meetings in my capacity as an academic as well as a concerned citizen. It was at such meetings that I became keenly aware (not for the first time) that there are people in Ethiopia, including some Tigrayans, who find it hard to accept the idea of Eritrea's separate identity and independent existence.

Even after Eritrea's independence became an undeniable fact of international relations, following the referendum of 1993, and its subsequent admission to the United Nations, that fact was unpalatable to such people. It is not beyond the realm of possibility, in the mind of such people, that somehow, sometime in the future, there would be a reversal of the situation. To these people the dominating thought is: How can Ethiopia remain a country without a port to call its own? Years of propaganda, including the seventeen years of the Dergue, had drummed into people's mind that Ethiopia could not exist without Eritrea. This was over and above the usual argument of historical ties and economic and social interconnections between the two. This was indeed a factor that had given ground for raising hopes and great expectations of cooperation between the two governments. The Badme War acted like a booster injection for hopes of reversal of Eritrea's independence, as borne out by remarks made in group meetings, public rallies, or private exchanges, some of which I myself witnessed.

As mediation efforts were launched by various international actors, notably—and most importantly—the United States of America, the Washington-based Center for Strategic and International Studies organized meetings to give representatives of Ethiopia and Eritrea an opportunity, in separate meetings, to explain their respective views on the origin and ramifications of the war. I was present as a member of the audience in both meetings. Following the remarks made by the Eritrean envoy presenting his country's case, I heard an Ethiopian woman—a former Dergue loyalist who wraps herself in the Ethiopian flag—interject vigorously, protesting that "Ethiopia's border is not Badme, it is the Red Sea." This sentiment seems to tally with Tekie Fessehatzion's thesis about the cause of the war. Tekie's view of the real cause of the war is the "Woyane government's need to extend its power and influence north into Eritrea because it's unsure of its future in tomorrow's Ethiopia" (Tekie, 2002). If Tekie is right, the Woyane's motive may be different from that of the Dergue loyalist; but both agree on the objective—the end of Eritrea's independence. However Tekie's view must be compared with Meles' view, which rejects any claim to "recover" any part of Eritrea (see next chapter).

In contrast to the Dergue loyalist, I met another person on the same occasion, following the end of the meeting—a man from Tigray whom I knew from my Addis Ababa days, and who happens to come from Adua, Meles Zenawi's birthplace. Instead of the tired slogans or vulgar imprecations of latter-day patriots of dubious worth, the man quietly accosted me and offered a chat over coffee outside the meeting hall. When we sat down for coffee, he mournfully expressed grave concerns about the loss of innocent lives. As he put it, "The two leaders have rushed into a war that will result in mutual annihilation of two brother peoples." What should we do to stop it? He wanted to know. "They must be stopped," he concluded, for this is a war between two "hard-hearted leaders who don't care about the fate of the ordinary people."

The man from Adua was not alone in the sentiments he expressed. It was a point of view shared by many from both sides of the border, but one that was lost to the "Hafash" (the masses) of both countries, subjected as they were to the bitter propaganda war in which both governments were engaged, pouring venom on each other. In a matter of days, the venom spread, corroding friendships and neighborly relations of hitherto friendly peoples in the two countries, all affected by the media wars, including those conducted on cyberspace. And diplomats were engaged in another kind of war in which the antagonists exchanged a war of words to win the mediators to their side.

Diplomacy While Wars Raged on All Fronts

Soon after the war broke out in May-June 1998, mediation efforts were launched to help avoid a conflagration of the conflict and to end it through negotiation. The United States joined Rwanda in pursuit of that end, with Rwanda's president, Paul Kagame, who was, or thought he was, a friend of both Isaias and Meles. President Bill Clinton sent a facilitation team to the region, led by Susan Rice, assistant secretary of state for African affairs. I was informed by a reliable source that president Clinton talked with both President Isaias and Prime Minister Meles on the phone several times, pleading with them to stop the fighting and resort to peaceful means to resolve the dispute, adding that he was hopeful of an early resolution of the conflict. Apparently, Clinton regarded both of them as his friends and hoped that his friendship would work like magic in getting them to the conference table to shake hands and end the war. He would be as disappointed as everyone else was who thought these erstwhile allies and comrades-in-arms would succumb to his well-known persuasive power.

Isaias had just returned from an unofficial visit to the United States and had met with Clinton a couple of weeks before the outbreak of the war. I happen to have met Isaias during that visit in Washington; we had a scheduled brief meeting at the Eritrean ambassador's residence and we also met one evening at a dinner-speech event where he was scheduled to deliver an address. Susan Rice and her Canadian husband were among the invited guests there. So was the Reverend Jesse Jackson, who was also a speaker in a sort of discussant's role.

I have reasons for making reference to that particular event. Two things have stuck to my mind about it. One was Jesse Jackson's comments about Isaias' speech; he reprimanded Isaias on a point he had made stating that democracy should not be imposed by outsiders on Africans. Commenting on the speech, Jackson gave Isaias an *ex cathedra* lecture on democracy, contending that there is but one universal democratic principle, and one should not derogate from that principle by advancing views that qualify or modify it. I am paraphrasing the comment; but that was the essence of it.

My reaction to Jackson's comments at the time was to wonder (loudly, as I recall) who the hell did he thinks he was, reprimanding the head of state of an African country, even a small country like Eritrea. I was annoyed not really because he reprimanded my country's leader—I was very much disillusioned with Isaias by then. It was actually the African in me that reacted, remembering that Jackson used to be vocal about supporting African liberation and all that jazz. In retrospect, in view of what has happened in Eritrea, I owe Jackson an apology.

The other bit of memory I have is Susan Rice's remarks to Isaias during an informal conversation on that occasion, demonstrating an attitude that seemed to me to be almost the opposite of Jackson's. I was introduced to Susan Rice for the first time at that event. Before that, I had heard her speak at the African Studies Annual Meeting shortly after she was appointed head of the Africa Bureau at the State Department. She was an impressive speaker. And so when I heard her cooing in admiration of Isaias, telling him to "Tell us what we should do...etc," I was surprised, to say the least. She was obviously taken by his charisma and the mystique of the guerilla leader—the "Che Guevara effect" in which her generation was weaned.

One theory favored by some is that American leaders assumed that the personal rapport Susan Rice had developed with Isaias, as well as Clinton's consideration of what he called the "new breed" of African leaders that he thought he had cultivated, would easily yield fruitful results in the mediation efforts. But apparently, somewhere along the line, when the mediation efforts were under way, the lovey-dovey relation soured. There is a story that President Isaias lost his temper and was abusive to Susan Rice. In an interview I had with a member of Susan Rice's facilitation team, I asked about the language Isaias had used; my informant declined to tell me the exact words, but said that it was strong, undiplomatic language. His subsequent remarks, dismissing her as an ineffectual diplomat—though apparently shared by some of the Ethiopian leaders—rankled American feelings.

It is generally believed among Eritreans that the United States favored the Ethiopian side in the Badme dispute. Even the U.S. mediation team (also called facilitators) have been accused of being partial to the Ethiopian side. Could it be that the American team felt more at ease with the Ethiopians because Ethiopians are, by and large, better diplomats than Eritreans, employing a more refined diplomatic language in their dealings? The story about president Isaias being rude to Susan Rice has been neither confirmed nor denied by anyone. In an interview with another member of the U.S. facilitation team, I tried to find out what Isaias had actually said. Again, while not denying that Isaias was rough, this informant also declined to reveal the exact alleged words of abuse.

It would be interesting, first of all, to know what exactly transpired between Isaias and Susan Rice during the meeting that so riled her; and second, if in fact the abuse had an effect in tilting the American view (and especially Susan Rice's view) toward supporting the Ethiopian position? Whether the abuse had an effect favoring the Ethiopian position or not, some Eritreans believed that it did. For example, Tekie Fessahazion expressed the view that the American government exerted pressure on the OAU to endorse the American proposal (i.e., the U.S.-Rwanda proposal), which Eritrea had rejected. Tekie went so far as to write that Rwanda was brought in "to provide a patina of African co-sponsorship, although it was purely an American solution, carefully crafted to help Ethiopia at the expense of Eritrea" (ibid,.45). In the same work Tekie claims that the Americans bent over backwards to accommodate Prime Minister Meles Zenawi, even to the point of using their clout in the donor organizations to facilitate securing over $400 million as reconstruction cost, to be used following the end of the conflict, which Tekie claims Meles applied to his native province of Tigray. Tekie does not mince his words:

> For too long, Prime Minister Meles has played the donor community as if they were a bunch of marionettes, always giving him assistance even when they knew it was being diverted for the war effort....The donors that funded Ethiopia's war cannot afford not to see the irony of what their assistance has done to the region and its people. No wonder they are trying to force a peaceful solution to the conflict.

It seems that Tekie is using the word "donor" as a code word for the Americans, since the World Bank is dominated by the United States. To an objective observer, "bribing" the Meles government to agree to a peaceful solution to end a disastrous war would seem to be salutary if not worthy of the Nobel Peace prize. But it does raise the question why the donors are being partial to Ethiopia. Does it not reflect negatively on Eritrea's side? Perhaps it is the lack of the requisite skill or will on the part of its leadership, at least at that point in the mediation process. Note that during the Algiers process, when Haile Woldensae (Dru'E) was the lead Eritrean negotiator, a level playing field seems to have developed, on which the Americans ultimately weighed in on the matter contrary to the desire of the Ethiopian side, as will be explained below.

As for the Eritreans'disappointment with Susan Rice, it became evident in the matter of the U.S.-Rwanda proposal. My first informant, who was present at the meeting, when Isaias used "rough language" toward Susan Rice, told me that the Eritrean side was disappointed with Susan Rice for taking the U.S.-Rwanda proposal to Ougadougou and using the OAU forum to bring pressure to bear on Eritrea. This information seems to tally with Tekie's view.

What, then, was the U.S.-Rwanda proposal? Before the conflict had degenerated into a full-fledged war between the two countries, a peace plan was offered jointly by the United States and Rwanda, on June 3, 1998. The joint U.S.-Rwanda peace plan was as follows:

1. Both parties should commit themselves to the following principles: resolving this and any other dispute between them by peaceful means; renouncing force as a means of imposing solutions; agreeing to undertake measures to reduce current tensions; and seeking the final disposition of their common border, on the basis of established colonial treaties and international law applicable to such treaties.

2. To reduce current tensions, and without prejudice to the territorial claims of either party: a small observer mission should be deployed at Badme. Eritrean forces should redeploy from Badme to positions held before May 5, 1998; the previous civilian administration should return; and there should be an investigation into the events of May 6, 1998.

3. To achieve lasting resolution of the underlying border dispute, both parties should agree to the swift and binding delimitation and demarcation of the Eritrea-Ethiopia border. Border delimitation should be determined on the basis of established colonial treaties and international law applicable to such treaties, and the delimitation and demarcation process should be completed by a qualified technical team as soon as possible. The demarcated border should be accepted and adhered to by both parties, and upon completion of demarcation, the legitimate authorities assume jurisdiction of their respective sovereign territories.

4. Both parties should demilitarize the entire common border as soon as possible.

It is in the nature of things that the response of the two parties to peace plans throughout the mediation process would differ depending on: (a) the belief of the party concerned on how the plan would affect its interests; and (b) the military advantage the party concerned has over its adversary. In other words, each party wanted to negotiate from strength.

Ironically, the U.S.-Rwanda peace plan that Eritrea rejected would, in essence, be the same as the final plan that became the basis for accord signed at Algiers. The reason why Ethiopia accepted the U.S.-Rwanda peace plan was that Prime Minister Meles considered it to be consistent with Ethiopia's demand in that: (a) it required Eritrea to withdraw from Badme to "positions held before May 5, 1998;" and (b) the civilian administration (of Ethiopia) would return to its previously-held positions in the Badme area. Eritrea was opposed to both requirements.

Eritrea considered this an unfair concession to Ethiopia, objecting in particular to the requirement that Eritrea restore the Ethiopian administration to the areas its forces occupied. The statement Eritrea issued on June 3, 1998, argues that "the question of temporary administration of the civilian centers in the demilitarized areas could be handled with necessary flexibility in the interim period, as the jurisdiction of the sovereign state would be reinstated as soon as the demarcation of the boundary on the basis of the established colonial treaties is completed." In other words, Eritrea wanted the redeployment of

Eritrean forces to positions held before May 6, 1998, to wait until demarcation of the border was completed.

The United States and Rwanda expressed grave regrets at Eritrea's refusal to accept their peace plan, and Ethiopia exploited this to the maximum. Prime Minister Meles issued a statement in which he blamed "the continued aggression of the Eritrean government...."

He directed the defense forces of Ethiopia "to take all necessary measures against the repeated aggression of the Eritrean Government and to safeguard the territorial integrity of the country...." He also called on the Ethiopian people to take all the necessary actions for safeguarding the country "according to directives to be issued by organs of the Government and the Defense Forces of Ethiopia." In other words, he took immediate steps to prepare Ethiopians for war.

I must note, in passing, the differences in the style of leadership of the two sides. Those differences are partly based on the different systems of government, and are in part due to the difference in the personalities of the two leaders—a difference that I describe in chapter 5. Meles consults with his parliament and Cabinet of Ministers; Isaias has no time for such niceties. Yet, as we shall see below, in his speech to the OAU Central Organ meeting in Ouagadougou on December 17, 1998, Meles did not mince his words in painting a picture of Isaias as an aggressive leader hell-bent on conquest.

Commenting on the U.S.-Rwanda peace plans, Tekeste and Tronvoll wrote, "Ethiopia's seeming duplicity in simultaneously accepting the peace plan and ordering the country's armed forces to prepare for military action—operationalized on June 5, 1998, when the Ethiopian air force initiated a first strike bombing sortie on Asmara airport—might to some extent explain the Eritrean position" (Brothers at War, 59). The Eritrean position to which the authors refer was one of skepticism regarding Ethiopia's peaceful intentions in accepting the US-Rwanda peace plan. Eritrean skepticism was not only about Ethiopia's intentions but also about the U.S. role in the mediation efforts. Eritreans' perception of American partiality towards Ethiopia was expressed during the mediation negotiations, in part because of the comparative lack of experience of the head of the U.S. team, Susan Rice.

Earlier expectations by the Eritrean leadership that Susan Rice and another member of the team (who asked for anonymity) might see things their way were naïve. One member of the team told me that Yemane Ghebreab made a statement in a private encounter expecting my informant to be on Eritrea's side. (Interview June 16 2008). According to Yemane, that same person was considered to be partial to the Ethiopian side because of a long-standing friendship with Meles and other top TPLF leaders.

Again, according to Yemane Ghebreab, the U.S. facilitation team was expected only to facilitate communications not to come up with a peace plan. The Americans apparently made serious efforts to persuade Eritreans to see things from the point of view of Meles' internal problems. They thought that Meles was at the time facing a serious challenge from TPLF hardliners who wanted him to make an all-out war and even use the opportunity to go beyond the border to bring about a regime change in Asmara. The Americans wanted Eritrean leaders to understand Meles's position and agree to withdraw from the areas they occupied. The subtext to this request was that if Meles were to be overthrown and replaced by the hardliners, Eritrea would face a much tougher situation.

An unnamed Eritrean leader explained to one of the authors of the *Brothers at War* that the Eritrean leadership rejected this American argument, and that they viewed Ethiopia as a whole unit in the conflict (ibid,. 60). That Meles had faced a serious challenge at the time was later revealed when he quickly mobilized his supporters in the TPLF Central Committee in the nick of time, barely escaping overthrow, a fact that retrospectively justifies the U.S. team's claim. Of the hardliners who posed a threat to Meles' position, only Abay Tsehaie, an old rival of Meles, has survived the purge and remains in the TPLF inner circle under Meles' good graces.

Whether as a function of the internal threat he faced from his adversaries, or for other unknown reasons, Meles decided to bomb the Asmara airport on June 5, 1998. The fact that the U.S. started evacuation of its citizens the previous day gave ground for Eritreans to suspect that the Americans had known about the intended bombing. This exacerbated the suspicion and mistrust that surrounded the mediation efforts. In response to the Asmara bombing, the Eritrean air force bombed Mekele (Tigray's capital), hitting a school and causing casualties among children and thus exacerbating the already-poisoned atmosphere.

Occurring only two days after the U.S.-Rwanda peace plan was announced, these events of bombing and counterbombing did not bode well for the prospects of peaceful resolution of the conflict. Even in terms of its content, the U.S.-Rwanda peace plan was skewed one way. As Tekeste Negash and Trenvoll put it, "The U.S.-Rwanda proposal was formulated and presented in a manner that put the blame for the conflict on one of the parties only, or, at least, it was perceived as such. Since all subsequent negotiation attempts build on the U.S.-Rwanda peace plan, this cemented the position, making it even more difficult to create a space for the two governments to maneuver within." (ibid).

As noted above, the OAU accepted the US-Rwanda peace plan. The conflict between Eritrea and Ethiopia became one of the major preoccupations of the OAU. It was a principal item of the agenda of the 68th Ordinary Session of the OAU Council of Ministers and the 34th Ordinary Session of the Summit of the Heads of State and Government held in Ouagadougou, Burkina Faso (June 1-10, 1998).

Eritrea finally accepted the peace plan and, without prejudice to the final settlement on the sovereignty of the disputed area, agreed to withdraw its forces and accepted the temporary security zone located twenty-five miles inside its own territory. Ethiopia's forces had penetrated deep into Eritrean territory; so that Eritrea was accepting a military fait accompli.

There was a point of psychology involved here—one of pride. Eritrea was reluctant to withdraw its forces unconditionally and considered the OAU's acceptance of the US-Rwanda plan as partial to the Ethiopian side. In his speech to the OAU, Meles poured salt on Eritrea's wounded pride by declaring Isaias a lawless adventurer. Meles continued his accusations that Isaias had attacked all his neighbors and is the source of continued instability in the region. In a speech before the OAU Central Organ on 17 December, 1998, he said:

> In five years, four of Eritrea's five neighbors had been assaulted, attacked. The only neighbor which so far has not been assaulted is Saudi Arabia. It is anybody's guess when and if this is going to happen. So Your Excellencies, there is a pattern of behavior here; Ethiopia was attacked as part of that pattern of behavior. This is not a freak event. This is a pattern of behavior of openly flaunting and openly rejecting the core principles of civilized conduct among nations; of shooting first, and talking later; of undue and exaggerated belief in one's military might and invincibility; of belief in might is right. (Quoted in Tekeste and Tronvoll, ibid).

Dismissing Meles's charges as "shrill and offensive language," Isaias made an attempt to persuade the OAU leaders of the justice of his case by pointing out that the issues of redeployment of forces and civil administration are linked with the location of the disputed area and with the source of the conflict, i.e. who used force, where and when. He continued:

> Since these vital questions have not been determined by an investigation, which Eritrea has been requesting for the past six months, any proposal for redeployment and administration need to take that fact into account. In regard to deployment, Eritrea holds that, with a ceasefire in place and military observers on the ground, demarcation can be done expeditiously without the complicated and time-consuming disengagement of hundreds of thousands of troops. Eritrea, however, has no objection in principle to redeployment in the framework of demilitarization. On the question of administration, Eritrea has repeatedly stated that, like all sovereign nations, it

cannot countenance alien administration of its own territory and over its own population. (Ibid).

Having heard the respective positions of the two parties to the proposals, the OAU Central Organ unconditionally endorsed the proposal for the Framework Agreement proposed by its High Level Delegation as appropriate to resolve the dispute and end the conflict.

The United Nations Security Council, which had not involved itself in the dispute until the beginning of 1999, passed a resolution supporting the OAU initiative and its proposal for a Framework Agreement, affirming that "the OAU Framework Agreement provides the best hope for peace between the two parties." (Resolution 1226 [1999]). The Security Council Resolution urged Eritrea to accept the Framework Agreement as the basis for peaceful resolution. Practically left with no room for maneuver, Eritrea raised procedural issues and this "dragging of its feet" was used as an excuse by Ethiopia to launch a major offensive. While the UN secretary general's special envoy to the region, Mohamed Sahnoun, was in the region, engaged in preparations for negotiations between the parties, Ethiopia launched a major offensive during the first week of February 1999.

Eritrea was caught between a rock and a hard place. On the one hand, accepting the OAU Framework Agreement would mean making concessions to Ethiopia on two key issues of contention—redeployment of its troops from the disputed area that it had occupied and acceptance of the restoration of an Ethiopian civil administration. On the other hand, continued refusal to accept what the entire international community accepted as a reasonable solution (the Framework Agreement) would lay Eritrea open to charges of unreasonableness, confirming Meles' contention that Isaias is a lawless adventurer. Indeed, Meles took advantage of Eritrea's "dragging of its feet," playing a game of poker with the OAU. In a briefing meeting to the diplomatic community in Addis Ababa, Meles praised the OAU for its work and urged member governments of the OAU "to exert all the pressure that you can possibly exert, directly and indirectly, to see to it that the OAU decision is implemented." And with a well-honed cunning, he added:

> Furthermore, we would expect all our brothers in Africa to understand that if some amongst us decide to play poker with the rule of law...if those very same forces have nothing but contempt for our collective decisions and continue to occupy the territory of a member nation, we would not ask you to come to our rescue and fight our wars. That request could be feasible, but we believe unnecessary. That request would be fair, but we believe unnecessary. But

we would expect you to fully understand our right to defend ourselves (Ibid).

After initial air raids on February 3, 1999, the large-scale offensive started the
following day on the Badme-Shiraro front. And as Tekeste and Tronvoll have
commented, "the conflict escalated rapidly into what has been estimated to be
the biggest battle on African soil since the expulsion of Nazi forces from Egypt
during the Second World War" (73).

Ethiopia waged war repeatedly with wave after human wave to overwhelm
Eritrea's positions and finally broke through the defense lines by the end of February. Badme and its environs, the bone of contention, were occupied by Ethiopian forces who drove back the 40,000 strong Eritrean defense forces holding
the lines. Ethiopia gained Badme; so presumably, the question whether Eritrea
accept the Framework Agreement became moot. But did it? Not according
to the Ethiopian point of view. In an interview given to one of the authors of
Brothers at War, Yemane Kidane (Jamaica), a high-ranking TPLF official, said
this:

> The rationale for the Framework Agreement was to avoid a war.
> Now that the war has erupted and we have won back Badme, the
> Framework Agreement is nothing. The conditions on the ground
> have changed, and the OAU process shall continue, they have to
> start over again to clarify the principles on the ground (ibid. 76-77).

Neither the OAU nor the United Nations could "clarify the principles on the
ground," and the deadly war continued through the spring and early summer of
1999, with huge casualties. It is reasonable to argue, as some Eritrean writers have,
that the Ethiopians were aiming for complete victory so that they could impose
terms in future "peace negotiations." Indeed, throughout the mediation efforts,
especially during the Algiers process, the Ethiopian position was intriguing, as
they made attempts to change the Framework Agreement in ways that would give
them a strategic advantage for future negotiations on the border issues. According
to the speech Haile Dru'E gave in Frankfurt, Germany, in the summer of 2000, it
was clear that the Ethiopians expected American-OAU collusion at the summit
in Lome, Togo's capital, to agree to Ethiopian demands, but that they were disappointed to find that the Americans did not comply with their demands.

Haile's speech, in which he pays tribute to the Algerians, as well as to the
final decision of the Americans to foil Ethiopian attempts at tinkering with
the Framework Agreement, contradicts Tekie's belief that the Americans were
biased in favor of Ethiopia. Tekie wrote of the US facilitators' "proclivity to
taking Ethiopia's side repeatedly including their latest tinkering with the OAU
Framework Agreement to appease Addis Ababa" (ibd. 246). In my interviews

with three members of the U.S. facilitation team, I quizzed each one of them about this point. All three said they could understand Eritrean suspicions, but that in the delicate process of negotiations in which mediators try to convince both sides to agree to a balanced and reasonable position, and above all to stop the killing, what they say and do may appear to both sides as partial to one or the other party. There is a sense in which Tekie's suspicions of American partiality are wellfounded; at least in appearance. The main reason is that the Ethiopian team tried to undo the peace package contained in the Framework Agreement, and whereas it would be reasonably expected for the mediators to reject out of hand such attempts, the Americans did not do that. A seasoned negotiator desirous of preventing the negotiations from sliding backward might act in a lukewarm fashion up front, while engaging in some tough talk in the background. This is my understanding of the American approach, based on my interviews with members of the U.S. team, especially with Anthony Lake.

From Ougadougou to Algiers

As is well known, Susan Rice was recalled and replaced by Dr. Anthony Lake as head of the mediation team, presumably following Isaias' disapproval. Anthony Lake had been national security advisor during President Clinton's first term; he was familiar with African affairs, and was well known for his patience and diplomatic skills. Meanwhile the chairmanship of the OAU had been transferred to Algeria's president, Abdulaziz Boutefliqa, and the U.S. facilitation team led by Lake shuttled between Algiers and the two capitals of the belligerent parties. After endless meetings and shuttle diplomacy, the OAU under the chairmanship of president Boutefliqa managed to persuade the two sides to agree to a final accord on the basis of the Framework Agreement, which was basically a rehashed U.S. peace plan.

The protracted mediation leading to negotiations held in Algiers finally ended in the Algiers Accord under which the parties agreed to submit their case to an international arbitral tribunal at The Hague in December 2000. The agreement took place under the chairmanship of president Boutefliqa, with co-mediator, Olusegun Obasanjo, the president of Nigeria. During the signing ceremony Boutefliqa did a Clintonesque act—he got the two antagonists (Isaias and Meles) to embrace in a brotherly hug. Boutefliqa, who was chairman of the OAU that year, succeeded where others failed because of a combination of luck and diplomatic prowess that Algerian leaders seem to possess. It is also likely that the antagonists had been exhausted, and the military issue resolved with Ethiopian troops having penetrated deep into Eritrean territory and having occupied the disputed territory around Badme.

According to an October 28, 2000 press release, coming out at the opening of the talks in Algiers under Boutefliqa's chairmanship, the two parties "renewed their trust and confidence in the Algerian mediation." According to Tekie, the Ethiopians "never felt comfortable because they knew that Algeria, unlike Burkina Faso, was even-handed in its approach and that it was determined to implement the OAU peace package" (Ibid. 247). My interview with Anthony Lake confirmed the crucial role played by Algeria's mediation, particularly by Algerian Prime Minister, Ahmed Ouyahia, who ably represented his president. Though Lake did not go all the way to agree with Tekie about Ethiopians' lack of confidence in the Algerians, he nonetheless confirmed that the Algerians were tough negotiators and did not play footsie with either of the parties in enforcing the OAU Framework Agreement. He also paid tribute to the foreign ministers of both Ethiopia and Eritrea.

In the end the dispute boiled down to three principal issues. The first was ceasefire, or cessation of hostilities, in the language of diplomacy. The second was border delimitation and demarcation. The third was deployment of peace-keeping forces. Additionally, there was the issue of compensation for war damages. The first question was taken care of under the June 18, 2000, Cessation of Hostilities Agreement. With respect to the second question—delimitation and demarcation of borders—the Lome summit also endorsed the June 18 agreement on cessation of hostilities throughout the negotiation process, which Ethiopia had insisted on dealing with the issue through arbitration. According to Eritrea's view, if accepted, this would have the effect of violating the Framework Agreement. Ethiopia's request had been floated in July of 1999 in a Washington, D.C. meeting; and, according to Eritrea's view, the facilitators appeared to go along with Ethiopia's request. At least they did not openly reject it as being contrary to the Framework Agreement (ibid. 246-247).

The mediation process involved, as facilitators/mediators: the U.S.—first together with Rwanda, then without Rwanda—the OAU and the UN. The OAU chairmanship went from Presdeint Campaore of Burkina Faso, to president Boutefliqa of Algeria. Then a funny thing happened in Lome, Togo, on the way to mediating a final settlement of the dispute. The OAU chairmanship had passed from Algeria to Togo; and so the OAU chairmanship was expected to pass to president Eyadema of Togo. To the disappointment of Ethiopia, the OAU summit decided to bypass Eyadema in favor of his predecessor, president Boutefliqa, to continue handling the mediation role. Another sign of a peaceful prospect was the UN Security Council's decision to send its head of UN peace-keeping mission to Eritrea and Ethiopia to start the process of UN peacekeeping in the area of dispute.

So the two parties had no choice but to go through the Algiers process under President Boutefliqa's chairmanship with his able prime minister, Ahmed

Ouyahia, doing the hard work of mediation, working out the nitty-gritty, and Anthony Lake facilitating. In his Georgetown University office, Lake has three posters hanging on his wall of sketches of maps drawn by the Eritrean and Ethiopian foreign ministers and by Ouyahia, indicating their respective versions of the disputed border. He obviously treasures these mementos. As Lake explained it, this sketching exercise was designed to "melt the ice" and reach a human level in the relationship of the negotiators of two adversarial parties. Doesn't this assume that the two foreign ministers had the power of deciding on disputed issues on behalf of their respective governments? Not always, was the answer, but there were times at critical stages in the negotiation when they could influence the course of events, provided they had the courage of their convictions and were not fearful of the consequences in case their respective leaders disagreed.

In this respect, Lake paid special tribute to Haile Dru'E, whom he described as incredibly courageous and one of the toughest negotiators he ever encountered in his career as negotiator. He also repeatedly paid tribute to the Algerians to whom he gave the overall credit for the success of the negotiation arriving at the Algiers Accord.

The Algiers Accord

On December 12, 2000, the two parties reached an agreement in Algiers to submit their case for a binding international arbitration. Article 4 of the Algiers Accord provides, among other things:

1. Consistent with the provisions of the Framework Agreement and the Agreement on Cessation of Hostilities, the parties reaffirm the principle of respect for the borders existing at independence as stated in Resolution AHG/Res.16(1) adopted by the OAU Summit in Cairo 1964, and, in this regard, that they shall be determined on the basis of [principles] pertinent with colonial treaties and applicable international law.

2. The parties agree that a neutral Boundary Commission composed of five members shall be established with a mandate to delimit and demarcate the colonial treaty border based on pertinent colonial treaties (1900, 1902 and 1908) and applicable international law. The Commission shall not have the power to make decisions *ex aequo et bono*.

Ex aequo et bono is Latin meaning "according to what is equitable and good." Under this doctrine, a decision maker is not bound by legal rules and may instead follow equitable principles. The commission is barred from applying this doctrine. According to the agreement, it was required to address three elements: (a) the specific treaties, (b) applicable international law, and (c) the significance of the reference to the 1964 OAU (Cairo) Summit Resolution. The relevant treaties are those of 1900, 1902, and 1908, respectively covering the central, western and eastern sectors of the Eritrea-Ethiopia borders. The commission considered the meaning of these treaties to be a central feature of the dispute. And in interpreting them, it said it would apply the general rule that a treaty is to be interpreted "in good faith in accordance with the ordinary meaning to be given to the terms of the treaty in their context and in light of its object and purpose." (Eritrea-Ethiopia Boundary Commision [EEBC], Decision, Chapter III, 3.4)

The reference to the Cairo Resolution concerns the 1964 decision of the African heads of state and government affirming the colonial boundaries. In the case at hand, the two parties had committed themselves, under the Framework Agreement, to respecting "the boundaries existing at independence," as stated in the 1964 OAU Resolution. The parties reaffirmed their commitment to these principles in the Agreement on Cessation of Hostilities concluded between them in June 18, 2000. The commission found that one particular consequence of the agreement is the parties have accepted that the date at which the borders between them are to be determined is that of the independence of Eritrea, namely, on April 27, 1993.

The UN cartographer was designated, under the agreement, to serve as secretary of the commission to undertake such tasks as assigned to him by the commission, making use of the technical expertise of the UN Cartographic Unit. The commission could also engage the services of additional experts as it deems necessary.

The commission could, and did, commence its work not more than fifteen days after it is constituted; and it undertook to make its decision concerning delimitation of the border within six months of its first meeting, with discretion to extend the deadline.

Upon reaching a final decision regarding delimitation of the borders, the Commission was required to, and did, transmit its decision to the parties and to the secretaries general of the OAU and the United Nations for publication. It was further required to arrange for expeditious demarcation.

The parties agreed to cooperate with the commission, its experts and other staff in all respects during the process of delimitation and demarcation, including the facilitation of access to territory they control. Each party agreed to accord to the commission and its employees the same privileges and immunities as are accorded to diplomatic agents under the Vienna Convention on Diplomatic Relations. The parties also agreed that the delimitation and demarcation determination of the commission would be final and binding, and that they would respect the borders so determined, as well as their respective territorial integrity and sovereignty.

Final Decision

As is well known, the problem of demarcation became intractable. We will consider this issue in the next chapter.

Chapter 9

NEIGHBORS THAT SHARE FIRE: BORDER DISPUTE AND PROXY WARS

———⟩⟨———

We have seen how so much hope had been pinned on the new governments emerging in Ethiopia and Eritrea after the fall of Mengistu's dictatorship in the spring of 1991, and that the hope proved illusory. What had seemed the dawn of a new era to the peoples of the two countries, who had passed a nightmarish experience for almost two decades, turned out to be wishful thinking unsupported by hard facts.

The new leaders, personifying the mystique of liberation fighters, lent credence to people's hopes and expectations of a better future. The mystique carried with it the belief that a freedom fighter does no wrong—a freedom fighter does not lie, does not deceive, does not steal, etc. Hopes and expectations had rested on such belief, a belief that was divorced from the reality. The fact that the first few years were marked by cooperative arrangements between the two governments fed the peoples' yearning for peace and prosperity, reinforcing false hopes, a dream of a bright, peaceful, and prosperous future.

The 1998-2000 war put an end to this dream. The war taught us all a lesson on the fallacy of hope—hope that the victims of war would not resort to war; hope also in the orderly progress of societies that had suffered oppression. The doomed alliance between the two governments, as much as the devastating war in the two poor countries, led commentators to describe the war variously as tragic, unnecessary, useless, fratricidal, etc. The fact that the two governments were wasting scarce financial and other resources on the purchase of arms lent poignancy to the tragedy, to say nothing of the loss of lives and the displacement of millions of people on both sides of the border.

Zero Sum Game of a Deadly Kind

An unresolved legacy of the 1998-2000 war is the "border dispute," the flashpoint that fired the war and, as we saw in the last chapter, remains unresolved.

Legally, the dispute over ownership of Badme, as well as other areas lying along the Eritrea-Ethiopia border was settled by the decision of the Eritrea-Ethiopia Boundary Commission (EEBC). The EEBC, which was constituted on February 20, 2001, pursuant to the Algiers Agreement of December 12, 2000 that ended the 1998-2000 war, handed down its decision on April 13, 2002.

According to the decision, some land claimed by Eritrea is to be returned over to Ethiopia, and some land claimed by Ethiopia is to be turned over to Eritrea. In the latter category is included Badme, the flashpoint of the war, a fact that would seem to vindicate Eritrea's claim that it did not invade Ethiopia because Badme has now been determined to be Eritrean territory. However, the commission put the blame squarely on Eritrea for starting the war rendering a decision that seems to be carefully calibrated in awarding territories along the long-disputed border to both sides and ordering that actual demarcation; that is to say, translating the map coordinates into pillars on the ground, to be done with the assistance of expert cartographers.

Unfortunately, implementation of the decision has been stalled for over eight years as we go to press. The two parties agreed to abide by the decision of the EEBC, and the decision is crystal clear; but the two sides have been expressing conflicting views regarding implementation of the decision. Indeed, each side has made ominous statements that give ground for fear that another war might break out. On November 26, 2006, EEBC notified the two sides that it would not wait indefinitely; that it would place the border coordinates on a map it provided as an annex, and that if the two parties do not demarcate the border, following the boundary points on the 1:25000 scale map it developed via a UN cartographer, or allow the EEBC to demarcate the border by November 2007, the boundary points (which are developed by high-tech gadgetry and accurate to within one meter) would be the legal border between the two states. This EEBC determination was rejected by the parties for different reasons: Eritrea contending that demarcation on the map is "a poor substitute for demarcation on the ground"; Ethiopia arguing that demarcation on the map is "a decision [that] is devoid of any legal force."

On first view, it would seem that the two sides are putting forward arguments to harden their respective positions and thus keep postponing the final solution of the "border dispute." On the face of it, Ethiopia's argument seems to be based less on technicalities and more on human considerations concerning the affected local populations. The contention is that, in consideration of the people in the border areas, there should be discussion on implementation of the demarcation. Eritrea argues that there is no room for discussion, since the Algiers Agreement makes the decision of EEBC final and binding. The EEBC, for its part, has consistently stated that, while the two parties are free to discuss and make changes that are mutually agreed to, it does not have the mandate to make changes.

The points of divergence between the two sides appear to boil down to the following:

Eritrea wanted to limit the discussion to article 4 of the Algiers Agreement that deals with the border demarcation. Ethiopia's response to this is that article 4 has to be considered together with article 1, which deals with cessation of hostilities. Subarticle 2 of article 1 in particular is related to the Temporary Security Zone (TSZ) and the UN peace-keeping mission (UNMEE). The EEBC was not impressed with Ethiopia's position and responded by asserting that its mandate is limited to demarcation. In an evident note of frustration, it finally declared that if the two parties are willing to provide free and secure access to its staff to position pillars, it would be sufficient to carry out its mandate.

Reviewing the transcript of one of the last meetings of the EEBC, one is struck by a Kafkaesque sense of the absurd or, to change the figure of speech, the exchange among the parties sounds like the proverbial dialogue of the deaf. The protagonists talk past each other, not to each other; and the EEBC president and his colleagues agonize over a problem that seems like an insoluble equation, trying to get the parties to talk to each other. The parties' legal representatives, who ordinarily would help untie the knots and help the commission in arriving at a fair and reasonable conclusion, are handicapped, as they are performing their professional duties as "officers of the court" by being obliged to do the bidding of their respective clients (bosses). They cannot make concessions without authorizations by the latter.

In view of the deadlock and the exasperation of the EEBC, as expressed in the final warning of its president, one is bound to wonder whether what is at stake is a contested national interest rather than a contest of wills between the two feuding leaders. The Eritrean side has been insisting on an unconditional implementation of the binding arbitral decision of the commission. The Ethiopia side, on the other hand, points to practical problems that would affect people on the border areas unless discussions are held to make adjustments to accommodate communities that might be badly affected by the new boundaries. To drive this point home, Prime Minister Meles, in an interview given in Tigrigna used a homely expression describing the relationship of the people on the border areas. He called the neighboring local people *melaminti hawi* (neighbors of fire, or neighbors sharing fire) to indicate the closeness of the various communities that have lived side by side and that would be adversely affected unless discussions are held to make the necessary adjustments.

Nobody can dispute the principle that the interests of the people should come first. In an ideal situation, the people of Eritrea and Ethiopia, given the chance, would mobilize to help provide solutions to this seemingly insoluble problem. This seems to have been in the mind of the EEBC president, Sir Eliahu Lauterpacht, when he made the following agonized but helpful statement:

> It is up to you to work out how to implement it [the decision]. It is up to you to consider such devices as open boundaries so that some of what you identify as manifest absurdities because a line cuts village[s] or a road several times can be overcome by allowing boundary to be open and nationals to pass freely from one side to the other or even cultivate their fields on the other side. *Those are not matters for us, those are matters for you.*

In the face of such admonition, nothing more needs to be said on this matter. In these circumstances, if a frustrated cynic were to exclaim, "A pox on both your houses," who could blame him?

A way must be found to end this absurd zero sum game. As we have seen, each side has stuck to its position. In terms of legality, Eritrea's insistence on implementation is obviously wellfounded, grounded as it is on the outcome of the binding arbitration. But Ethiopia's insistence on a human consideration, on remembering the populations that would be affected by automatic implementation, cannot be dismissed out of hand. How can one ignore what lies behind the homely phrase of neighbors sharing fire, as elucidated by the nimble Meles? He has thrown the moral gauntlet at his archrival's feet. And Lauchterpact's call for mutual accommodation—"those are not matters for us, those are matters for you"—puts extra pressure on Eritrea.

The title of this chapter, Neighbors That Share Fire—invoked because of the close, neighborly relations between the people of Eritrea and of Tigray living along the border—is a compelling phrase that reminds all concerned of the simple life of peasants who depend on one another for simple domestic needs like fire. In the absence of matches, when fire is out in one household, that household takes it from its closest neighbor. Meles was making the point about people living on either side of the border, people who share a common culture and face the same hazards, be they natural or man-made.

The point about the longstanding neighborly relation between the two peoples across the border is not a matter of subjective judgment of interested parties. It has been the subject of scholarly writings and journalistic comments. For example, Richard Reid, who toured the border area, scene of the war, immediately after the end of the war in the summer of 2000, notes the complexity of the nature of the relationship, but also gives many examples attesting to the longstanding amity and general good relations, on the basis of lengthy and varied interviews of villagers, with a few people expressing views about Tigrayan "duplicity," especially among some veteran liberation fighters.(Reid, "Old Problems and New Conflicts," 2003 Africa, 375-376). On the basis of his research, done along the border areas, in the wake of the war, Reid notes:

> There is the idea that good relations had always existed across the border, that highland communities on either side of the Mereb River were indelibly intertwined, shared cultural links, were socially involved with one another (in terms of weddings, funerals and religious feast-days, for example), and were commercially dependent on one another.(ibid, 377).

As already noted, the point about sharing fire has been invoked as emblematic of the closeness of relationship of the people living along the disputed border. Fire is a vital domestic item in peoples' lives. Fire can also be destructive, and thus the symbolism of fire can extend to war. The war reportedly caused by the unresolved border dispute may have ended; but it has been replaced by a condition of no-war—no-peace. An expression of this condition is the fact that the two states support opposition movements against one another. Daniel Ayana, an Oromo scholar has expressed the matter eloquently thus:

> Fire is the source of life, regeneration, and rebuilding. From simple cooking to the preparation of farmland, fire is the necessary ingredient to sustain life. For industrial societies fire symbolizes power, passion, energy, and love; a variation on the same theme. On another level the difference between pre- and post-industrial societies can be gauged by the magnitude of taming fire for life necessities. Yet in reasonable societies, reasonable men and women tame fire to produce basic life necessities. The idea of taming fire on a large scale is a road everybody imagines, but less traveled in the Horn of Africa. (Ayana, October 18-21, 2007).

Professor Ayana extends the logic of his analysis on the uses and abuses of fire by contending that what he calls unreasonable men persist in trying to adapt the world to their own desire. Applying his analysis to the case at hand, Ayana writes, "Unreasonable men formed different organizations under different names to mobilize reasonable men. While many failed, only two, Isaias and Meles, succeeded militarily as leaders. Reasonable men expected from these successful new leaders a new project of taming fire on a large scale instead of the continued ...use of fire in creative destruction." According to this analysis, the process of "creative destruction" promotes itself "with an invisible hand" of the seduction of power; and the unreasonable men resent the reasonable men's demand for freedom, and the two worlds collide. It is a valuable insight explaining why two highly intelligent and seemingly reasonable men have been the cause of so much destruction. And the fire has spread across national boundaries in the form of proxy wars.

Proxy Wars: Manifestation of Deadly Feud

Both Eritrea and Ethiopia have been involved in the ongoing conflict in Somalia.

Their involvement is an expression of the yet unresolved conflict between the two countries. The Hobbesian condition of post-Siyad Somalia has left the country virtually without a state. The forces that were opposed to the Siyad regime and that played a part in overthrowing the regime fell out among themselves, leading to chaos and warlordism, inviting foreign intervention. Several efforts were made to create a government of national unity involving a constellation of clan-based political groupings. Every time such attempts were made, there would be disaffection and breakup, until finally a government of national unity was formed calling itself the Transitional Federal Government (TFG). It was supported by most interested foreign governments including Ethiopia; indeed Ethiopia sent elements of its armed forces to back the coalition TFG.

Meanwhile, several factions of young Somali men were not only critical of the slow process of reconfiguring the Somali state but were disaffected by the nature and behavior of the state itself as well as by what they saw as a slowly decaying civil society; decided to reclaim Islamic Sharia as the only way to resolve Somalia's perennial unrest and chaos. These forces eventually coalesced into the Union of Islamic Courts (UIC) and openly and vociferously challenged the coalition government backed by Ethiopia and other states. One or two factions of the UIC espouse extremist Islamic tenets and are said to have links with Al Qaeda.

Somalia thus became an object of US interest in its campaign against international terrorism in the aftermath of the September 11, 2001, attack on America.

Somalia and Ethiopia

From the time of September 11, 2001, when America's foreign policy was dominated by preoccupations with international terrorism, complications began to occur in the politics of the Horn of Africa. This politics involved the intervention of the rival governments of Eritrea and Ethiopia in Somali affairs, each side being intent upon advancing its own national policy. Ethiopia's intervention took the form of dispatching a large military contingent to Somalia at the end of 2006, on the face of it, to hunt down Islamist extremists wanted for alleged terrorist activities. Whether this intervention was done at the behest or with the encouragement of the United States has been disputed; but there are indications that there had been consultations between the two governments. U.S. assistant secretary of state for African affairs, Jendayi Fraser, hinted at an antiterrorist pact between Washington and Addis Ababa beyond the declaration of the anti-Saddam Hussein "Coalition of the Willing." The United States wanted to hunt down terrorists, including those suspected of blowing up US embassies in Kenya and Tanzania in 1998.

Following Ethiopia's intervention, several Somalis, who also hold citizenship in other countries in Europe and North America, were captured by Ethiopian troops on suspicion of being associated with Islamic terrorists, and this created an uproar with Ethiopia being accused of creating another Guantanamo center in its own territory and allowing American special agents to interrogate the captives. Meanwhile, the intervention that was conceivably designed as a short-term surgical operation turned out to be a deadly occupation with some unexpected complications. Attacks were launched against members of the Ethiopian armed forces by armed guerillas belonging to factions of the UIC. What had been planned as a mopping up operation to help the TFG get rid of the Islamic forces ended up in entangling Ethiopians in a Vietnam-type war. Not only were the Islamists not defeated; they dispersed regrouping in smaller guerilla units that attacked Ethiopian troops and even Ugandan peace keeping troops. President Musseveni apparently decided to send troops as a gesture of good will toward the Ethiopians and perhaps to curry favor with the Americans. And when his troops became the target of missile attacks from UIC, he traveled to Eritrea to beg Isaias to use his influence with the UIC to cease and desist from carrying out the attacks. Isaias, who was sojourning in Massawa, received Musseveni there, reportedly told one of the leaders of the UIC factions not to attack the Ugandan troops, and the attacks had stopped. Eritrea had become a player in Somalia's messy politics. Unfortunately for Uganda, the Islamic extremist faction of the UIC, the Shabaab, carried out a terrorist attack in Kmpala during the Soccer final match in July 2010, killing over seventy people. In the aftermath of that attack, US congressman Ed Royce called on the US government to declare Eritrea a terrorist sponsoring state.

Eritrea's Role in Somalia

There is an ongoing debate as to whether Eritrea's involvement in Somali affairs was an act of solidarity with the long-suffering Somali people, and a payback for Somalia's support of the Eritrean struggle, or whether it was an exercise in power politics of the worst kind in which people have become pawns in the conflict between the two feuding Habesha leaders—Meles and Isaias. The response given by Isaias to the charge that he was supporting terrorist groups in Somalia is that he was motivated by a desire to help the process of Somali national reconciliation and unity—a "reconstitution" of the Somali state, as a he repeatedly calls it in several interviews, (for example, in interviews with a Swedish journalist, a *Financial Times* journalist, a BBC journalist and a German radio journalist). During the final days of the George W. Bush administration, U.S. assistant secretary of state for African affairs, Jendayi Fraser issued a threat that Eritrea might be placed on the list of Terrorist Sponsoring States. The U.S. claim that Isaias had supported terrorist groups in Somalia was backed by a UN Monitoring Group making the same accusations. Her warning fell on deaf ears.

In the latest accusations of providing help to the Shabaab Islamic extremists, the U.S. ambassador to the United Nations, Susan Rice, warned Eritrea on the same subject in the wake of a UN Security Council resolution condemning Eritrea for its role in Somalia. The UN Security Council resolution supports an African Union (AU) resolution condemning Eritrea for supporting Islamic extremist groups. In early August 2009, the U.S. Secretary of State, Hillary Rodham Clinton, issued a stiff warning to Eritrea to stop providing aid to the Somali Islamic extremists, threatening that "action" would be taken by the U.S, government.

At about the time when Frazer issued her charge accusing Eritrea of being involved in supporting terrorist groups in Somalia, and for some time thereafter, Asmara was hosting Somali dissident groups, including members of UIC's leadership such as Sheikh Hassan Dahir Aweys. Far from relenting, Isaias seemed to be defiant in the face of a serious charge that, if sanctioned by the United States, as Frazer seemed to suggest, Eritrea could be in dire straits. His response to the latest warning and to the UN Security Council resolution, as well as to the AU resolution is the same as before—defiance. Is his behavior a gambler's bluff, or is it the act of a true believer defying the world's lone super power in a manner of Fidel Castro of old or of Hugo Chavez today? But Castro had Soviet backing, and Hugo Chavez has his oil wealth to bank on. What or who does poor Eritrea have? China? The European Union? If Isaias believed this, he might as well have believed the Brooklyn Bridge is for sale, as the New Yorkers say.

All of the above reflection proceeds on the assumption that the U.S. threat would or might be carried out. Some believe that the U.S. has become a toothless old bulldog and was too preoccupied with Iraq and Afghanistan to bother about tiny Eritrea. In any case, the Bush administration was in its last days, and Isaias might have thought that it would not undertake any new and costly actions. It is reasonable to assume that Isaias might have banked on that fact, as well as on the unwieldy nature of the U.S. government, with the State Department and the Pentagon locked in endless bureaucratic battles on most issues of international security. Others argued that the "Bushies" were hell-bent on smashing international terrorism, and that if they did indeed believe that Isaias was helping Islamic terrorists in Somalia, they would impose sanctions on Eritrea.

Whichever of these theories is correct, two things have become clear in retrospect. First, Meles made an error in invading Somalia. His original plan was premised on quick victory and early withdrawal, ensuring a TFG take over from then on. It didn't work out according to that plan; and he became entangled in a Vietnam syndrome, facing a cruel dilemma: If he withdrew his troops, the TFG would collapse and the Islamists would take over, returning Somalia to the status quo ante. So, he stayed—with some horrific consequences in loss of life, both Ethiopian and Somali. Second, Isaias, an inveterate gambler, was risking everything to create a problem for Meles; thus his policy of destabilizing the Meles regime.

Isaias Afwerki's interest in post-Siyad Somali affairs goes back to the early days when he favored Mohamed Aidid among the warring factions. Why he favored Aidid over his rivals is not clear; it could be personal chemistry or his perception of Aidid being a strong man and able to dominate the others. But Aidid was no less a war lord than Abdullahi Yousuf, the president of TFG, which raises the question why Isaias was favoring Islamic extremists against a secular former warlord. The only answer to this conundrum is that Isaias supported the Islamic extremists because Meles was against them, acting on the old logic: The enemy of my enemy is my friend.

What are the implications of the mutual hatred and seemingly endless feud in which these two erstwhile comrades-in-arms are locked for both their two countries as well as for the Horn of African region? And what is the Obama administration policy going to be in that regard? All indications are that America is stcking with supporting the Meles government, banking on the thinking that Ethiopia is committed to fighting international terrorism, particularly in its manifestation in the form of the Somali Shabaab, who are believed to have links with Al Qaeda. Nonetheless, judging by the statements of State department officials with regard to Eritrea, there seem to be hopes of bringing Isaias back to the fold. The question becomes: How can U.S. policy makers reconcile Meles and Isaias, who seem to be on a collision course, demonstrated by the unresolved border dispute; the U.S. government has been either unwilling or unable to cause the implementation of the verdict of the Hague Commission. A joint U.S. European Union strategy to untie this "Gordian knot" may offer solution; but the outlines of such a policy are not yet visible. Meanwhile, Isaias keeps maintaining a defiant posture, even flirting with the Iranians.

The following section will put the matter in historical perspective.

The Horn Region and US Strategic and Geopolitical Interest

From the onset of the cold war in the late 1940s, the Horn of Africa has been of interest to American strategic policy. It was in terms of that interest that the right of the Eritrean people to self-determination and independence was denied in favor of Emperor Haile Selassie's demand that Eritrea be joined to his empire. Former secretary of state, John Foster Dulles' 1950 statement in support of Ethiopia's claim, and in denial of the justice of the Eritrean cause, was plain and unadorned with diplomatic niceties. Dulles said:

> From the point of view of justice, the opinions of the Eritrean people must receive consideration. Nevertheless, the strategic interest of the United States in the Red Sea basin and considerations of security and world peace make it necessary that the country has to be linked with our ally, Ethiopia.

At that time, the Soviet Union and its satellites opposed the U.S. and supported Eritrea's right to independence. International relations being what it is, however, when a reversal of alliance occurred following Mengistu Haile Mariam's ill-fated romance with the Soviet Union, the Soviets changed their original support and opposed Eritrea's independence. In international relations, there are no permanent friends and permanent enemies; only permanent interests, as noted before, quoting nineteenth century British statesman, Lord Palmerstone.

In the post-September 11, 2001 world, international terrorism has replaced communism as the adversary of choice in U.S. strategic thinking. The Horn of Africa region, and especially Somalia, is an area of great interest in that respect, partly because of the chaos that followed the fall of the Siyad Barre regime in 1990, and in part because of the emergence of extremist Islamic forces. Add to that the context of increased Saudi (*Wahabist*) influence, which provided a breeding ground for extremism.

After the ill-fated Black Hawk incident in the first few months of Bill Clinton's first term, in which American soldiers were shot down and their bodies dragged through the streets of Mogadishu, shocking American sensibilities, the American intervention dubbed "Operation Restore Hope" that president George Herbert Bush launched in response to the humanitarian disaster was terminated by his successor, Bill Clinton. In the wake of the withdrawal, and in the absence of a security umbrella provided by a lawful and authoritative government, Somalia descended into chaos characterized by famine, warlordism, and violence—a Hobbesian condition of the war of each against all. Not until September 11, 2001 and the appearance of Islamic extremists, did the U.S. policy makers revive the idea of intervening in Somalia, but not in the direct form of the early 1990s. Once more Ethiopia assumed greater importance in the scheme of things from U.S. strategic interest.

Ethiopia is the core of the Horn of Africa region, geographically and in other respects. That Ethiopia should be the center of attention for U.S. (and other) policy makers should, therefore, come as no surprise. In the years following the fall of Mengistu's regime and the advent of the current government, Ethiopia has been a favored recipient of assistance. Partly because of this, but in part because of America's partiality to Ethiopia historically, many Eritreans believed that the Americans took Ethiopia's side in the 1998-2000 war between the two countries. Some claimed that U.S. satellite pictures of Eritrean troop positions were made available to Meles. Whether this claim is true or not, the subjective belief among Eritreans played a part in their perception of the American attitude toward Eritrea then, and continues today, fanned by the periodic anti-American attacks made by Isaias.

Eritreans generally believe that the American government has not exerted the necessary pressure on Ethiopia to implement the decision of the EEBC requiring demarcation of the border; and to Eritreans, this is proof positive of U.S. partiality toward Ethiopia. In Eritrean minds this translates into U.S. bias against Eritrea; and considered in the historical perspective of U.S. denial of Eritrea's independence, revives old fears, including a suspicion that the United States may even favor a reversal of Eritrea's independent statehood. The party platforms of Ethiopia's main opposition forces, especially the CUD have not accepted Eritrea's independence, reinforce such suspicions.

It is necessary to pose some questions in order to clear away such fears and suspicions.

First, do the U.S. policy priorities of favoring Ethiopia include a negative bias against Eritrea?

Second, if so, does such bias extend to encouraging or tolerating Ethiopian intransigence?

Third, is there any sign of any kind indicating U.S. support for the demands of extremist Ethiopian parties for the reversal of Eritrea's independent statehood or for lopping off the port of Asab and it environs and giving it to Ethiopia, as some extremists have demanded?

As regards the first question, there is no way of proving the existence of such bias at the highest government level; such bias may be purely personal, based on individual subjective feelings. In the recent past, especially before independence, some American diplomats and policy analysts have been known to voice negative views about Eritrea's viability as an independent state, citing internal divisions and comparing Eritrea to Lebanon. A prominent proponent of this stance was Paul Henze. But even those who voiced such biased views came round to supporting Eritrea' independence after the EPLF military victory and also praised the Eritrean leadership until the 1998-2000 war.

The answer to the second question is covered by the answer to the first question. Moreover, in the experience of the present writer, the relevant officials in charge of the Ethiopia and Eritrea desks at the State Department, going through regional directors right up to the assistant secretary of state, from Susan Rice to Jendayi Fraser, have been even handed, despite official Eritrean complaints to the contrary. In all fairness to Jendayi Fraser, her apparent bias, particularly after her statement on Eritrea's support of Somali terrorists, must be seen in the context of Isaias Afwerki's policy of support of the Union of Islamic Courts led by Aweys and the shabaab, and his behavior, refusing to meet with U.S. officials, including Jendayi Fraser, at their facilitation missions.

In actual fact, there was a time during the armed struggle when Eritrea's historical victimization and underdog status as well as the proud history of its lonely fight had earned it a rare place of honor and a fund of goodwill before it was squandered thanks to the behavior of its leader. Certainly, both during the mediation efforts at the height of the 1998-2000 war and after the decision of the EEBC, there had been no record of U.S. government bias favoring Ethiopia to the detriment of Eritrea. The Ethiopian government's foot dragging on the question of demarcation of the border, and the American government's failure to induce appropriate action from the Ethiopian government, would seem to have more to do with internal Ethiopian politics than with American support of Ethiopian resistance. Nonetheless, some Eritrean writers disagree with this assessment, arguing that the international community (meaning the United States and the United Nations that does its bidding) is unfairly biased in favor of Ethiopia. For example, Redie Berketeab writes:

> Broadly speaking, the international community and many scholars and commentators seem to have agreed with Ethiopia on the basis of the simple but apparently compelling logic that might is right. They seem to think that because Ethiopia had won the military confrontation, the EEBC should have rewarded Ethiopia by awarding it Badme (Redie Bereketeab, 2010: 111).

The scholars/commentators that he claims support such a position are Zondi and Rejouis(2006); Healy and Plaut (2007); Clapham(2003); and Plaut (2005).

In apparent conflict with this position as far as American policy is concerned is a statement in favor of enforcement of the EEBC ruling made by one US State Department officer that I personally heard. During the brief period of my membership of the leadership of the Eritrean Democratic Party, I was part of a delegation that met with Ms. Connie Newman, Jendaye Fraser's predecessor as assistance secretary of state for African affairs. When we suggested to her that the US position was lukewarm at best, and biased at worst, in response she told us that she had recently told Seyoum Mesfin, Ethiopia's foreign minister, that the US position was that Ethiopia must implement the EEBC verdict on demarcation, much to his chagrin, according to her. We had no reason to doubt the veracity of her statement.

As pointed out before, the reason for Ethiopia's delay in or resistance to implementing the EEBC ruling has been explained by Prime Minister Meles in terms of the practical difficulties it would create to some local communities if implemented without adjustments. Eritreans, including some Eritrean writers, respond by invoking "Tigrayan duplicity." There is also local political resistance on the part of some TPLF hardliners, a constituency that Meles is apparently careful not to alienate

As to the third question whether American policy favors the revanchist elements of Ethiopian politics that want to reverse Eritrean independence, one way to answer this hypothetical question is to look at what Meles and other top level members of his party and government say regarding the issue of Eritrea's independence; for US diplomacy is aligned to support Meles in view of the convergence of interests concerning the fight against international terrorism. For example, some of the extremist factions of CUD, if not its mainstream, lay claim on the port of Asab as rightfully belonging to Ethiopia and demand that the Ethiopian government should take aggressive steps to make good that claim, arguing that such steps should include the deployment of international diplomacy aimed at the "recovery" of Asab. Meles' answer is a much needed lesson in history: that such a demand is based on the wrong assumption that Eritrea was originally joined with Ethiopia in a federal union in the early 1950s through diplomacy. He reminded them that the federal arrangement made by the UN to join Eritrea with Ethiopia was done in response to the divided voice of Eritreans, with one segment (the highland Christians) favoring union with Ethiopia while the other segment (the lowland Muslims) favored independence. His advice to the revanchists and to everyone else—and this during an election—was to forget about recovering Asab or any other part that is Eritrean.

In view of this, it is fair to ask: why hasn't Meles taken the necessary steps to implement the EEBC ruling and get on with the job of demarcation of the border? Is his thesis of the *"Melaminti Hawi"* (Neighbors that Share Fire) based on a genuine concern of potentially divided communities along the border areas, or is this a clever ruse? On the face of it, a concern for local communities seems a rational and reasonable position for a leader to take. And his request for talks that would lead to an adjustment of borders to accommodate local communities accords with basic human values. So, the question becomes: Why is Isaias allergic to such talk? Does he consider such talks as capitulation or surrender of principles? Is it a matter of pride, or is it a tactical ploy designed to maintain a status of tension the better to make life difficult for Meles?

Now, if the claim that local political considerations of not wishing to anger or alienate local Tigrayan communities and their leaders is true, wouldn't acceptance of the offer to talk and complete the demarcation strengthen Isaias's hand in his feud with Meles? That is to say, assuming Isaias wants demarcation and eventual normalization of relations between the two countries. That is an assumption that may be false, particularly if it is the case that Isaias is wedded to a strategy of no-peace—no-war; and the allied strategy of continuing a proxy war in Somalia to weaken Meles. If that is the case, there will be no border demarcation as long as Isaias is in power. On the other hand, if Meles is also wedded to the same strategy on the belief that it will eventually lead to the fall of Isaias, this too will ensure a continued tension with the consequent problems to the Eritrean people, especially those who live in the border area.

Chapter 10

THE "BERLIN MANIFESTO" AND THE G-15: A SQUANDERED OPPORTUNITY

There are moments throughout history that mark a turning point. By the same token, when the significance of such moments is either not perceived by historical actors as such or not acted upon with sufficient alacrity and due care with eyes fixed on the future, such moments can be classified as missed opportunities. The events surrounding the action taken by the people who have become known as the G-13 and G-15 surely belong to such turning points in postindependence Eritrean history.

There is also a sense in which the two—the G-13 and G-15—are related, though not in the way that the Isaias regime's spinmasters have attributed to them. Contrary to what the regime's leaders have said, there was no collusion or even any contact between the members of the two groups. However, one group's daring and timely action inspired or emboldened the other. The G-13's letter to Isaias, though meant as a private communication between the group and the president, was leaked to an Eritrean website, Dehai. The letter, variously called the Berlin Letter or the Berlin Manifesto, (see appendix I) seemed to galvanize Eritrean public opinion and revive the somnolent opposition in the Diaspora. One way to describe the immediate effect of the letter is to say that it, or rather its writers, became radio active, at least in the eyes of Isaias loyalists. The latter were caught unprepared for the deluge of public sentiment against the war and the way it was conducted, which the Berlin Letter highlighted. They lost no time in castigating the writers of the letter as traitors to the cause of Eritrean sovereignty and territorial integrity. The regime's supporters and mouthpieces abroad echoed this tune and talked about the dire consequences of criticizing a government in time of war when the very survival of the nation was at stake. etc., etc.

The Berlin Letter was private; its writers never wanted it to be public. How it was leaked is the subject of great mystery worthy of investigation by the likes of Sherlock Holmes. And the leak became the main bone of contention at the meeting the G-13 group had with Isaias in November 2000, convened at his own request. But whoever is responsible for leaking the letter, once it entered the public domain, thanks to the Internet, it produced unexpected results with historic significance. One of the results is, of course, its catalytic effect on the emerging conflict within the higher echelons of the PFDJ; conflict that had been simmering below the surface and that the debacle of the Badme War brought to the surface. Indeed, one of the pleas expressed by the letter writers (the G-13) was to urge Isaias to resolve his differences with his erstwhile comrades-in-arms and friends in view of the imminent danger facing the unity of the nation.

Contrary to some earlier impressions by some members of the public, the G-13 was not a political group. It was a random gathering of Eritrean academics and professionals who were gravely concerned about the fate of their nation in the wake of the third offensive in the 1998-2000 war when, in the early summer of 1999, Ethiopian troops had broken through the defense lines of the Eritrean Defense Forces (EDF) and penetrated deep into Eritrean territory. As expressed in one of the paragraphs of the Berlin Letter, there was genuine fear that the very independence of the country might be at stake. Needless to say, the supporters of the Isaias regime did not have a monopoly on patriotic feelings and concern, though they obviously think they do.

The Different Effects of the Berlin Letter

Due to the bold and timely action it took, the G-13 group was generally viewed with awe and admiration by many concerned Eritreans in need of reassurance at a crucial point of their nation's life. The Isaias regime, on the other hand, considered it as a subversive group out to discredit and destroy the president and his government. Presumably in a state of panic, Isaias resorted to cyber warfare in defense of his regime, making wild accusations. In one of his postings on the Internet, written under a pseudonym, he asserted that I was the initiator and organizer of the G-13. The name Isaias used as a pseudonym was Bereket Fedai Niguse, and he unhesitatingly put the blame of the work of the G-13 on me because of, as he put it, my "inordinate hatred" of him. The Tigrigna words he used were "...*kitur Xil'i silezelewo.*"

When I read that, I became convinced for the first time that the man suffered from paranoia. As it happened, far from hating him, I had sung his praises for years, much to my regret later. Yet the man believed I hated him. I was intrigued by his insistence and remembered the words of an American journalist, a reporter of the *Washington Post.* It was in July 1991, at the end of a press conference in Addis Ababa held by both Meles and Isaias on the occasion of the conference convened by Meles and his victorious EPRDF party.

The journalist had tried to engage Isaias in a discussion concerning the issues of Eritrea-Ethiopia relation at an auspicious moment when relations between the two countries were at their best. Isaias not only frustrated her, but his manner was dismissive and rude, in stark contrast to Meles' smooth and poised performance. It is possible that Isaias was frustrated by being upstaged by Meles, whom everyone praised and lionized. The American journalist herself saw the contrast between the two leaders. Her remark regarding his behavior has stayed with me as a perceptive and haunting question; for she had wondered wistfully: "Why do I have the feeling that this man wants me to hate him?" Her question reflects disappointment with her attempts at ingratiating herself with him, which had been coldly rebuffed.

Speaking of Isaias and hatred, in 1975 a cousin of mine, who is more prescient in such matters, once used disparaging language in describing Isaias in a conversation with me, judging him harshly on the grounds of the reported case of the group that he eliminated in the early 1970s—the group known as Menka'E. My cousin had known some of the members of the group, notably Yohannes Sebhatu, who had been his classmate when they were students at Haile Selassie I University. I remember getting cross with my cousin and telling him about many positive things that I had seen in Isaias, having dealt with him in my capacity as founding chairman of ERA, in the first few months of that year. And I always try to bear in mind my own initial open support and positive view of Isaias as a factor in explaining why his comrades-in-arms tolerated and even supported him while he committed atrocities over the years. It is not fair to blame others in light of one's own judgment, proving how easily one can be misled into believing, based on first impressions and superficial knowledge, complex and deceptive characters like Isaias.

My Namesake, the Mystery Man

Before relating the story of how the G-13 happened to meet in Berlin and write the famous (or notorious, depending on your viewpoint) letter, I need to mention one curious fact that adds to the mystery of the whole episode—the identity of Bereket Fedai Niguse. I was told by an informed source that there actually exists an Eritrean by that name who lives somewhere in the mid-west of the United States. My informant knows this man personally and believes that he is not only known to Isaias but that he is in contact with him. I asked the inevitable question: Does this man know that his name is being used as a pseudonym in a vicious campaign—that is to say, assuming that he did not write the piece himself? My informant did not know the answer to that question, or whether the real Bereket Fedai Niguse did his best to avoid him. But he did find out that a brother of Isaias is a close friend of Bereket Fedai Niguse and lives in the same area of America. Moreover, according to my informant, the real Bereket Fedai Niguse is utterly apolitical and does not have a capacity to write the kind of politically sophisticated piece that appeared twice on the Internet bearing his name. So, one has to wonder why such an unaffected person would allow his name to be used in a scandalous campaign. The question will remain one of the mysteries of the whole curious episode, and will perhaps become fodder for future researchers.

Before we were informed that there is a man by that name, another Eritrean, personally known to me, wrote a response to the article boldly asserting that Isaias was the author of the piece and rebuking and ridiculing him for using a name like "...Fedai Niguse" with its subliminal suggestion of royalty and revenge. And out came a reply to the response stating that the author was indeed who he said he was—Bereket Fedai Niguse—and that he (the writer of the response) was mistaken in assuming otherwise. It was at this point that my informant told me that there was indeed a man carrying that name, that he was a former student in the Soviet Union who studied science and that he had never involved himself in politics of any kind, including the politics of liberation during the armed struggle, unlike other fellow Eritreans studying there.

We were convinced that the author was Isaias, and this was on the basis of two factors. One was the style of Tigrigna, which resembled that of Isaias. The second factor, and the clincher, was a passage in the article making reference to a conversation he claims to have had with me in the recent past. The reference coincides with a conversation I had with Isaias during an interview I conducted with him (for a book project) in the winter of 1997-1998. I had never had a talk of any kind with any Bereket Fedai Niguse; nor did I know anyone by that name.

One of the blessings with which I am endowed is a good memory (knock on wood!). Evidently, in writing thus, Isaias had forgotten the fact that I had conducted the interview in which I said what he claims that I said. A liar or simulator easily forget facts and contexts; and the truth has a way of emerging to dispute and discredit the lie. Clearly, the habit of simulation and lying has become second nature to a man who uses it as part of his armory in waging his own hidden struggle, for years, against contestants to his power—real or imagined . It had become second nature and continued even after the end of the armed struggle.

The Authors of the Berlin Letter and Its Reception

Who were the thirteen Eritreans who met in Berlin in late September, 2000 and how did they come to get together?

The majority of them are academics and professionals who live in the United States and Great Britain; the rest live in different parts of Europe, and one lives in South Africa.

Of the thirteen, two would defect and make their peace with the Isaias regime for different motives, which need not detain us. One, the poet, Dr. Rusom Haile, died a few years later. The group's professional background ranged from medicine, science, law, accounting, public administration, and literature. In terms of political affiliation, half of them were members or supporters of the EPLF; while the other half comprised members or supporters of the ELF and nonaffiliated, independent supporters of the liberation struggle. What united them and got them all to meet was a keen sense of national sentiment and patriotism.

The venue was chosen because a German foundation offered to fund the conference, and one of the conditions made was that the meeting take place in Germany. In the press fallout that followed the publication of the letter, the person who facilitated the funding, who happened to be an Eritrean with German citizenship, was singled out for vicious calumny by the regime's attack dogs. Even her name was sliced and diced in an attempt to paint her as an Ethiopian loyalist, even though she was known to be an Eritrean patriot who had made a significant contribution to the cause of national liberation.

Evidently, Isaias and his close collaborators in the PFDJ inner circle had become disturbed by the Berlin Letter. Its publication coincided with the emergence of a free press in Eritrea with many veteran EPLF fighters writing as reporters and editors of several newspapers. Immediately after it appeared on the Internet, commentators began calling the letter the "Berlin Manifesto." This fact of naming such a document a "Manifesto" brings to mind other manifestos of history, like the Communist Manifesto of 1848, which announced to the European world the coming struggle to be led (as it was asserted by Karl Marx) by the emerging and suffering European masses. Indeed, Marx had proclaimed in it his famous thesis, "The history of the world has been the history of class struggle."

The Berlin Letter, so named because it was drafted at a meeting held in Berlin, as already mentioned, had become a weapon of struggle by disaffected Eritreans, including those elements of the government and party who were thinking of raising issues of democratic transition and asking for the implementation of the constitution. Perhaps that was why it was called the Berlin Manifesto; some Eritreans even believed that the thirteen academics and professionals were a proto-political party committed to challenge Isaias and his PFDJ party.

As we shall see in more detail below, the members of another group, the G-15, seized on the political opening provided by the letter to make their own specific and historic challenge, and Eritrea's new private newspapers afforded them the opportunity to voice such challenge. It was a brief but exciting period—so exciting that I called it "Prague Spring," comparing it with the short-lived democratic opening in Czechoslovakia in 1968. With breathtaking speed, the reporters and editors of the newspapers conducted interviews with prominent members of the government and the party, who were eager and willing to give their comments. These veteran EPLF leaders, who had been nursing hidden psychic wounds inflicted by a ruthless leader and former comrade-in-arms, seized on the open season of freedom of the press and vented their feelings and expressed their views to the amazement of the reading public. It was literally incredible—people could not believe their eyes, reading criticisms of the regime's politics of domination and exclusion, accompanied by demands for the implementation of the constitution and democratic transition.

Alas! The "Prague Spring" of free expression was to be short-lived; but it left in its wake a mixture of hope and bitter disappointment. A struggle ensued between Isaias—a hard-boiled, ruthless leader and his inner circle, determined to hold on to their monopoly of power—and a few prominent veteran leaders determined to challenge Isaias, demanding democratic change. The opposed group of veteran leaders that ended up as the G-15 began with a larger membership; but as the Isaias regime reacted with a vicious campaign of recrimination and fabricated allegations of treason, only fifteen were left standing their ground and facing the consequences—the wrath of Isaias and his party machine.

The Contents of the Berlin Letter (See Appendix to this book)

As mentioned before, the writers of the Berlin Letter became known as the G-13, because they comprised thirteen individuals. They were academics and professional people who took it upon themselves to address a personal letter to President Isaias, gravely concerned as they were about the fate of the country in the wake of the Badme debacle. The Eritrean public seized on every word of the letter and gave it their interpretation to suit their various purposes. The seven-page letter was couched in courteous terms but was unusually bold and assertive. It addressed Isaias as Mr. President, even though most of the writers begrudged the fact that he was an unelected dictator who imposed his will on the nation by force, not by law.

The letter is divided into eight segments, including an introductory paragraph that acknowledges the contribution Isaias had made as leader of the EPLF in the national liberation. It then expresses grave concerns about the potential peril that the nation faced in the wake of the Badme War. It commends the heroic role of the Eritrean national defense forces whose tenacity and willingness to sacrifice saved the nation. It engages in a critical national self-interrogation, inquiring how we came to this point of peril: How did the two countries rush to war, and why couldn't the conflict be resolved through peaceful means, including with the help of the mediation efforts of third parties?

A matter of great concern to the authors of the letter, and one on which they lay heavy emphasis, was the humanitarian disaster befalling Eritreans, both those who had been displaced from the areas affected by the war as well as the over 70,000 Eritreans and Ethiopians of Eritrean origin who had been expelled by the Ethiopian government. On the issue of Ethiopians living in Eritrea, the G-13 commended the reported humane handling by the Eritrean government of Ethiopian residents in Eritrea and urged the government to follow international norms in future handling of issues of foreigners living in Eritrea. The G-13 condemned the Ethiopian government's violation of the human rights of Eritreans and made a commitment to help mobilize support for the victims of such violations. At the same time the letter is critical of the way our government dealt with private voluntary organizations including those that stood by us during our long liberation struggle.

Perhaps the single most important segment of the letter, and one that most probably irked Isaias, was the G-13's using the occasion of the war to question some of the policies and politics of the government and his leadership style. The letter makes reference to the collective style of leadership followed during the armed struggle in which there was a modicum of accountability, and it condemns, in no uncertain terms, the abandonment of that style in favor of "one-man rule."

The letter writers believed in the primacy of unity and reconciliation. They remind all concerned that it was by such unity and resolution of differences that we achieved our independence. The letter goes on to urge the leaders of Eritrea and Ethiopia to resume the earlier spirit of amity that existed between the two governments. It further reminds the government leaders of the need of creating the right environment to enable individual citizens and groups to make their fair contribution in the reconstruction and development of the war-ravaged country. It points out that the absence of such an enabling environment has damaged our society and induced a sense of hopelessness and alienation among a significant segment of our population.

Reiterating the role of collective leadership and accountability during the struggle, the letter boldly asserts that the time-tested style was abandoned and that Eritrea is being ruled by one man. It laments the fact that many of the veteran leaders were sidelined and frozen for reasons that are not clear. "It is not clear to us," the letter says, "why they are not being utilized to make their contribution at a time of national peril" during the ongoing war. The letter poignantly reminds the president that an individual, however gifted, cannot match or replace the collective wisdom and capacity at the disposal of many veteran leaders. This point was and is indeed a sticky one to Isaias, for he had refused to ask for the contribution of veteran leaders whose role in the liberation war was crucial, including people like Mesfin Hagos, Petros Solomon, and Uqbe Abraha, all of whom had made critical contributions to the success of the victorious EPLF army. All these and others could have made a difference in the outcome of the war had Isaias asked them to take part in the prosecution of the war.

There have been stories to the effect that all of them reported for duty, offering themselves for military service in defense of the nation in its hour of peril; but they were rebuffed. Isaias apparently thought he could snatch victory in a war of his own making. He did not want to share the glory with anyone else. Indeed, some commentators argue with good reason that Isaias might feel upstaged because he did not play an active part in the frontline, though he was commander-in-chief of the EPLF army, especially during the last years of the liberation struggle when leaders like Mesfin Hagos, Sebhat Efrem, Petros Solomon, and Ugbe Abraha each played crucial roles in the frontline leading to Eritrean victory over the Ethiopian army. The fact that the rank and file *tegadelti* idolized people like Petros and Mesfin did not sit well with Isaias; and some commentators argue that Isaias provoked the Badme War in part because he wanted to claim victory alone and thus nullify, or at least water down, the glory attributed to others in the liberation war.

One of the issues the G-13 looked on with disfavor was the role of the PFDJ party in the political and economic life of the country, pointing to the unhealthy (incestuous) relationship between the party and the government. The Berlin Letter makes a serious recommendation that there should be strict separation of party and government, and that the private sector of the economy should be left to play its rightful role in the economic life of the country. The domination of the PFDJ-based economic organization in the economic life of the country militated against the idea of foreign capital investment coming into the country; and this has hurt the economy and society.

The letter's concluding paragraph deals with the ratified constitution of 1997. The letter demands the implementation of the constitution immediately, without any precondition. It mentions the fact that the constitution was the result of popular participation, that it represents the culmination of the Eritrean struggle for which many gave their lives, that it was the property of the people, and that no one has the right to change it, or tamper with it. The letter complains that much of the practice of the government is contrary to the letter and spirit of the constitution and is, therefore, a mockery of the constitution. For this reason, and for many others, the constitution must be implemented immediately.

The G-15 and their Dilemma

Many a postmortem has been done on the "mistakes" of the G-15. Some arm-chair commentators dismissed the G-15 as naive. The contention of such critics is that the members of the G-15, being veterans of the liberation war who knew Isaias very well should have anticipated his negative reaction. Are such comments fair and accurate, or did the commentators wise-up after the event, a sort of "Monday morning quarterbacking," to use an American sports metaphor?

The criticism raises several other questions:

First, what else could the G-15 have done, and what other options were available to them apart from a peaceful demand for change?

Second, did they discuss other options, and why did they stick to democratic dialogue with its risks of failure?

Third, who were these people anyway, and what exactly did they do?

The answer to the first and second questions offered by critics of the failed attempt is that the group should have planned a mini coup, placing Isaias under arrest or even taking him to a remote place where he could do no harm to them or to their cause. An extreme suggestion is that they should have killed him. There are unconfirmed reports that one of them had suggested this last drastic step, but that his suggestion was readily rejected by all the others.

Were they willing and able to use coercive methods? There is anecdotal evidence that coercive methods were discussed, and that most of them opposed it, being of the view that it would land the country in a spiral of violence that would defeat the aim of democratic change and discredit the overall aim of our revolutionary struggle. One of them is reported to have vigorously argued against coercive methods, saying that we Eritreans did not engage in such protracted struggle to end up like other African states engaged in military coups. It is worth pointing out that this sentiment of Eritrean "exceptionalism" is a sort of a double-edged sword; while it can be the source of legitimate pride in view of Eritrea's heroic struggle, it can also produce in non-Eritreans a resentment leading to charges of arrogance.

All questions about whether the G-15 considered the use of coercive means assume that the members of the group had control over any military unit to enable them to do that without repercussions? Even if any one of them or all of them had such a power or control, it is anybody's guess whether they could have accomplished it without bloodshed? More importantly, would a decision to use coercive methods have led to division and conflict between pro-Isaias and ant-Isaias forces, thus leaving the country vulnerable to foreign attack? One writer at least has answered this question with an unhesitating yes. The prolific political commentator known as Berhan Hagos has written several pieces on this question. In one of his writings (*Bro Q's Afe'Arkbu*, posted in Nahrnet.com, February 24, 2009, Berhan argues that the approach of the G-15 "was absolutely correct and wise in foresight and hindsight." Expanding on his point he asks his readers to consider several points as follows:

> As we recall, the G-15 pursued legal means to address burning issues
> of the day in 2001 because they wanted to create a positive prece-

dence. Knowing PIA's (President Isaias Afwerki) political antics, had G-15 pursued to remove the regime by force in 2001, other problems could have been created precipitating civil war in Eritrea worse than the situation today:

a. The Eritrean population could have been divided into pro-PIA and anti-PIA camp creating a possible bloody conflict. The fact that more Eritreans have awoken to PIA true nature in 2009[sic] doesn't mean they carried the same views in 2001.

b. Similarly, Eritrea's leadership could have split into power-competing groups resulting in infighting if a more forceful approach is used. The fact that PIA is using illegal means to maintain power wouldn't have justified the use of illegal means to remove him. Had G-15 used illegal means to remove PIA, their illegal actions would have torn the reform movement and our long-term inspirations.

c. The vast majority of Eritreans living abroad, and many within Eritrea, could have condemned G-15 for pursuing such dangerous acts while the border problem remains unresolved.

d. Generally, based on persistent lessons of human history, those who attain power through coups and violent means are most difficult to dislodge.

e. If chaos was to ensue in Eritrea, this could have given Ethiopia impetus to reinvade Eritrea in the hope of ensuring the outcome of the border or attain their ultimate motives.

The writer of these words does not seem to have any doubts about the possibility of worse things happening had the G-15 resorted to coercive means. He seems to think that it is better to err on the side of caution than regret later and, in the circumstances, he is probably right. In any case, in choosing the path of dialogue with a man who does not believe in dialogue, the G-15 gambled and lost, paying with their freedom and some even with their lives.

The third question we posed above concerns the identity of the members of the G-15. Who were they, and what was their historic role? To understand the events of 2001 that ended up in the arrest and detention of the majority of the G-15 as well as the editors and reporters of the private newspapers, we need to give some background narrative of events that culminated in the historic confrontation and fallout. It is also necessary to give a sketchy profile of the principal leaders who challenged Isaias in the post-Badme War.

First then, some background.

Background to the Historic Confrontation

There is a sense in which the challenges of the G-15 are linked to the Berlin Letter. That document broke the frightful silence that had enveloped the nation, giving voice to a hitherto gagged population, including members of the government, and opening the floodgate of criticism of the policies and politics of Isaias Afwerki. The coincidental opening of a free press, owned and operated by young veteran fighters added momentum to the cause. Several members of the G-13 knew members of the G-15. Indeed, some were comrades-in-arms during the liberation war. But, contrary to the claims of the Isaias regime, there was no organic connection between the two groups in any shape or form beyond sharing a common belief in democracy and the rule of law, as ordained in the constitution.

To understand the source of the historic confrontation, a brief review of the structure and operation of the EPLF leadership, and the place of some of the principal actors of the G-15 is necessary. The principal members of the G-15 were also members of the EPLF's Central Committee, the "legislative" organ of the front. Six of them had been members of its most important organ, the Political Bureau (Politburo). These were: Petros Solomon, Haile Woldense'e (Duru'E), Mesfin Hagos, Mahmud Sherifo, Okbe Abraha, and Berhane Gerezghiher. As the Berlin Letter points out, the central leadership of the EPLF enjoyed a measure of collective leadership, even as Isaias gradually assumed a monopoly of power, sidelining the other members of the Politburo.

During the first years after the first congress, following the Chinese system, the EPLF politburo had a four-man Standing Committee: Isaias, Romodan Mohamed Noor, Ibrahim Afa and Haile Duru'E, that met every month and was the highest executive organ in between the meetings of the thirteen-man Politburo. The Standing Committee was discontinued after the second congress in 1987.

Despite its dubious value through much of its operation, the notion of collective leadership was useful; at the very least, it provided an institutional structure whereby the group could conceivably exercise a degree of control over the principal leader. The constitution of the front certainly gave the members that power. Paradoxically, the members of the Politburo subscribed to the belief that the fiction of collective leadership had some residual value, as Isaias issued executive orders in its name, while gradually emasculating it. When this became more widely known over time, many ordinary members of the EPLF began to voice criticism of the other members of the Politburo for allowing Isaias to get away with it. They were, of course, bound by the Leninist doctrine of "democratic centralism," which requires obedience by the members of the Politburo—obedience of all the chairman's orders. The Leninist doctrine established a military like chain of command; once a decision had been made, orders flowed from top to bottom—all members from the highest level to the branches had to obey the commands of the superior.

In theory, democratic centralism implies democratic debate before decisions are made. In the EPLF's case, questions were frequently raised by rank-and-file members whether the members of the Politburo exercised their democratic right to advance their views and thus exercise a degree of control over the chairman. Interviews with members of the secret party close to members of the Politburo reveal that, though some of the Politburo members quietly complained about Isaias's growing dictatorial tendencies, they did not take steps to stem it or to organize against it. They were averse to criticizing him or to acting collectively, (a) because they did not trust each other, and (b) because he dominated them intellectually and emotionally. An interview with a former Politburo member made it clear to me that his domination was excused or tolerated because of his "dedicated efforts beyond the call of duty." About the time of the second EPLF congress (1987), there was clear evidence of these tendencies; yet there was no evidence of any collective voice expressed in protest of these tendencies. By the time of the third EPLF congress (1993), it was too late; he had already decided to purge them and replace them with the "new blood" of yes-men who would do his bidding.

To their eternal disgrace, and eventual regret, members of the politburo behaved as though they would never be replaced by others, even as Isaias hinted at it by repeatedly making statements like "the leadership is corrupt" (*Iza meriHnet meshmisha'ya*). Isaias revealed his intentions of an imminent purge to members of the secret party at a secret meeting at Valineki (Adi Nifas) on the eve of the third congress, during which some critical issues of party policy directions were discussed. At that meeting, it became obvious, at least to the clear-eyed members, that the old guard would be changed; only the self-deluding members of the old guard thought that Isaias would spare them from the purge. One clear indication of things to come was the fact that Isaias assigned Yemane Gebreab (nicknamed monkey) to answer some controversial questions raised by members of the party. Yemane would become the top political ideologue of the front, second only to Isaias in that role, and one of the top four members of the Executive Committee, which replaced the old Politburo. This was confirmed at the third congress, where the entire old guard was replaced.

There were a few feeble attempts to challenge the manner of the selection of items of the agenda and the conduct of the meeting at Valineki. But the entire old guard accepted their fate (their defeat) quietly and meekly, even though eyewitness accounts said they could not hide their disappointment. There was nothing they could do about it; hence their meek acceptance of a fait accompli by a master tactician who ruthlessly used them and discarded them when they were no longer useful to him or could pose some challenges to him. Also, most of them were appointed to ministerial posts, which seemed to have mollified them.

When they eventually did put up a challenge, it was too late. Isaias used the cover of the attack on the Twin Towers of New York by Al-Qaeida, while the attention of the world was diverted, to order the arrest and detention of eleven members of the G-15 as well as of the editors and reporters of the ill-fated free press.

The Six Members of the "Old Guard"

What follows is a brief sketch of the six leading members of the G-15 who had been members of the Politburo. The order of their appearance here follows their presumed rank in terms of their political importance or future leadership potential in the eyes of EPLF members and of the wider public, which is of course a subjective judgment and therefore one susceptible to dispute.

1. Petros Solomon

Petros joined the EPLF in 1972, and was elected to the Central Committee (CC) and to the Politburo at the first congress (1977). In the judgment of many people that I interviewed, Isaias regarded Petros Solomon as his natural rival, and thus monitored his movements with extra attention over a long period, including the latter part of the armed struggle, when Petros performed spectacularly as the EPLF's head of military intelligence. Petros possessed all of Isaias's qualities of intelligence, dedication, and single-minded pursuit of his aims. And Isaias knew these qualities. Like Isaias, Petros was indefatigable, working day and night, monitoring all his chief aides at all hours of the day and night, interrogating them, guiding them, and (unlike Isaias) giving them encouragement and needed support. Unlike Isaias, Petros had social skills and a capacity for empathy that enabled him to connect with anyone at any level. He was funny and could make anyone feel at ease with him. All his comrades at what was known as 72 (the military intelligence) adored him, and it was this popularity that marked him as Isaias's primary target, as a man to watch.

As if he had been waiting for the right opportunity, Isaias used the 1993 mini-uprising of the EPLF veterans who challenged his program of work without salary to remove Petros from the key intelligence post, accusing him of neglect of duty for "allowing the uprising to happen!" with an unstated hint that he was behind it. What is worse, in the judgment of many thoughtful Eritreans, in terms of national security and healthy institutional development, Isaias recklessly dismantled 72 thus exposing the nation to hazards that became clear during the 1998-2000 war with Ethiopia. The shadowy institution of military intelligence known as 72 comprised the best and brightest Eritreans with the requisite training and experience suited for the job. I have heard it said that even Isaias occasionally admitted (perhaps after he had had one too many) that Eritrea's independence was secured primarily due to the work of 72.

By way of covering his intentions of emasculating Petros, Isaias "kicked him upstairs" by appointing him minister of foreign affairs. Apart from meeting him socially several times over the years (including during the armed struggle), I had occasion to observe Petros closely in his role as foreign minister, at least three times; on all three occasions, he impressed me with his lightness of touch, humor, and discipline. One such occasion was when he asked me to give a seminar on constitutionalism to his principal aides at the foreign ministry, which included some ambassadors and all department heads. His aim was obviously to show them all his wholehearted support of the constitution making process in which we were engaged. He knew the risk of upsetting Isaias, but he was past caring about that by then.

Another occasion was during the visit of German President Roman Herzog. Dr. Herzog had been president of the German Constitutional Court, before his election as president of the country. Having been informed by the German ambassador that an interesting constitution making process was under way in the country headed by a constitutional lawyer, President Herzog expressed a desire to visit the headquarters of the Constitutional Commission. Foreign minister Petros alerted me to the fact, and that he was acting as his personal escort to visit my office. During the visit we had an interesting conversation with the president as constitutional lawyers on the intricacies of constitution-alism. Throughout the exchange, Petros was like a model student, absorbing everything and saying nothing. A few days later he called me and asked for a few moments of discussion with me on my work. He came to my office, and we had a good exchange on the importance of the constitution to our country's transition to democracy.

The third occasion was a chance meeting at the Asmara airport. We were both going to Addis Ababa—Petros for a meeting with his Ethiopian counter-part, Mr. Seyoum Mesfin; and I for a public meeting to give a lecture to Eritrean residents of Addis Ababa on the process of the constitution-making. We traveled together, and when we arrived at the Addis Ababa airport, Petros insisted that I join him in the VIP lounge where envoys of Seyoum Mesfin waited. The envoys took us to the Hilton Hotel, where the meeting was to take place, and where we met Seyoum Mesfin. What made that meeting memorable to me, and a testimony to Petros's social skill, was the way the two related to each other, laughing and joking about each other, referring to things that now would be misunderstood as politically incorrect. I felt so proud of the two of them, espe-cially of Petros, and was so hopeful of the future of our two countries. Alas! All of that came to naught with the outbreak of war; but there is reason to believe that Seyoum still holds Petros in high regard.

Another person who holds Petros in high regard is veteran journalist and writer Dan Connell. Connell uses, as epigraph for his book, *Conversations with Eritrean Political Prisoners*, a quote from a statement made by Petros that was published in the newspaper, *Tsigenai*. The statement speaks volumes; Petros is quoted as saying, "When confronted with criticism, it is not useful to think in terms of digging up trenches and launching counter-offensives. Criticism should be accepted with an open heart and in an environment of tolerance. No person or institution has a monopoly on wisdom and foresight." (Connell, 2005).

Does anyone wonder who he had in mind when he spoke of monopoly of wisdom or foresight!

2. Haile Woldetensae (Duru'E)

Haile was a close friend of Isaias from childhood. They were classmates at the Lu'ul Mekonnen Secondary School and comrades of the armed struggle from at least the mid- 1960's. The reader is referred to Dan Connell's account of their advent to the field when they joined the ELF, and their disappointments. (*Conversations*, 2005).

Because of conditions that they found unacceptable and unchangeable, Haile and a group of other freedom fighters defected in the summer of 1967; he reenrolled in Haile Selassie I University and completed his university education. He then joined the EPLF in 1972, was captured by the Ethiopian military, tortured and imprisoned until he was liberated by a daring ELF prison attack in 1975 and rejoined the EPLF. I met Haile for the first time in early 1975 in the village of Weki, where Isaias had set up his temporary headquarters. After introducing himself to me and explaining how he was able to rejoin the EPLF, Haile showed me his back which was horribly scarred with beatings that he suffered under interrogation.

Haile was by all accounts the closest friend Isaias ever had; but it is not their friendship alone that explains their collaboration as members of the Politburo. Isaias knew from early on about Haile's intellectual qualities. Haile was one of the best political theoreticians and most eloquent writers of political tracts in the EPLF, at least as far as writings in Tigrigna is concerned.

After the first EPLF congress (1977), and his election as a member of the Politburo, he became head of political affairs in charge of all cultural, information, and educational matters—Tigrigna section. (Alamin Mohamed Said was his counterpart for the Arabic section). In that capacity Haile was in charge of all political education, including heading the school of cadres, which meant he was responsible for the indoctrination of thousands of EPLF cadres. As head of the cultural and information departments, he was responsible for the ideological and propaganda orientation of the organization, including the production of important monthly and quarterly periodicals or pamphlets. Indeed, some Isaias fans with whom I had casual conversations in the United States feared that, in the event of any power struggle, Haile might use the organizational leverage he had acquired by virtue of the fact that hundreds, if not thousands, of high-ranking cadres who had passed through his hands and occupied key positions in the organization, including the EPLF army, might be his basis of support.

What people who entertained such fears might not have realized is that, in addition to his wily monitoring system, keeping all potential rivals on a short leash, Isaias himself selected those who occupied the key positions. To anyone participating in the second congress (1987), as I did, any questions as to Iaisais's popularity were answered by the phalanx of arms thrust forward during the proceedings of election of the Central Committee (CC) of the EPLF. This massive demonstration of popularity occurred during the election of the leadership and after one participant nominated Isaias for the membership of the CC and the presiding officer of the congress asked for someone to second the nomination. It obviously warmed Isaias's heart, for he giggled with pleasure at the sight of the phalanx of arms. Incidentally, the presiding officer at the congress was Haile Duru'E together with Alamin Mohamed Said.

Haile was invariably in charge of the organization's election preparatory committees, as well as drafting its important documents, including the postindependence EPLF charter. After independence he became head of the Department of Economy and Finance; and as such he gave several interviews to the local media and in English to some foreign correspondents, though he showed discretion in not claiming authorship of any documents, as he must have been aware of its effect on Isaias. There had been a cooling of their friendship for a number of years. But the serious fallout occurred after Haile became minister of foreign affairs, particularly over the handling of the Algiers negotiations as we saw in chapter 8. The "crime" attributed to him was a statement he made in Germany during the Badme War in which he admitted that Eritrea had messed up. The exact words he used that were used as a pretext to accuse him of "defeatism" were, *aTalaQiyomna neirom'yom*. The video showing that historic speech has been since distributed widely. It is a very instructive video, showing Haile who repeatedly referred to the Weyane (the TPLF) as enemies, contrary to the trumped-up charges that were designed to mark him and his other fellow detainees as sell-outs and defeatists.

Haile is credited with being the principal draftsman of the "Open Letter to All Members of PFDJ," dated May 5, 2001, which the G-15 distributed to members of the Central Council of the party and the National Assembly, challenging Isaias. Although it is the collective work of the group, the quality of incisive analysis and synthesis for which Haile was known can be discerned in the statement. The document makes a historical review of the experience of the EPLF before liberation (1970-1991) and after liberation. It is a good summary of the record of achievement and failures of the front in a clear, concise but comprehensive manner, providing students of the subject with an important point of departure for study. From that document, it is clear that Haile and the other members of the G-15 were determined to have it out with Isaias and thereby also make amends for their past mistakes in keeping silent while he arrogated power to himself.

One of the guards of the EEra-EEro secret detention camp, who defected recently to Ethiopia, reported that several members of the G-15 and journalists imprisoned with them have died as a result of the harsh conditions of their imprisonment and lack of medical care. The same guard has reported that Haile, who suffers from diabetes, has become blind.

Here is a man who was Isaias' best friend and comrade who spent the best years of his life fighting for freedom and justice. And Isaias threw him into a dungeon where no one can visit him, no medical care of his or his family's choice can be provided, and he becomes blind as a result. He is placed in solitatry confinement where he hears no other human voice, except the occasion clang of iron doors and the silent shuffling of feet pushing his meals by guards who are forbidden to talk to him. He speaks to nobody, knows nothing about his family's fate or of what goes in outside the prison. He is a lonely blind man waiting for death to deliver him from this cruel fate. Can one think of a more horrifying end?

3. Mesfin Hagos

Mesfin Hagos is one of the earliest founding members of the EPLF and one of Isaias' closest comrades. Like Isaias, he went to China for military-cum-ideological training; and like him, he was a member of the ELF, which he abandoned to help form the EPLF. The reasons why they all left the ELF to form another organization is an involved story that has been covered by other writers such as John Markakis and Ruth Iyob. (Markakis, 1987, Ruth Iyob, 1995). In conversations I have had with Mesfin, Isaias and other EPLF leaders, the reason they advance for breaking away from the ELF is that it was impossible to reform it from within; and that their lives and those of others were in danger, following the murders committed against leaders like Kidane Kiflu. The ELF narrative explaining the split and the creation of the EPLF disputes this, stating that there was a reform movement within the ELF that Isaias and the others who split could have helped but that they chose to break away for reaons of personal ambition and sectarian (i.e., Highlnad Christian) reasons. This is obviously one of the issues that historians will argue about for years to come.

Mesfin is the consummate military man—reticent, disciplined, and organized. Though a man of few words, he can be very articulate in explaining his beliefs and positions on any issue. A brief interview with him reveals a mind like a steel trap, but with a social skill deficit. Mesfin was popular among the forces he commanded and respected by his colleagues. His popularity was demonstrated during the election of the Central Council of the EPLF (later PFDJ) at the third congress in 1993. In his strategy to sideline his former comrades (the "old guard"), Isaias had omitted Mesfin's name from nomination for the membership of the Executive Committee. The congress participants, in a rare challenge to Isaias' power, elected Mesfin. In fact he came short by a few votes of upstaging Isaias for being number one. Isaias was forced to appoint him minister of defense, partly in an apparent show of deference to the "common will" and in part in order to use him to appease the restive EPLF armed forces, following the 1993 "mutiny."

As in all other cases, Mesfin's popularity did not sit well with Isaias. Their relationship has been a troubled one from early on. Mesfin was popular with the *Massaween*, the Tigre-speaking members of the Red Sea component of the EPLF formation. They referred to him affectionately as *Wed'Hagos,* speaking with him volubly in Tigre, in which he is fluent, whenever they met. It has always seemed curious to me that he was more relaxed in their company than in that of his own highland Tigrigna group! But there is one member of the *Massaween* whom Mesfin did not seem to like or respect—Romodan Mohamed Noor. Romodan was the titular head of the EPLF for ten years (1977-1987), but it was Isaias, as head of the secret party, who ran things behind the scene, sometimes openly putting Romodan "in his place." It was obvious to any keen observer that Romodan was a mere fig leaf for Isaias's raw power. Apparently, the fact that Romodan allowed himself to be played upon by Isaias displeased Mesfin, as my interview with him made clear (Taped interview in Frankfurt, August 2008).

Isaias had systematically divided the members of the top leadership of the EPLF. Clearly Romodan must have come to the conclusion that there was no point in trying to upset Isaias, whom he held in awe; and it must have been this attitude that led him to become a laid-back leader, and that caused Mesfin to hold him in low esteem. The overall effect of these character traits, exacerbated by the systematic division that Isaias fostered among his colleagues, would have a disastrous effect on the action of the G-15. Mesfin was not on speaking terms with Petros Solomon and Sebhat Efrem. Petros was not on speaking terms with Sebhat Efrem, and neither of them was on speaking terms with Haile Duru'E, who was not on speaking terms with Mesfin, etc. It was a bloody mess, and they knew it; they would not speak about it for fear that it might be reported to Isaias, who would react by demoting them. Human nature being what it is, none of them welcomed demotion; and so things went on forever with Isaias doing what he pleased with no opposition of any kind. They muddled through years of endless, thankless labor of love—until the Badme debacle gave them ground on which to coalesce and challenge Isaias. And Mesfin became a natural anchor on which the group could lean because of his history and popularity with the armed forces. There was obviously a need to mend fences between Mesfin and Petros; in a precipitous but genuine spirit they decided to let bygones be bygones for the sake of the national cause. Their meetings were semisecret; they met in cars, in small groups, and held discussions while driving out of the capital.

There is also the case of Sebhat Efrem. Historians will puzzle over what his role was in all this. He was part of the early discussions, but he decided it was too risky, so he thought personal safety is the better part of valor, and quietly—and perhaps not so quietly—abandoned them. He remains a puppet minister of defense at the beck and call of the commander-in-chief. None of the G-15 has volunteered any opinion on the role of Sebhat Efrem beyond saying cryptically that the whole affair was voluntary, and everyone has the right to be, or not to be, part of it. But there is more there than meets the eyes, and one day it will all come out into the open as to what role the smooth and slippery Sebhat has played.

4. Sherifo

Of all the members of G-15, Sherifo was the one in whom each of them seemed to have confidence. In that respect, and in view of their history of disunity, it is possible that he was the linchpin that held them together through the brief period when they stayed focused on their fateful mission. Sherifo also had the trust and confidence of Isaias until they fell out, as I will explain shortly. Sherifo enjoyed Isaias' confidence for two reasons.

First, Sherifo did not pose any threat to anyone. Though immensely popular, Sherifo did not cause any uneasiness with Isaias because his popularity was of an avuncular kind. Or, to vary the metaphor, it was similar to the popularity of an intelligent jester at a king's court.

Second, Sherifo did not have a solid base of followers that would constitute a threat to Isaias' power. That threat could only come from the Tigrigna group. Sherifo is from the Saho group; and while he might conceivably pose a threat if he had an additional base of support outside that group, he did not seem to have or want to have such support. Sherifo's ambition, if he had any, was perceived generally by the mass of EPLF members to be related to service to the Eritrean cause. Isaias' perception did not differ from the general one—that is to say, until the moment of truth that arrived at the 13th session of the National Assembly, held in September 2000.

An eyewitness account of the meeting (a member of the G-15) told the author of some drama-filled exchanges. According to this informant, the moment of truth unfolded after Isaias appointed Sherifo to lead the committee entrusted with drafting the law on the much-expected political party formation. With apparent belief that Sherifo would not disappoint him, Isaias left to his discretion the task of nominating the other members of the committee. He expected him to choose members that were to his liking. However, to the utter shock of Isaias, Sherifo named Haile Duru'E as the first member. My informant said that he observed Isaias' face when

Sherifo began by naming Haile Duru'E as the first member. Even the tone with which Sherifo announced that choice had a sort of "in-your-face" quality, one of defiance. He told me that the rage visible on Isaias' face was frightful; it was as though he had seen a ghost. The Tigrigna word my informant used was "*xilil ilu*" (He was raving mad). He was speechless; he was crushed.

By the time of this happening, everyone knew that Isaias and Haile had fallen out; and for Sherifo to choose Haile as his principal colleague in the most important committee in the whole attempt at democratic transition—in the historic challenge the G-15 was posing to Isaias—seemed like a deliberate moral slap. But Isaias had gambled that Sherifo would remain loyal to him; that he was just playing along with the G-15 without understanding the dangerous nature of the matter. As it turned out, Sherifo had remained loyal not to Isaias but to the principles for which he had fought. The "court jester" had turned out to be a true believer in the cause of freedom and democracy. And in the weeks that followed, during which Sherifo acted as chair of the committee, he insisted on conducting a popular consultation. Whereas Isaias wanted the committee to report to him, Sherifo insisted that he would report to the body that appointed him, namely, the National Assembly; whereupon Isaias ordered his dismissal and also dismissed him from his post as minister of regional government.

That act by Isaias sealed the fate of the project of democratic transition. The resolution of the 13th session of the National Assembly had required a national election to be held by December 2001. All of that was set aside as Isaas issued a decision dismissing the committee on elections with immediate effect. From then on it was just a matter of a convenient time before Isaias would spring his trap. The opportune moment came with the Al-Qaeda attack on the Twin Towers on September 11, 2001. He ordered the arrest of the eleven members of the G-15 on September 18. They were taken to an unknown place first to Embatkala, and later to EEra-EEro where they have been held incommunicado, ever since.

The rest is history, and Sherifo is an important part of that history. Reports of his death and that of other members of the group have been made by a former guard who defected to Ethiopia, as noted above.

5. Okbe Abraha

Okbe Abraha is (was) a highly respected intelligent and gentle man. He was among many whom I had interviewed for a book I had planned to write in late 2007. He was minister of social affairs at the time; and I found him to be one of the most considerate, courteous and perceptive ministers. At the time of our first meeting in Sahel in the early 1980s, he was in charge of the economic affairs of the EPLF and suffered from severe asthma. Despite that disability, he went out of his way to greet visitors and explain the problems of his work. When I made a request for an interview in 2007, asking for the best time for me to come to his office, he offered to come wherever I was staying, adding, "After all, you are our revered elder"(*ayyan'ndiKa*). I will never forget that; I went to his office of course, and he gave me a lengthy taped interview.

Earlier during the liberation war, following his tenure of the economic department of the EPLF, he was appointed commander of a regiment in the northeastern front, and my information about the role he played during some crucial battles was that it was outstanding. He was also considered an expert on logistical matters in the EPLF army. For reasons that I never discovered, Okbe was dropped from the list of Poliburo members at the second congress, as were Mesfin Hagos, Berhane Gerezghiher, and Mohamed Said Barre. Again, for reasons not made clear, Okbe had fallen out with Isaias but did not complain of or express any form of grievances, behavior that was typical in the EPLF. At the time of the Badme War, Okbe was chief of staff of the armed forces; but, as always, Isaias held the key to all matters, and Okbe was a frustrated man when war broke out. Imagine, the chief of staff of a national armed forces offering his services in a time of war and being ignored. Only in the Eritrea of Isaias! The reports of Okbe Abraha' death in detention has now been confirmed by the guard who defected to Ethiopia. Okbe died before the detainees were transferred from Imbatkala to EEra-EEro. He attempted to commit suicide, and later died of the wound inflicted in the attempt.

6. Berhane Gerezghiher

At the time of the Badme War, and thereafter until the G-15 debacle, Berhane was head of the Eritrean militia, a reserve army that did not cut much ice; it was not endowed with resources. Isaias had not been pleased with Berhane for some reason, for they had been in good terms previously as friends and former classmates at the Prince Mekonen Secondary School. When I first met Berhane in Sahel in the summer of 1975, I was traveling in the field in the company of a member of the German relief group, Asme Humanitas, that did much to help the Eritrean Relief Association (ERA). Isaias assigned Berhane to escort the group, or more correctly, to report on their activities, and mine. Whatever he might have reported in the end, I found Berhane's handling of the German guests appropriate—very civil and helpful. They were very impressed with his assistance. A year-and-a-half later, I learned that he had been elected a member of the Politburo, which confirmed that he was in Isaias' good book.

Berhane was also a good friend of Petros Solomon, and that fact, among other unknown factors, might have precipitated his fall "from grace." As a fairly well educated man and a conscientious one, it is also possible that he may have noticed the dictatorial tendencies of Isaias, wich might have led him to seek change along with like-minded people, including his friend Petros. During the early phase of our constitution making, Berhane was administrator of the Hamasien region (later diced and sliced and renamed Central region, in a diminished size). In conversations I had with him during that time, he showed eagerness to help in the success of the constitutional "enterprise," as he called it. He was a popular administrator and did much during his brief tenure to launch some commendable projects, a feat that couldn't have failed to anger Isaias. The people of the region showed their appreciation at banquets they organized for him on the eve of his departure—another point against him in the eyes of Isaias. For those who need proof of the validity of the saying, "no good deeds go unpunished" let them come to the Eritrea of Isaias.

MEMBERS OF THE CONSTITUTIONAL COMMISSION
OUTSIDE THE COMMISSION'S MEETING HALL
(THE HALL OF THE NATIONAL ASSEMBLY), JANUARY 1995.

COMMISSION MEETING IN NAKFA.
A PEASANT PARTICIPANT MAKING A POINT.

Interview meeting with Dawit Yohannes, Speaker of Ethiopia's Parliament at his office. January 1998.

UNC Chapel Hill campus. Spring 1999, with Wole Soyinka and a Nigerian student.

OCTOBER 2000. ABUJA, NIGERIA, WITH LONG-TIME
FRIEND AND COLLEAGUE GEORGES NZONGOLA.

BERAKI GEBRESELASSIE HOLDING HIS INFANT SON AT
HIS GARDEN. (OCTOBER 1997).

TOKYO, JUNE 1999. WITH ANDREAS ESHETE, DURING BREAK OF
MEETING CONVENED BY PEACE BOAT.

TOKYO, JUNE 1999. MEETING CONVENED BY PEACE BOAT. TO MY RIGHT
IS DR. ASSEFAW TEKESTE; TO MY LEFT IS KIFLE WODAJO.

IDRIS GELAWDEOS DURING BREAK OF MEETING OF THE COMMISSION.

A GROUP OF MEMBERS OF THE COMMISSION
OUTSIDE THE MEETING HALL

Nov. 1997. Mendefera,
A MEETING OF THE REGIONAL ASSEMBLY OF THE DEBUB REGION.

OCTOBER 1997. CHIEF JUSTICE TAEME BEYENE AT HIS OFFICE.

SOME MEMBERS OF THE COMMISSION, OUTSIDE THE MEETING HALL,
DURING BREAK

JANUARY 1995 CONFERENCE, PROF. OWEN FISS PRESIDING.

ETHIOPIAN ARBEGNAS IN MOSCOW. ERITREAN PATRIOT HAILE BEYENE
IS ON EXTREME LEFT OF THE PICTURE. TO THE RIGHT OF THE YOUNG
WOMAN GUIDE.

THE AUTHOR AT THE INAUGURATION OF THE U.S. PEACE INSTITUTE
BOOK, *FRAMING THE STATE IN TIMES OF TRANSITION*.

FIRST YEAR SEMINARS

Please consult ConnectCarolina and the FYS website for the most up-to-date information about FYS offerings and availability.

kings, Presidents, and Generals, led by Professor Bereket Selassie, AFRI 050

AFRICAN STUDIES

AFRI 050: Kings, Presidents, and Generals: Africa's Bumpy Road to Democracy

Communication Intensive (CI); Beyond the North Atlantic (BN)

Bereket H. Selassie
TR, 11:00 am–12:15 pm

This seminar is designed to introduce first year students to Africa's modern history and politics. Starting with a brief, recent history of the continent, we will focus on the variety of systems of government in Africa and the challenges facing them. Traditional institutions, juxtaposed with modern institutions, will be discussed with a special focus on the types of leadership involved in such institutions. A major part of the course will pose questions such as:

- What has been Africa's record in the march toward democracy?
- What are the obstacles to democratic transition and how have Africans tried to overcome such obstacles?
- What are the roles of the constitutional systems and the forms of government in advancing democracy?
- What is the role of leadership?
- What difference does the type of leadership (monarchy, republican, etc.) make in the march toward democracy?

Bereket Selassie is the William E. Leuchtenburg Professor of African Studies, and Professor of Law at UNC, Chapel

Hill. *After over 20 years of engagement in government, law and diplomacy, Professor Selassie chose university teaching as a career. He has always enjoyed teaching, even when in government, and he has been engaged in full-time teaching for 29 years. Professor Selassie's roles in government service have included serving as Attorney General and Associate Supreme Court Justice of Ethiopia, among other positions. More recently, he served as the Chairman of the Constitutional Commission of Eritrea (1994-1997), and he has been a senior consultant on the drafting of constitutions in Nigeria, Iraq, and other countries.*

AFRO-AMERICAN STUDIES

AFAM 050: Defining Blackness: National and International Approaches to African American Identity

Social and Behavioral Sciences (SS); U.S. Diversity (U$)

Timothy McMillan
TR, 9:30 am–10:45 am

America is an increasingly multicultural and diverse nation. And yet, the central concepts of race and diversity are often poorly defined. Racial categories have been used in the U.S. from the earliest colonial times, but their meanings have changed with every generation. What makes a person black in the 21st century is increasingly complex and a subject of much debate. In this seminar, we will focus on politics and race in the U.S. and internationally. How did blackness and whiteness play out in the election of Barack Obama? The intersection of race and educational policy in the US, France, and Kenya will be explored. Position papers responding to films, readings, and blogs; class discussion; and a final documentary project exploring race and society will be used to evaluate students' understanding of the meaning of blackness in the U.S. and the larger global community.

Timothy McMillan is an adjunct assistant professor in, and the associate chair of, the Department of African and Afro-American studies. He received a Ph.D. in Anthropology from UNC–Chapel Hill in 1988. McMillan has taught Afro-American studies, African studies, and anthropology at UNC–Chapel Hill, at NC State, and at Humboldt State University. His research has included fieldwork in Kenya;

ARTICLE ABOUT ME ON UNC WEBSITE WITH MY PICTURE, LECTURING IN CLASS

Chapter 11

THE DIASPORA AND A
DEMOCRATIC OPPOSITION
MOVEMENT

Background and Significance of the Diaspora

It is not generally known that over one-quarter of Eritreans live outside Eritrea. An estimated four hundred thousand Eritreans live in the Sudan, some three hundred thousand in Ethiopia, and another three hundred thousand in Europe, North America, and the Middle East, combined, which is a large number considering Eritrea's total population of four million. Moreover, those living in the Diaspora comprise a significant number of the rising professional and entrepreneurial class, and an increasing number of them are young. The importance of the Eritrean Diaspora is demonstrated by the fact that the annual remittance it sends to the homeland has been the basis of a large portion—if not the largest portion—of the Eritrean government's foreign exchange account, as will be explained in more detail below.

Historically, emigrants from Eritrea to neighboring countries were of three kinds; (i) a few educated men and (ii) many skilled and semi-skilled men and women. The first group comprised highly educated men who were products of early missionary education (both Catholic and Protestant), then sent abroad for higher education, mostly for the priesthood; and eveventually defected to Ethiopia at the completion of their education. The best known cases are Blatengheta Efrem Tewolde-Medhin (Protestant) and Blatengheta Lorenzon Taeza (Catholic); both were high-ranking officials in Emperor Haile Selassie's government who, after their dedicated and distinguished service, ended up as disappointed men soured by the treatment they received from the Emperor and his Shoan kinsmen. There were many others who provided the Emperor's government with much- needed skills at a time when Ethiopia had few educated personnel, notably in technical services.

The second group consisted of merchant adventurers as well as unskilled and semiskilled workers who sought better opportunities for self-improvement in a much larger and richer Ethiopia. An even larger batch of Eritreans, constituting the third group, crossed over the border to Ethiopia, defecting from the Italian army and placing their services at the disposal of their Ethiopian brothers when Italy invaded Ethiopia in 1935. Many of these later served with distinction as part of the liberating forces, both with the returning Emperor Haile Selassie and with the British forces in the southern and easern fronts. General Michael Aman Andom was part of the first group, and colonel Haile Beyene was an exemplar of the second group. For a fuller account of Aman Andom, the reader is refered to Volume 1 of these memoirs. As for Haile Beyene, a great representative of the *Sime Turu Hamasienoch*, he had been among those detained by the British in Kenya, then a British colony, until 1941. Haile Beyene rose to the rank of colonel and head of the Signals department of the Ethiopian army, until an imperial spy falsely implicated him in the Crown Prince's camp (and thus against the Emperor!), whereupon he was kicked upstairs to become a senator. But he remained a highly respected arbegna, i.e., patriot. (See picture).

Following the restoration of his kingdom by British and Allied Forces in 1941, the Emperor named this group *Sime Turu Hamasienoch* (the Illustrious Hamasiens) and gave them land grants at Shashemenna in southern Ethiopia. In those days, Ethiopians referred to Eritreans as *Hamasienoch* (the people of Hamasien). Many of these Eritreans, as well as others who were part of the Italian colonial forces (known as askaris by Italians and as bandas by Ethiopians) decided to remain in Ethiopia. They formed part of two or three generations of a large Eritrean Diaspora in Ethiopia that included many of those who were deported by the Woyane (TPLF) authorities in 1999.

In later years another batch of Eritreans who went to Ethiopia consisted of mostly students who attended the various faculties of the university in Addis Ababa and elsewhere. During the ten-year period of the Ethio-Eritrean federation (1952-1962) and thereafter, until the government of Emperor Haile Selassie was overthrown in 1974, thousands of Eritreans attended these colleges. Countless others also attended secondary and technical or vocational schools. To the students were added workers—both skilled, semi-skilled and thousands of unskilled laborers—who crossed over to Ethiopia in search of a better life. As mentioned in the Introduction to this book, Ethiopian government policy of degrading the industrial capacity of Eritrea led to thousands being unemployed and migrating to Ethiopia and other neighboring countries. Such migrations continued through the 1960s and 1970s; even the overthrow of the Emperor's government did not lead to easing any of the pressures.

Several hundreds of the college and secondary school students joined the Eritrean armed struggle in the late 1960s and early 1970s. Others, who received scholarships from different sources, traveled to the United States, Canada, and Europe for higher studies. In the early and mid- 1980s, these batches were joined by thousands of others, for the most part comprising former members of the Eritrean Liberation Front (ELF). Almost all of these have struck roots in the countries of their refuge, where they received citizenship and many settled down with jobs and families. The first jobs for the majority of these refugees were concentrated in the service industries—hotels, restaurants, gas stations, and working as security guards, and parking lot attendants, etc. Many enterprising types among these continued their education, including learning English, and acquiring skills that landed them in better-paying jobs.

Since the vast majority of these refugees left their homeland, escaping the oppressive Ethiopian occupation, one would expect them to return home following Eritrea's independence in 1991. However, studies show that while many, if not most of them, returned to Eritrea to visit family members, very few have returned to resettle back home permanently. One student of the subject has explained the reason why most decided against repatriation as follows:

> Many did not return home because the home they left does not exist anymore after thirty years of war and destruction. The people they knew are either old, or dead, or have left. Their family members have changed in the long period of separation. Their peers and friends are either dead or have also left the country. Those who stayed have been changed by the thirty-year war and the Dergue's reign of terror. New faces and new people live in the villages, towns, and places they once considered home. Even the vocabulary and linguistic expressions...they used when they were young has changed...they found themselves alienated from the villages, towns, and cities they considered home because their own experience in exile in the Sudan, the Middle East, Italy, and other European countries they lived before being granted refuge in the US has changed their sense of self and personhood....The "home" they know remains only in their memory, which they could cherish and remember while continuing their lives in self-imposed exile (Tekle Woldemikael, 1998).

In the cited study Dr. Tekle also mentions economic reasons to help explain the decision against going back home. Most people earn infinitely more money than they would if they went back to live in Eritrea, their homeland. Indeed, most send money to family members back home who would not survive without such assistance. This fact has become even more important since the article appeared over a decade ago. As conditions have gone from bad to worse, the memory of "home" is a pale imitation of what they once knew—moderately happy families who, though not wealthy, lived better lives filled with hope of better days to come with independence. The disappointed hope added to the worsening condition is an important factor, causing many members of the Diaspora to join or support the opposition movement in one form or another.

The latest batch in the swelling ranks of the Eritrean Diaspora comes from what the Eritrean government dubbed the Warsai generation. The members of this generation are mostly in their twenties and thirties and participated in the 1998-2000 war with Ethiopia. They are veterans of the Sawa experience.

What Constitutes the Eritrean Diaspora?

Much of the following is taken from a paper I presented at the founding conference of a civic organization, Citizens for Democratic Rights in Eritrea (CDRiE), held in London on January 11, 2009, as well as a first keynote address delivered at the symposium convened by Eritrean Global Solidarity (EGS) on June 20, 2009. Both the papers and the following discussion are based on research I conducted over the last couple of years, especially during the spring and summer of 2008.

In recent years, there has been a wave of mass exodus of Eritrean youth. This question of the massive exodus of Eritreans from their homeland to various foreign countries, mostly Europe and North America, is a subject deserving serious study. It should be a legitimate topic for students of political science, sociology or history to research both for academic aims and for organizational purposes. This should be a matter of grave concern for all Eritreans, particularly for organized bodies, be they civic society groups or political parties. The mass exodus has swelled the numbers of the Eritrean Diaspora. The Diaspora today comprises five groups, which are more or less distinct, but which interact with one another socially as members of a Diaspora community, meeting in their churches or mosques or at weddings, funerals, and other social gatherings.

First, there are the active members of the opposition who belong to the various political parties and different civic organizations. Though small in number, these active members have been marked by their dedication and willingness to sacrifice time and money in order to bring about change in Eritrea. The core members of the opposition political parties are former members or supporters of the historic Eritrean liberation organizations, the ELF and the EPLF. Until recently—until the creation of the Eritrean Democratic Alliance (EDA), a coalition of the various factions—the members of the two groups did not see eye to eye for the most part even as they met at social gatherings. Indeed, there was much acrimonious exchange between many members across the factional divide, and a great deal of time and energy has been squandered causing dismay among the rank-and- file Diaspora opposition and causing much delight to Isaias and his supporters; Isaias occasionally referred to the opposition as midgets who were ignorant of the conditions of their country.

One of the effects of the fact of coalescing into the EDA has been to reduce the previous condition of mutual suspicion and recrimination prevalent among the respective members of the historic fronts and to lay down a better foundation for cooperative efforts. The recent movement toward unification between the Eritrean Democratic Party (EDP) and the Eritrean Peoples Party (EPP) is an example of promising developments. But much remains to be done, as witness the yet unfulfilled reunification between the major factions of the former ELF formation, namely, the former ELF-RC (renamed the EPP) and other factions of the ELF. The same is true with the three parties formed by former members of the EPLF. The reason, or basis of disagreement, among the leaders of these factions is almost always found to be nonsubstantial; it can be summed up as personal animosity or conflicting ambitions. Some of it may also be based on grudges held during the days of armed struggle, compounded by personality conflicts or colliding egos. Some of these speculations are based on my own observations during my brief membership in the EDP as a founding member and as an integral part of the original leadership, particularly during the time when the EDP was known as the EPLF-DP, and when I was privy to frequent clashes among some members of the leadership. This is not an opportune moment to go into details on this matter, but I reserve the right to do so in the future.

Second, there are those who provide moral and material support to the opposition but are not engaged in their activities. Their support is based either on their hostility to the Isaias regime and/or on their sharing of the aims of one or more of the opposition parties. There is no available record of their numbers, but it is reasonable to assume that it fluctuates. The reason why members of this group and those in the next group do not come out openly in support of the opposition has to do with their fear that the regime back home might penalize their relatives. It is not an unreasonable fear, but if one could assume a united mass protest, a time might come when the regime would find it difficult to penalize these supporters and their relatives because they would comprise too many people.

The example of the Charter Movement in former Czechoslovakia is instructive in this respect, and worth studying. A proper task of the opposition movement is to imagine or search for the last straw that would break the Camel's back so to speak; the opposition movement needs to continue planning and organizing activities to induce and embolden the Eritrean people to challenge the government. In this respect, there are some encouraging developments back home The reported freeing of detained parents of those living in the Diaspora by elements of the armed forces, if true, should provide a point of inspiration for more courageous action. Any oppressed people need an inspirational point of opening in order to take bold action. The Emperor is naked, but it takes only one daring person to point out that the Emperor is not wearing any clothes for the rest to join in the chorus of denunciation.

Third, there are the passive supporters who are critical of the regime, but who do not come out openly in support of the opposition. It is even harder to know the number of this group. The comments in the preceding paragraph also apply to this group, for it is the same fear that has paralyzed them into silence and submission. When the Emperor is known to be without clothes this group will be among the first to shout the loudest in denunciation.

Fourth, there are the PFDJ supporters. No systematic study has been made aimed at assessing the strength of this group or of any of the other group for that matter; all we have are estimates based on attendance at meetings and rallies. The numbers of this group tend to be exaggerated by agents of the regime. Puzzled people often ask why this group continues to support a regime that has kept a nation hostage and is seen to be bankrupt in all respects. Material interest and downright opportunism is one reason, of course. Land grants expropriated from community-owned traditional property and given for building houses is one material incentive for such people. Another reason is a misguided feeling of validation based on psychic need to be associated with the center of power.

This is particularly true among those educated Diaspora elites who act as the purveyors of the regime's propaganda. The moral blindspot of such purveyors of the regime's propaganda is difficult to fathom, as many of them deny the facts staring them in the face. An example of such facts is the sad spectacle of elderly mothers quietly begging on street corners for alms to feed their starving children. Another is the emptiness of the much-vaunted roads and other "infrastructure"—marvels of the "National Plan." The beguiled elites do not bother to ask why there are no vehicles on the marvelous roads and what is the use of infrastructure while people go hungry?

Fifth, there is the group that we may call the Sawa refugees.

Members of this group are the recent arrivals, the young escapees. A few of these have joined one or more of the political parties; some have joined civic society organizations. The vast majority remain outside of the groups, tending to go with the flow, and concerning themselves with the daily problems of survival and wishing to forget the harsh life they left behind. Many indeed express extreme sentiments about their experience and do not want to be reminded of it or even of Eritrea. They simply assert that they have amply paid their dues and tell recruiters of political parties or civic organizations to spare them preaching about nation and people, which to them sounds like utterly sanctimonious nonsense—Where were you, smart asses, when we were tortured in the dungeons of the regime? They seemed to say. They are bitter, and it is anybody's guess as to whether they can ever be persuaded to recover their faith in the nation that they left behind. Many seem to see their future in the country of their refuge, not in the country of their birth. This is one of the saddest aspects of the current Eritrean reality; it raises some serious questions with deeper implications about Eritrea's future. How many more of such escapees is Eritrea going to lose? If such numbers reached a critical mass, it raises the question of what impact it will have on Eritrea's future as a nation-state; for, after all, the future of a nation is made up of its youth.

The Diaspora and the Opposition

In my recent research travels in Europe, I was informed by members of the evangelical churches that some four thousand of what I called the Sawa refugees have joined their churches. This number comprises those living in the United Kingdom and continental Europe. Apparently, their number is increasing; and as evangelical Christians, they seem to be motivated to lead a purposeful life— to study, get a good job, and raise families—and are better placed to receive assistance from their fellow evangelicals in the countries of their refuge, the United Kingdom being a prime example. Clearly, the opposition, especially the civic segment, needs to consider these Eritreans with all the seriousness they deserve and involve them in their constructive activities. The governing principle should be: All Eritrean must be part of all decisions affecting their destiny as a people.

It would be interesting to find out if other denominations or confessions— be they Christian or Muslim—offer similar assistance. Since providing aid and comfort to Eritrean refugees is of prime importance, it is reasonable to assume that opposition civic societies would look for similar sources of support—official and unofficial—for other Eritrean refugees. In the spring of 2008, a task force comprising a group of Eritreans took the initiative to approach the European Union (EU) for support of the Eritrean opposition. If the opposition civic society organizations could unify their efforts in this task, the EU might open its considerable resources to help refugees in different ways such as support for education and skill-enhancement projects.

It may be fairly assumed that most, if not all, Eritreans share one thing in common—their love of their homeland. Yet they are divided, as we saw, on the question of who supports the regime and who is against it. Whether the majority support the opposition remains unknown. Even the vast majority of the young refugees who escaped from the forced labor camps in Sawa and are dead set against the Isaias regime are not necessarily supporters of the opposition camp. This fact is indeed the great challenge facing the opposition camp. Since the vast majority of Eritreans in the Diaspora have chosen to remain out of the opposition camp, and since the opposition has not so far demonstrated the ability either to change the regime or to cause change in its policies and politics, the question arises: What is to be done? What does the organized opposition, both civil and political, need to do to change the situation? Consider the following options:

a.   continue as before
b.   admit defeat and submit to the regime, forgetting all ideas of struggle
c.   find an alternative framework of struggle.

I cannot imagine anyone, other than the regime's supporters, adopting option *b*. Nor is continuing as before, i.e., option *a,* acceptable to most Eritreans. So the answer seems to be *c.* If that is the answer, then the question becomes what kind of framework of struggle will get us home? Clearly, it would be neither desirable nor feasible to advocate doing away with the present opposition camp. It is not desirable because it is ready-made political and social capital that has a history, capital in which people have invested much in terms of life-time service and dedication. It is not feasible because, human nature being what it is, it is impossible to persuade people who have invested in the political parties and civic organizations to abandon their respective parties or organizations. Indeed, it would be counterproductive to do so.

So then, what is to be done?

Practical Suggestions

1.   First, and foremost, the Diaspora *Opposition must continue their work of opposition*. This is an obvious point but one worth emphasizing in view of the understandable complaints voiced by some citizens concerning the slow pace of movement towards unity among the various parties. There is a clear need to encourage all the existing parties and civic organizations to continue their work and to urge them to redouble their efforts. At the same time, Eritreans need a transformative, transparty, transorganizational body that draws on the organizational and personal capital of the existing opposition camp, but one that goes beyond their factional or corporate objectives and creates a movement designed to arouse the public at large. Such a movement must depend on the fund of goodwill and the variety of skills of all Eritreans, and on innovative, transparent, and accountable leadership.

2.   *National Reconciliation.* In order to accomplish the above-stated objective, a genuine national reconciliation is required. Eritreans need to think "outside the box" of past divisions, whatever their origin and history. Past biases have to be abandoned in favor of a national patriotic goal as summed up in the goal of *Midhan Hager* (national salva-

tion); and to that end, even members of the regime's party, the PFDJ, should be welcomed; indeed, they should be encouraged in one way or another. We presume that they are the silent majority who put patriotic duty or the needs of the country above factional politics. The Tigrigna word *Midhan Hager*, as used here, embraces both the notion of *"salvation"* as well as *"survival."* Salvation implies restitution of the values and ideals that drove the liberation struggle and for which so much sacrifice had been paid. And the idea of survival is invoked because the very existence of our nation may be at stake.

3. *Crime and Punishment versus Forgiveness and Unity.* In order to achieve national reconciliation, it is necessary to let bygones be bygones, that is to say, forgive past crimes committed during the armed struggle. What about crimes committed after liberation? Many would find it hard to accept forgiveness in this respect, particularly in view of the absence of remorse on the part of Isaias Afwerki, who continues to act in a predatory manner, arrogantly dismissing any idea of change or of accepting blame for his errant deeds. Whereas members of the G-15 opened up to the possibility of answering for any past wrongs in statements made to the free press during the "Prague Spring" of 1998, Isaias has never admitted to committing any wrong. The likelihood of his ever doing so is next to zero, which makes the notion of forgiveness and reconciliation in his case a moot point.

4. *The Only Option.* In view of the above, and given the outrageous statements Isaias has made in interviews with several newspaper reporters in which he has defied international public opinion, being hell-bent on continuing his dictatorial rule and disastrous policies with their risk of leading the nation to utter ruin and even state collapse, there remains but one option. The Diaspora opposition and the internal opposition that looks to the Diaspora for guidance is left with no alternative but to unify and effect a strategy of struggle to change the Isaias regime with a democratic system.

As I proposed in my keynote address to the EGS symposium of June 20, 2009, the opposition needs to agree on a common plan of action. To that end, they need to go beyond factional and confessional divisions. They have to leave the divisions of the past behind and agree on an agenda for national salvation, what I have called *Midhan Hagher*. In pursuit of a common agenda, they need to support the emerging progressive websites that are doing a good job mobilizing our people and giving a sense of hope, hope of change, especially to the rank and file of our defense forces. Moreover, civic society organizations and political parties must establish joint committees everywhere—wherever Eritreans live in large numbers—with the aim preeminently of helping new arrivals. The help should include legal and logistical matters such as contacting immigration lawyers with a view to finding housing and jobs and facilitating access to health and educational services. Last but not least, the opposition organizations should establish a coordinating committee to set the above recommendations in motion.

The Diaspora and a Legacy of Division

In the history of Eritrean liberation struggle, the most critical role played in the Diaspora in support of the struggle was by Eritreans in North America, originally known as Eritreans for Liberation in North America (EFLNA), followed by their counterparts in Europe, Eritreans for Liberation in Europe (EFLE). This is not to forget the role played by Eritreans in the Middle East. They too were divided between those under the influence of the ELF (for the most part guided by Idris Gelawdios), and those under the influence of the EPLF, or more specifically the Sabbe wing of the EPLF. The first were organized under the GUES (General Union of Eritrean Students), headquartered in Baghdad, Iraq.

As I elaborate in chapter 13, I will never forget the evening in Baghdad, in the spring of 1975, where I addressed a group of Eritrean students. I had just come out of Sahel, having participated in the conciliation efforts in the ongoing war between the ELF and the EPLF, and then having helped in forming the Eritrean Relief Association (ERA) together with other Eritreans. My aim in traveling through the Middle East was twofold: first, to encourage continuation of the ongoing process of conciliation, and second to mobilize support in the effort of raising relief for Eritrean refugees and internally displaced persons. Not only did I fail in my mission, but I was subjected to merciless attacks by the assembled students as a lackey of the Sabbe group and the *Thawra Mudadda* (counterrevolutionary) EPLF.

I had been warned not to even go near the Baghdad group, but I considered it my duty to talk to my fellow Eritreans, who were almost entirely from the western lowlands. It was a disaster; though there were a couple of more mature people like Omar Jabir who helped save the day and opened up to me and were gracious in their apologies for the lack of civility that greeted me in the meeting. (See chapter 13 for details).

Omar Jabir, a veteran ELF freedom fighter, was a leading organizer and the first chairman of GUES Iraq, who has recently stated that the GUES played a crucial role in helping to introduce the Eritrean cause to international organizations of the day. Its membership of the International Union of Students (IUS), based in Prague, exposed it to the socialist camp of the divided world during the cold war. Omar Jabir also claims that the GUES played a role in national service whereby it persuaded students to serve in the field in the ELF in various capacities. (See Interview of Omar Jabir with Woldeyesus Amar, August 4, 2005, published in Nharnet.com).

GUES-Baghdad was affiliated to the ELF. The ELF-EPLF divide meant that a rival organization would inevitably be created. Since GUES-Baghdad was associated with Idris Gelawdios—arch rival of Osman Saleh Sabbe—the latter engineered the creation of GUES-Cairo. Omar Jabir claims that the Cairo-based GUES did not have any international dimension or weight, whereas GUES-Baghdad was so effective that the Baathists of Iraq, who apparently could not dominate it, created a Baathist-based Eritrean student union in Baghdad and "planted many hurdles against our organization." (ibid).

The subject of the Diaspora's contribution in Eritrea's history of struggle for independence has attracted the attention of scholars in recent years. Tricia Redecker Hepner, for example, has researched and written on this subject (Hepner, 2005).

Many of the principal points covered in Hepner's work, are confirmed by the experience and close observations of the present writer. The North American organization of Eritrean students and workers originally known as EFLNA played a crucial role in providing financial, logistical and intellectual support to the EPLF. Many distinguished individuals even went to Sahel to be part of the armed struggle, several of them ending up as members of the Central Committee of the EPLF and as officials of the post-independence government. The crucial fact in all this is that, despite the preponderance of intellectual weight favoring the Diaspora, it was the EPLF that called the shots in terms of ideological orientation and regimentation. Hepner records meticulously what was known generally that the Diaspora followed the "field."

In this respect a pivotal moment was the EFLNA's reprinting, in March 1973, of *Nihnan Elamanan* (Our Struggle and Its Goals), prefacing it with an analysis of the split in the ELF that led to the creation of EPLF. The analysis reflected a predisposition to favor the perspective of the authors of the document which casts the ELF in a negative light. Hepner sums up the EFLNA's EPLF-oriented narrative as follows:

> The framing of the issues reflected the growing naturalization of the EPLF's position among EFLNA members that the class-based, religious, and regional tensions within the ELF were problems of the Front's structure and ideology, and not necessarily contradictions within the Eritrean nation. EFLNA highlighted the religious, regional, and class solidarities in ELF as an explanation for the otherwise vague ideological differences between the Fronts. It associated the ELF in general and its leadership in particular with Islamic chauvinism, regional and kin-based patrimonialism, and

petty-bourgeois class interests. Its ideology was described as "deficient, reactionary, and sectarian," and its ties with Arab countries vexed those who advocated a nationalism divorced from religious identity altogether. ELF's ties with Arab states led to charges of "narrow nationalism" and "Arabism." In contrast, EFLNA presented EPLF as the antithesis of ELF: explicitly multicultural, religiously inclusive, and ant-regionalist or anti-patrimonial, and mass-based; hence progressive, democratic, and revolutionary"(Ibid).

I will consider, in more detail, the issues concerning religion, regionalism, and democracy in the next chapter. At this point, it suffices to note that the division of the Eritrean struggle between two fronts was confirmed with EFLNA taking sides with the EPLF for the reasons outlined in the above-cited quotation from Hepner's work. I further note that as a member of the EPLF mass organization in North America (1977-1991) I observed first hand the process in which members of the mass organization were "socialized" (brainwashed would be too harsh a term) to believe that the EPLF showed the way forward to the liberation of Eritrea—liberation of the land from Ethiopian colonial occupation and of the people from feudal and bourgeois exploitation. Indeed, the EPLF's open adoption of Marxism-Leninism as its guiding ideology was replicated in the organizational manuals and indoctrination sessions of EFLNA. Marxist ideology was the wave of the times, espoused by most liberation movements throughout the world.

It should also be mentioned that the core EPLF leadership had created a secret Marxist-Leninist party, as early as 1972, as previously mentioned. By the mid 1980s, selected leaders of the Diaspora organizations were appointed to the secret party's membership, a fact that explains, in retrospect, some of the antidemocratic conduct of the selected leaders and their chosen cronies. Such conduct included refusal to account for money collected from the public and other irresponsible behavior that amounted to corruption. One word that sums up the behavior of the EFLNA leaders is *impunity*; and we were later to find out that such impunity characterized the conduct of the EPLF leadership itself and became the bane of the Eritrean people's life.

Interviews I conducted with prominent members of the Eritrean Diaspora in North America, and former members of the EFLNA, as well as my own personal experience, attest to the fact of the general tendency of the members of the EFLNA to accept word coming from the "Field" as gospel truth. The ideological blinders imposed by the leadership of the EFLNA, itself playing a subaltern role to the EPLF leadership, in addition to the sense of guilt felt by those who did not go to the field to fight, ensured total submission to the dictates of the EPLF. The EFLNA's original autonomy gave way to total acceptance of what Hepner calls the "EPLF discourse," totally rejecting the ELF's version of the liberation narrative. The EFLNA's original autonomy was based in part on the fact that before the appearance of the EPLF on the scene, especially between 1971 and 1975, Eritreans had developed a strong sympathy for the ELF, which had remained the dominant face of the liberation struggle. It lost that autonomy completely when, in 1976, it converted itself from a supportive organization to a member mass organization of the EPLF, virtually at the beck and call of the EPLF leadership. I happened to be in Bologna, Italy, in August of 1976, attending the annual festival of the EFLE, and was privy to some of the critical debates when it was "persuaded" to become a member organization.

It had become customary by then for the EFLNA to send delegates to attend the EFLE's festival, and I heard the arguments among members of both organizations both during the formal sessions as well as during lunch breaks and in the evenings. Sebhat Efrem, the Politburo member and head of the mass organizations of the EPLF, was present, doing his "persuading" by using various techniques both subtle and not so subtle as he went round talking to principal leaders with the help of the EFLE leadership. It was clear to me that he had convinced the latter before the formal sessions were held. A delegate of EFLNA who was close to me explained to me that the die had already been cast: that both the EFLE and EFLNA would become mass organizations affiliated to the EPLF. He was not quite sure himself of the wisdom of the step, but argued that the EPLF had critical need of the membership in the Diaspora organizations, for, otherwise the Sabbe forces (and the "reactionary line") would triumph over the "correct" line.

It is worth recalling that, a few months earlier, Osman Saleh Sabbe had severed relations with the EPLF, taking with him all financial aid coming from Arab sources; he was also eager to dip his hands into the Diaspora sources of the EPLF or at least to cause disruption of the fast-developing link between the EPLF and the Diaspora organizations. In volume 1 of my memoirs, I described Sabbe's attempt at recruiting me to head the European and north-American Diaspora on his behalf, an attempt that I rejected. We are, therefore, talking about a critical phase of the struggle from the perspective of the EPLF's strategy and even its survival at that particular time. From that perspective, most Eritreans, including myself were persuaded that, in order to survive, the EPLF had no choice but to require the EFLNA and the EFLE to become affiliated members. It was also a moment when the EPLF was beginning to score some notable military victories over the Ethiopian armed forces.

What about the ELF? The efforts to reconcile the ELF and the EPLF had failed. Instead, Eritrea had become a divided country with two spheres of influence controlled by one or the other organization. Sahel was the EPLF's base, and Barka was the ELF's base, with the inhabitants of the respective areas living under the influence and control of one or the other group. The people of the highlands were similarly divided in their allegiance, with the people of Hamasien and Akele Guzi mostly falling under the EPLF influence, and those of Seraye falling under the ELF influence. In each case, there were pockets of resistance to the control of either organization, and some people suffered imprisonment and sometimes worse punishment for asserting their allegiance.*

The Diaspora after the ELF's Exit from the Field

When, in 1981, the "civil war" between the ELF and the EPLF ended in the ELF's defeat and exit from the field of combat, its members were dispersed throughout the world—Sudan, Saudi Arabia, Europe, Australia, Canada, and the United States. By the mid-1980s, former ELF members swelled the ranks of the Eritrean Diaspora, in some areas, quadrupling the number of Eritreans. Up until that time, there were very few vocal supporters of the ELF, who were usually shouted down whenever they tried to put forward the ELF narrative of events in the Eritrean struggle. The coming of a large number of ex-ELF fighters emboldened these few stalwarts, but, on the whole, most ex-ELF members were preoccupied with making a living and raising families. Many, indeed, joined in the efforts to support the EPLF in its final life-and-death struggle against the Dergue army, i.e., attending fundraising events. A few even decided to become active members of the mass organizations.

In my capacity as EPLF representative at the United Nations (and as an academic) I traveled widely in the United States and Canada as well as Europe. At meetings that I addressed, there were occasional discordant notes expressed by some ex-ELF fighters denouncing aspects of the EPLF's policy and conduct and defending the ELF's narrative of events. As much as possible, I tried to avoid unnecessary controversy and concentrated on seeking the support of all Eritreans in the common struggle. But on a couple of occasions I made the mistake of defending the EPLF narrative of events concerning the civil war, particularly when it concerned events that I had witnessed or took part in, such as the attempts to mediate in the mid-1970s.

In one particular incident in Battle Creek, Michigan, where I had given a lecture, I was drawn to controversy in which I made a remark that I would later

---

* My own brother-in-law was kidnapped from the village of Shimanegus La'Elai and sentenced to die by the ELF military tribunal for being an ardent member of the EPLF peasant organization. He was taken to Barka, tried and condemned for execution. The execution was delayed, awaiting the confirmation of the chairman of the ELF, who happened to be away on travel abroad. Meanwhile the final battle between the two organizations took place in 1981; the ELF lost out and left the field for good. My brother-in-law and other detainees were rescued by the EPLF army and taken to Sahel, where I met them later that year.

regret. It was a remark made in the form of a joke, the kind that supporters of two teams make after one team loses to the other. My remark was something to the effect that it was no use crying over spilt milk—no use regretting the "ELF's sunk ship." Well, the ex-ELF members, who were the majority in the audience, were not amused. Instantly, the friendly atmosphere changed into a hostile camp; the levity and camaraderie that had characterized the meeting was altered, becoming charged with raw emotions. Normally, I am very careful not to offend people and had always been particularly attentive to ELF sensitivities; but on that particular occasion I slipped—a slip of tongue occurring amid momentary levity did not tally with the fact that for the ex-ELF fighters the memory of loss was too fresh, and that I had touched raw nerves. One ex-ELF fighter, who had commanded a battalion, took me to task, protesting and expressing astonishment that such a statement could come from the likes of me, etc.etc. He said he was proud of having served in the ELF, which he described as being among the best days of his life. Evidently, he spoke for the rest, as I could see from the vigorously nodding heads accompanying his remarks.

I cringed. I was quick to apologize. I said that it was an unfortunate remark made in a light moment of levity. Although the man said he forgave me, the mood of camaraderie had disappeared. Years later, I met him, and he reminded me of the incidence; but he was gracious and made a joke of it, putting me completely at ease by saying that he had overreacted to a simple joke. He is a decent and honorable Eritrean. In fact the vast majority of former ELF fighters aligned themselves behind the national cause for independence, making contributions in different ways. As I always said to some narrow-minded EPLF-hardliners, the ELF was a mother front, and its contributions cannot be wished away by EPLF hard-liners or anybody else; nor can we forget that their martyrs are our martyrs, for they paid the ultimate sacrifice for the same cause.

Unfortunately, the legacy of division persisted in different forms. One manifestation of the division was in the area of humanitarian assistance and allied activities such as the formation of communities in the different parts of North America. The EPLF mass organizations were adept at dominating community activities; so some former ELF members decided to create rival community organizations, and this led to dissention and contestations. For instance, after the 1978 debacle of the EFLNA, some members of the dissident group (followers of Mengisteab Isaac) joined forces with some ex-ELF members in forming a community organization in the Washington, D.C., area, competing with the one controlled by the EPLF mass organization. This led to some bitter controversy and failed negotiations, lasting until liberation day in 1991.

Postindependence Politics

Up until the 1998 war with Ethiopia, two events, and issues connected with them dominated Eritrean Diaspora politics—the 1993 referendum and the 1994-1997 constitution-making exercise.

The referendum, which was monitored by UN-appointed personnel and several private observers, asked Eritreans to choose between independence and remaining as part of Ethiopia. The result showed 98.8 Eritreans opting for independence. Some members of the Diaspora opposition groups, particularly the ELF-RC (since changed to EPP) decided not to participate in the referendum for reasons that are not understood by most Eritreans, but which go back to the ELF-EPLF enmity. Many ex-ELF members and some of their supporters did not wish to be part of an Eritrea liberated by the EPLF, as I was surprised to find out in a lecture I gave in Los Angeles on the eve of independence. One young ELF supporter said, during the question-and-answer session, that he was not ready to accept independence secured by Isaias Afwerki.

I remember responding to him in a one-liner: *Mihret Yewridelka*! (May God cure you!). In view of what Isaias has done to the nation that young man's remark is understandable but few, if any, foresaw that we would find ourselves in the present predicament.

On the other hand, though I do not have the figures, I am sure that the vast majority of Diaspora Eritreans participated in the referendum. I even met some—lining up to vote in a polling station in Asmara, including my niece Zifan and Tesfai, her husband (both ex-ELF members). I was pleasantly surprised to learn that Abdella Idris, a prominent ELF leader and mortal enemy of Isaias, decided to vote and told his followers to vote, setting aside his personal feelings and arguing that this was what we all fought for. The referendum was, after all, a formal act of confirmation, lending legitimacy to what was acquired by military victory, confirming to a hitherto skeptical world that the Eritrean people desired complete autonomy. In response to the mediation efforts that were organized by well-meaning people like former President Jimmy Carter who sought a peaceful resolution of the long war in order to avoid further blood shed, the EPLF had earlier proposed that a referendum be held. The Dergue rejected the proposal, knowing full well that the Eritrean people would decide in favor of independence.

The other issue that engaged the attention of Eritreans in the Diaspora was the constitution-making process. The process took three years to complete, from March 1974 to May 1977; and, as already discussed in chapter 6, it involved the participation of Eritreans both at home and in the Diaspora. For more details, I refer the reader to my book, *The Making of the Eritrean Constitution* (2003). The participation of the Diaspora was organized by members of the Constitutional Commission as well as by prominent Eritreans residing in countries where there is a large Eritrean community. The latter group was appointed by the Constitutional Commission. Naturally, all Eritreans, irrespective of their ideological leanings or political background, including former members of the ELF, were encouraged to participate in the process. Indeed many former ELF members played a prominent role in organizing and conducting meetings in the United States, Canada, and several European countries.

However, a segment of the ELF Diaspora membership boycotted meetings or expressed opposing views as to the legitimacy of the process, when in attendance of meetings. As previously explained, the basis of the objection was that the process was an EPLF process, which excluded the participation of other political forces, especially the ELF. I was engaged in debates with the leading exponents of such views, urging their participation individually and that they make their contribution. Making my own views clear, I even made reference to a piece of my own writing (published on the eve of Eritrea's independence) in which I had openly advocated the recognition of the ELF as a potential opposition party and its participation in the postliberation political process. Unfortunately, the EPLF leadership did not see fit to accept the proposal, which is one of the causes of our sad political predicament. I appealed to the ELF members to take part and try to influence events in that capacity. But to no avail; there was too much bitterness between the two fronts that lingered to haunt Eritrean politics, and no individual effort like mine could change that sad legacy. It still haunts us to this day.

Chapter 12

STATE AND RELIGION

————◇◇◇————

A Sign of the Times

On August 1, 2009, I happened to be in Washington, D.C., visiting a family friend who was in hospital following serious surgery. As I was about to leave the hospital, a brother of the patient—a man I have known for many years and regarded as a friend—was also leaving and told me about a meeting being held at the *Medhane Alem* Orthodox church in down town Washington. He is a member of the church and said that the meeting was an annual congregation of Orthodox Christians, which was being held in Washington, D.C., at the time. I was curious to know about the meeting because the church, and especially the Orthodox church, is a potent force opposed to the regime in Eritrea, bringing together social forces critical of the policies and politics of the regime, including many individuals who had once belonged to opposition political organizations. I expressed an interest to attend the meeting; so we went there together.

When we arrived a young cleric was conducting a seminar for a congregation of over six hundred men and women on aspects of the Bible's teachings . At the end of each segment of the seminar, simple hymns were sung in Tigrigna by the whole congregation, to the accompaniment of huge drums carried by two young men beating traditional church rhythms on the drums, and going back and forth with women ululating when the drum beat reached a climactic point. It all took me back nostalgically to the good old days when I used to experience such sights and sounds during celebrations in my village of origin, during my youth and many times thereafter in my adult life.

When the seminar was over, and before lunch was served in the basement of the church building, my friend introduced me to several young Orthodox clerics, some of whom held graduate degrees, including one who holds a Ph.D. in science. I was impressed by their youth, dedication, and eagerness to serve as priests and deacons while working in their various fields of knowledge. I met a few people I had known during the struggle for independence, who were members of Eritreans for Liberation in North America, as well as others who are new arrivals to the United States; in fact, the vast majority are people who left Eritrea in recent years, including the young priests and deacons, who belong to a new generation of Eritrean Orthodox Christians dedicated to modernizing and revitalizing the church. As we shall see later, these are representatives of a new breed of men with irresistible ideas who have collided with the resistance of the immovable object of hidebound traditionalism of people who felt insecure in the face of the dynamism, knowledge, and enlightenment presented by the young priests. Again, as we shall see later, some of their fellow priests have been imprisoned, held incommunicado like the other prisoners of conscience, both Christians and Muslims, including a medical doctor and the only trained psychiatrist in the country.

Another seminar was conducted after lunch by Dr. Tseggai Isaac, who related, citing passages in Geez, the fascinating story about the life and work of Saint Abranyos, an Eritrean mystic and religious leader. Dr. Tseggai is a professor of political science, and I was surprised by his knowledge of Geez, which he read fairly well albeit dragging the course of the seminar somewhat, to the annoyance of some members of the congregation who did not know Geez, the church's liturgical language. The seminar was in fact brought to a close before Tseggai could finish what he had started. Qeshi Gebremichael, a respected priest and community elder, ended the seminar rather abruptly, decisively brushing aside complaints from some of the female members of the congregation. Neither the women's complaint nor the abrupt ending was clear to me; no explanation was given.

Another surprise came from Dr. Tseggai himself with his contrite statement of apology to me for writing negatively about me in the recent past, siding with the government on some issues that I had forgotten. In fact he had made his apology privately to me before climbing to the podium to deliver his speech, and I had told him that I hold no grudges whatsoever: I don't even remember what he had written about me. He was gracious in his confession of wrong-doing, and I was touched that he made his confession in public, asking me to stand up and identify myself to the congregation, which I did (rather embarrassed), to prolonged applause. It took unusual courage on his part to own up to a mistake—a rare thing these days.

By and large, judging by the speeches and questions and answers following the speeches, the meeting exhibited a positive spirit, one that demonstrates a new vitality and an aroused social consciousness with a clear political content. This meeting is one of many being held on Sundays throughout North America, in both the United States and Canada, wherever there are Eritrean communities. It is part of a new trend whose origin and impact on Eritrean society and politics we need to explore together with other religious movements, or at least to express religious grievances—both Muslim and other Christian denominations—leveled at the ruling regime.

Nation-State and Nationalism: A Historical Perspective

There are three powerful forces driving modern politics—nationalism, religion, and the demands of constituent parts of a state in national politics, such demands being based on the shared values of democracy and justice. This truism applies to Eritrea; and in this chapter we explore aspects of religion in connection with the policies and politics of the Eritrean government regarding these issues. Issues connected with regional politics, including the land question are taken up in the next chapter. Some aspects of the issues, and the forces aligned behind the issues, have been subsumed or even articulated in some of the preceding chapters.

As to nation and nationalism, let it be said that the combination of these two concepts has been the primal force driving Eritrea's quest for self-determination and independence. Nationalism was the "melting pot" (to use a much-abused phrase) that united the disparate groups making up the nation and mobilized them against an alien occupying army, eventually leading to the country's independence.

To begin with nation, let me first repeat the obvious about the idea of nation. Nations are born; they grow and die. Nevertheless, the idea of nation as a historical phenomenon is an enduring fact of the constitution of human society. The modern imagination is hard put to think of the idea of a person without a nation. I well remember during the Eritrean war of independence a popular slogan was, *bizei hager kibret yellen* (There is no dignity without nation). Sometime back I read a story written by a Frenchman who lived as an exile in Germany during the Napoleonic period. The story was about a man who lost his shadow. (Can you imagine that!). It is a parable about a man without a nation. There cannot be a shadow without corporeal substance; a man without shadow has no substance. A man without a nation (an émigré) defies the ordinarily accepted categories and provokes at best pity; at worst, revulsion. Perhaps in a nation of refugees like America this may not be applicable. Although having a nation is not an attribute of humanity, in our own time having a nationality is a human right. Consider the predicament of the Roma nation also known as Gypsies; they have at least a strong sense of nationhood, albeit handicapped by their lack of an actual state.

A distinction must be made between nation and nationalism. The latter can be and has been used in defense of the former; nationalism in fact holds that state and nation are meant for each other. One without the other is incomplete, as the tragic predicament of the Somali people demonstrates.

In connection with nationalism, it will help to put the idea of nation and state in context. In modern times—roughly in the last one hundred fifty years—with the demise of large empires, like the Ottoman, and Austro-Hungarian empires (and later the European colonial empires), the nation became the only internationally legitimate state form. On the debris of the disappearing empires, nation-states appeared, many basing their sovereignty on ancient identities. In the case of the former European colonial empires of Africa, the sovereignty was defined in terms of the colonially fixed boundaries enclosing within them different ethnolinguistic entities. When the League of Nations assembled in 1920, in the aftermath of World War I, they inaugurated an era in which the nation became the legitimate unit of the international legal order. American President, Woodrow Wilson, then championed self-determination as the defining idea proclaiming that every nation has the right to determine its political future, thereby providing the philosophical/moral justification for the dissolution of the Austro-Hungarian and Ottoman empires and the emergence of several new nations out of those empires; in the Balkan region of Europe and in the Middle East.

In more recent times, in the post-cold war era, an explosion of new nationalisms broke out in Europe. In fact, the world seemed to be witnessing two diametrically opposed trends: one involving the creation of larger unities out of many nations typified by the European Union; the other witnessing the rise of national movements breaking out of larger, multi-ethnic nations. At the start of the 1990s, Yugoslavia had disintegrated, and the Union of Soviet Socialist Republics (USSR) had divided into independent states.

The power of nationalism has intrigued scholars who wondered why so many ordinary people were willing to lay down their lives for nations that their grandparents had never heard of, to say nothing of the ethnic cleansing and the other atrocities that were committed in the name of nationalism. Some scholars explained the phenomenon of nationalism in terms of the dislocation caused by modern industrial society, which destroyed traditional rural communities and drove millions of people into wholly strange factories and urban centers and defined by a new identity (See, for example, Earnest Gellner, 1983). Presiding over and shaping the change is, of course, the modern state with its powerful institutions of coercion and programs of standardized public education for everyone within its reach, aided by a mass market in communications—books, newspapers, radio, and television. These factors combined to create a new sense of community, of "subjects" transformed into citizens.

To this "functionalist" analysis of nationalism must be added religious and cultural elements to explain its emotional appeal. These elements give nationalism a deeper historical grounding or a longer attachment stretching to an antiquity, real or imagined. But, to reiterate, the most significant factor in the construction of nationalism is the rapid expansion of literacy and the development of a mass newspaper readership, or a radio listening audience. In all this, language assumes a critical role as a means of communication and a national leadership using it skillfully. Hence the importance of language in modern political discourse and the fact that there is much debate on language in national politics, including the wisdom or otherwise of having an official national language designated under a constitutional provision.

Nationalism in Eritrea

Eritrean nationalism is based on the creation of the territory as an Italian colonial state. Like the rest of colonial Africa, its identity as a nation-state was defined by the boundaries created after Italy declared it as a colony in January 1890. This historical fact, reaffirmed by the postcolonial African legal order under the 1964 Cairo Resolution of the OAU, is buttressed by the factors discussed in the preceding paragraphs about the construction of nationalism. Italian industrial investment and the urbanization and consequent mixing of different ethnic groups in factories, plantations, and shantytowns created a sense of a community among the colonial subjects who were transformed into fellow citizens following the departure of their colonizers. The struggle against a common occupier—first the Italians, then the British, and finally the Ethiopians—eventually culminated in the triumph of national independence.

When we consider the two defining factors that figure in the analysis of the construction of nationalism, discussed above—namely industrialism that destroys traditional communities, on the one hand, and the emotional appeal of religious and cultural antecedents, on the other—in Eritrea's case, the former prevailed over the latter even though an uneasy symbiosis continued between them. The claim of Ethiopia's governments, from Emperor Haile Selassie to the Dergue, contending that Ethiopia had ancient religious and cultural ties to a major part of Eritrea proved to be untenable. Eritrean nationalism, forged under Italian colonial rule and reinforced thereafter through bitter struggle, triumphed over that claim.

In any case, even if the religious and cultural factor were to apply, it would only be relevant with respect to the Christian highland populations; for Eritrean nationalism embraces both the Christian highland and the Muslim lowland populations, a fact conveniently ignored in the Ethiopian narrative when it suits the purpose of the moment. This fact is not limited to the imperial or Dergue ideologues, as the recent writing of Shaleqa Dawit Woldegiorgis illustrates (Dawit, 2009). Christian Ethiopian identification of the Habesha as being inclusive of Eritrea assumes that Eritrea is composed of the Christian highland only. This is a serious error that glosses over a vital element of Eritrean nationalism—the fact of its being a composite of a Christian (highland) and Muslim (lowland) mix forged during the colonial era. It is important to remind writers like Shaleqa Dawit that the attempt to drive a wedge between the two in the form of the Bevin-Sforza Partition Plan failed owing to the united opposition of Eritreans under the leadership of the Muslim-Christian United Bloc.

The remaining part of this chapter—the major portion—deals with religion and the state, As noted above, I deal with ethno- regional politics in the next chapter.

Religion and the State—a Delicate Dialectical Relation

Religion is a universally recognized fundamental human right, so fundamental that it is taken for granted by most people. Yet it has been the subject of violation even in this day and age; and the state—the supposed protector—has been a guilty perpetrator of, or an accessory to, the fact in such violation. What is, or what should be, the proper relation between religion and the state? Historically, different countries have given different answers to this question; but the one constant factor is the ideal search for the autonomy of religion from the demands of parochial or national politics.

In 1996, in the midst of Eritrea's constitution-making exercise, I convened a meeting of the principal religious leaders of Eritrea—the head of the Eritrean Orthodox church, the Mufti of Eritrean Muslims, the representative of the Catholic church, and the head of the Protestant church. The meeting was held in the assembly room of the headquarters of the Constitutional Commission of Eritrea. In opening the meeting, addressing the distinguished religious leaders, I said that first of all we needed their prayers, and that as chairman of the commission, I asked them to pray for the success of our work because we were engaged in a historic national task. Next, I told them that my colleagues at the commission and I believed that religion is a fundamental human right, and that the future constitution that we were preparing would contain a provision to that effect. Finally, I told them that we believed in the separation of religion and state, and that this too would be provided for in the future constitution.

In the commission's preliminary set of ideas—the precursor to the constitutional draft, known as the proposals—the concept of secularism was posited as an expression of our idea of the separation of religion and state. During the extensive public debate that followed the publication of the proposals and of the actual draft constitution, many members of the public expressed concern that the use of the word *Alemawinet,* the Tigrigna word for "secularism," might create misunderstanding. *Alemawinet* conveyed a different and potentially misleading sense, one that was associated with worldliness in the negative sense of the word. In this respect, it is worth noting that in earlier English usage, the word *secular* was interchangeable with *profane*. For example, the renowned scientist, Sir Isaac Newton, is reported to have said, "I find sure marks of authenticity in the Bible than in any profane [secular] history whatsoever."

In my book, *The Making of the Eritrean Constitution* (2003), I discuss the question of secularism in the context of the idea of separation of church/mosque and State, summarizing the public debate on the subject and the concerns expressed by some citizens. In the book I wrote the following:

> The Commission used the opportunity to ask itself some probing questions related to religion, state and society in a country like Eritrea. That there must be separation between state on the one hand and church and mosque on the other was a matter beyond dispute among the vast majority of Eritreans including the leaders of the two main religions. A theocratic state was neither desirable nor practicable; it would be a prescription for disaster. (p. 107)

Following the public debate, the Constitution Commission decided not to include an article declaring secularism as a principle, leaving such a matter to be handled extra-constitutionally. I went on to comment that the commission recognized the dialectical relation between the sacred and the worldly, between spiritual and material wellbeing, and the preamble to the constitution reflects this recognition. Indeed, such a dialectical relation was essential, a timeless and creative aspect of Eritrean society. The consensus was that the state and religion may have to be separated but, to borrow the language of the law of domestic relations, they could not be divorced from each other. There was too much at stake for the state not to be concerned with religious matters and for religion to be aloof from all politics. As I put it in the concluding paragraph of the section of the book dealing with the issue, "Although the golden medium of their relationship was not amenable to a cut-and-dry formula, it was dialectics, and had to be worked out in the manner of all dialectics—with patience, caution and acumen." (ibid)

What is then, the source of religion's authority, and how does it tally with state power?

In primordial social organizations, where there was no differentiation of functions, there was unity of faith and power. Indeed, in much of earlier human history, the religious leaders enjoyed near-absolute power of life and death. Differentiation of functions in social organization marked degrees of higher evolution. Such specialization of functions involved, among other things, a type of control of religious bodies over those who exercised political power with the use of commonly accepted principles or shared values. An example of such control is given in the Orthodox Christian mythology of the mysteries of the Virgin Mary (*Te'amire Mariam*), as mentioned in a previous chapter. In that story, the Virgin Mary, mother of Jesus, is taking her son on a tour of hell, where he sees people tied to columns of fire, suffering without respite. When he asks her who they are, she informs him they were princes who abused their power, doing injustice to people when they ruled over them in their earthly life.

There is a similar injunction in Islam attributed to the Prophet Mohamed (peace be upon him). "Pharaoh turned into a tyrant on earth, and discriminated against some people. He persecuted a helpless group of them, slaughtered their sons, while sparing their daughters. He was indeed wicked." (Surah 28:4).

And from the Hadith: "If anyone walks with an oppressor to strengthen him, knowing that he is an oppressor, he has gone forth from Islam. (Bukhari Muslim).

And again: "I heard the Prophet (saaws) saying 'Any man whom Allah has given the authority of ruling some people and he does not look after them in an honest manner, will never feel even the smell of Paradise.'" (Sahih Muslim – volume 9, book 89, number 264, narrated Ma'qil)*

Thus was religious doctrine conceived by religious authorities in attempts to keep rulers in check by the threat of eternal punishment in the hereafter if they did harms to their subjects, nor was this limited to religious authorities. Dante's *Divine Comedy* contains passages in which rulers that he did not look on with favor, like the Count Ugolino, were consigned to the Purgatory. (Dante Alighieri, *La Divina Commedia, il Purgatorio*).

It is open to question whether such injunctions deterred princely rulers from abusing their powers and doing harm. But it is conceivable that it might have had a restraining effect on at least some of them some of the time.

Religion relates to politics in a number of ways. It interacts with the nation-state, which, as mentioned before, is the standard political arrangement in modern times. Many religions are powerful forces with global impact that can play crucial roles in conflict situations either in intensifying or in helping resolve them. Religious institutions like churches and mosques themselves play roles within nations in different ways, either pacifying conflict situations or inflaming them. And often religious values are invoked to justify and legitimize political action. Also at times the policies or actions of political leaders may be motivated by religious beliefs, even in countries like the United States of America that practice separation of church and state. As noted above, state and religion may be separated, but they cannot be divorced. To vary the metaphor, the spiritual and the material are two sides of the same coin.

---

*   I am indebted to Semere Habtemariam for providing me with these quotes.

State and Religion in Eritrea

Eritrea's principal religions, embraced by the overwhelming majority of its population, are Christianity and Islam. A small minority of people (most Kunama) are followers of traditional African religion, also known as animism. The vast majority of Christians are adherents of the (Eastern) Orthodox religion, the remainder being Catholics and Protestants. The Muslims are adherents of the Sunni branch of Islam.

Christianity was introduced to Eritrea in the fourth century of the Christian era, when much of today's Eritrea was an integral part of the Axumite kingdom. But the Catholic and Protestant branches of Christianity were introduced for the most part in the middle of the nineteenth century by European missionaries. Earlier attempts to introduce Catholicism in the region were made by Portuguese Jesuits by converting the reigning king during the Gondarine dynasty in the sixteenth century. The attempts were foiled by stalwarts of the Ethiopian Orthodox religion, who were heading a public protest, charging that the converted king had become prey to the influence of foreign powers. As a result, the converted monarch was overthrown and succeeded by his son, the renowned King Fasil. From then on Ethiopian (Abyssinian) Orthodox leaders and their followers, with the support of the monarch, as defender of the faith, have had to contend with the gradual encroachment of Catholic and Protestant missionaries. For over four centuries the (Ethiopian) "Mother Church" has thus been on the defensive, as the two other branches increased their membership, fielding a host of priests and ministers with modern education in contrast to the Orthodox priests, most of whom were stuck with their old ways until recent times.

In Eritrea, as mentioned at the beginning of this chapter, there is a new awakening among Orthodox clerics led by the new blood of educated and conscientious clergy. This, as we shall see in more detail, has been part of the current problem facing the Eritrean Orthodox church and its relation with the state.

In terms of the Christian-Muslim relation, the two religions have interacted in complex ways for centuries, having been forced by circumstances to find ways of coexisting. In view of the role that religion seems to have played in recent conflicts in many African countries, it is crucial for students of the subject as well as for policy makers to devise ways of properly understanding the interaction of the adherents of the two religions. And it is especially the duty of scholars to think of how an objective study of their relationship might be conceptualized. One scholar of religion writing on the subject has suggested two methodologies for understanding interfaith relations in Africa: 1) Sociological and practical, and 2) Doctrinal and theoretical.

He explains:

From a sociological and practical analysis, we must inquire into what is taking place on the ground at the moment, as well as what the historical background might be for what we are now experiencing. We must address how members of the Christian and Muslim faith communities relate....The doctrinal and theoretical analysis will require, among other things, an inquiry into the teachings of Christianity and Islam in order to appreciate the religious principles that motivate the attitudes of the individuals or communities in question. (Laurenti Magesa, 2007, "Contemporary Catholic Perspectives on Christian-Muslim Relations in Sub-Saharan Africa: The case of Tanzania," in Islam and Christian-Muslim Relations, Vol.18, No. 2)

I would lay special emphasis on the need for historical perspective; the writing of historians on the subject provides invaluable insight into interfaith problems and methods of resolving them.

Historically, Christianity and Islam have coexisted in the Horn of Africa region, including Eritrea and Ethiopia for centuries, beginning shortly after the rise of Islam in the seventh century and following its gradual spread. Ethiopian kings, being titular heads of the church, viewed the spread of Islam with some trepidation, particularly following Islamic conquests or incursions into their kingdom. Indeed, on a few occasions, there have been religiously inspired wars of conquest and resistance. The most famous of such wars, and one that left a deep impact on interfaith relations in the country, was the one conducted by Imam Ahmed bin Ibrahim, popularly known among Ethiopians as Ahmed Gragne (the left-handed), whose forces swept across much of the Ethiopian highland kingdom in 1529 converting thousands to Islam. In 1542 the Ethiopian king was able to defeat Ahmed bin Ibrahim's forces and recover the lost ground with the help of Portuguese troops. One of the significant consequences of the Ahmed Gragne conquest, and the void it left in southeastern and central parts of Ethiopia, was a demographic change. The void left was filled with the advent of the Oromo from their southern strongholds to the southeastern region and to central parts of Ethiopia, forever changing Ethiopian politics and society.

Problematic Coexistence in Ethiopia

Until the emergence of Eritrea as an independent state, the Eritrean Orthodox church was part of the Ethiopian Orthodox church. Hence an account of the life of Christians and Muslims of earlier times is relevant for our analysis. Eritrean Orthodox Christians looked up to their Ethiopian Christian brethren. Those with resources would go all the way to Axum to be ordained priests; for Axum was the original center of Christianity in Ethiopia. Indeed, many went beyond Axum, all the way to Gondar for higher education. Even the creation of Eritrea as an Italian colonial state did not sever the link completely. In other words, there was a strong religious and cultural bond between Eritrean Christians and Ethiopia via Orthodox Christianity. Historically, the king was the head of the church, which means, among other things, that no one could ascend the throne unless and until he professed the Orthodox Christian faith. Church and state supported each other, with the state providing the security umbrella and material support for the church, while the church provided ideological support for the state. There is a tradition whereby the state is supposed to allocate one-third of its land to the church (*Siso le-qedash...*).

At the micro level, relations between Christians and Muslims in Ethiopia were seemingly harmonious, having demonstrable friendly coexistence and mutual tolerance. Linguistic commonality (Amharic, etc,) and geographic proximity helped: The fact of sharing a common language and living in the same locality enabled members of the two communities to participate in one another's lifecycle rituals of birth, wedding, funerals, and other social occasions. In the Wollo region, they even intermarried. On the other hand, in the wake of the Ahmed Gragne conquest, barriers emerged, the most notable being Christian avoidance of meat slaughtered by Muslims, and vice versa. It is interesting that such a barrier does not exist outside Ethiopia (and Eritrea).

At the macro-level, the interfaith relationship definitely shows Muslims relegated to a position of second class. They had no role in running the affairs of the Christian state. As a consequence, the policy and attitudes of the (Christian) ruling elite filtered down to all levels, creating a situation in which Muslims were perceived as inferior to Christians. The relationship of tolerance and coexistence was thus a façade hiding a divided society. Not even during Haile Selassie's comparatively more liberal reign did Muslims gain equal rights with Christians. Apart from a few token appointments, Muslims were excluded from employment in public offices and from holding higher ranks in the army.

It should be pointed out that the imperial government's policy of exclusion and domination was not limited to religion; it also applied in the ethnic area. The Oromo were excluded from key positions, as the story of Tadesse Birru illustrates. Tadesse was an Oromo army general who was appointed to head the Police Rapid Deployment Force, and who played a key role in foiling the 1960 attempted coup to overthrow the Emperor. Following the failed coup, Aklilu Habtewold, the Emperor's prime minister, was consulting with him on recruitment and promotion policy concerning the security services. Tadesse happened to have an Amhara-sounding name and spoke impeccable Amharic; so the prime minister, on the assumption that he was Amhara, warned him to keep Oromos out of key security positions. Tadesse was outraged but did not show his feelings; instead he proceeded to help organize an Oromo resistance known as the Mecha-Tulema movement for which he was later tried and executed.

To return to the position of Muslims, it would change suddenly with the Italian invasion of Ethiopia and its five-year occupation (1935-1941), which marked a break with the past. The Italian policy of divide and rule was aimed at devaluing the Christian ruling group and empowering Muslims by giving them equal status for the first time. The policy included financing construction of mosques and *madrassas*, employing Muslims in administrative positions, and subsidizing propagation of Islam and pilgrimages (*Hajj*) to Mecca.

The next time Muslims found their voice was after the overthrow of the imperial regime. Some 100,000 Muslims conducted a massive demonstration in Addis Ababa in April 1974, and called for the recognition of Muslim festivals as public holidays, financial support for the construction of mosques, and permission to establish a National Islamic Council. After the fall of the Dergue government, the new EPRDF government gave Muslims more rights, lifting restrictions on Hajj and the ban on Islamic religious literature as well as restrictions on the construction of mosques. Newspapers and magazines began to appear published by Muslim groups. However, there was a reversal of some aspects of the new government's liberal policy in the wake of violent incidents resulting in the death of some worshippers around the *al-Anwar* mosque in Addis Ababa.

The Church in Eritrea, under Italian rule, maintained a tenuous link with its Ethiopian counterpart. Italian policy sought to undermine the power of the Ethiopian Orthodox church by encouraging autonomy, if not complete severance of ties between the two churches. At the same time, while taking care not to interfere in religious affairs, Italian policy aimed at encouraging the Catholic church to spread its wings, and undermined the role of the Ethiopian Orthodox church. But, to give the devil his due, so to speak, the Italians respected the office of the priesthood, a fact demonstrated by their policy of exempting priests from being conscripted to the military.

Muslim-Christian Coexistence in Eritrea

As we saw, Ethiopian Muslims had found their voice during the brief period of Italian occupation but had to wait another sixty years before they could gain equality. By contrast, in Eritrea, throughout the fifty-odd years of Italian colonization, Muslims had equal rights with Christians in all respects. Interestingly enough, Catholic evangelization aimed at converting Orthodox Christians to Catholicism and stayed away from Muslim areas where the colonial government encouraged building mosques and *madrassas.* Moreover, Arabic was taught in the government-run schools where Muslims mixed with Christians as they also did on the plantations and in the factories as well as in the colonial army.

Muslim-Christian relations at the microlevel have been peaceful, characterized by a neighborly spirit of live and let live and participation in social events like weddings and funerals. Friday prayers are festive affairs for Muslims, particularly in the cities, where one can see one's neighbors, flocking to the mosque, dressed in their best. Among the Blin and the Mensa'E in Senhit, interreligious interaction is reinforced by ethnic solidarity. In the central highlands of Akele Guzai and Seraie villages, though the inhabitants are predominantly Christian, there are significant numbers of Muslims—Saho in the one and Jeberti in the other. In Hamasien, there are pockets of Muslims in several villages. All of these are members of farming communities, tilling their plots of land and living the life of typical villagers.

In the village where I was born there were some twenty Muslim families, who organized their own Qur'anic school at the elementary level for their children. One of my childhood friends would repeat to me, after his class, the Arabic alphabets (*Alif-ba-ta-...* etc.), and I would repeat to him the Tigrigna alphabets (*Ha-hu-hi...* etc.). Since we did not have paper and pencils, we would write on the ground one another's alphabets. To us children it was a kind of innocent game. That was before I left the village life and went to Asmara to continue my education, as I described in the First Volume of these memoirs. I saw my childhood friend a couple of times before I left to Ethiopia; I never saw him again.

My kinsman, Dr. Nerayo, narrated to me that when he was attending elementary school in our village, they had one teacher for the two grades—grades one and two. The teacher divided the class into morning and afternoon sessions, teaching first grade in the morning and the second grade in the afternoon. Nerayo, who was a precocious child, asked his mother if it was alright for him to attend Arabic lessons in the village Qur'anic school when he was not attending his class. His mother, a devout Protestant, agreed, thus enabling Nerayo to study the Arabic alphabet; and he says he can still remember the first part of the Arabic recitation that Qur'anic students learn—*Bismi'Allahi Arrahman Arrahim...*etc.

What was more surprising to many, Nerayo and my brother Elias (Nerayo's childhood companion) frequently ate at the household of IndaBoy Ibrahim. The meals included meat, which meant they were crossing the barrier of taboo, defying the meat avoidance practiced by Orthodox Christians. As an important part of this barrier, at weddings, the hosts prepared separate dishes for Christians and Muslims. Clearly, the Protestant parents of Nerayo and Elias had shown their children the way of breaking a taboo—a taboo that Eritrea's founding fathers, Ibrahim Sultan Ali and Woldeab Woldemariam, ritually broke as a gesture of political unity of Muslims and Christians.

As is well known, in one historic meeting, Woldeab and his fellow Christians agreed to eat chicken meat slaughtered by a Muslim, and Ibrahim and his fellow Muslims agreed to eat chicken meat slaughtered by a Christian. It was indeed a moment of epiphany, if I may be forgiven for using a Christian concept. Ahmed Raji informs me that the Arabic equivalent is *tajally,* or *lahtha tajally,* signifying a moment of clarity. In one symbolic gesture of unity, they broke an irrational taboo that had existed for over three hundred years, since the time of Ahmed Gragne. Eritrean freedom fighters—both ELF and EPLF, Muslims and Christians—pushed the barrier-breaking practice one step forward, eating goat meat together, similarly slaughtered as described above. Incidentally, a few of the Christian freedom fighters had lived in predominantly Muslim countries like Egypt and Sudan, where no such taboo existed.

Muslim-Christian relations during the years after Italian colonial rule followed a similar pattern of peaceful coexistence for some years. A point of divergence occurred during the years of political agitation concerning the future of Eritrea (1942-1950), with Muslims generally supporting independence and Christians for the most part supporting some form of association with Ethiopia. The divergence led to negative expressions of mild forms of mutual animosity at the microlevel with Christians referring to Muslims (as well as Christians who favored independence) as *rabiTa,* and Muslims and Christian independence supporters calling the union supporters as "*andinet.*" The words—rabiTa and andinet—meaning "league" and "union," respectively, did not carry any stigma in themselves; but in time, when repeatedly and loudly hurled by one side at the other, became terms of abuse. Indeed, there were extreme expressions of hostility resulting in tragedy. A great independence leader, Abdulkadir Kebire, was assassinated; and Woldeab was the target of nine assassination attempts, forcing him into exile in Egypt. Both the Kebire assassination and the attempts on Woldeab's life were carried out by Andinet extremists and instigated by the Ethiopian government.

Leaving to historians the analysis of key events and the role of historic figures of the period, let me just note in passing that the federation period, and especially what followed after Emperor Haile Selassie's abolition of the federal arrangement, was marked by the gradual demolition of whatever autonomy Eritreans enjoyed. The period saw the subordination of Eritreans to Ethiopians, with an implicit diminution of the role of Muslims in a government presided over by a Christian emperor. Nonetheless, the alienation of Eritrean youth and many among the generation of their fathers was accompanied by a common—Muslim-Christian—sense of grievance with different expressions of solidarity. Such solidarity was epitomized by the adoption of the underground project known as *Mahber Shewate* by Christian highlanders who knew its roots to be in Port Sudan and that it was created by Muslim Eritreans under the name of *Haraka.* This was in the late 1950s and early 1960s, before the declaration of the armed struggle led by Hamed Idris Awate in 1961. Awate instantly became a national hero, and the ELF that he led became a potent expression of Eritrean nationalism.

Muslim-Christian Relations in the Armed Struggle

When it started, and for a few years afterward, the ELF was an all-Muslim organization. Its birthplace was Barka and its leadership comprised Muslim lowlanders. One of the points of difference between the ELF and Haraka was that the latter was an all Eritrean (Muslim-Christian) organization. However, in deciding to eliminate Haraka from the field, the ELF was not as motivated by religious sentiments as much as by turf—territorial monopoly. Religion may have contributed to the crisis in the ELF; indeed, according to the principal leaders of the EPLF who had been members of the ELF, it was the leading cause. *"Nihnan Elamanan,"* the original manifesto of the core group of what would later become the EPLF, categorically claims that Christian members of the ELF were singled out for victimization, and many were assassinated. To what extent this claim is true, and whether religion was the only, or the single most important reason, we leave for historians to sort out together with other issues of dispute connected with the armed struggle. One thing is certain and worth reiteration—Isaias Afwerki, the principal author of *Nihnan Elamanan*, has himself much to answer for in what he did in the thirty years of his leadership of the EPLF, not to mention the postindependence period.

In conducting research for the purpose of writing this chapter, I prepared a simple questionnaire that I distributed to a select target audience of twenty-five prominent Eritreans, both Christians and Muslims. One of the items in the questionnaire was the role of *Nihnan Elamanan* in the politics of Eritrea's armed struggle. A majority of those I approached responded to my questions. One respondent, a former ELF member and critic of Isaias, described *Nihnan Elamanan* as follows:

> a Christian message of agitation intended to control the struggle by rallying Christians as oppressed by Muslims....Its writers chose to go it alone when there were many progressive Eritreans risking their lives to achieve reformation of the ELF: *Islah* is the name of the first attempt for reforming the ELF, which Isaias ignored to advance his wish to be seen as the only reformer by the sectors he was rallying.

In support of his argument, the writer of this piece raises the question of veracity: such claims as the ELF killing of hundreds of Addis Ababa University students , he avers, have not been substantiated. Admitting that although "some Christians were wrongly killed in the ELF," the writer claims that dozens more Muslims were killed, and that "Isaias made it look as if it was Muslims targeting Christians."

In contrast to this respondent's claims and arguments two other respondents (one Christian and one Muslim) maintain that as a document Nihnan Elamanan is not a problem. We will call the two respondents A and B. In fact, they both contend that it is one of the best political documents ever written in the history of the Eritrean struggle, articulating as it does the mission and the vision and the core values of the EPLF and the people who made it. On the other hand, both respondents point to the fact that the document made the cultural, religious, and geographic divide a permanent fixture in Eritrean politics. In defense of the EPLF's split from the ELF, respondent A contends that, rightly or wrongly, "the people that made the EPLF/PLF felt that they could not make a difference by staying within the ranks of the old ELF." In the end, he says with a touch of pragmatism, that success is what counts, and that while the EPLF approach succeeded, that of the ELF did not. And respondent B adds that, given its importance in shaping our history in one way or another, "the document should now be part of Eritrea's heritage to help us understand our contemporary history."

Another critical respondent gave a less strident and a rather nuanced analysis of the content and effect of *Nihnan Elamanan*. His summary of the document's content is as follows: The message reassured its target audience (Tigrigna highlanders) that its authors had no religious agenda, only nationalist aspirations. He cites one of the most memorable phrases of the document where its writer(s) claim that they chose "sitting on the edge of a razor blade," that is to say, the choice they faced was between surrendering to Ethiopia, or surrendering "to the bigotry of ELF leadership." The "poison in the document," the respondent says, was:

1. That the ELF leaders were jihadists and religious fanatics
2. That they had no political agenda
3. That they persecuted Christians and civilians, and butchered hundreds of fighters and civilians
4. That they stole property from highlanders, and with the proceeds, took up multiple wives in Sudan.

Perhaps the most damaging and misleading message of Nihnan Elamanan was, according to the respondent, that it did not disclose that there was a contest in the ELF between traditionalists (reactionaries) and reformers (both Muslim and Christian). Instead it spoke of a contest between hardliners and Christians.

What emerges from the above narrative of mostly ELF-oriented commentators is that *what EPLF supporters consider a historic document that was billed as justification for the split was in fact a fraud perpetrated by Isaias Afwerki in order to assure himself the support of Christians. And in doing so, he committed a crime against the Eritrean nation by causing a dangerous religiously-based division.* (Emphasis added)

After I received these and other responses, Ismail Omar-Ali (whom I didn't know and did not, therefore, solicit his views) wrote a thoughtful piece in Awate. com (September 19, 2009). Ismail believes that, contrary to Ali Salim's view, religion—not ethnicity and regionalism—is the most salient issue of division in Eritrea. He calls *Nihnan Elamanan* an apocalyptic vision of a Christian leader. However, despite his belief that there has been a persistent pattern of inequality through regime changes, his conclusion is a positive and salutary one. He writes:

> We find that Muslims and Christians have shared common struggles, dreams, and aspirations; that they lived side by side for centuries in peace and mutual respect (for the most part); that they fought side by side to rid themselves of occupation; and that even today, they are struggling together to bring about freedom and democracy to Eritrea.

Isaias and Muslims in Independent Eritrea

Ever since the early days of independence, there have been reports of Muslims arrested by Eritrean security forces. No reason has been given for their arrest, nor has there been any report on their fate. As recently as August 13, 2009, Awate.com's *Gedab News* reported that about thirty religious Eritrean Muslims, including teachers and students, were rounded up in Asmara by government security officers. Among those arrested was a seventy-year old scholar, Shaikh Abdella, a graduate of Al Azhar University who used to provide regular afternoon *derse* (short Islamic lectures) at the Masjid Khulafa Al Rashidin (Asmara's Grand Mosque), after the Asr prayers. Such lessons were banned by the government in 2002. That was the year when the government arrested many Muslim teachers whose fate is still unknown but are feared dead. In point of fact, such arrests had started in the early 1990s.

The Gedab News story offers a possible reason for the arrest; it says that the arrest may be related to an intra-Muslim feud that has been going on in the Maichehot neighborhood of Asmara between the traditional (Sufi) practitioners of Islam and the more strict (Selefi) proponents. Apparently, their differences had become so irreconcilable that the Selefists had splintered and founded their own mosque.

According to the Gedab News, the deputy mufti, Salem Ibrahim Al-Mukhtar, is reported to have played a role in the wave of arrests. It is stated in the same news account that when Eritrean Muslim elders petitioned the government to name Salem Ibrahim as a successor to the current mufti, their hope and expectation was that he would emulate his father, the renowned Ibrahim Al-Mukhtar Ahmed Omar, Eritrea's first mufti (1939-1969), to show courage and compassion. The great Ibrahim Al-Mukhtar Ahmed Omar was not only a respected scholar but a man of principle who stood for the rights of Muslims, defending his flock against Ethiopian interference.

The question now is whether his son Salem has become an enforcer of PFDJ's policies, completely abdicating his religious (mediating) responsibilities, as the Gedab News seems to suggest, or are there other reasons why the arrests were made? If so, what are the reasons? At times, it may boil down to questions of loyalty or allegiance, or of conflicting loyalties, to be more exact. Are the followers of any sect loyal to the country to which they belong first, or do they owe allegiance to the sect of which they are adherents? There are instances where a *Talib,* (pupil of a shaikh), or a *deqe mezmur* (Christian disciple) knows his master before his king or president. This fact led a French scholar of Senegalese society to remark, "In Senegal, one is often a *talib,* disciple of a Marabou before being a citizen of a state." (Coulon, 1981).

Whatever the reasons, whoever is responsible for arresting people has the responsibility of providing reasons; and the government has a constitutional duty to give reasons for the arrest and to follow the rule of law in bringing detainees to an open court. If Salem has been just an instrument of the government, enforcing its orders without ensuring that the legal rights of the detainees are observed, or at least requesting that they be observed, then he has indeed become a willing tool of the government. This raises the question of the role of government in religious matters.

As previously stated, government institutions and religious bodies are different entities and should be separate. Unlike political organizations, religious bodies are not entities that can be formed or abolished at will like political organizations. Accordingly, the PFDJ government, even though it is led by atheists, has not deigned to order the closing of the generally recognized religious institutions. At the time of independence, the EPLF (later the PFDJ) government did not have an institution to oversee the activities of religious institutions. The question was considered closely related to national security; and the responsibility for religious affairs was first given to Isaias loyalist Naizghi Kiflu, who reported directly to the president. Naizghi's first challenge was to organize the election of a mufti for Eritrean Muslims

The Mufti

I have been able to obtain information from a reliable source that had an intimate knowledge of the work of the government office on religious affairs and on the relationship of the government and religious institutions, including the office of the mufti. The following account, and that of the Orthodox Church (to be given later), is based on this information.

With regard to the election of a mufti, all districts were required to present a candidate for the post of mufti from among people who were learned Islamic clerics known for their patriotic sentiments. The Security Department then presented a list of people who were considered as potential candidates. Then suddenly, before a proper election was conducted from among the list of candidates, Shaikh Alamin was selected by the government as Mufti of Eritrea. This was done because, in addition to his religious education, Shaikh Alamin was a supporter of the EPLF. His selection, without proper election procedure, was resented by the Muslim community.

According to my informant, the mufti was under government control; clear evidence of government control of the mufti is the resources made available to his office. The government allocated an annual budget for the mufti's salary, for administrative expenses, and for logistical support that included an office building together with office furniture and other facilities.

It is necessary to point out that obtaining government support should not, in and of itself, be regarded as a mark of compromising one's religious autonomy or religious duties. If the mufti (or the patriarch of the Ethiopian Orthodox church for that matter) can maintain the integrity of his office in being a proper mediator between conflicting forces as "an honest broker" or a neutral reconciler in the case of feuding Islamic sects, he can conceivably justify himself. After all, as Omar Jabir recently reminded us, even the churches of some secular governments in northern Europe obtain financial support from their governments. That does not mean they do the bidding of the governing party on any issue, even where the leaders of the government and of a given church in Europe may or may not agree on policy issues.

The fact that the mufti is associated with the government has made him enemies among Eritrean Muslims, some of whom have occasionally made threatening phone calls to his office. There have been repeated complaints about the manner by which Shaikh Alamin was selected mufti of Eritrean Muslims, many Muslims asserting that his selection was contrary to accepted modes of election. Moreover, there are Muslims who are followers of the Ansar Alsunna sect who do not accept the present mufti. Following the repeated threats made on Shaikh Alamin's life, the government decided to move his residence from Akria to Tiravolo where most of government ministers reside. The mufti also receives constant protection through individual security detail.

Those suspected of making the threatening calls—presumably followers of the Ansar Alsunna Sect—though few in number are scattered, living in Keren, Ginda'E and in the Akria and Maichehot sections of Asmara. According to my informed source, they also have ties with Saudi Arabia and with other Middle

East forces that have designs of extending their influence in Eritrea. Their worldview and religious orientation is inimical to the worldview of PFDJ and its government.

A word on the composition of Eritrean Muslims will be helpful in understanding the conflict that might have led to the recent arrest of Muslim teachers and students as well as to earlier arrests. As noted before, most Eritrean Muslims are Sunni. Muslim Sunni belong to four schools of thought following four jurors. The four jurors are:

1. Ibn Hambel, whose adherents are called Hanabla
2. Abu Hanafi, whose adherents are known as members of Hanafiyya
3. Ashafi'e, whose adherents are known as members of Shafe'eyya
4. Ibn Maliki, whose adherents are members of Malikyya.

There are a few Qadiriyyah and other smaller sects within the Sunni Muslims of Eritrea, but the overwhelming majority in Eritrea and Eastern Sudan are Khatmiyya Sufis. Khatmiyya is a Sufi denomination of Islam; and Khatmiyya means the end, or the seal—Mohammed being the seal and believed to be the last prophet after Jesus. Khatmiyya's founder is Al Mirghani and Khatmiyya and Mirghaniyya are used interchangeably. The Khatmiyya, being Sufi, are advocates of spirituality and meditation and chanting. The (Saudi-based) Wahabi are strictly opposed to the Sufis.

My informant and guide on this subject wryly notes, "Now you know the Jehovah equivalent of Islam!" He also points out the fluidity in the adherence to the four schools. According to him, Eritrean Muslims follow the four schools of thought and one does not even see the difference. "Sometimes even Muslims do not see the difference," he notes, "for one can follow one juror on one case and another on a different issue."

It is worth stressing that as far as the PFDJ government is concerned, no organization— be it political or religious, Christian or Muslim, mainstream or sect—is tolerated if it cannot be controlled. The PFDJ (and the EPLF before it) has never tolerated any view that is outside its own worldview and that it cannot control. In this, as in other matters, the government of Isaias Afwerki is an equal opportunity oppressor.

The Christian Churches

From the outset, the government recognized four religious bodies: the mainstream Islam led by the mufti, as described above; the Eritrean Orthodox church, the Catholic church and the Evangelical Lutheran Protestant church. The Catholic and Protestant churches depend on donations from their members as well as from outside bodies with which they are associated. The government has devised ways and means of monitoring the activities of these churches, including their external sources of finance. Infiltrating them is one such means. As to the Orthodox church, the manner of exercising control over the activities of its leaders is not much different from that used in the office of the mufti.

Just as the government has banned Islamic sects opposed to the Khatmi-yya and to the leadership of the mufti, it has banned what it has branded as new Christian religions. Included in this category are the Pentecostals, Faith Mission, Presbyterian Church, Jehovah's Witnesses, and the Seventh Day Adventist Mission. How some of these churches like the Seventh Day Adventist, which has been present in the country for a century, could be called new religions is beyond comprehension.

The Jehovah's Witnesses were targeted for special exclusion not meted out to members of the other banned religions. Not only were they prohibited from practicing their faith; they were denied ordinary rights of citizens like practicing a trade or profession. They were driven out of their villas, which were distributed to high-ranking members of the government. Their trade licenses were withdrawn, thus literally being deprived of a means of livelihood.

Why were the Jehovah's Witnesses treated this way? The reason advanced for these denials and prohibitions are twofold. First, adult members of the Jehovah's Witnesses refused to participate in the 1993 National Referendum of Eritrea, on the ground that they believed that their kingdom is not of this earth. Second, they refused to participate in the national service, asking to be given social service tasks instead of military service. Unsubstantiated accusations were made that their motive was driven by Ethiopian politics, and that some of them participated in similar national service during the time of the Dergue, such as the rural development campaign known as "*Yegeter Zemecha.*" As for the first reason for their harsh treatment, it is an open question whether a citizen can be forced to participate in a national event like a referendum; in a nation of laws, this would be tested in a court of law. Eritrea has no such "luxury!"

The decision regarding the Jehovah's Witnesses was taken by Isaias himself, who ordered the then minister of the Interior, Ali Said Abdella, to execute it. Ali then sent a circular to all Ministries and other organs of government requiring them all to do as they were told, including denying working and trading licenses. As it happened, the details of the circular were leaked; and the American embassy obtained a copy. President Clinton is reported to have mentioned this to Isaias in one of their meetings. When Clinton asked him Isaias is reported to have responded by saying that the Jehovahs believe their kingdom is in Heaven, so what are they doing coming to Clinton, who leads an earthly government? Apparently, Clinton, who is known for his wit and linguistic prowess, was left speechless, and the matter ended in laughter!

With regard to the second reason, again in a nation of laws, there is such a thing as a conscientious objector who can decline performing military duties or service on religious or moral ground, opting for an alternative like performing medical service or other social services.

Members of other "new religions" have also been treated harshly in connection with the so-called national service in Sawa. Clergymen of some of the other churches, including the Orthodox church, also protested on being forced to do military service; but to no avail.

Isaias and the Eritrean Orthodox Church

At first, religious affairs were run randomly, with Isaias issuing orders to Naizghi and Ali Said. Then about 1995-1996, a Department of Religious Affairs was created within the Ministry of the Interior. It was later transferred to the Ministry of Regional Administration until the abolition of that ministry. Finally it was put under the direct control of the president's office, where it remains today. The Eritrean Orthodox church, being the church whose adherents constitute the majority of Christians in Eritrea, has received special attention in a manner similar to that of the mufti's office.

The Orthodox church has been administered under the office of the patriarchate. Abune Philipos was the head of the office, with Abune Yacob as the principal administrator. Abune Philipos headed the synod. Even though Abune Yacob was higher in rank as archbishop and was considered more learned in theology, Abune Philipos had the advantage of having been inside Eritrea longer and of being a well-known Eritrean patriot who stood up to the Dergue. When the synod decided to change the office from a bishopric to a patriarchate, the issue of who would be the first Eritrean patriarch became the number one item on the church agenda. The head of the Egyptian coptic church, Pope Shinoda, was persuaded to send his envoy, Bishop Bishoy, to witness the occasion.

It was a time when there was keen competition for the post of the first patriarch between the two contestants: Abune Philipos and Abune Yacob. The competition divided the church into two camps, with regionalism rearing its ugly head. Abune Philipos rallied supporters from the Akele Guzai region, and Abune Yacob rallied supporters from the Hamasien region. One high cleric, Abune Makarios (whom Eritreans in America knew as Aba Petros), a younger and comparatively better-educated cleric, was expected to play a mediating role. He made some half hearted attempts at mediating but, according to some informants, he was overcome by vaulting ambition and apparently seemed to follow the maxim "between two contestants a third will win." But he did not win; instead, Abune Yacob was persuaded to bow out on the understanding that he would be the next patriarch. So Abune Philipos became the first patriarch of Eritrea at the ripe old age of ninety-six.

A point worth emphasizing here is the fact of the historical link between Egypt and Ethiopia, whereby the archbishop of Ethiopia was traditionally anointed by the patriarch of Egypt. This was changed in the mid-1950s, when Abune Basilios became the first patriarch of Ethiopia, thus altering the historic link. According to some Ethiopian commentators of the time, this was considered one of Emperor Haile Selassie's historic achievements, second only to his "recovery" of Eritrea, when he abolished the UN-arranged federation in November 1962. The "Nile Question" being uppermost in the Egyptians' strategic thinking and policy priorities, despite their reluctance in ceding the prerogative of anointing Ethiopian bishops and thus maintaining a symbolic link with Ethiopia, Egyptian leaders settled on maintaining a cordial but watchful relationship with Ethiopia. The Nile being the lifeblood of Egypt and the major source of the Nile being Ethiopia, their relations cannot but remain cordial and watchful.

Similarly, even though one of the Nile's tributaries flows from Eritrea, it is much smaller than either the Blue or White Nile. Nonetheless, Egypt's interest in Eritrea is no less important for strategic and geopolitical reasons; and its relations with Eritrea will be no less cordial and watchful. The link between Egypt and Eritrea continues in a somewhat altered state, with the elevation of the head of the Eritrean Orthodox church to the position of patriarch, thus asserting Eritrea's full national autonomy in this matter.

It is regrettable to learn that the relationship of the two top clerics—Abune Philipos and Abune Yacob—after the former's elevation and anointment, was not one of cordiality. Abune Yacob retired to his home, where he remained until the death of Abune Philipos and his own anointing as patriarch. In all of this drama, Isaias did not relinquish his control; on the contrary, one could see his hand in all the critical affairs of the church, including his approval of the elevation of Abune Philipos to patriarch, thus settling the dispute. He was also responsible for the decision to banish Abune Makarios, rejecting the latter's last-minute offer to be part of the synod as a simple bishop and at the same time expressing remorse for his earlier plots campaigning to become the first patriarch.

With regard to the finances of the Orthodox church, the government plays a major role. The income from the faithful, such as it is, does not go beyond covering the expenses of the church leaders; so the government makes an annual budget allocation of over two million nakfa. This is in addition to the provision of vehicles and other logistical support. Also the Egyptian Coptic church had made a donation of some $100,000 for the purpose of building a theological college. This fund was supposed to take care of the preliminary studies and the architect's plan. The government knows of this, but no one knows where the money has gone; and there is no college building in sight. Moreover, ten young students of theology were selected for training under the auspices of the Coptic church. Among these, one prominent priest, Keshi Gebre-Medhin, is now in detention, together with Dr. Fitsum and other clerics.

The arrest and indefinite detention of these two educated and dedicated priests is symptomatic of what ails the Eritrean Orthodox church and religious life in Eritrea today. Many other young priests and other religious people have been arrested and remain in detention incommunicado. What we do know about Dr. Fitsum and his companions is that they are dedicated priests who have a firm commitment to serve the Orthodox church and to revitalize and modernize some of its methods of managing its affairs. An example of the programs of change is a proposal made by the young priests that the sermon be given in Tigrigna instead of in the traditional Geez, so that the community of faith can understand its message better. Second, they proposed that the church service be conducted at noon, instead of the early morning, so that young congregants could attend. The response of the older and tradition-bound priests was to accuse the young reformers of being *Pentes* (Pentecostals). They were thus accused of straying from the "correct line" of the Orthodox church.

Clearly, in their commitment to modernization and revitalization, the young educated priests were engaged in the proverbial contest between the irresistible idea and the immovable object. The latter was in the form of older and tradition-bound priests who saw in this new approach a threat to their vested interests. What is intriguing is how the dispute led to the arrest and detention of the young priests, including Dr. Fitsum, a dedicated psychiatrist who performed commendable medical/psychiatric service to patients over and above his pastoral duties. How and why did the dispute land at the president's desk and why did he order their arrest? This question is connected with the dethronement of His Holiness Patriarch Antonios, Eritrea's third Patriarch. What Isaias did is comparable to the desperate acts of despotic kings of old like Henry VIII of England.

The President and the Patriarch

Patriarch Antonios is a man of God whose primary pastoral concern has always been the wellbeing of his "flock." Unlike some other high priests of the Eritrean Orthodox church, he was not involved in the competition to ascend to the office of patriarch. The office was hoisted on him by virtue of his seniority as well as by his piety and humility. When Isaias began detaining the young progressive priests, Patriarch Antonios, who had seen the value of the young priests' view, which is modernizing the church, expressed strong disapproval of their detention and requested their release. The president also removed the associates and sympathizers of the young priests, thus leaving the church open for sycophants and yes-men who would do his bidding, under the leadership of Mr. Yoftahe Dimetros, whom Isaias appointed to run the affairs of the Orthodox Church. In noting the irony of choosing Yoftahe, one wonders what unknown relationship there might be between Isaias Afwerki and the son of Keshi Dimetros!

It is also obvious that Isaias thought Antonios would be easy to manipulate. As the website, In Chain for Christ (ICFC) aptly put it, "Isaias mistook the piety and humility of the Patriarch for docility and thought he could walk all over him as he was accustomed to doing to so many others." (See Special Report: http:www.inchainsforchrist.org/index.php?option=com_content&vie...)

He would discover that beneath the piety of a monk was "a defiant and unshakable granite of a man." When he could not manipulate him, Isaias did something that no temporal authority should do with respect to a spiritual authority—dismissing an anointed patriarch. According to tradition and canonical law, no political leader may intervene in church affairs and depose an anointed patriarch. A patriarch can only be deposed by a properly constituted ecclesiastical body on the grounds of proof that he is found in a compromising sex act, or that he becomes mentally unfit to hold office.

But the outrageous act of deposing the patriarch did not go unchallenged; on the contrary, there was a massive protest. Again, to cite ICFC, by the time of the deposing of the patriarch, "the only orthodox body that could pose the threat of any organized resistance to this gross interference in the Eritrean Orthodox Church was the Diocese of North America." And to counter that, the Isaias regime decided to send a bishop/cadre to America. The candidate for the job was Bishop Sinoda, who was dispatched to Washington, D.C., in October 2005. ICFC claims to have documents showing that Sinoda and his handlers at the Eritrean embassy launched a campaign of vilification against the leaders of the synod in North America, coupled with words of intimidation to the larger community of faith of the Orthodox church. It was a campaign tactic lifted from the pages of the PFDJ manual conducted against members of the political opposition.

With the active participation of heads of the PFDJ cells in North America, the bishop was involved in these campaigns, which included attempts to sully the name of H.H. Patriarch Antonios, as well as many leading members of priesthood in North America. But the table was turned on the plotters. To begin with, Patriarch Antonios, who had not been deposed yet but was aware of what was happening, wrote a letter informing the North American diocese and followers of the Eritrean Orthodox church that Bishop Sinoda had been sent to America without his knowledge and approval, and that he denounced the appointment as illegal.

In a massive demonstration of solidarity with the deposed patriarch, and in opposition to Sinoda, the North American diocese and the community of the faithful rose up in protest. They inundated the Eritrean embassy in Washington, D.C., with letters of protest, making it impossible for Sinoda to succeed in the campaign. Eventually Sinoda saw that he was engaged in an impossible mission. He gave up on his assigned project, breaking with his masters and has reportedly applied for asylum in America. If this is true, one wonders as to what grounds he cited as reason for his asylum request. The vast majority of Orthodox Christians are committed to delivering their church from the clutches of the regime. They owe loyalty to the one legitimate patriarch and opposed to the illegitimate successor who was appointed by the president. There is only one legitimate Patriarch, and his name is Antonios.

The struggle continues.

Chapter 13

ETHNO-REGIONAL POLITICS

Eritrea's Geographic Division

Eritrea's geography is divided into the highland mountain region, and the lowland plains. We must distinguish this geographic divide from the administrative divisions that are man-made, and which have been changed from time to time according to the whim and caprice of whoever happened to be ruling the country. For example, there is an oral tradition that says the Italians lopped off a southern portion of Hamasien and added it to Seraye. They did this to spite the Hamaisen traditional ruling elite that had apparently proved obdurate. And in our own time, Isaias, in his infinite wisdom, chopped up Hamasien, distributing pieces of it to various "Zobas" (regions). The reason advanced for changing the structure of the historic administrative division was geoeconomic and environmental—I heard, for the first time, the expression *Mai-ko'O* (watershed) used at the time of the introduction of the new law changing the structure and names of the regions.

Also subjected to the merciless scythe of the grim reaper are the historic names of Eritrea that were unceremoniously disposed of and buried. They were abolished by a presidential (or rather royal) decree and substituted with neutral-sounding geographical expressions—Maekel, Debub, Anseba, Semenawi Qeyih Bahri, Debubawi Qeyih Bahri. The abolition of the historic names was explained by some well-meaning government supporters in terms of the EPLF's commitment to a progressive, national (nation-building) agenda transcending ethnic and "subnational" sentiments. Such sentiments were associated with a feudal mentality and condemned as unfit for a progressive organization. In fact, in the EPLF vocabulary of vilification, "subnational" replaced "feudal" as a term of abuse.

The only region that was allowed to retain its name is Gash-Barka. This is a region rich in agricultural and other resources, and the government has designated it for development. As such, it has become a subject of a great deal of contention with far-reaching political implications, as we shall see.

The highland geographic land mass is predominantly inhabited by Christians, while the eastern and western lowlands are inhabited by Muslims. There are Muslims in the highlands, of course—Saho in Akeleguzai and Jeberti in Seraye; and the majority of the inhabitants of Senhit and Sahel are Muslims, with Christian communities among the Blin and the Mensa'e. The inhabitants of the highlands are predominantly farmers, while those in the lowlands are pastoralists and agropastoralists. In the eastern lowlands, along the Red Sea coast, particularly among the Afar, fishing is also a way of life. The recent attempts to promote fishing and the consumption of fish, an important component of nutrition for Eritreans, may have persuaded some non-Afar Eritreans to become interested in fishing; but such attempts are limited in scope and a far cry from what needs to be done. This question is related to the different modes of production and of ways of life of Eritreans living in the different regions, and how it is linked to the national interest.

Tigres and Tigrignas

Once more I shift gears to inject a personal note before I resume the academic, analytical mode, hoping that the reason for this temporary shift will become clear later. In the recent cyber space discourse among Eritreans, to which I will return, my name was mentioned a few times by one particular writer in a context that was distorted, presumably with the aim of drawing me into a cyberwarfare. I did not think that would advance our common cause of democracy and justice, but would rather please the enemies of that cause, especially those who are ruling over our people. In terms of our common cause, I thought it better to wait for an opportune moment and decided to treat the subject dispassionately. My shift to a personal narrative is aimed at demonstrating that there is more that unites highland and lowland Eritreans as a people than divides us. Our recent history of struggle is a living testimony of this fact.

I begin with reference to my childhood perceptions of people who seemed to me the same as myself and my kind, though they spoke a different language. Tigres and Tigrignas are related peoples, as can be seen in the closeness of their two languages, with Geez as their common pedigree; and of the two, Tigre is closer to Geez. I have pleasant childhood memories of Tigre-speaking people visiting us from nearby Ad'Shuma or distant Habab with their camels or flock of goats. I loved to hear their language though I never had the opportunity to learn it. My paternal grandmother, Iteghe Sebene, was the one who spoke volubly with the occasional visitors, sipping coffee and eating *qolo* (roasted grain), or *qiCha* (local bread).

In terms of the relationship of the two peoples, historically, there developed a distance between them, a distance that was both physical and cultural, bridged by occasional interaction in the form of an exchange of goods and services. I'll offer some personal anecdotes to help provide a comparative perspective and human dimension to the relationship of the two peoples.

In the area where I grew up until the age of twelve, the occasional arrival of lowlanders with their camels and goats was greeted with excitement by us children, as the men would stop in the villages for respite and coffee. We were fascinated by the sight of camels set loose by their owners, who left them to forage on the acacia trees. Those villagers with a smattering knowledge of Tigre showed off their knowledge by addressing the guests in Tigre and chatting with them over coffee. Some of the Tigre-speaking Muslims from nearby Ad-Shuma frequently exchanged salt for grains. There was one man in particular from Ad'Shuma whom I remember with fondness; his name was Omar Hussein, and he was a frequent visitor to our household. He was a builder and spoke fluent Tigrigna; he often stayed in our house for a few days, proudly telling us young ones that he built the *mereba'e* part of our compound (modern structure) where I slept. I loved talking to Omar Hussein (or Merhishen, as we called him).

The other group that came once a year were Asgede from Sahel. These were distant relatives of the inhabitants of my village, Adi Nifas, which was founded by our common ancestor, Asgede.

The next time I came in contact with Tigre-speaking people I was at a mature age, decades later when I joined the Eritrean struggle in 1975. Actually before I linked up with the liberation fighters in the highlands around Asmara, I came in contact with Saho-speaking ELF fighters in Akeleguzai; but my contact there lasted only a few days. It was in Sahel that I finally came in contact with Tigre-speaking people; only it was among smaller groups during resting time that I heard Tigre spoken by some of the fighters from Semhar, or when some of the fighters were addressing the Sahel *"ghebar"* (non-combatant), a term that I resented because of its demeaning connotation. The fighters spoke among themselves either in Tigrigna or Arabic.

On the whole, I found the Tigre-speaking fighters a more open and relaxed lot, compared to the highlanders. Comparing Isaias Afwerki (a highlander) with the lowlander Romodan Mohamed Nur, for example, I found that the latter spoke more openly even in the Sahel context that I would later discover to be a repressive milieu. Later, when I met wounded fighters in Aden and Beirut, where they were sent for medical treatment, the same openness and candor characterized the lowlanders. For example, the veteran fighter (and martyr) Shaikh Omar of blessed memory, with whom I spent some time in Beirut in the summer of 1975, spoke more openly and taught me much of the history of the struggle from the early days when it started.

In contrast, earlier, when I had tried to learn the same history from some of the highlanders, including leaders like Mesfin Hagos, getting it out of them was like extracting teeth with the associated pain. Ibrahim Afa, a Semhar Tigre, responded to my questions without hesitation or reservation; even the prevailing culture of silence of the EPLF did not restrain him. In retrospect, it is not hard to imagine that Ibrahim's candor and openness, in addition to his heroic status and popularity among the *tegadelti*, earned him Isaias' enmity.

In general, I came to the conclusion, as I mentioned in the first volume of these memoirs, that the lowlanders are a more open and sincere people than we highlanders; we tend to be secretive for the most part. We may possess other qualities like discipline and tenacity, but in my view, our Tigre brothers surpass us in this respect. (N.B. The Ethiopian equivalent of this phenomenon is found in the juxtaposition of Somali-Amhara character in which the Somali are open and direct whereas the high-land-Amhara are secretive. I emphasize the term highland-Amhara advisedly, because I noticed that Amharas born and brought up in Harar are more open and direct like the Somali and unlike those from highland Shoa).

I am not so foolish as to turn this into a general theory, because my view is not based on a rigorous scientific inquiry. But let us take it as a working hypothesis. If it is correct, as I think it is, it should be followed by a conclusion, namely, that such openness and sincerity are valuable assets in our national ethos that can contribute to transparency and democratic health. Consequently, as a nation, we have a duty to preserve and promote it. Above all, lowlanders are a vital and constituent part of our Eritrean national heritage, particularly the generation of freedom fighters who have been through thick and thin together and fought shoulder to shoulder, finally bringing about an independent Eritrea. No particular segment of Eritrea, highland or lowland, can claim the lion's share in that glorious history; it is a common heritage, a shared patrimony. Accordingly, no one side can or should be allowed to claim a monopoly of power or control of resources. Eritrea belongs to all her people; and the government is the government of all the people. To the extent that any government disputes or deviates from this is proof that it is not fit to govern.

And WE THE PEOPLE bear a responsibility to prevent this from happening. Nevertheless, the question remains: How do we do this, and what are some of the issues that need to be addressed in this respect? These are topics for another day. At this point it is enough for us to take stock of what ails our country and at the very least try to reach a common understanding of the emerging tragic reality in all its manifestations.

When Things Fall Apart

It is time to face up to the grim reality. Eritrea is in crisis. To borrow a line from the great Irish poet, W.B. Yeats' 'Second Coming,' "Things Fall apart; the center cannot hold..." The great Nigerian writer Chinua Achebe, has written a novel under this title. The theme of the novel is the destruction of traditional Igbo values under the onslaught of European colonial rule. In essence, what we are facing in Eritrea today is similar—our liberationist ideology of freedom, justice, and democracy are under attack from a system led by people who seem to know the price of everything, but the value of nothing; in short, people with whom we do not share common values, despite their pretense, tricking us with what I have called an immaculate deception.

We must now look deep into our national soul, as it were, and reexamine what has held us together. What was the glue that held things together in Eritrea's case? What principles underlay the relation of the "center" and the "periphery"? Again, to paraphrase Yeats, will the center hold, or is "mere anarchy...loosed" upon our nation?

A few Eritrean writers who do not seem to believe in Eritrea as a viable nation, presumably want us to join (or rejoin) and reclaim common nationhood with our larger neighbor to the south. Such writing presumably subscribes to the "*Greater Ethiopia*" hypothesis advanced by Donald Levine. There is nothing wrong in aspiring to belong to a larger unity, transcending local dividing lines, provided certain conditions are fulfilled, as experience has taught us Eritreans. One of those conditions is mutuality of respect and acceptance of some fundamental rights, including democracy and the right of self-determination. We have had our cautionary experience under the ill-fated, UN-arranged federation, which was unilaterally abrogated by Emperor Haile Selassie and led to the thirty-year war of liberation.

At the other end, there are Eritreans who hold the "*Tigrigna Supremacist*" hypothesis, imagining a scenario of a possible breakup of Eritrea in which the lowlands join Sudan and the highlands join Ethiopia. It is not clear whether this scenario is based on fear or wish; but the idea of such a prospect would cause Bevin and Sforza to turn in their graves and declare from beyond: "We told you so!" Two other people who would turn in their graves with consternation are Shaikh Ibrahim Sultan Ali and Memhrey Woldeab Woldemariam, the leaders who spearheaded the movement to defeat the Bevin-Sforza conspiracy to partition Eritrea. And among the living, it is not hard to imagine Ethiopians like Shaleqa Dawit Woldegiorgis rubbing hands with glee in contemplation of such a gratuitous political gift; and Dawit's celebration would be joined by a chorus of "Amen!" from the revanchist crowd known as *Kinijit*.

But the man who would laugh loudest is none other than Isaias Afwerki himelf, dutifully joined by his captive inner circle and sycophants. To him the "Opposition" is a washout. I told you, he would cry triumphantly, all this *qebeT-beT* of the lowlanders and the confusion of the midgets calling themselves the Opposition shows the failure of Western democracy and the so called freedom of the press, which is a tool of the CIA. Isaias considers all the controversy among Eritreans in the Diaspora as a validation of his iron grip, and a reminder to doubters within his ranks that his way is the only way to go. I can hear him shout: Give me an Iron Rod—or give me Death!

As many people know, in the recent past a vigorous debate has been raging in cyberspace concerning the right of ethnolinguistic groups and minorities within a nation, including their land rights and legitimate representation in national power sharing. Some Eritrean lowlanders, like Ali Salim, have argued that the Eritrean government as presently constituted does not represent them; that it has launched an evil scheme whereby it will expropriate lands historically belonging to people in one part of the country—the lowlands—and settle people from another part—the highlands. The writers contend that the PFDJ regime has used (or rather abused) the Land Proclamation, and the 1997 Constitution that undergirds it, to launch this dangerous program of wholesale expropriation of lands of lowlanders. They further contend that the program of forcible settlement of highlanders in the lowlands is part of a long-term strategy of a massive resettlement of highlanders on lands that should be reserved for lowlanders who are wasting away in Sudanese refugee camps. Moreover, the writers also accuse the government of deliberately delaying or even blocking the repatriation of the refugees to their ancestral lands. This, they argue, is in order to settle highlanders there under a strategic scheme that one of the writers calls demographic engineering by "Tigrigna supremacists and neo-Nazis."

Leaving aside the strident nature of the writing with its tendency to brand people with extreme epithets, we need a rational approach and a calm response. An appropriate response would be, first to determine whether what is being said is well-founded: Is there incontrovertible evidence to support these charges? Second, to determine what our duty is as concerned citizens: What should we do if it turns out that the charges are well-founded? Clearly, these statements raise some serious questions concerning rights and responsibilities, equitable sharing of resources, power sharing, highland-lowland or "center-periphery" relations, and generally the future health of our nation. These are questions that all Eritreans must face squarely.

When we examine the expressions of disillusion of some of our disaffected citizens, even those couched in strident language and provocative form, we need to understand that persons with grievances sometimes tend to go to extremes in expressing those grievances. We need to exercise restraint and make a calm and rational appraisal of the situation. Any attitude of outright dismissal of the charges just because they are couched in extreme language is not helpful, any more than the resort to branding of a whole category of people with hateful language is helpful.

Now, in terms of fundamental principles and mechanisms of resolving issues of contention, and to answer the kind of questions we are addressing, the universally recognized basic framework for settling such issues is a national constitution. In Eritrea's case, there are two problems in this regard. First, the Isaias regime has trashed a constitution that its parliament approved, and a Constituent Assembly ratified. Isaias is on record for calling the constitution "just a piece of paper." Second, some Eritreans, including the lowland writers mentioned above, do not accept a constitution made under the aegis of the EPLF. Therefore, in the circumstances, it would appear that we cannot expect a resolution of the issues at hand in the framework of the 1997 Eritrean constitution, despite its potential for achieving the objective. When one side charges that the constitution is "a manual for land grabbers," and the culprit regime will not hear of any constitutional dispensation, it would seem futile to insist on the point. It would seem that we are talking about a moot question; accordingly, in terms of logic, we may have to look elsewhere for resolution. The question is: Where do we look—what do we do?

To begin with, it is a matter of record that the government has taken the first steps to implement the resettlement scheme. My own reaction to such government folly was and is, first of all, that forcible resettlement of people is contrary to generally recognized human rights law. Second, such a policy has historically proven to be disastrous. We don't have to go far to prove this point. The Dergue's attempts in neighboring Ethiopia ended up in failure with collateral damage to thousands of people. Additionally, the policy would constitute double jeopardy; that is to say, lowlanders are being dispossessed of their land and highland villagers are forced out of their ancestral lands and placed in harm's way by such forced imposition.

Let us examine this further by separating the issues. Can the government uproot people against their will? The answer is that it has the power to do so because it has a monopoly on the instruments of violence. And it is forcing people against their will and relocating them to the lowlands. But that does not mean it is right; clearly it is not. In fact, as mentioned already, it is a crime. At the other end, can the government take other people's land against their will and give it to other people? Here we need to introduce the subject of state ownership of land, a matter that has also been the subject of considerable debate.

Those of us who had been under the spell of socialist ideology during the revolutionary era thought that state ownership of the means of production, distribution and exchange (the standard definition of socialism) was the best prescription for Eritrea. We are suffering from the hangover of that belief, as witness article 23(2) of the 1997 constitution, which provides: "All land and all natural resources below and above the surface of the territory of Eritrea belong to the State. The interests citizens shall have in land shall be determined by law."

Not that public ownership of some key elements of what they now call the commanding heights of the economy is a bad thing; even in capitalist America there is the doctrine of eminent domain, and there have been government interventions in times of need. Moreover, as the next subarticle of article 23 of the constitution provides, the state may "in the national or public interest take property, subject to the payment of just compensation and in accordance with due process of law."

The problem is that a predatory state owning key economic resources like land can do more harm than good, as we have learned in Eritrea. As one of the founders of the Eritrean Democratic Party and a member of its top leadership, until I resigned, I became convinced of the need to reverse the mistake we made by declaring that article 23(2) of the constitution should be amended to restore land to its rightful owners—the members of the village community. However, I still believe in the right of the government to own land for development purposes, as opposed to wholesale unrestricted ownership. In this respect, the Isaias government's abuse of the constitution and the Land Proclamation has taught us an expensive lesson.

Another amendment the founders of the Eritrean Democratic Party agreed upon was: making Arabic and Tigrigna official languages of Eritrea. (I hope that Idris Aba-Are will survive his imprisonment and live to see this change).

Another issue concerns the belief by some highly-educated lowlanders that a Tigrigna-based (exclusionist) government is determined to create facts on the ground that cannot be reversed—facts that are bound to have adverse (perhaps tragic) effects for people and the nation as a whole. If the government scheme of mass resettlement from the highlands in the lowlands goes forward, and there are clear indications that it will, this scheme is an invitation to some serious consequences. We are talking about a tragedy in the making. Hence the introductory, rather dramatic words—Will the center hold, or will things fall apart?

What are the requirements for the center to hold and to avoid a meltdown or collapse? Does the Eritrean nation need to be reconstituted so that all regions and ethnic minorities—those in the periphery—can be secure in their respective regions with a constitutionally guaranteed and equitable share of power and control of their resources? In what way can the 1997 constitution be adjusted to provide for such an accommodation? The issue of land ownership and the policy of the Isaias regime to pursue a strategy of massive settlement of highlanders in the lowland raise some serious questions pertaining to law and politics. The related question of state ownership of land, ordained under the constitution of 1997 and the Land Proclamation that preceded the constitution, has been cited by some in these debates as a source of the problem. Indeed, one writer goes to the extreme conclusion that the constitution and the Land Proclamation were designed by the government with the aim of dispossessing lowlanders and settling highlanders. (Ali Salim, Awate.com, 2009). The same writer also accuses the government of deliberately blocking the resettlement of lowlanders who are still living as refugees in Sudan.

This accusation as well as the policy of forced resettlement by the Isaias regime cannot be taken lightly. But we need to separate facts from opinion. If there is truth in the charge of deliberately blocking Eritrean refugees from returning to their homeland, it is tantamount to a crime against humanity, if not genocide. Even an egregious neglect of helping the refugees to return to their homeland amounts to the same thing in the context of a deliberate policy of demographic restructuring, assuming the charges are true. Are these charges true?

There has been some research on the subject of repatriation of Eritrean refugees. The following findings are neither complete nor up-to-date but are indicative of the early policy of the government. According to the statistics of the U.S. Committee on Refugees (USCRI), some 250,000 Eritreans had repatriated to their country of origin by 2004. (See USCRI Eritrea Report from 1999 to 2003). When it comes to the place of their settlement, most were settled in Tessenei, Goluj, Gergef, Tebeldia, Alebu, in the surrounding areas of Tessenei; the majority were settled in towns, especially Tessenei. This means that their livelihood is not based on agriculture. According to the reports of researchers on the subject, the large majority of the refugees, including those who originally hailed from different parts of Senhit, including the Maria area, Halhal, Anseba, Barka, Kebesa, had settled in the 1950s, 60s and 70s in Gash Setit area before they fled to Sudan.

From Antipathy to Empathy

Much of the public discourse among Eritreans has been marked by the bitter exchange of tirades. The underlying spirit in such exchanges can be summed up as *antipathy*. A legacy of pseudo-Marxist ideology of "class struggle," which was espoused by a generation of Eritreans that had matured during the 1960s and 1970s, may partly explain the bitterness—but only partly. Marxist ideology aside, there is a sense of alienation experienced by a segment of our population on the grounds of actual or perceived exclusion from participation in the political and socioeconomic life of the nation, One of the most articulate expressions of such exclusion is the recently published document under the heading "The

Eritrean Covenant." A distinguishing feature of this document is the absence of bitterness or antipathy; on the contrary, it exudes *empathy*.

Apart from its brilliant analysis and acuity of conclusion, the document abounds with concern for the common good, for which it should be embraced. And you don't have to be a Muslim to embrace it, for it is a national document, comparable with (some would say antithetical to) *Nihanan Elamanan*. I read it twice and hope to read it again. When I reached the part that refers to Jesus Christ as "Our Lord," I couldn't believe it; so I consulted a Muslim friend and asked him for the Arabic version, and he confirmed that it means the same in Arabic as it does in the English. Since then I have started referring to the Prophet Mohammed (peace be upon him) as "Saidna Mohammed." That is mutually reinforcing empathy—fellow Christians, take heed!

Omar Jabir: An Empathetic Sage

In this segment I have decided to include a response to a piece that Ustaz Omar wrote about me under the intriguing title, "Dr. Bereket Habteselassie: From the Unknown to the Uncertain" (Awate, Mar 07, 2010). The relevance of Omar's piece to the subject at hand will become clear later. When I read the piece, at first I thought that some unkind person had misinformed him about my departure to the "great unknown" from which no one returns. That kind of title usually refers to the "dearly departed" and God knows that there are a few types who dearly wish me a hasty departure, especially among that ungodly crowd in Asmara and their mindless agents in the Diaspora.

On further reading, however, I realized that my first reaction was misplaced, realizing that the gentle Omar was paying me a compliment, putting some parts of my past life and service in perspective, covering a period of over thirty years. He gives a rough outline of aspects of my life and role in some historical events. The reality is more complex; but rather than write a correction here, I prefer to send him a book of my memoirs with my compliments. Omar also raises questions concerning my views on a couple of issues, which makes his piece relevant to the subject about which I am writing; and therefore questions I need to answer. But before I respond to the questions he raises, I thought it might be relevant to give a brief review of the historical circumstances of our meeting. After all, this segment is an excerpt related to my memoirs.

My Journey from Sahel to the Middle East

It was in the spring of 1975. I was on a mission—part humanitarian and part political. Having spent some time in the highland areas of the "field," helping in the popular efforts to stop the "civil war" between the ELF and the

EPLF, I had traveled to Sahel and thence abroad, with a mandate to mobilize relief supplies for Eritrean refugees and displaced persons whose number had increased exponentially after the Ethiopian military offensive in early 1975.

I journeyed from Sahel on board a small boat captained by an EPLF fighter, an Afar named Vasco, and we crossed the Red Sea on the way to Aden in what was then the Democratic Republic of Yemen. We had traveled together with some wounded fighters in the company of Romodan Mohammed Nur and Woldenkiel Gebremariam. The late Osman Saleh Sabbe came from Beirut to meet us in Aden. He made all the necessary plans for us to travel to Beirut for a meeting of the foreign mission of the EPLF, which he headed. After that meeting he arranged for me and my traveling companion, Redazghi Gebremedhin, to tour the Middle East, including Iraq.

When we discussed things to do and not to do—people to meet and places to visit—with Romodan and Weldenkiel, I remember Weldenkiel telling me not to meet the Eritrean group in Iraq; they belonged to GUES Baghdad. He told me in no uncertain terms to avoid them like the plague (*KeytiQerbom*!). Weldenkiel was the EPLF representative in Aden, and Romodan was a member of the EPLF provisional leadership. It was a time of bitter division; hence Weldenkiel's counsel, which may sound strange to an uninformed listener. Eritrean politics was poisoned by factional fights exacerbated by the deadly "civil war"; and one of the reasons for the tour was to help put an end to this sad condition, i.e., to promote unity as well as to mobilize relief. The mandate to mobilize relief was decided in a meeting at Deqetros in the Hamasien highland, which was attended by Isaias Afwerki representing the EPLF and by Ibrahim Totil representing the ELF. To that end, we later created the Eritrean Relief Association (ERA) of which I was the founding chairman and Redazghi Gebremedhin the secretary.

I did not heed Weldenkiel's counsel to avoid the GUES; on the contrary, I told him that as an Eritrean elder working to promote unity of the two fronts and seeking relief for the distressed, I was duty-bound to meet any and every Eritrean who came my way. And when I met Osman Sabbe in Beirut, I told him that I wanted to meet all Eritreans, whichever front they supported. Sabbe raised no objections; indeed, he made several arrangements for meetings throughout the Middle East.

An Encounter with GUES Baghdad

Baghdad was our last stop. We first met Abu Ala, a Syrian-born official of Iraq's Baath party and head of the party's department dealing with Africa. Having completed our "official" visits, I asked to see Eritrean students who were grouped around GUES Baghdad. Our tour guides informed us that there was a death in the family of one of the students, and that most of them were sitting in mourning. Could we wait until the mourning was over? I said, I would like to visit the place where the mourning was held; and we did go there to pay our condolences. A couple of days later, we attended a meeting of a few dozen Eritrean students. I believe it was there that I first met Omar Jabir at the end of the meeting.

The meeting began calmly. Naturally, everyone was curious to know who I was and why I had come to Iraq. Speaking in Tigrigna, and with an interpreter sitting by my side at the table translating, I started my speech with warm greetings before I delved into the topic at hand. Before I could continue some members of the audience voiced protests. There followed a period of shouting and a general atmosphere of riot—*igirgir!* It all took me by surprise (at that point I remembered Weldenkiel's counsel—*keitQerbom*!). Turning to the interpreter, I asked him what was happening; he told me that they were protesting my speaking in Tigrigna! I told him to let them know that I was capable of making the speech in English if need be. He did, and some voiced approval, while others objected. The *igirgi* continued.

At that point, a distinguished-looking man, who appeared to be more mature in years than the average member of the audience, got up to address the assembly. When he spoke people quieted down and listened to him with rapt attention. At the end of his speech when he sat down, my interpreter told me that I could speak in Tigrigna. I said quietly, "*Alhamdlillahi*, I can speak in my own language!" Some of those sitting in front heard what I said and laughed at the irony of the point of my remark. I also asked the interpreter in a whisper who the distinguished man was who calmed the riot down. He whispered back, "His name is Omar Jabir."

I gave the gathering a summary of the nature of our mission and also briefly described the ongoing mediation efforts aimed at creating national unity with the reconciliation of the two fronts as a crucial element. At the end of my speech, there was polite applause, a politeness eclipsed by what followed during the question and answer session. I was mercilessly attacked by a few outspoken members of GUES Baghdad for what they were convinced I was—an emissary of *thawra muddada* (Arabic for counterrevolutionary), which was what the ELF cadres called the EPLF. There were, of course, a few questions that were relevant to the topic of my speech. In the end, exhausted and disappointed, I sat down to lick my wounds and to wonder whether Weldenkiel was right in warning me against meeting the Baghdad group. Was I a fool in search of a hopeless cause of unity? I thought not, and I doggedly set forth in pursuit of that noble cause and was pleasantly surprised to find a kindred spirit in Omar Jabir, a wise man and gentle soul who encouraged me to continue the cause of unity that he shared wholeheartedly.

Persistent Questions

In the concluding part of his piece, introduced above, Omar Jabir wrote:

> ...I would like to pass to Dr. Bereket some remarks that I heard from some observers who follow (his) contributions (mainly Muslims): I hope he will consider the following in the struggle for a new Eritrea (Haddas Ertra)...
>
> - Some say that you are concerned about the post independence influx of Eritrean Refugees, that is natural and appreciated, but you should equally be concerned about the "original" refugees—more than a quarter of a million—who should be returned home by now and settled in their liberated land.
> - Some believe that you are a strong advocate for democracy and against dictatorship—something that is highly appreciated: but you do not go far enough to call for the dismantlement of the structure and composition of the present state that is dominated by one ethnic group. And those observers ask:
> - If the composition of the state—its departments, channels and personnel are all from one ethnic group—how can we have justice and equality?—How can we guarantee justice and equality if one ethnic group owns the wealth, resources, assets and everything else in Eritrea?

My Response

In a posting on Awate.com, I gave the following response

> - To me, all refugees deserve our attention and support. When I helped establish ERA, I was only aware of the refugees in the highlands around Asmara whose villages the Ethiopian army had destroyed. Indeed, the creation of ERA was begun in response to those events in early 1975, events that I personally witnessed. It was not until I went to Sahel that I started learning about the "original" refugees in other parts of Eritrea in the lowlands. I remember one particular song of Idris Mohamed Ali in Tigre in which he asks: *"Ayye guesset Kubuda....Semsem Guesset interrb...Semsem guesset interrb!"* etc.etc I asked what the song was about and was told it was about the earlier Eritrean refugees driven from their homeland by enemy attacks. And when we created the ERA my companion Redazghi and I went to the refugee areas in Sudan to make assessment of needs. So I have been aware of, and had the same concerns for, the "original" refugees as for the new ones. To me a refugee is a refugee. The

preeminent consideration is motivated by a human concern, and should not have anything to do with the ethnicity or nationality of the refugee.

- The claim that the original refugees have been denied their right of return has disturbed me ever since I heard about it; and I made attempts to verify its veracity. That there are a huge number of Eritrean refugees still in Sudan is beyond question though their exact number is disputed. Also disputed (by some) is the allegation that the Isaias regime has denied and deliberately blocked their return. My comment on this last part has been twofold. First, we all have a duty to see to it that all Eritrean refugees are helped to return to their homeland, and that the government has a solemn duty to do everything in its power toward that end. Second, I am on record for stating that if the allegation of deliberate blockage is well-founded, the government is liable to charges of crimes against humanity. I stand by that statement. (See my last posting in Awate.com, March 1, 2010).

- As to the question regarding my position on the dismantlement of the structure and composition of the present state, the point is that the current state is dominated by one ethnic group, the Tigrigna: How can there be justice and equality under such a situation?

My Response

Concerning this question, I give the following threefold answer:

- First of all, the domination of the Eritrean state by the Tigrigna ethnic group is not subject to question. This is a fact and only those suffering from self-delusion can deny it. The facts and figures marshaled by researchers like Ahmed Raji prove this to be the case beyond doubt.

- Secondly, there are historical and other reasons to explain the fact of the Tigrigna domination of Eritrean political life. The ethnic question is connected to the religious question as I tried to describe and analyze in my previous posting referred to above. Comparatively more educational and other opportunities were available to the Christian (Tigrigna) highlanders. As I observed in the earlier posting, one of the effects of abrogation of the UN-granted federation of Eritrea and Ethiopia was to diminish or downgrade the role of Muslims in the Eritrean government.

- Thirdly, the question now is where do we go from here: what is to be done in order to redress the balance, to remedy the situation in the new Eritrea? In this respect, owning up to the facts of inequality and agreeing on the basic principles of democratic equality among Eritreans is a first prerequisite. Democratic equality is guaranteed under the 1997 constitution, which the ruling regime has suspended. Eritreans who do not accept the constitution on the grounds that it was drafted under the aegis of the EPLF government should review chapter three of the constitution. Those who find fault with the constitution on any other ground should be reminded that it has amendment provisions; it can be improved. One such amendment, in addition to the one mentioned in my previous posting, may be the need to provide for more devolution of power from the center to the regions. This can be discussed dispassionately.

Let me be clear on one thing: Anyone who expects me or members of my commission to apologize for being responsible for drafting the constitution is simply providing an illustration of what I called an antipathetic spirit. I will not apologize for taking a major role in drafting the constitution, as some have demanded. On the contrary, except for the part of the constitution which I agree may need amendment, it is my firm belief that the constitution can and should be taken as an important weapon in the struggle for democracy and justice. The tendency of Eritreans opposed to the EPLF to condemn members of the EPLF and expect them to apologize for the part they played as members in various capacities, including being part of the constitution-making process, is not only wrong but damages the cause of a united struggle for democracy and justice.

Granted that many evil deeds were committed by the top EPLF leadership for which they should be answerable both in law and at the tribunal of history. *But the EPLF members should not be confused with the errant leaders; they should certainly not be expected to apologize for liberating Eritrea from enemy occupation. By the same token, I should not be expected to apologize for helping write a constitution, which, despite some defects, has been hailed as exemplary by many observers and experts.* (See, for example, "Framing the State in Times of Transition," US Institute of Peace Publication, April 2010).

The Need to Cultivate Empathy

By way of contributing to the resolution of the deadlock in current Eritrean opposition politics, I have come to the conclusion that there should be a conscious decision by Eritreans to cultivate empathy towards their fellow Eritreans. It is very easy to be antipathetic to "the other," especially in political discourse;

and, conversely, it is hard to cultivate empathy. But the practice of empathy holds the key to resolving our problems. This may be dismissed as idealistic dreaming; *but minds keener, and hearts greater than mine throughout the ages have ordained that, far from being a dreamer's wish, empathy is, in essence, utterly realistic because it facilitates the establishment of a framework for harmony among people.*

I am sure each one of us can give examples of people who practice empathy and have thus contributed to harmony and social solidarity. In this chapter I called Omar Jabir an empathetic sage. I did that both on the basis of his behavior at the meeting in Baghdad, which saved an occasion from turning into a disastrous encounter, as well as on his writings. Omar strikes me as a man dedicated not only to democracy and justice, but also to decency and empathy to people holding views different from his own.

I chose the heading for this section of the chapter, "The Need to Cultivate Empathy," because I have come to the conclusion that we Eritreans, as different ethnic and religious communities, are in dire need of empathy toward one another, if we are to survive as a united country. We are at the crossroad; our people are going through a traumatic experience, suffering under a tyrannical regime controlled by a ruthless, narcissistic leader. Yet, tragically, the opponents of the regime remain divided, and the *hafash* are confused—helpless victims of a situation beyond their control. The country gained its independence, but the people are not free. The promise of freedom, equality, and justice for all, for which our martyrs paid the supreme sacrifice, was betrayed. Moreover, vertical divisions, in part fostered by the regime and in part manipulated by the inordinate ambition of some incorrigible individuals, have plagued us and threaten to tear us apart.

Even as the regime is precariously hanging on to life, the members of the opposition camp are, for the most part, engaged in recriminations and endless squabbles, a condition that psychologists describe as *group regression*. This is a phenomenon in which a perceived leadership vacuum causes groups or teams to retreat to less adaptive modes of functioning, *pointing fingers at one another instead of focusing on the true adversary*. And amid the furious war of words waged among the ever-increasing number of fronts, political groups, civic society organizations, and assorted individual voices, now amplified by the advent of the Internet, something seems to be missing. Something vital has been lost—the original "founding myth" of the Eritrean story. That compelling story, which had fascinated the world, a world that had betrayed it and later dismissed it as a lost cause (do you remember?)—that story has inexplicably morphed into orphaned victimhood.

Today, the lions of yesteryear moan and groan. Of late, they have been fighting over turf—turf that is still the private domain, the hunting preserve of the Brute. Roaring frightfully, these proud guerillas of the Red Sea now mobilize their respective pride, growling at one another—highland versus lowland. This—as if they didn't forge a national will for the common goal, shedding precious blood, sweat and tears together! To witness their "turf fight" is to be tempted to abandon hope and cry, "A plague on both their houses!" But then for whose benefit? To whose advantage? Certainly not to those people for whom the war of liberation was waged and for countless heroes who paid the supreme sacrifice. Abandoning hope would dishonor the sacred blood of martyrs. It would deny the noble sentiment, that spark of human liberty, of universal freedom and brotherhood that was the source of the "founding myth." That noble sentiment, that spark of liberty, constitutes the core value defining the essence of Eritrean identity. And it was that core value that launched our freedom fighters to wage a national war of liberation. Yes, we won liberation of the land, but not the freedom of the people, which was frustrated by the betrayal of a tyrannical regime.

A Paradigm Shift at Last?

The expression "turf war" used in the preceding paragraph may appear vague. So let me make it clearer using more familiar language to those who have been following the raging debate over the past year. A particularly bitter controversy of what I call a turf fight concerns a region-based complaint that highland Eritreans are taking over land belonging to the lowlanders. After months of seemingly endless debates, it appears that comparative calm has descended on Eritrean opposition cyberspace. A major cause of the calm is the appearance, out of the blue, of an extraordinary piece of writing known as the "Eritrean Covenant," which shifts the grievance from region and centers it on religion, namely, Islam. In the wake of the posting of this document many writers have approvingly hailed it as a historic document. I join those writers in welcoming the Mejlis Muktar Ibrahim "Eritrean Covenant." From now on, I hope and trust that the debate will take a more positive and constructive turn and create a basis for united action against the common adversary—the tyrannical regime in Asmara.

Chapter 14

CONCLUSION

———◇◇◇———

In this concluding chapter I pin-point some key issues discussed in the preceding chapters. Though we are primarily concerned with Eritrea and Eritreans, it is also necessary to think in regional terms, going beyond national boundaries. In this age of globalization, which imposes limits to national sovereignty, the challenging question for all of us is: How do we reconcile the hard-won national independence (based on the principle of self-determination) with the demands and advantages of interstate and regional cooperation? An answer to this question to the satisfaction of all concerned would require extraordinary vision and courage and leaders with such qualities.

The need, in Africa in particular, to think beyond national borders, most of which are artificial creations of former colonial rulers, is a prerequisite for peace and stability as well as for sustainable development. In the final analysis, a mutually advantageous regime of cooperation would be irresistible to all neighboring nations. This is certainly the case with respect to countries lying along the Nile basin. Seen against that context, clearly, all conflicts must give way to peaceful resolution, followed by a regional strategy of rational utilization of resources, including water and other natural resources.

Recurrent Themes and Lessons Learned

An important part of this concluding chapter consists in outlining some of the recurring themes and lessons learned from the past. To that end, I make reference to seven themes and outstanding issues confronting Eritrea and the Horn of Africa region as a whole. The first of these issues is conflict.

Conflict

A constant theme in discussion of all states, and of African states in particular, concerns conflict—its causes and consequences, its regional and international ramifications. An earlier work by the present writer, under the title, "*Conflict and Intervention in the Horn of Africa*," dealt with this subject toward the end of the cold war when the United States and the Soviet Union were aligned behind their client states in the region. Compounded by drought, which hits it on a regular basis, the Horn of Africa region was plagued with wars almost from the start of the period of decolonization. There was the war between Ethiopia and Somalia over the disputed area of southeastern Ethiopia known as the Ogaden; and there was the Eritrean war of liberation, or secession depending on who is speaking. And then there were also rebellions in various parts of Ethiopia.

Somalia claimed the Ogaden as part of "Greater Somalia"; and having failed to secure its claim through diplomacy, went to war. At the start of that war (1977-1978) the Soviet Union was on Somalia's side, while the United States sided with Ethiopia, which it considered an important ally in the global contention between the two superpowers. Then a strange thing happened: There was a switch of alliances in which the Soviet Union changed sides from Somalia to Ethiopia, at the time ruled by a self-proclaimed Marxist-Leninst regime led by Colonel Mengistu Hailemariam. Such a switch of alliances threw American diplomacy into a turmoil that lasted until the end of the cold war in 1989. By that time, the regime of General Mohammed Siyad Barre of Somalia was in its death throes, and Mengistu's regime was on the defensive in the face of the onslaught of a combined Eritrean and Ethiopian liberation forces that would end in victory over Mengistu's armed forces within two years.

The most important liberation movements were: the Eritrean People's Liberation Front (EPLF), the Tigray People's Liberation Front (TPLF), the Oromo Liberation Front (OLF), the Western Somalia Liberation Front (WSLF) fighting to liberate the Ogaden, and the Ethiopian People's Revolutionary Party (EPRP). The EPRP had broken up into various factions, with one faction joining up with the TPLF to form an all-Ethiopian movement under the name of Ethiopian People's Revolutionary Democratic Front (EPRDF). Today, the EPRDF and the EPLF are the ruling parties, respectively, of Ethiopia and Eritrea. With the collapse of the Somali state, the WSLF went through a period of confusion and disarray. Then one of its factions agreed to accept the post-Mengistu federal arrangement fashioned by the EPRDF government under which the Ogaden (western Somalia) would be administered autonomously by Somalis of the area.

As for the OLF, whose political program calls for the liberation of Oromo-inhabited areas of Ethiopia and forming a separate state of Oromia, its leadership was persuaded to join the EPRDF in a coalition government following the fall of the Mengistu regime as noted previously. The OLF remained part of that coalition for a little over a year, but fell out with the senior partner and withdrew from the partnership, resuming its separatist, liberationist agenda. However, the EPRDF had managed to persuade Oromo elements to form a partner party created in the image of the EPRDF, under the name of the Oromo People's Democratic Organization (OPDO).

This brief account forms the historical context for some of the continuing conflicts in the region. The contending forces may have changed their colors and adjusted their claims under the post-Mengistu EPRDF constitutional dispensation. But the issues of contention are virtually constant: It is about fundamental rights and power sharing. It is also unfortunately about petty ambitions and empire building on the part of some leaders. Examining these forces and issues of contention is beyond the scope of this book; it is being addressed here in a sketchy fashion as part of the overall, regional context in which the Eritrean story has played out and is still playing out.

Conflict is a part of life; the question is how to resolve it. This is as true at the personal or local level as at the national level. In the language of Marxist pedagogy, there are primary and secondary contradictions, the first being between irreconcilable foes—or class enemies. Such contradiction can lead to serious conflict, while the secondary contradiction should be amenable to easy resolution. When it comes to conflict between nations, it is usually about resources like land or water. As already stated, there is no reason, apart from failure of leadership, why such conflicts cannot be resolved rationally and amicably, given goodwill and common sense. Things get complicated in the case of colliding egos or conflicting ambitions between the leaders of the nations concerned, as was exemplified by the 1998-2000 war between Eritrea and Ethiopia. At the height of the war, when people were getting killed by the thousands on both sides, we noted the obduracy of the leaders in pursuit of their respective interests or ambitions. We leave the question of guilt or blame to the judgment of history.

Interstate Cooperation

The border dividing Eritrea and Ethiopia is of recent origin—a little over one hundred years old. Most postcolonial African borders are similarly of recent origin. One of the ironies of modern African history is that despite the brevity of this history, the identity of the nations found within the states has been defined by these borders. And wars have been fought based on disputes arising from claims and counterclaims of small pieces of land along borders. The 1998-2000 Eritrean-Ethiopian war has the dubious distinction of being the most deadly of such wars. The earlier promising start of cooperation between the erstwhile allies who seemed to share a progressive ideology was thrown overboard. While European colonial history was foisted on the peoples of the two nations, which, like much of Africa, they were not able to reverse, yet the common history of struggle against a common enemy as well as a shared historical and sociocultural heritage should have provided the leaders of the two countries reason enough for charting out a strategy of cooperation and eventual unity. It did not; and all right-thinking people from both countries bear an awesome responsibility to reexamine what went wrong and make serious efforts to encourage a policy of reconciliation and cooperation.

To those ends, the regional bodies like the African Union (AU) and IGAD should help; but it is incumbent upon the educated elite of both countries, including professional and civic organizations, to break the ice and spearhead a movement aimed at reconciliation and mutual accommodation. The beginning can consist of modest and well thought-out programs of confidence building measures. This can be followed by more elaborate programs of study and research focused on common resource endowments and public meetings to discuss such programs. Cultural exchanges and arrangements of friendly sports tournaments should serve as lubricants to facilitate the process. There is enough precedent of such exchanges and friendly sporting events going back to the recent past, before the dogs of war tore us apart.

Issues of Concern among Eritreans

The principal axis of division among Eritreans is support of the PFDJ government and opposition to it. This book has determined the cause of such division as being the nature of the government in Asmara and the character of its principal leader. My description of the cause of Eritrea's predicament—our winter of discontent—as immaculate deception, characterizing it as the original sin of Eritrean politics, has intrigued some readers of the draft when a segment of it was posted on the Internet. The chief architect of the elements of the immaculate deception, Isaias Afwerki, is wedded to a lifetime occupation of the high magistracy of the state considering no possibility of sharing it, let alone of handing it over to anybody else. In pursuit of the capture of the power, first of the guerilla organization that he led, then of the state that was based on that organization, Isaias committed many crimes for which he is answerable at the bar of history and the law, if and when he is unseated from power.

Meanwhile, Isaias has installed a tyrannical regime, and those opposed to his regime remain divided. As the chapter on the Diaspora and democratic opposition described, there is a continuing mass exodus among the young that raises serious questions about the future of Eritrea as an independent state. A country devoid of youths cannot endure. An allied issue of concern is the emerging division along religious lines. The appearance of the "Eritrean Covenant" from Mejlis Mukhtar Ibrahim represents at once an expression of such a divide, and a call for a rational dialogue between Christians and Mulims. A recognition by Christians of the sense of alienation experienced by their fellow Eritreans as Muslims will go a long way in creating a necessary bridge of understanding between the two communities. There is a need for empathy across religious and other lines of division. Such empathy can generate a reciprocal empathy from the other side.

Associated with the religious divide is also a regional or ethnic divide. Chapters 12 and 13 of this book make an attempt at providing a historical background of enduring kinship and mutuality of interest among members of the two communities. There is a need to expand and deepen such mutuality. The absence of empathy and lack of sensitivity to the plight of "the other" is a problem that needs to be explored, and mechanisms must be created to enable people to understand the concerns of their compatriots who come from a different religious or ethnic background. The experience of the *Ghedli* had created an exemplary ethos of understanding and empathy. Alemseghed Tesfai's *"Two Weeks in the Trenches"* gives a vivid picture of the values of comradely empathy created in the Ghedli. Daniel Semere Tesfsfai's epic novel in Tigrigna, *Halaw'ta Werqawit Ghereb*, also provides a rich context of the life of the ELF *tegadelti*. The *Ghedli* demystifiers need to read these books and ponder; but, by and large, the further away we have come from that experience, the dimmer the memory of that valuable experience becomes.

National Reconciliation Among Eritreans

Before we can speak about regional cooperation, we need to have a national reconciliation as Eritreans. Eritreans need to think outside the box of past divisions, whatever their origin and history. The opposition organizations have to abandon past biases in favor of national patriotic goals aimed at national salvation. To that end, even members of the regime's party, the PFDJ, should be welcomed with open arms; indeed, they should be encouraged in one way or another. Such encouragement is based on the assumption that they are the silent majority that would put patriotic duty above factional politics; the same assumption applies, of course, to the members of the opposition. The notion of national salvation (*Midhan Hager*) embraces preservation or restoration of national integrity and survival as a sovereign nation. It implies restitution of the values and ideals that drove the liberation struggle and for which so much sacrifice had been paid. And the idea of survival is invoked because the very existence of our nation may be at stake.

The emerging realignment of opposition political forces under the umbrella of the Eritrean Democratic Alliance (EDA) has shown signs of hope toward the end of national reconciliation. The realignment into two segments—the Eritrean People's Democratic Party (EPDP) and the *Tadamun* seems to follow a historic pattern of division along the Kebesa- and Metahit (lowland)-based Eritrean communities, the one predominantly Christian, and the other predominantly Muslim. Any long-term resolution of the tensions and disputes arising out of such division will have to be based on democratic principles and mechanisms transcending the regional and religious divide that was espoused during the national liberations struggle. This too requires vision and courage and a leadership possessing these qualities.

Crimes and Consequences

The question of whether Eritrean national leaders of the era of armed struggle should face criminal prosecution has elicited different responses. In order to achieve the objective of national reconciliation is it necessary to let bygones be bygones, that is to say, forgive past crimes committed during the armed struggle? What about crimes committed after liberation?

For many it would be difficult to accept forgiveness of crimes in this respect, particularly in the absence of remorse on the part of the main culprit, Isaias Afwerki, who continues to act in a predatory manner, arrogantly dismissing any idea of change or of accepting blame for errant deeds.

While members of the G-15 opened up to the possibility of answering for any past wrongs in statements made to the free press during the "Prague Spring" of 1998, Isaias has never admitted to committing any wrong. The likelihood of his ever doing so is next to zero, which makes the idea of forgiveness and reconciliation a moot point. In view of this, and given the outrageous statements he has made in interviews with several media reporters in which he defied international public opinion, forgiveness seems to be foreclosed. He is hell-bent on continuing his dictatorial rule and disastrous policies with their risk of leading the country to ruin and even state collapse. This leaves us no option but to unify and coordinate a strategy of struggle to replace Isaias' dictatorial regime with a democratic system. With a successful change of regime, Isaias and his top aides can be brought to trial together with whoever else in the regime might have committed crimes.

Easier said than done? Quite right. The Eritrean opposition movement, including the various political parties (or fronts), together with the civic organizations, need to agree on a plan of action. To that end, they need to go beyond factional and confessional division. They have to leave the divisions of the past behind and agree on an agenda of national salvation. In pursuit of a common agenda, they need to support and facilitate the coordination of the progressive websites that have been doing a good job of mobilizing our people and giving them a sense of hope, hope of change, especially the rank and file of our defense forces. The increasing mass exodus of Eritrean youths leaving Eritrea and finding themselves in neighboring countries as well as Europe and North America imposes a responsibility on the opposition movements to establish joint committees—of political parties and civic organizations—to meet the challenges faced by the thousands of youths. The help should include legal and logistical matters such as contacting immigration lawyers aimed at finding housing and jobs as well as facilitating access to health and educational services. In order to accomplish these tasks the opposition organizations should establish coordinating committees in Europe, America, Canada, Ethiopia, and Sudan.

Lessons Learned or to Be Learned

It is clear now that we trusted too much and we have lived to suffer from the consequences. The emphasis is *"too much"*. Historically it was impossible to not trust; we could not afford not to trust especially a government of freedom fighters. It is counter intuitive not to repose a trust on the government of freedom fighters, people who sacrificed their youth and much else for a cause that is greater than themselves. In the case of these people verification of trust was not applicable—at least not in the early years when the abuse and misuse of power was not apparent. Maybe some discerning people outside the rank of the tegadelti could see through them; most of us did not.

So, the lesson we learn from the bitter experience of disappointment—of betrayed trust—is to be always skeptical, if not cynical, of all high-sounding ideas and proposals coming from anybody. We need to be critical; to paraphrase, Hamlet, we have to be cruel to be kind. Now such a personal commitment is all well and good, but personal commitment in this case needs the support of institutional guarantees to enable it to be activated without fear of contradiction. Democracy provides a general framework to enable people to question and critically assess all government measures, that is to say, accountability. That is where the constitution and constitutionalism comes into play; and that is where the misadventure of the 1997 constitution, i.e., its suppression by a government that had enthusiastically supported its making, becomes a poignant lesson learned. The regime's apparent support of the making of the constitution, and its suppression after its ratification, has puzzled many people.

It is now clear that this is a prime example of what we have called immaculate deception. Isaias wanted to appear democratic in order to be in the good books of the providers of development assistance. He thought he could control the process of the making of the constitution as well as the outcome of the process, i.e., the content of the constitution. Having approved its making, he could not stop it in midstream even when he realized that he could not control its making and content. So he waited for an opportune moment and actually provoked a war with Ethiopia, thinking that he could browbeat Meles and his EPRDF. Meles proved a tough nut to crack. Indeed, he outsmarted him in all respects. Result? A humiliating defeat and the loss of a sizable area of his sovereign land. One wonders whether he has learned a lesson, or whether he is capable of learning from his mistakes. Evidently, he did not learn a lesson; but we as a people must learn the lesson.

A related lesson Eriteans must learn has to do with the democratic opposition. Although Isaias is in a class all his own as the villain of the piece, there is a sense in which many of the leaders of the opposition are chips off the same block. Their experience of the guerilla way of life has made them incapable of dealing with Eritreans having a different experience. In the liberation war experience, the leaders were used to military modes of relationships, which is to say, command and obedience. In civilian life, they must persuade and compromise. Most of them find it hard to do either, with the result that their following is miniscule in proportion to the size of the Diaspora population. And they are too old to change.

The reality is that the real owners of the struggle today are the young, and they bear the brunt of the suffering caused by the misguided policies and repressive politics of the Isaias regime. The rest of us should act in a supportive and advisory capacity to them. In fact, in my considered opinion, no one above fifty should be elected to a leadership position of all opposition parties. Those over fifty can back up the younger leaders, acting in an advisory capacity as council members. I am sure this will not endear me to the old leaders of the opposition parties; but I am inured to any negative reaction from any quarters.

Cultural and Psychological Context

Finally, there is a need for most of us Eritreans (and others in the Habesha category in Ethiopia) to look into our inner self and examine it in the context of our inherited cultural context. There have been some studies on our cultural context, some of them esoteric; others of practical significance and worth examining. One recent study, which is concise but insightful, is by Salaam Yitbarek, an Ethiopian researcher who has written an article titled "*Dysfunctional Behavior among Habesha.*"

The writer begins his piece by asking why many Ethiopians, individually and collectively, find it difficult to get along, or why Ethiopian organizations, groups, or collectives seem unable to work well or to resolve conflicts. He issues a challenge calling on "academicians and development practitioners" to make awareness of intragroup conflict a top priority for study and intervention. The writer then offers an explanation as to why there is so much intragroup conflict. One explanation is related to the culture that engenders "Dysfunctional behavior," which hamper effective communication. This diagnosis sounds familiar; after all, the Habesha factor is a common feature with a significant segment of our own nation.

Yitbarek lists eleven dysfunctional behaviors; they are:

1. Personalization of Issues;
2. Parochialism;
3. Chronic Suspicion and Mistrust;
4. Paranoia, i.e.viewing everyone as a threat;
5. Lack of empathy and empathetic understanding, i.e. the ability to identify with or understand;
6. Inability to suspend judgment or give others the benefit of the doubt.
7. Character assassination, spreading hostile rumors;
8. Lack of Openness. Openness facilitates effective communication. The absence of openness or secrecy of the EPLF and the PFDJ is an example;
9. Holding grudges; understanding or forgiveness is considered weakness.
10. Envy: Instead of endeavoring to improve our position, working to weaken others;
11. Stubbornness and Lack of Compromise. Stubbornness and inability to compromise is certainly one of Eritreans' weaknesses.

In terms of a long term solution, the writer makes two notable recommendations, that are of relevance to us: (1) to organize/create a campaign of awareness raising,and (2) to make a collective attempt "to stigmatize" dysfunctional behavior. His prescriptions proceed from an assumption of an open, democratic milieu acceptable to everyone concerned. This begs the question principally because a democratic deficit is one of the causes of the dysfunctional behavior—not the only cause, but an important cause. The cultural milieu under which our communities operate—both Ethiopian and Eritrean—is rooted in a precapitalist, feudal or semifeudal society. Add patriarchy to the equation, and you get a picture of a culture that does not favor interactions that are open and constructive. So I can't help wondering if Salaam Yitbarek's insightful analysis is a cry from a voice in the wilderness that will not be heeded or alternatively, if the young generation of Ethiopians and Eritreans might take heed, in this age of democratic opening. I have hopes that the young will respond positively to this kind of prescription. The audacity of hope is how Barack Obama would put it. Or, if I may cite an older saying, Hope springs eternal.

Appendix I

LETTER TO H.E. ISAIAS AFWERKI, BERLIN, OCTOBER 3, 2000

———◆———

Berlin, October 3, 2000
H.E. Isaias Afwerki
President of the State of Eritrea
Asmara, ERITREA

Dear Mr. President:

We, the undersigned, Eritrean academics and professionals, concerned with the predicament facing our country, have agreed to meet in order to make a sober appraisal of our country's current problems and to suggest appropriate solutions. Fully cognizant of your role in leading our nation to independence and mindful of your continued importance as a national leader, we decided to address this letter for your consideration and action.

Your comrades-in-arms trusted you as their leader during the liberation struggle. Your assumption of the office of President is a function of that trust. That trust and the responsibilities that it implies have never been more important than at this crucial moment of our history. We, as concerned Eritreans, also feel the weight of this responsibility. It is for this reason that we have come together to voice our concerns, and to exchange views and ideas which we submit as follows.

We would like to begin by expressing our unreserved support for our government in its defense of our country's sovereignty and territorial integrity, and our admiration for the Eritrean defense forces and the entire Eritrean population for their role in foiling the Ethiopian aggression. But it is our firm belief that the military threat posed by Ethiopia cannot be dealt with separately from the political and economic challenges that confront us as a new nation. We are aware that the great promise of peaceful reconstruction and development has been shelved by considerations of national survival. However, we are also convinced that we can meet the present danger and future challenges if we unite our efforts and correct our past mistakes. The current crisis presents an opportunity to those ends.

I. A Hard-Won Independence Was Nearly Lost

Mr. President,

The experience of the last two years has been particularly painful but enlightening. As a nation we have been devastated by the Ethiopian invasion of our sovereign land. Indeed, the wound inflicted upon us by this war has been a chastening experience. Destroying towns and driving thousands of innocent citizens from their homes and even to foreign lands, the Ethiopian army's deep penetration inside Eritrea and our sudden retreats shocked every Eritrean to the core and shook our nation to its very foundation. The very independence and sovereignty for which Eritreans paid with their lives and limbs was put at risk. We believe, had it not been for the resistance waged by our heroic defense forces and the unflinching support of our people, Eritrea would have almost been destroyed.

How did this come to pass? What are the causes of this tragic war? Why and how did the Ethiopians manage to penetrate deep into Eritrean territory with such speed and devastating effect? This war has not only cost us dear in life, property and in the suffering of our people. It has also raised grave questions about the conduct of Eritrean affairs both domestic and foreign, and about the nature and style of our leadership in the post-independence period.

Mr. President,

To ask why we have come to this impasse—to inquire into what went wrong—and to reflect upon the cause and conduct of the war, and whether it might have been avoided, is not only legitimate, but it is also the duty of every citizen. We hope that the Eritrean leadership, in its recent meetings, has done some soul searching and endeavored to provide satisfactory answers to these questions. We, on our part, took it upon ourselves, as concerned citizens who made modest contributions to our national struggle, to express our views on our nation's current predicament and to offer some proposals as remedies. We hope and trust that you will consider these views in the spirit in which they are given, i.e., on the strength of our patriotic duties and our people's proud tradition of love of truth and respect for the opinion of others.

The initial impulse that brought us together is manifold. First and foremost, it is the humanitarian crisis facing our people as a result of the war with Ethiopia. But we would be remiss, as concerned citizens, were we to ignore the other burning issues exposed by the current crisis facing our nation—political, social, and economic, as well as crisis in leadership.

II. Humanitarian Crisis and Eritrea's Image

On the humanitarian question, we express deep concern for the tragic conditions of Eritrean victims of war. We are particularly concerned with the plight of the hundreds of thousands of Eritreans who have been affected by the war and the over 75,000 compatriots who were expelled from Ethiopia, and our citizens who are in refugee camps in the Sudan as well as those still languishing in Ethiopian jails and concentration camps. While we appreciate the Eritrean government's principled stand on the issue of deportation, we hope and trust that any deportation that may take place in Eritrea, if necessary and legitimate, would adhere to international law, and be in accordance with the previous practice of the Eritrean government.

We support the Eritrean National Assembly's recent resolution condemning the criminal acts of the Ethiopian government, and we condemn the many egregious acts of violence, vandalism, rape and theft that have been perpetrated, and are being perpetrated, by agents of the said government against innocent Eritreans. In this respect, we pledge to commit our intellectual and financial resources in the ongoing effort to mobilize support. We trust the government to facilitate the timely delivery of humanitarian aid to our people in this time of need and we call upon every citizen to lend a helping hand in this effort.

Turning to another issue of concern, i.e., Eritrea's image, we wish to assure you, on the basis of close observation, that Eritrea's image has never been as bad as it is today. Indeed, it has hit rock bottom. There should be no illusions about this. Despite our belief in the rightness of our position, much of the world community, including our fellow Africans, perceive the Eritrean government and its leadership as aggressive and irresponsible. Eritrea's leadership has been cast, particularly since the start of the war with Ethiopia, as contemptuous of international law and accepted norms of behavior.

Although Eritrea's worsening image may have been affected by these charges, it is also true that we have alienated our friends and allies, including those who stood by us during the liberation struggle. Even the commendable policy of self-reliance, which many applauded, has now been portrayed as an aspect of arrogance. In our view, the problem is not the policy but its implementation. We know that there is a lot of room for improvement in the matter of implementing policies and in the manner of handling representatives of foreign bodies. Hence, there needs to be a critical reappraisal of policy and praxis.

III. The War and Critical Issues it Brought to Light.

We have followed with great interest and anxiety the unfolding of events since the outbreak of the war with Ethiopia. This tragic war has induced in us a need for critical review of the post-independence developments in Eritrea and particularly in our government's performance. We recognize the fact that there are notable achievements in the fields of infrastructure, education, and social services. However, we have also noted developments that cause us considerable uneasiness and serious concerns about the future of our country.

Despite these disquieting developments, we remained remarkably silent. The reason for our silence was not due to apathy or lack of interest but rather due to the pervasive phenomenon of self-censorship. This self-censorship was particularly acute during the last two years because we all felt that criticism would give aid and comfort to the enemy who might distort it to suit its purposes. Now it is time to speak and speak plainly. Further silence can only endanger the interest of the country as well as compromise our historic responsibility. We must now say that, in our considered opinion, the government has lagged behind in the development of democratic institutions, including mechanisms for ensuring accountability and transparency. We respectfully submit that this is the most important matter for you to ponder and face squarely in whatever reappraisal of government policy and practice you may be undertaking, as we hope you are.

IV. Reconciliation and National Unity

We are convinced that we reflect a widely held view among Eritreans that there should be national reconciliation. Eritrean military victory and the assumption of sovereign nationhood should have been accompanied by a spirit of reconciliation fired by magnanimity—the same magnanimity shown towards Ethiopians. Wisdom and statesmanship required a call for reconciliation extended to all Eritreans irrespective of belief or political affiliation to join hands in rebuilding a shattered society and economy. It is an opportunity that was lost but that can still be reclaimed. The EPLF (PFDJ) leadership should be willing now to provide political space for groups or individuals. The absence of such space has severely affected the development of civil society and has fostered a feeling of alienation among segments of our society. The constitution, about which we shall say more below, requires such space in no uncertain terms.

V. Collective Leadership and Popular Participation

Mr. President,

Considering the practice of the EPLF during the armed struggle, we believe that one of the grave mistakes that the government has made has been the abandonment of collective leadership. You do not need us to tell you that the practice had created trust and mutual confidence among the leadership and between the leadership and the rank and file. The heroic struggle of Eritrean fighters—their tenacity and resilience in the face of overwhelming odds—would not have been successful without such trust and confidence and the collective leadership based on it.

After independence this practice was abandoned and replaced by one-man leadership. It is also distressing to learn that individuals who were part of the leadership during the struggle have been inexplicably sidelined, in some cases with a loss of their use in this crucial time of crisis. This is inexcusable, and whatever the explanation for this negative development, we feel that it must be rectified. No individual leader, however gifted, can be a substitute for values that come with collective reflection and action in national affairs. The advent of one-man dominance has had the effect of suffocating a variety of ideas from blossoming and denied meaningful popular participation. It has inevitably prevented the growth of democratic institutions. A new nation with very limited and under-developed resources facing enormous challenges in all fields—political, security, economic, social—cannot afford to have a government that depends only on one person.

In fairness, the blame must also be shared by other members of the leadership to the extent that they did not object to the negative practices. They may have put up some feeble complaints, but we have heard of no such protests. So, they too have failed the nation along with you in allowing power to be concentrated in the hands of one man. The absence of any record of protest is also a function of the absence of freedom of expression which has prevented the citizens from exercising their rightful duty of restraining the undue accumulation of power in the presidency. Thus it is no exaggeration to say that, despite some notable progress to its name, the government has failed the nation in some important respect.

VI. Crisis within the Leadership

Mr. President,

It is not a secret that there is a serious contradiction and a major rift among the leadership. We cannot over-emphasize our apprehension of what may ensue. We deem it to be too serious and dangerous to be handled in a confrontational manner. Hence, we appeal to you and the rest of the leadership to handle it carefully, and to resolve all future conflicts within the framework envisaged by the constitution. Any further delay in resolving the crisis within the leadership will have grave consequences for our nation. We cannot minimize the potential weakness that this crisis may create if not handled properly, considering the opportunity that it can give the enemy to exploit our internal contradictions.

VII. The Role of PFDJ in Politics and the Economy

Mr. President,

We are particularly concerned about the parallel institutions of the PFDJ and the government. We see lack of clarity in functions. We see duplication and a bewildering variety of tasks and actors. We feel this involves confusion and waste of resources which a small nation with scarce resources can ill afford.

We would like to see a clear definition of what the PFDJ is. We would also like to see it confined to party activities and refrain from activities that are the proper province of government. The PFDJ's economic activities are a cause for concern and an abuse of the goodwill and trust of the people. While it cannot be denied that PFDJ/government business activities have solved many problems by providing timely and affordable commodities to our people, this cannot be said anymore. In point of fact, PFDJ/government economic activities are contrary to the government's policy of "a dynamic, private sector-led ...market economy...and a commitment to private sector development..." More to the point, PFDJ companies have no clear mechanism of accountability and transparency. At least, there is none that is known to the public. We believe that this is a recipe for disaster and for fostering corruption, cronyism, and favoritism. This climate discourages genuine and credible investors. We strongly believe that the current business practices of the PFDJ will act as corrosive agent of the political, social, and economic life of the nation. In any case, and in view of the record of the PFDJ, it is important to seriously reassess the whole question of a party running business.

VIII. Implementation of the Constitution

Eritrea has a constitution—the most sacred document of the nation. This constitution represents the consummation of the Eritrean struggle which was fought for self-determination, democracy, social justice and the rule of law. It was crafted with the participation of the people and was ratified by their representatives. It is the people's document and no one has the right to suspend it or otherwise tamper with it. You were right when you said in your recent interview that the time for the implementation of the constitution was yesterday. *[Iwanu t'mali'yu neiru.]* We agree, but we say: better late than never.

The constitution must be implemented immediately. A ratified constitution means that it is already in effect and that the Eritrean people should be enjoying their constitutional rights. We are dismayed to witness the operation of institutions that are clearly and flagrantly in violation of the spirit and letter of the constitution. We are astounded to hear of practices that are contrary to the provisions of the constitution continue today. We, therefore, solemnly request that you take the necessary steps to ensure the full and immediate implementation of our constitution.

As a sign of goodwill and seriousness of intent, again, we would like you to abolish the "special court" which is undermining the rule of law and creating disaffection among a segment of our population. People have been languishing in jail for many years without being formally charged of any crime, let alone sentenced. They have been waiting to appear before the special court. This stands in stark opposition to the letter and spirit of the constitution and is an affront to elementary notions of justice. We urge you to set these people free immediately or have them brought before a court of law.

Another disturbing practice that is contrary to the spirit of the rule of law is the resort to arbitrary practices of freezing civil servants in what is popularly known as ***midiskal.***

This harsh and unfair practice, presumably intended to instill fear, seems to have been self-defeating. If the intent was to correct or rehabilitate the victim, or otherwise bring something good to government or the nation, it has not had that effect. The overall effect of the practice has been disillusionment, confusion and waste of valuable resources.

Conclusion

Mr. President,

Eritrea is at a crossroad. A portion of our land is under foreign occupation. A significant proportion of our population is displaced. It is time for a serious soul searching by all concerned, starting from the leadership. Let the leadership and the entire nation conduct an open debate. People should not be denied this right which they have paid for with their blood, sweat and tears. We urge you most sincerely to seize this moment of crisis and turn it into an opportunity to reclaim your hard-earned reputation as a leader. You owe it to yourself and to the nation and to the wonderful people that has followed you through thick and thin.

On our side, we will spare no effort to help secure Eritrea's territorial integrity and national sovereignty. At the same time, we will endeavor to promote a culture of openness, tolerance, accountability and rule of law. To these ends, we intend to broaden our base by convening a larger meeting which will consider your response to this letter. The idea is to begin and institutionalize a government/civil society dialogue on a continuing basis as a critical part of a healthy development of our future.

Respectfully yours,

Araya Debessay	\<debessay@udel.edu\>
Assefaw Tekeste	\<assefaw@uclink.berkeley.edu
Bereket Habte Selassie	\<bselassi@email.unc.edu\>
Dawit Mesfin	\<d.mesfin@unl.ac.uk\>
Haile Debas	\<hdebas@medsch.ucsf.edu\>
Kassahun Checole	\<awprsp@castle.net\>
Khaled A. Beshir	\<khaled9@yahoo.com\>
Lula Ghebreyesus	\<aipa@iafrica.com\>
Miriam M. Omar	\<meriam35@hotmail.com\>
Mohamed Kheir Omar	\<mohamed.omer@veths.no\>
Mussie Misghina	\<Mussie.Msghina@chello.se\>
Paulos Tesfagiorgis	\<paulos88@hotmail.com\>
Reesom Haile	\<reesomh@hotmail.com\>

Contact person in Asmara—Paulos Tesfagiorgis

Appendix II

INTRODUCTORY REMARKS BY DR. HAILE DEBAS, DURING THE MEETING OF THE "G-13" WITH PRESIDENT ISAIAS IN ASMARA, ERITREA, ON NOVEMBER 25, 2000

Your Excellency President Isaias,

Allow me first, on behalf of our group, to express our deep appreciation for inviting us to this face-to-face discussion of the issues we raised in our letter to you. I am not entirely sure why the group asked me to make these introductory remarks. I suspect it is because of my age and my naiveté in all matters political. And please forgive me for speaking in English.

I would like to begin by telling you something about the group. We are individual Eritreans from all walks of the academic spectrum, from different parts of Eritrea, from different political and religious persuasions. We do not represent a political group and none of us has any personal political agenda. Our only common bond is the love of Eritrea, a passion for its sovereignty and its success as a new model country in Africa. We are also bound by a common perception and a set of concerns that have convinced us that the country may have veered off from the initial trajectory that inspired so much hope within the Eritrean Community at home and abroad, and within the world community of nations. We are unreserved about our support and commitment to our motherland and we feel that we have a huge stake in the success of Eritrea as a nation.

Allow me to introduce the members of this group, some of whom you know very well: <u>Dr. Araya Debessay</u> is Professor of Accounting at the University of Delaware in the United States; <u>Dr. Assefaw Tekeste</u> is the Dean of the faculty of Health Sciences at the University of Asmara and is currently on a sabbatical at the University of California at Berkely as research fellow of Public Health and working for Ph.D. in Public Health;

Dr. Bereket Habteselasie, is Professor of Constitutional Law at the University of North Carolina. Dr. Bereket could not be here today but wholeheartedly supports our meeting with you and pledges to accept its outcome; Mr. Dawit Mesfin is systems network Administrator at the University of North London. He is also studying for a Ph.D. degree in Education at the University of London; Mr. Kassahun Checole is Publisher of Africa World Press and the Red Sea Press; Dr. Khaled Beshir is Senior Engineer in Motorola in Chicago; Ms. Meriem Mohammed Omer is currently student in Economic Development and Administrative Management at the University of Manchester in England; Dr. Mohamed Kheir Omar is lecturer at the University of Asmara, currently undertaking Ph.D. studies in Norway; Dr. Mussie Msghina is Associate Professor of Neuroscience at the Karolinska institute in Sweden; Mr. Paulos Tesfagiorgis, whom you know very well, is lecturer in Law at the University of Asmara; Dr. Reesom Haile is a roving poet living in Asmara and Brussels, Belgium; and I am Haile Debas, Dean of the School of Medicine and Vice Chancellor for Medical affairs at the University of California, San Francisco.

The meeting we had in Berlin was prepared at a short notice, and was not a secret meeting. Indeed, we had asked and hoped that a member of your government could attend. As I said earlier, the group is neither a political organization nor does it have a political agenda. It has no leader, and indeed, many of us did not know each other well before our meeting in Berlin. We are very distressed, as we are sure you must be, by the leak to the press of the highly confidential letter we sent to you. We can solemnly assure you that none of us was responsible for the leak. In fact we do not know who did it and we hope you will support our efforts to identify the perpetrator. Believe us Mr. President, the last thing we wanted was to embarrass you and give comfort to the enemies of our country and our leader. Once in the public domain, the letter has incited a lively debate within and outside the country. We are pained to see how unfairly our intent has been covered in the official Eritrean press, which has waged a sustained and unfair attack on us without making public the contents of the letter itself. We, who believe in the absolute sovereignty of our country and cherish our Eritrean identity and commitment, are offended by the depiction of us as traitors to our country. The people, who do not know that the letter was meant to be a confidential communication to you, understandably ask how we can be openly critical of our government and leader at this time of conflict with Ethiopia. The truth of the matter is we were writing to you confidentially and we were not responsible for its being made public.

Mr. President:

We respect you as our leader and as the first President of our new nation. We are enormously proud of the early achievements of the Eritrean government. Nothing has made us more proud than our government's spirit of self-reliance and the absence of corruption, two attributes that in the early and mid 90's won an enviable image of Eritrea in the eyes of the world. We understand the enormous constraints our country has in the resources it needs, in being situated in a geopolitically unstable region. In our letter, we wanted to share with you our genuine concerns about our perception regarding the delay in the establishment of democratic institutions, the disregard of the rule of law, issues of collective leadership, the dominant role of the PFDJ in the economic life of the nation, and the need for national reconciliation and unity.

Above all else, what we want is to discuss our concerns in a positive way and see if we can develop a win-win solution.

We stand by the concerns we have raised and feel that we have a moral obligation to convey them to you and to support you develop solutions and strategies to address them. I, for one, would be prepared to step down from my incredibly busy position as institutional leader, at the University of California, in order to devote more time to help polish the image of Eritrea in the U.S. and to work hard to help my country in the area where I have some knowledge and expertise, that is, health care and medical education. I also know that each and everyone of my colleagues have a similarly passionate commitment to serve the Eritrean nation in their respective areas of expertise.

If I had two wishes for the outcome of this meeting, and these wishes are shared by all of us, they are:

First: that we come out united and indicate to the world that we are together and united. This act will take away any comfort our enemies may have felt from the perception of division within our ranks. It will also go a long way to restore our own reputation within the country, a reputation that has been damaged by unfair press.

Second: We would like to help mobilize the Academics and Professionals abroad and to harness their collective and special knowledge and expertise to help address the legitimate concerns we have raised.

Mr. President,

Thank you very much for your indulgence and patience in hearing my remarks.

Again, let me express our deep appreciation to you for inviting us to this face-to-face discussion.

We have a huge stake in the success of Eritrea. Glory to our martyrs and our admiration for and solidarity with those men and women at the front fighting to guard our freedom and the territorial integrity of our country.

References

Select Bibliography

Alemseghed Tesfai. 2002. *Two Weeks in the Trenches: Reminensces of Childhood and War in Eritrea*: Trenton: Red Sea Press.

Ali Salim. Awate.com website [Augus, September, 2009, and March, 2010].

Bereket Habte Selassie. 2003. *The Making of the Eritrean Constitution*. Trenton: Red Sea Press.

Berhan Hagos. *BroQ's Aferkbu*. Nharnet.com website (2009).

Connell, Dan. 2005. *Conversations with Eritrean Political Prisoners*. Trenton : Red Sea Press.

Daniel Ayana. *Neigjbors that Share Fire*. New York: African Studies Association Annual Meeting (2007).

Daniel Semere Tesfai. 2009. *Halaw'ta Weqawit Ghereb*. 34537 Bad Wildungen, Germany.

Dante Alighieri. 1997. *La Divina Commedia (Purgatorio)*. Fierenze : La Nuova Italia Editrice, Scandicci.

Dawit Woldegiorgis. *The Way Forward for Ethiopia and Eritrea*. www.ethiomedia.com (2009).

Gaim Kibreab. 2008. *Critical Reflections on the Eritrean War of Independence*. Trenton: Red Sea Press.

Gelner, Earnest. 1983. *Nations and Nationalism*. Oxford: Oxford University Press.

Geertz, Clifford. 1993. *The Interpretation of Cultures*. Basis Books.

Hepner, Tricia Redeker. *Transnational Tegadelti: Eritreans for Liberation in North America and the EPLF*. Trenton: Eritrean Studies Review, vol. 4, no. 2 (2005).

Human Development Index (HDI), UNDP HDI Report (2006).

Jaspers, Karl. 1947. *The Question of German Guilt*.

Magesa, Laurenti. Contemporary Cathlic Perspectives on Christian-Muslim Relations in Sub-Saharan Africa: The Case of Tanzania, in *Islam and Nuslim-christian Relations*, vol. 18, no.2 (2007).

Markakis, John. 1987. *National and Class Conflict in the Horn of Africa*. Cambridge: Cambridge University Press.

Ruth Iyob. 1995. *The Eritrean Struggle for Independence: Domination, Resistance and Nationalism 1941-93*. Cambridge: Cambridge University Press.

Saleh Younis. [Response to Ghedli Skeptics]. Awate.com website (June 3 2008).

Tekest Negash and Tronvoll, Kjetil. 2000. Brothers at War. Oxford: James Curry.

Tekie Fessehatzion. 2002. *Shattered Illusions, Broken Promise*. Lawrenceville: Red Sea Press.

Tekle M. Woldemikael. 1998. Ethiopian and Eritrean Refugees in the United States. *Eritrean Studies Review*: 2(2). 89-109.

United Ntions Economic Commission for Africa (UNECA)/USSIP Symposium. 1993. Communique of Symposium.

United States Committee on Refugees (USCRI) Eritrea Report from 1999 to 2003: (http://www. Refugees.org).

Woldesus Amar. 1997. *The Role of Asmara Students in the Eritrean Nationall occasionsist Movement, 1958-1968*. Trenton Red Sea Press.

Yosief Ghebrehiwet. *Romanticizing the Ghedli*. Asmarino.com website (2008).

Interviews and Responses to Questionnaire

Note. The following list represents people with whom I conducted interviews and from whom I received response to written questionnaire, or who wrote comments on parts of the draft manuscript. The list does not include the scores of people with whom I had informal conversations in efforts to obtain as much information as possible from a cross-section of Eritrean society on the Eritrean condition. The numbers in the square brackets represent the date when the interview was conducted.

Ahmed Raji [8.10. 2009]
Amanuel Hidrat [10.3.10]
Amha Domenico [28.7.08]
Araya Debessay [8.27.08]
Berhane Adhanom [20.5.08]
Berhane Gebrenegus [27.8.08]
Berhane Haile [20,5.08]
Bawtree [Vicky 2.8.08]
Dawit Mesfin [6.7.08]

Daniel G. Mikael
Elias Habte Selassie
Gabe Tseghai
Gaim Kibreab
Habtom Yohannes [6.8.08]
Habtu Ghebreab
Haile Menkerios [informally, on several occasions]
Houdek, Bob [2.2.08]
Lake, Anthony [20.6.09]
Mesfin Hagos [29.7.08]
Michael W. Eyob [20.5.08]
Noel Yosef [11.7.08]
Okbai Gebremedhin [20.5.08]
Prendegast, John [20.6.08]
Saleh Gadi Johar
Saleh Younis
Selam Kidane [11.7.08]
Semere Habtemariam
Seyoum Tesfaye [26.8.08]
Shengeb [10.6.08]
Smith, Gayle [17.6.08]
Sulayman Hussein[8.7.08]
Surafiel Yacob [8.7.08]
Tesfu Zewde [24.7.08]
Tewolde Stifanos

Index